Culture and Customs of Greece

Greece. Cartography by Bookcomp, Inc.

Culture and Customs of Greece

ARTEMIS LEONTIS

Culture and Customs of Europe

GREENWOOD PRESS
Westport, Connecticut • London

Library of Congress Cataloging-in-Publication Data

Leontis, Artemis.
 Culture and customs of Greece / Artemis Leontis.
  p. cm.—(Culture and customs of Europe)
 Includes bibliographical references and index.
 ISBN 978–0–313–34296–7 (alk. paper)
 1. Greece—Social life and customs—21st century. 2. Greece—Civilization.
 3. Popular culture—Greece. I. Title.
 DF741.L46 2009
 949.5—dc22   2008051962

British Library Cataloguing in Publication Data is available.

Library of Congress Catalog Card Number: 2008051962
ISBN: 978–0–313–34296–7

First published in 2009

Greenwood Press, 88 Post Road West, Westport, CT 06881
An imprint of Greenwood Publishing Group, Inc.
www.greenwood.com

Printed in the United States of America

The paper used in this book complies with the
Permanent Paper Standard issued by the National
Information Standards Organization (Z39.48–1984).

10 9 8 7 6 5 4 3 2 1

Contents

CONTENTS

Series Foreword

THE OLD WORLD and the New World have maintained a fluid exchange of people, ideas, innovations, and styles. Even though the United States became the de facto world leader and economic superpower in the wake of a devastated Europe in World War II, Europe has remained for many the standard bearer of Western culture.

Millions of Americans can trace their ancestors to Europe. The United States as we know it was built on waves of European immigration, starting with the English who braved the seas to found the Jamestown Colony in 1607. Bosnian and Albanian immigrants are some of the latest new Americans.

In the Gilded Age of one of our great expatriates, the novelist Henry James, the Grand Tour of Europe was de rigueur for young American men of means, to prepare them for a life of refinement and taste. In a more recent democratic age, scores of American college students have Eurailed their way across Great Britain and the Continent, sampling the fabled capitals and bergs in a mad, great adventure, or have benefited from a semester abroad. For other American vacationers and culture vultures, Europe is the prime destination.

What is the New Europe post–Cold War, post Berlin Wall in a new millennium? Even with the different languages, rhythms, and rituals, Europeans have much in common: they are largely well educated, prosperous, and worldly. They also have similar goals and face common threats and form alliances. With the advent of the European Union, the open borders, and the Euro and considering globalization and the prospect of a homogenized Europe, an updated survey of the region is warranted.

Culture and Customs of Europe features individual volumes on the countries most studied and for which fresh information is in demand from students and other readers. The Series casts a wide net, inclusive of not only the expected countries, such as Spain, France, England, and Germany, but also countries such as Poland and Greece that lie outside Western Europe proper. Each volume is written by a country specialist, with intimate knowledge of the contemporary dynamics of a people and culture. Sustained narrative chapters cover the land, people, and brief history; religion; social customs; gender roles, family, and marriage; literature and media; performing arts and cinema; and art and architecture. The national character and ongoing popular traditions of each country are framed in an historical context and celebrated along with the latest trends and major cultural figures. A country map, chronology, glossary, and evocative photos enhance the text.

The historied and enlightened Europeans will continue to fascinate Americans. Our futures are strongly linked politically, economically, and culturally.

Preface

Every day the sun rises on the speakers of a language as fabled for its longevity as its difficulty. These people stand poised to do many things, but perhaps nothing with greater enthusiasm than speak Greek. A language with more than 3,200 years of documented history, Greek in their mouths takes the shape of broad vowels, staccato consonants, long words, and endless expressive possibilities. Although Greek users value their language's communicative power, they are also deeply aware, with each proud syllable they dispatch, that they are keeping an old language alive. Some even claim that Greece exists for this purpose, to preserve Greek: "Greek the language they gave me / ... My only care my language on Homer's shores."[1]

Greeks care deeply about their language. In the past they even sacrificed lives over language disagreements. Today's language debates don't reach quite that pitch, yet questions fly: Doesn't text messaging impoverish young people's communication skills? Must people translate older texts into today's Greek? Shouldn't children learn ancient Greek at a younger age? How threatening are foreign lexical imports such as *e-mail* or *debate* to the integrity of Greek? Will Greece's recent immigrants learn Greek or remain forever Greece's latest *varvaroi* (barbarians, speakers of *bar-bar*, or gibberish)? With each passing day, people feel the survival of their culture is on the line, and the least they can do is to argue about it in beautifully articulated Greek.

Greek culture presents many themes. Urbanization is one, with Athens taking center stage in the country's development and consequently in this book. Athens is home to almost half of Greece's population and is the administrative and cultural center of the country. It's impossible to ignore. The performative side of Greek culture is another: the way people play their parts for one another, onstage and off. And the living relationship of inhabitants to the distant past is a third.

A key theme is that the Greek language is central to Greek culture. Greek defines the modern nation; anchors religion; relates Greeks to their ancient ancestors and to their Septuagint and New Testament religion; ties diasporic Greeks with their homeland; gives oral and visual order to poetry and prose; creates emotional ties through song; gives people weighty words for petitions, protests, slogans, and debate; and lies at the center of artistic expression. Knowledge of Greek is essential for entering Greek culture fully.

Even without Greek, it's possible to make inroads into the labyrinth of Greek culture simply by observing. Here people are arguing with equal intensity about how to buy a watermelon and whether illegal immigrants bring to Greece essential services. There a large crowd is noisily misdirecting a driver as she squeezes her car into an impossibly small parking space. It seems people in Greece can create a crisis out of nothing, then face real threats with equanimity. And they don't mean exactly what they say. They shake their head back in a gesture of *ohi!* (no) inviting the other person to share. Their downward nod of *nai!* (yes) can provoke an argument. Words of praise may signify envy, while criticism is a sign of affection. Promises are made to be broken and threats rarely carried out. Perhaps most illuminating, people of all ages, classes, and occupations take delight in deliberation: testing all sides of an argument, finding the most effective way to impose themselves on others.

In every dimension of culture, Greece is a country of paradox, politics, and pleasure in speaking, arguing, chanting, singing, cooking, and performing Greek.

NOTE

1. Odysseus Elytis, *The Axion Esti*, "The Passion II," trans. Edmund Keeley and George Savidis (Pittsburgh, PA: University of Pittsburgh Press, 1974), 18, lines 1 and 3.

Acknowledgments

THIRTY-SIX years ago on my first visit to Greece, I found myself on a precipice looking down into deep, mysterious waters. I would not have taken the plunge into Greek culture without the help of beloved family members and friends. This book owes its finer insights to them. *Efharisto*. I am grateful to colleagues from various institutions who shared syllabi for their courses and students who asked probing questions in my classes at the University of Michigan and Ohio State University. Yiorgos Anagnostou, Peter Jeffreys, Peggy McCracken, Panayiotis Pafilis, Yopie Prins, Yona Stamatis, and Liz Wingrove gave me detailed feedback on drafts. Stella Elena Acornicesei, Traianos Gagos, Van and Janet Gegas, Kimberly Johnson, Maria Kakavoulia, Neocles and Vassiliki Leontis, Bill and Daniel Loumpouridis, Despina Margomenou, Katerina Michaelidou, Carrie Romant, Stephen Snyder, Efi Spyropoulou, Fani Tufano-Mallouchou, Stratis Valakos, Vasileia and Yiannis Varvarigou, and Pavlos Vasileiou, offered images, information, sounds, ideas, flavors, museum visits, and excursions. Ben Acosta-Hughes, Mariette Baker, Bruce Frier, Richard Janko, and Ruth Scodel helped me find extra time to write. Stacie Harris, Perry Katsikas, Daphne Lambropoulos, Sophia Roumanis, and Laurie Talalay propped me up with intangibles. Editor Kaitlin Carmiello prodded me on. To Vassilis Lambropoulos, for the sheer joy of twenty-five years of exploring Greece together and for his terrific archives, I dedicate this book.

Chronology

STONE AGE (28,000–3000 B.C.)

c. 23,000–3000   Inhabitation of Franchthi Cave in Peloponnese.

6000–2500   Agrarian settlements centered in Thessaly spread to Macedonia, Boeotia, Attica, Argolis, and Messenia. Cretan settlements.

4300–3200   Aegean settlements.

BRONZE AGE (3000–1200 B.C.)

3000   Beginnings of Minoan settlements in Crete.

2100–1650   Arrival of Mycenaean Greeks in Greece.

1850–1400   Inscriptions of hieroglyphic-derived Linear A for writing pre-Greek Minoan.

c. 1600   Great volcanic eruption on Thera (Santorini).

1450   Inscriptions of Linear B script derived from Linear A for writing Greek.

1200–1150   Collapse of Mycenaean civilization. Writing disappears and material culture is in decline.

DARK AGE (1150–750 B.C.)

1150–1100   Doric and Aeolic settlements in Greece.

c. 1025   Iron replaces bronze for weapons.

9th–8th century   Geometric period. Rise of first Greek city-states. Beginning of Delphic oracle.

ARCHAIC PERIOD (750–480 B.C.)

776   Traditional date for first Olympic Games.

8th century   Composition of Homeric and Hesiodic poems.

750   Greek inscriptions written in Greek alphabet.

c. 600   Coin currency introduced.

534   Thespis is first recorded winner of dramatic competition in Athens.

508–507   Cleisthenes' democratic reforms in Athens.

499–448   Persian wars.

490   Greeks defeat Persian army at Marathon.

480   Athenians defeat Persian fleet at Salamis.

CLASSICAL PERIOD (480–336 B.C.)

478   Founding of Delian League under leadership of Athenians.

461–429   Age of Pericles inspires building of Parthenon, Propylaia, Erechtheion, and Temple of Nike on Athenian Acropolis, and other cultural programs.

431–404   Peloponnesian wars between Athens and Sparta, ending in Sparta's victory over Athens.

430   Plague in Athens.

399   Trial and execution of Socrates.

387   Founding of Plato's Academy.

338   King Phillip II of Macedon defeats Theban and Athenian forces at Chaeronea. End of Greek cities' independence.

HELLENISTIC AGE (336–30 B.C.)

336   Death of Phillip II and accession of Alexander.

335   Founding of Aristotle's Lyceum.

334–326   Alexander conquers Persian Empire and reaches Bactria and India.

323	Death of Alexander. Division of his empire among his successors.
316	Founding of Thessaloniki by Kassandros.
148–31	Roman conquest of Greece. Octavian (Augustus) defeats Marc Antony and Cleopatra at Aktion and brings Greek world under Roman control (31).

ROMAN PERIOD (31 B.C.–A.D. 330)

| A.D. 117–138 | Roman emperor Hadrian sponsors major building projects in Greece. |
| 313 | Constantine I issues edict of Milan, proclaiming religious toleration of Christianity. |

BYZANTINE PERIOD (A.D. 330–1453)

330	Constantine rebuilds Byzantium, renames it Constantinople and Second Rome. This becomes center of Vasileia Romaion (Greek for Kingdom of Romans), the eastern Roman or Byzantine Empire.
5th–6th century	Emperor Theodosius II closes pagan temples in Greece (435); Emperor Justinian closes philosophical schools in Athens (529); Parthenon is converted into Christian church.
961–1000	Athanasios the Athonite builds Great Lavra on Mt. Athos and lays foundations of coenobitic monasticism on peninsula.
1054	Great Schism divides Eastern (Greek) Orthodox and Western (Roman) Catholic churches.
1204	Fourth Crusade captures Constantinople. Crusaders rule much of Greece for at least half a century.
1210–1645	Venetians occupy Crete.
1430–1456	Ottoman conquest of Thessaloniki (1430), Constantinople (1453), and Athens and Peloponnese (1456).

OTTOMAN PERIOD (A.D. 1453–1821)

1482–1797	Venetians occupy Zakynthos and other Ionian Islands until Napoleon conquers Venice (1797).
1492	Ottomans give asylum to Sephardic Jews expelled from Spain. Over time Thessaloniki becomes a predominantly Jewish city.
1687	Venetians besiege Athens and bombard Acropolis.

1770	Russian count Alexis Orloff attempts but fails to establish Greek principality.
1798	Rigas Feraios, advocate of revolution against Ottomans, is assassinated.
1814	Secret Filiki Etairia (Friendly Society) formed to organize Greek revolution against Ottomans.
1815	Ionian Islands placed under British protection.

GREEK WAR OF INDEPENDENCE (A.D. 1821–1832)

1821	Greek revolution against Ottoman rule breaks out (March). Ottomans hang Patriarch Gregory V of Constantinople in retaliation (April).
1822–1823	First constitution for an independent Greece. Ottoman massacre of civilians in Chios wins foreign sympathy for Greek revolution.
1822–1826	Ottoman siege of Messolonghi (1822, 1823, 1825–1826). Lord Byron's death there (1824) and Ottomans' harsh treatment following victory over Greeks inspires Eugène Delecroix's painting *Greece Expiring on the Ruins of Missolonghi* (1827) and stirs foreign sympathy for Greek cause.
1827	Combined British, French, and Russian fleet destroys joint Ottoman-Egyptian fleet at Navarino Bay (Pylos).
1828	Count Ioannis Kapodistrias becomes president of First Hellenic Republic in capital city of Nafplion.
1830	France, Britain, and Russia (Great Powers) recognize independent Greece.
1831	Kapodistrias is assassinated.

KINGDOM OF GREECE (1832–1974)

1832	Great Powers offer Greek throne to 17-year-old Bavarian Prince Otto, who becomes the first King of the Hellenes.
1833–1834	Otto arrives in Nafplion. His regents declare the church of Greece autocephalous and name Athens the capital of Greece.
1843	Military coup and popular demonstration (September 3) forces Otto to give Greece a *syntagma* (constitution). Square in front of palace where people demonstrated becomes known as Syntagma.

1844	New constitution defines Greece as constitutional monarchy. Ioannis Kolettis articulates Megali Idea (great idea) challenging Greece to expand its borders to encompass historically Greek territories with large Greek populations.
1862	King Otto forced to abdicate.
1863–1864	Prince George of Denmark becomes King of the Hellenes. Ionian Islands are incorporated into Greek state as coronation gift to King George. New constitution defines Greece as crowned democracy.
1881	Province of Thessaly and region of Arta in Epirus incorporated into the Greek state.
1883–1893	Era of Harilaos Trikoupis's reforms, building of railway and Corinth Canal.
1893–1920	Greece declares bankruptcy (1893). Mass labor emigration of nearly five hundred thousand people from Greece to United States.
1896	First modern Olympic Games held in Athens.
1896–1897	Cretan rebellion leads to Greco-Turkish war and Greek defeat in Thessaly. Crete gains autonomy.
1901, 1903	Riots over vernacular Greek translation of New Testament (1901) and Aeschylus's *Oresteia* (1903).
1903	Beginning of Greek campaign for accession of Macedonia.
1909–1910	Military officers' revolt at Goudi topples government, imposes reforms, and brings Eleftherios Venizelos into national politics.
1911	Italian forces occupy Dodecanese Islands.
1912–1913	Greece gains Macedonia, Epirus, and Crete as a result of Balkan wars. King George is assassinated in Thessaloniki and succeeded by his son Constantine.
1915–1917	National schism: Venizelos and King Constantine clash over World War I: King advocates neutrality and Venizelos presses for alliance with Triple Entente. Venizelos establishes revolutionary government in Thessaloniki. Constantine forced to abdicate, succeeded by his son Alexander. Venizelos returns to Athens and declares war on Central Powers.
1917	Great fire of Thessaloniki devastates city (August 18–19).
1919–1920	Greece rewarded as victor in World War I with territory in Thrace and mandate to administer Smyrna.

1920	King Alexander dies from monkey bite. Venizelos loses elections. Constantine returns to throne.
1919–1922	Greco-Turkish war in Anatolia between Greek army and Turkish nationalists led by Mustafa Kemal Atatürk ends in Greek defeat, burning of Smyrna, and ravaging of Christian population in Asia Minor. King Constantine abdicates, replaced by his son George II. Venizelos returns to power.
1923	Treaty of Lausanne (July 24) establishes boundaries between Greece and Turkey and imposes mandatory population exchange of 1.3 million Greek Orthodox Christians in Turkey for more than 350,000 Muslims in Greece.
1924–1935	Second Greek Republic follows plebiscite rejecting monarchy (1924), until failed antiroyalist coup leads to return of King George II (1935).
1936	King George II endorses suspension of key articles of constitution (August 4), enabling caretaker Prime Minister General Ioannis Metaxas to assume dictatorship.
1940	Greek mobilization (October 28) against invading Italian forces drives Mussolini's army back into Albania, the first Allied victory in World War II.
1941–1944	Joint German, Italian, and Bulgarian occupation of Greece.
1941	Greece falls to Germany (April–May) as King George II and government retreat to Egypt. Two law students take down swastika flag from Acropolis (May 30) in first act of resistance to the occupation.
1941–1942	Estimated 250,000 Greeks perish in great famine (winter). International Red Cross distributes food (summer 1942).
1942–1944	Resistance to occupation by communist-led National Liberation Front (EAM) and National Republican Greek League (EDES). Internal strife between left- and right-wing resistance groups.
1943	Germans begin mass deportations of Jews from Thessaloniki and other areas of Greece. An estimated fifty-five thousand Greek Jews are exterminated.
1944–1945	German army evacuates and Greek government under Prime Minister George Papandreou repatriates (October 1944). EAM demonstration in Athens (December 3) leads to battle between EAM supporters, police, and British troops. Varkiza Agreement (February 1945) halts fighting.

1945–1949   Greek civil war between Communist Democratic Army of Greece (DAG) and Greek government with U.S. support ends in communist defeat.

1946   Royalist party wins elections. King George II returns to Greece following national referendum favoring constitutional monarchy.

1947   Dodecanese Islands ceded to Greece by Italians. King Paul succeeds his brother George. Truman Doctrine grants massive aid to Greece.

1950–1974   A second wave of about 1 million people leave Greece to find work in the United States, Canada, Germany, South Africa, and Australia.

1952   Women given right to vote. New constitution declares Greece parliamentary monarchy, bans Communist Party, and imposes restrictions on human rights. Greece joins NATO.

1955–1961   Constantine Karamanlis appointed prime minister after death of Prime Minister Papagos (1955). Radical Union Party under Karamanlis wins elections (1956, 1958, 1961).

1955–1965   After pogrom directed against Istanbul's Greek minority (1955), tens of thousands of ethnic Greeks from Istanbul immigrate to Greece.

1963   George Seferis wins Nobel Prize for Literature. Right-wing extremists assassinate Parliament deputy Grigoris Lambrakis. Karamanlis resigns after confrontation with King Paul. George Papandreou's Centre Union Party wins elections.

1964   Constantine II succeeds his father King Paul. Centre Union Party under Papandreou wins elections.

1965   King Constantine II clashes with Prime Minister George Papandreou over monarchy's intrusion in military and political affairs.

1967–1974   Dictatorship. Junta of colonels seizes power in military coup (April 21, 1967) and suspends elections indefinitely. Constantine flees country after abortive countercoup (December 1967). Colonel George Papadopoulos names himself prime minister. Hundreds of political activists arrested. Strict censorship imposed.

1973   Dictatorship sends tanks into Athens Polytechneio (November 17) to disband student-led demonstrations. Papadopoulos overthrown in bloodless coup by Brigadier-General Demetrios Ioannidis.

1974   Dictatorship collapses (July) after its failed attempt to topple Cyprus's President Makarios leads to Turkey's occupation of 37 percent of Cyprus. Constantine Karamanlis returns from exile to serve as prime minister in transition government. His center-right New Democracy Party wins landslide in November elections.

HELLENIC PARLIAMENTARY REPUBLIC (1974–PRESENT)

1974   Greece becomes republic following successful referendum (December) to abolish monarchy.

1975   New constitution declares Greece a parliamentary republic with some executive powers vested in the president.

1980   Odysseus Elytis wins Nobel Prize for Literature.

1981   Greece joins European Economic Community. Panhellenic Socialist Movement (PASOK) led by Andreas Papandreou wins October elections.

1982–1983   Revision of Greece's family law section of the civil code liberalizes definition of family members' roles and relations.

1985   PASOK under Andreas Papandreou wins June elections.

1989–1990   Two deadlocked elections fail to produce government (1989). New Democracy forms government under Constantine Mitsotakis after securing majority (1990).

1991   Yugoslav Republic of Macedonia declares independence. Greece objects to name and flag of republic on grounds that they imply territorial claims on Greek Macedonia.

1993   PASOK under Andreas Papandreou wins October elections.

1995   Greece normalizes relations with Former Yugoslav Republic of Macedonia.

1996   Former Prime Minister Andreas Papandreou dies; Costas Simitis elected leader of PASOK and prime minister. Tensions flare between Greece and Turkey over disputed Aegean islet of Imia. PASOK wins September elections under Simitis.

1999   Greece and Turkey initiate "earthquake diplomacy" and achieve breakthrough in bilateral relations after earthquakes hit both countries (summer) and generate outpouring of mutual assistance. Greece supports Helsinki accords, acknowledging Turkey's eligibility for EU membership.

2000   PASOK wins April elections under Simitis. Church leaders organize mass demonstrations and petition against government decision to eliminate religious data from national identity cards. Government rejects petition.

2002   Greece joins Eurozone. Euro replaces drachma.

2002–2003   Suspected members of November 17 terror group responsible for bombings and twenty-two killings arrested (July 2002), tried, and convicted (December 2003).

2004   New Democracy under Kostas Karamanlis wins March elections over PASOK under Giorgos Papandreou, successor to Simitis. Karamanlis becomes prime minister. Athens hosts Olympic Games (August 13–29).

2006–2008   Regular mass demonstrations protesting government-proposed reforms of education and pension system.

2007   Summer wildfires ravage country, culminating in inferno in Euboea and Peloponnese (August–September) and leaving eighty-four people dead and 670,000 acres destroyed. Despite criticism of handling of fires, Prime Minister Karamanlis's New Democracy Party wins September 16 elections.

2008   Karamanlis becomes first prime minister to pay official visit to Turkey. Greece vetoes Former Yugoslav Republic of Macedonia's bid to join NATO because of unresolved issues over republic's name and territorial aspirations. Police shooting death of 15-year-old boy in Athens (December 6, 2008) sparks country-wide demonstrations and riots.

1

The Land, People, and History

LAND AND WATER

RUINS DOT GREECE's landscape. Whether revered relics of older eras or scorched remains from last summer's firestorms, they lie scattered everywhere: in densely populated cities, open fields, and the remotest places. Wherever one treads, the past seems eerily present. Lord Byron called the Greek earth "haunted, holy ground."[1] To the outside world, the cool, silent stones of the classical era (480 to 336 B.C.) represent a timeless Greece next to which later eras seem timeworn. Excavation frequently meant the destruction of newer histories to reach those older layers. Today's archaeologists are changing their approach, however, in order to create a more complete record of Greece's rich history from the Stone Age to the present. The Hellenic Ministry of Culture lists about five hundred archaeological sites it actively oversees.[2] There are twenty-five-thousand-year-old remains from inhabitation at Franchthi Cave; traces of a Neolithic lakeside settlement from 5000 B.C. in Dispilio; a volcano-buried Bronze Age town at Akrotiri; Minoan centers at Knossos and Phaistos; late Bronze Age Mycenaean citadels at Mycenae, Tiryns, Thebes, and Pylos; Bronze and Iron Age mounds in central Macedonia; ancient temples, theaters, wells, homes, shops, workshops, schools, shrines, altars, and baths everywhere; Venetian fortresses all around Greece's coastline; the best-preserved medieval European town in the Old Town of Rhodes; Ottoman bridges, mosques, and bazaars in Epirus, Macedonia, and Thrace;

Ruins on the island of Delos. Photo by author, September 2008.

and the Athenian Acropolis, where people from all eras have fortified themselves. This is just scratching the surface.

The fact that more than twenty-five thousand years of human habitation are preserved in the Greek landscape is a miracle of the land, a seismic zone that regularly turns itself over. Even more miraculous is the diversity of living things at this unstable juncture, where the Eurasian and Anatolian tectonic plates meet and collide. Greece is a beautiful land with an insecure geography. Lawrence Durrell put it succinctly: "You should see the landscape of Greece. It would break your heart."[3]

Greece has infinite variety on a human scale. Its 50,949 square miles of territory feature three climate zones: Mediterranean, mid-European temperate, and alpine. A long coastline surrounds two peninsulas—the mainland and the Peloponnese—joining them together by a narrow, 4.2-mile land bridge at the Isthmus of Corinth. The coastline touches the Sea of Crete and the Ionian, Aegean, and Libyan seas and encloses twenty-one lakes. It brings tempering winds that soften the blow of winter and cool the sweltering plains but also fan fires in the summer. There are close to 8,000 islands and islets,[4] 170 of them inhabited,[5] from Crete with a population of 601,131 to the smallest islands with one or two lonely goatherds.[6] The plains of Thessaly; the rich farmlands in Macedonia; and the cool, alpine forests of Epirus offset desertified islands in the Aegean. Rare species of marine and terrestrial life vie against development. Thessaloniki and Athens sprawl: two great modern cities, a study in contrasts. All these are packed tightly into one impossibly small area.

Mountains and hills cover 80 percent of Greece. Eighteen mountains reach heights of more than 7,381 feet. The two tallest are Mt. Olympus (9,570 feet)[7] and Mt. Smolikas (8,651 feet).[8] The Pindus range, a southern prolongation of the Dinaric Alps, is Greece's craggy spine. It runs north to south through Epirus, Macedonia, and Thessaly. Then it breaks briefly at the Gulf of Corinth before it rises again as the mountains of Arcadia and the Taygetus range. It falls into the Mediterranean at the Peloponnese's southern tip and resurfaces as Kythira and Crete. The range cuts the country in half, blocking rainfall from west to east, so that Greece's northwest is significantly wetter than its southeast. Its folds rise and fall dramatically. Vikos Gorge in Epirus near Ioannina reaches a depth of 2,952 feet and is the world's deepest canyon in proportion to its width.

The mountains also produce a rush of melting snow. They feed twenty-one rivers, none of them navigable—too dangerous in winter, too dry in summer. Mountains, rivers, and gorges make land transportation difficult, as the folk song "The Bridge of Arta" records. The ballad, which takes its name from a beautiful Ottoman bridge that spans the Aracthos River in northwest Greece, tells of forty-five builders and sixty apprentices who could not secure foundations to build a bridge. So they immured the builder's wife, who then cursed the bridge: "'If the wild mountains tremble, may the Bridge tremble, if the wild birds fall, may those who cross it fall.'"[9]

Many places in Greece appear landlocked. Yet no point on the Greek mainland is farther than eighty-five miles from the sea. Greece has the longest coastline of any European country, 8,205 miles (the United States, which is 70 times bigger, has just 11,954 miles of coastline), which meanders lazily in and out of gulfs and capes, around two large peninsulas, and follows the contours of so many islands.[10] Compare this to the 734 miles Greece shares with its neighbors of Albania, FYROM (Former Yugoslav Republic of Macedonia). Bulgaria, and Turkey.[11] Easy access to the sea has meant easy communication by water. Whereas mountains have contributed to isolation and localism, exposure to the sea has encouraged travel, trade, migration, and cosmopolitanism. At the same time the sea has exposed Greece to raids by bands of marauding pirates and invasions by imperial armies. These have periodically sent people back into the mountains.

Greece's geography is divided into ten geographic regions. Moving from west to east, Epirus, Macedonia, and Thrace are the northernmost provinces. Epirus is wet, wild, rugged, and mountainous, with an alpine climate; a rich animal life of bears, deer, wolves, foxes, and wild boar; and the lowest population density in all of Greece. It is most famous for its dairy products, woven goods, polyphonic ensemble singing, coniferous trees, abandoned villages, and the cities of Ioannina on Lake Pamvotis and Igoumenitsa on the Ionian Sea. The view of snow-strewn mountaintops from the town of Metsovo, with its traditional stone houses, takes one far afield from the standard image of blue sky, azure water, and whitewashed houses.

The province of Macedonia, bordering FYROM, is Greece's largest and second-most populous region. It is a place of contrasts. Mount Olympus, where the ancient Greeks imagined a pantheon of deities rubbing against the sky, straddles Macedonia and Thessaly. Rich farmlands around Macedonia's river basins produce rice, wheat, legumes, olives, tobacco, and all kinds of fragrant fruit. Mount Athos, a self-governing peninsula of Greek Orthodox monasticism, occupies the last of three fingers of Halkidiki in Macedonia's southeastern corner, a place of legendary beauty. The other two are Cassandra and Sithonia, popular waterfront vacation destinations. Thessaloniki is Greece's second-largest city, with a metropolitan population of more than 1 million people. Its historical and official name recalls the *nike* (victory) of the Thessalians under King Philip II. Thessaloniki was a great Byzantine city, second in power to Constantinople, and it remained the most important city on the Greek mainland from late antiquity until the nineteenth century. Other versions of "Thessaloniki"—"Selanik," "Salonico," and "Salonica"—link the city to its midlife as the "Mother of Israel" or "second Jerusalem," a story that came to an end tragically when Nazis occupying Greece during World War II deported 48,974 Jews from northern Greece to Auschwitz and so effectively erased the city's once-vital Jewish presence.[12] The Via Egnatia, a Roman-built road, still cuts through Thessaloniki, as it did in Roman and Ottoman times. Traveling east, it meets Kavala, another port city and a crossroads between the Aegean and the Balkans, Europe, and Asia. Philippi, an ancient site located a few miles from Kavala, was St. Paul's first port of call in Europe as he traveled west from Asia.

Thrace, the northeastern corner of Greece, shares its name with neighboring regions in Bulgaria and Turkey. It is a place of great environmental and cultural diversity, and it is strategically critical to Greece as a border province with a mixed population. More than one hundred thousand Muslims live in Thrace.[13] The Rhodope Mountains in the north separate Greece from Bulgaria, although Pomaks, Bulgarian-speaking Muslims, live on both sides of the border. Wetlands around the Evros River, the dividing line between Greek and Turkish Thrace, shelter wintering birds from Europe and Asia. The Evros Delta also contributes to Thrace's rich soil in its lowlands. In rural Thrace, tobacco, corn, rice, and grapevines are cultivated. Minarets, church domes, and storks' nests fill the villages' horizons. Alexandroupolis, a coastal town surrounded by fishing villages, is Thrace's largest city, with a metropolitan population of about seventy thousand.

At the center of Greece's mainland lie Thessaly and Sterea Ellada, comprising Central Greece and Attica. Thessaly is identified almost exclusively with its coveted plain and Greece's biggest crop of wheat. Yet it is also home to dramatic geographic variety. Melting snow from a ring of mountains feeds the Pineus River and enriches the plain. A more significant deluge of water in the distant past probably carved out Meteora, a karstic landscape of steep, gutted boulders rising from the surrounding valley and, most unexpectedly, housing twenty-four monasteries perched precariously on its peaks. This is one of sixteen UNESCO-declared World Heritage Monuments in Greece.[14] People occupy themselves with agriculture, hunting, raising cattle, and forestry. Larissa, Thessaly's largest city, with 250,000 people in its metropolitan area, is a transportation and agricultural hub and a university town. Volos, an industrial town of eighty thousand, is Thessaly's only port city.

Sterea Ellada is home to Delphi, site of the ancient oracle, nestled between Mt. Parnassus and a silvery-green valley of olive groves that stretch down to the Gulf of Corinth. Further west is Messolonghi, a Venetian fishing town located in a swampy lagoon between the Acheloos and Euenos rivers. The death of Lord Byron on Easter Monday, 1824, during the Greek revolution against the ruling Ottoman Empire made it famous, as did the Turkish-Egyptian siege and massacre of ten thousand Greek rebels on April 10, 1826, and a poem by Greece's national poet Dionysios Solomos on the subject. Central Greece is perhaps Greece's richest battleground, home to countless mythical and historical conflicts at Plataea, Chaeronea, Thermopylae, and, in the twentieth century, Distomo, where on June 10, 1944, Nazis killed 218 citizens in cold blood. Sterea Ellada also includes Attica, a triangular peninsula jutting into the Aegean Sea and Greece's most densely populated region. The mountains of Hymettus, Aigaleo, Parnitha, and Pendeli surround a large basin, Athens's container. Beyond the mountains lie plains of terra-cotta soil, where people have traditionally cultivated grapevines, pistachios, figs, olives, and small gardens but are now selling plots to suburban homesteaders. Besides Athens, Greece's commercial, cultural, and administrative center, Attica's cities are Piraeus, Eleusis, Megara, Lavrion, and Marathon. Its islands are Salamis, Aegina, Hydra, Poros, Spetses, Kythira, and Antikythira, with a population totaling more than 4 million people (the official number was 3,894,573 in the 2001 census). Athens (2,805,272) and Piraeus (553,450) account for 86 percent of that population.[15]

The Peloponnese is a hand-shaped peninsula spreading its fingers outward to reach the Ionian and Aegean Seas. Its extreme northeastern corner connects to the mainland at the Isthmus of Corinth, a 3.91-mile-wide land bridge cut through in 1893 by the Corinth Canal. The 1.7-mile-long cable-stayed Harilaos Trikoupis Bridge completed in 2004 connects Rion in the peninsula's northwest corner to Antirion on the mainland. The Peloponnese is a microcosm of Greece. Nikos Kazantzakis saw in it "the face of Greece," a "palimpsest of twelve major overlapping scripts: the modern, 1821, the Turkish occupation, the Frankish occupation, Byzantium, the Roman Empire, the Hellenistic Age, the Classical Age, the Doric middle ages, the Mycenaean, the Aegean, and the Stone Age."[16] Inhabitation of the Peloponnese's east coast reaches back to the Stone Age. Corinth's isthmus harbors the story of countless invasions and migrations. Mystra is witness to the Frankish occupation in 1204. Patras, Greece's third-largest city and a leader in trade with Italy and Europe, is the only port facing west. Every square inch of the Peloponnese echoes with stories: from Atreus's sordid house to the toughest years of Ottoman rule. Here, too, were important battlegrounds in Greece's War of Independence (1821–1828), Nazi occupation (1941–1944), and Civil War (1945–1949). Places have their legendary associations: Lerna with the many-headed Hydra and Hercules' labors; Laconia with parsed speech; Sparta with thrift and military determination; Mani with feuding families and fierce independence; Kalamata with smooth, dark, football-shaped olives and a sinuous, kerchief-led line dance; Arcadia with Pan. And hundreds of thousands of emigrants and their children in the United States, Australia, and Canada remember all the Peloponnese nostalgically as the poor homeland that could not feed them. Yet Greeks everywhere identify the Peloponnese as the region with the greatest access to political power in the modern era.

Greece's islands are like tesserae in a rich mosaic, each with its own color, reflection, reason, and place. No two islands are alike. The Ionian Islands blanket the west coast of Greece. They are (from north to south) Kerkyra (Corfu), Paxi, Lefkada, Ithaki, Kefalonia, and Zakynthos (Zante). (Kythira, or Cerigo, off the southern tip of the Peloponnese, is traditionally although not officially part of this grouping. Officially it is part of Attica.) The islands are famed for their writers, musical speech, tracts of verdant forest, sandy beaches, and catastrophic earthquakes. Powerful earthquakes in 1953 practically leveled Kefalonia and Zakynthos. Kerkyra, Homer's mythical Phaeacia, has the largest permanent population. The town of Corfu has a cosmopolitan air, a strong tourist economy, and the most enduring marks of Venetian and British occupations. Lefkada's spectacular cliffs recall legends of the poet Sappho's suicide, while its islet of Skorpios is home to the almost-mythic family of Aristotle Onassis. Ithaki, the small island Lord Byron once considered buying, almost sinks under the weight of associations with the *Odyssey*, though archaeology has not produced hard evidence to support the Homeric text. Kefalonia, in contrast, is rich in archaeology but sparing in its reputation, apart from the islanders' conviction that they are the craziest Greeks. Their oddball humor may serve to lighten the load of history's pain. At the end of World War II, following the Allies' armistice with Italy, Kefalonia became a killing field where Nazis rounded up and executed more than 4,500 disarmed Italian soldiers of the Acqui Division.[17] Aging local inhabitants in Kefalonia still observe the memory of the Italian dead, even though they had endured more than 2 years of Italian occupation prior to that brutal event. Zakynthos is the birthplace of great poets: Ugo Foscolo; Andreas Kalvos; and Greece's national poet, Dionysios Solomos.

Hundreds of islands comprise the Aegean Archipelago, which is officially divided into three peripheries, the North Aegean, South Aegean (comprising the islands of the Saronic Gulf, the Cyclades and Dodecanese), and Crete. Most are mountainous, dry, and barren, although a few are rich in forests and farmlands. The climate of the Cyclades is the driest in Greece. In contrast, the Sporades off the east coast of the mainland, the Dodecanese in the southeast Aegean near Turkey, and the islands of the North Aegean (Chios, Samos, Lesvos, Limnos, Thassos, and Samothraki) tend to be more humid. Evia, Greece's second-largest island after Crete, is practically a piece of the mainland, divided by the narrow Evripos Strait. The strait's shifting currents reverse directions several times a day. Lesvos has a permanent population of about ninety thousand and is a treasure house of biological and geological diversity with a petrified forest. Its inhabitants take pride in their music, ouzo, and poets: from the ancient Sappho to Odysseus Elytis. Millions of tourists annually overtake Rhodes. Chios has a rich, cultivated beauty representing its prestige as an island of shipowners and producer of mastic, the original chewing gum. A dark hour in its history was the massacre or enslavement of tens of thousands by the Ottomans in 1822 in retaliation for the Greek War of Independence. The Chios massacre inspired Eugène Delacroix's painting *Le massacre de Scio* and gained European sympathy for the war. Samos is known for its wine, waterfalls, and native son Pythagoras; Limnos, for its volcanic landscape and strategic importance near the Dardanelles Straits. Naxos is the largest, most fertile island in the Cycladic cluster. Andros is home to famous shipowners such as the Goulandris family, which endowed the island's outstanding Museum of Modern Art. Karpathos, a mountainous, windy island in the Dodecanese, has preserved its ancestral villages, including Olymbos, an eighth-century refuge from pirates perched high in the mountains to the north. In summertime it fills with loyal expatriates from the United States, Australia, and Canada. Kos memorializes its native son Hippocrates with a huge old plane tree, said to be the place where he used to teach. In the Ottoman period, the island was a meeting ground for Orthodoxy, Catholicism, Judaism, and Islam, with houses of worship representing all these religions still surviving today. Ikaria is known for its dense forests, wild landscape, and traditions of poetry, art, and political protest. Besides these large islands, smaller ones each have their special associations: Tinos with marble workers and the annual pilgrimage on August 15; Syros with its neoclassical buildings, shipyards, and parallel Greek Orthodox and Catholic communities on adjacent hills. Finally Mykonos, with its windmills, churches, and seaside buildings, and Santorini, dangerously perched over an eruptive caldera, epitomize the Aegean as a tourist destination. The fragile destinies of these two poster children of Greece truly represent the mind-bending range of histories, traditions, and landscapes found in the Aegean.

Crete, the largest of Greece's islands, has occupied a place of its own since it broke away from the landmass connecting Greece and Asia Minor 10 million years ago. It lies between Greece and Libya at a spot linking three continents and bordered by four seas. Along the southern coast its climate resembles that of North Africa. In some ways Crete is another microcosm of Greece. Its oblong landmass is 160 miles long from east to west and between 7.5 and 37 miles wide.[18] A mountain chain with scores of peaks crosses from east to west, divided into three ranges: the White Mountains in the west, Ida or Psiloritis at the center, and Dikti or Lassithi in the east. This chain morphs into fertile plateaus, fabled caves, dramatic gorges, and two lakes. Around its edges lie natural harbors, sandy beaches, and small tracts of coastlands used until the recent past only for summer grazing. Not long ago, the majority of Cretans herded animals or farmed mountainsides for internal consumption. But the island is capable of producing food in excess of the islanders' needs. With Greece's accession to the European Union, Cretans have found export markets for olive oil, citrus fruits, bananas, grapes, and carob. Changes in land use go beyond the reorientation of Crete's farming and livestock-breeding markets for export. The building of roads and airports destroyed summer grazing lands and so erased a traditional way of life. Yet roads also improved communication. While olive growing and processing remain a significant industry, tourism is now a basis of the economy. People have moved to cities to embrace the life of consumers rather than producers. Of Crete's population nearly half live in the prefecture of Iraklion. Most are city dwellers in Crete's northern-facing cities—Chania, Rethymno, Iraklion, and Agios Nikolaos. Sitia and Ierapetra, the southernmost cities in Europe, face south.

Crete is a powerful player in Greek culture. It has produced major politicians, artists, writers, composers, and musicians. Though decidedly a part of Greece, Cretans proudly embrace their particularity. They feature their turbulent path from prehistory to the present, distinctive dialect, and defiance in their songs. They reflect on their love for Crete in rhyming *mantinades* accompanied by traditional instruments: "Whatever Cretans have to say, in plain words they won't speak/in *mantinades* they will greet, in *mantinades* weep."[19]

The landscape in the remotest regions of Greece, far from the madden-
ing drill of Greek conversation, teems with life. Rare brown bears, wolves,
roe deer, wild goats, foxes, and wild boars roam forested hills and mountains. Monk seals, sea turtles, fish, dolphins, and whales swim over mollusks.
Thousands of lizards live in precarious isolation on barren islands.[20] Bees visit
thyme, orange blossoms, fir trees, and pine.

Most Greeks witness little natural diversity in their daily lives. In the past
half century, the majority of Greeks have turned from the mountains to the
coastal plains, from rural to city life. Nearly half the country lives in the great
cement expanse of metropolitan Athens. Here people experience an ambivalent togetherness and find ever-new reasons to talk: a sudden deluge of rain
flooding the metro and streets, discovery of some magic corner of the city,
complaints about parking, plans for weekend escapes. Sometimes they catch
glimpses of lizards running into masonry cracks or swallows circling above
penthouse terraces. For a fleeting moment, they may remember the natural
beauty of their abandoned villages.

PEOPLE

Greece's boundaries contain more than 10 million people who identify
themselves as Ellines (Greeks). The 2001 census figure was 10,964,020,[21] and
the 2007 estimated population was 11,190,000.[22] Of these, 761,813 were foreigners with permanent residence.[23] There are many uncounted, illegal immigrants. Self-identifying Ellines represent the *ethnos*: the national group sharing a narrative of their continuous presence in Greece from prehistory to the
present. History, culture, the Greek Orthodox religion, and above all the pride
they feel as speakers of Ellinika (Greek)—the language "known to have been
well established in mainland Greece and Crete by the [thirteenth] century
[B.C.]"[24]—give them a strong sense of cohesion.

The demographic pie can be cut in different ways. Language is the most
obvious, as Greeks consider language their clearest identity marker. Greek is
the mother tongue of more than 92 percent of the population. According
to the 2001 census, Albanian is spoken by just under five hundred thousand people. Statistics for other languages vary. An estimated 160,000 speak
Romany; 100,000 Turkish; and more than 50,000 a Slavic language or
dialect.[25] Arvanitika, the dialect that evolved five hundred years ago from
Albanian and as recently as 1970 was spoken by 150,000, and Vlachika
(Aromanian or Vlach), an eastern Romance language, have a diminishing
number of younger speakers.

Ethnic identification presents a slightly less homogeneous picture. The
2006 report "Foreign Population by Citizenship and Sex," by the general

secretariat of the National Statistical Service of Greece, lists 481,663 people holding Albanian citizenship, the largest minority in Greece. More than 100,000 are from other countries of Eastern Europe, including Bulgaria (43,981), Romania (25,375), Ukraine (19,785), and the Russian Federation (13,635). Also, 70,674 come from Asia and 15,237 from Africa.[26] Of ethnic groups with older ties in Greece, about 200,000 identify themselves as Roma,[27] and 120,000 as Turks, Pomaks, or Roma in Thrace.[28] Eighty thousand are formerly nomadic Sarakatsans, who are Greek speakers and also self-identify as Greeks. About 5,500 are Jews, many of whom also identify themselves as Greeks.[29] The 1951 census counted 39,855 Vlachs, but their numbers are fewer today.[30] Slavic Macedonians are especially difficult to count, given the Hellenization campaign that began before World War II, large numbers that fled Greece after the Civil War, complexities of self-ascription, and different terms of identification: Dopioi (local people), Greek Macedonians, Aegean Macedonians, Macedonians, and Ellines.[31] Estimates range from ten thousand to fifty thousand.[32]

Although religious identification shows great uniformity, immigrants are introducing diversity. More than 97 percent of Greek citizens identify themselves as Greek Orthodox, whether or not they are practicing. There are more than one hundred thousand Muslims in Thrace and another four thousand on Rhodes and Kos. Catholics are estimated at fifty thousand, Protestants at thirty thousand, and Jehovah's Witnesses at fifty thousand. People practicing the religion of the Dodecatheon, or "12 Gods," claim forty thousand members. Among Greece's recent immigrants the number of Muslims is growing, with about 150,000 Muslim immigrants now living in Athens. Greece's 5,500 Jews are a small remnant of the 100,000 who lived in Greece prior to World War II.

That the general picture of Greece has an overwhelming majority identifying themselves as Ellines should not be surprising. Greece sought independence from the Ottoman Empire in 1821 in order to create a sovereign nation-state for Greeks. It built the Greek language and Greek Orthodox Christianity into its foundations. Yet the Greek territory in its beginnings also housed a diverse population in terms of Greek dialects and other Balkan languages, ways of life, ideology, political aspirations, and, to a much smaller degree, religion. Whether Greek or other, people identified more closely with their local villages or regions than with the emerging state. Personal connections mattered more than abstract principles. And people trusted no one more than their inner circle of close relations. A number of developments in Greece's history worked to bring people to identify more closely with the nation-state. First came the forging of a standard language from Greek dialects. Then, gradually, came the Hellenization of the population. As Greece expanded its borders to its present size, it incorporated the greatly diverse populations living in its fringes in Crete, Macedonia, and Thrace; but a mandatory population exchange between Greece and Turkey in 1923 shifted the balance decisively by both sending about 350,000 Muslims from Greece to Turkey and between 1.2 and 1.5 million Orthodox Christians from Turkey to Greece.[33] In the 1950s another 350,000 Greeks arrived following pogroms that pushed them out of Istanbul.[34]

Nothing has extinguished regional differences as successfully as the post–World War II mass migrations from mountain villages to coastal towns. Nothing has erased the eccentric variety—still present before World War II, when Cretans, Koutsovlachs, Karagounides, Arvanites, Tsamides, and Sarakatsans crossed mountain peaks to find new pastures—as effectively as Greece's transition to a country where roads lead to cities, and where 65.7 percent of the population is now urban dwelling.[35] Perhaps this demographic analysis cuts to the heart of contemporary Greek culture. With 35 percent of the population living in metropolitan Athens and 22 percent in Thessaloniki and nearby towns and cities in Macedonia, this leaves just 43 percent distributed throughout the remaining eight regions of Greece. Less than 30 percent of the population is rural.

Sixty years ago, the situation in Greece was different. Rural, mountainous Greece—whether on the mainland or the islands—defined the country's ethos. Through much of Greece's history of the past five hundred years, *to vouno* (the mountain) functioned as a safe retreat. Mountains sheltered people from the dangers of insecure, unhealthy lowlands. Mountains also represented a potent idea. They stood for a hard, unforgiving life, where women labored like men. They promised freedom from the dominance of others. And they forced people to embrace the family as the indivisible social unit. Mountains also promised stealth in guerrilla warfare. They were places where local knowledge could overwhelm global power. Greeks list battles fought in the mountains from the time of the Ottoman occupation, when Klephts, a special brand of bandits, vexed the enemy, to World War II and the Greek Civil War. Life in the mountains contrasted with life in the plains. According to a folk song, mountaineers scorned "young men down in the plains" for their soft life and found joy instead eating snow and dew up in the hills.[36] The song fails to mention the dangers people of the plains faced from invaders, malaria, tax collectors, and greedy landlords.

Despite the symbolic weight the people gave to mountains, they abandoned them in the second half of the twentieth century. Economic and political pressures conspired to turn them into plains dwellers. Prior to World War II, the farming population in Greece was 54 percent. European Union subsidies following Greece's entry into the community in 1981 brought substantial resources to the country. They developed agricultural holdings especially in Macedonia, Thrace, Thessaly, the Peloponnese, Central Greece, and Crete. They also reshaped Greece's labor force, as fewer farmers could work for greater profits under better conditions. According to 2007 statistics, 11 percent of 4.9 million in the country's labor force is involved in agriculture, livestock, and fishing, in contrast to 11 percent in manufacturing; 8 percent in construction; 23 percent in trade, restaurants, and hotels; and 8 percent in banking, insurance, or management of real estate. The unemployment rate is 8.1 percent.[37] Poetry, nostalgia, some products from the village, and a holiday retreat are all that remain of a former way of life. People may still be haunted by memories of their villages. "My body walks the streets of the city, but look for my soul in the shadows of my village," a folk song reminds the migrant.

Yet Greece's cities are dynamic places. City dwellers have developed their own ways of combining old patterns of thinking with new means of deploying them. Internal migrants who made their home in cities in the past 50 years carry on their shoulders a siege mentality. They feel the threat of outside scrutiny, whether from too-curious neighbors or intrusive governments. To fortify themselves, they consume news as a kind of national sport, competing to uncover the big story everyone else missed. They see conspiracies everywhere, or tragedies in the making. People don't take for granted the security they experience, but instead anticipate that circumstances may betray them. One way they react to perceived threats is with protests. They go out on the street to march for a cause, whether against an international war or privatization of public institutions. Just as easily, however, people throw all caution to the wind to advocate a life passionately devoted to the present moment.

Politics, suspicion, protest, and living for the present moment: How did Greece become a country of politically minded urban consumers?

HISTORY

Greece's modern state begins with the War of Independence fought by Greek Orthodox Christians and their allies against the Ottoman Empire from 1821 through 1832. The Ottomans occupied Greek territory after they captured Constantinople in 1453. Greeks remember the Turkokratia (Ottoman rule) as a period of heavy taxation, *paidomazoma* (the forced gathering of Greek Orthodox male children to be raised Muslim and enrolled in the Ottoman army), and decline. The Greek revolution of 1821 found its inspiration in the desire to overthrow an alien, oppressive ruler and in two other sources: nationalism, on the one hand (the belief that people sharing the Greek language and culture constitute a group and have the right to self-determination) and philhellenism, on the other (the idea that the world owes

Greeks their independence in return for rich legacies received from their ancient ancestors). A precursor was Rigas Feraios (1757–1798), an Enlightenment figure of Vlach descent who produced a constitution for a free federation of Balkan states, detailed map of Greece, and inspiring revolutionary *thourios ymnos* (war hymn) against tyranny, with a famous line: "Better one hour's freedom than forty years' slavery and prison."[38] In 1814, the secret Filiki Etairia (Friendly Society) formed to organize the war with financial backing from wealthy Greek merchants. They found the Orthodox Christian peasant population in Greece ready to fight, as it was so worn down by decades of harsh, arbitrary rule that it had nothing to lose and everything to gain. They seized the opportunity when Ottoman armed forces were tied up fighting Ali Pasha, the Ottoman governor of mainland Greece. The revolution's beginning in 1821 is commemorated each year on March 25, the feast day of the Annunciation, which also carries the message of divine salvation. Legend has it that Bishop Germanos raised the flag of revolt at the monastery of Agia Lavra in the Peloponnese on this day. That same month, Alexandros Ypsilantis issued a proclamation of revolt in Wallachia (present-day Romania) and led a small rebel group into Turkish territory in hopes that Orthodox Russia would quickly dispatch support for the Greek rebellion, but he found himself abandoned and renounced. Ottomans retaliated by hanging the Patriarch Gregory V of Constantinople. This harsh act of revenge against the Greek Orthodox *ethnarch* (national leader—the Ecumenical Patriarch of Constantinople was the Ottoman's administrative leader of its Greek Orthodox population), in addition to bloody massacres at Chios (1822), Psara (1824), Kassos (1824), and Messolonghi (1826) and the death of Lord Byron at Messolonghi, gained foreign sympathy for the Greek cause. The war was bloody, with many civilian casualties on both sides. Greek rebels achieved early successes and met to form an assembly (January 1822), but internal fighting broke out among rebel groups. In 1825 Ibrahim Pasha, of Egypt, son of Mehmet Ali, reconquered the Peloponnese for the Ottomans and held it until 1828. The turning point for the rebels came when the Great Powers, Britain, Russia, and France, sent in a joint naval squadron that destroyed the Ottoman fleet in the naval battle of Navarino (October 20, 1827). The Russian army continued to wage war on the ground near the Ottoman capital of Constantinople, forcing the Ottomans to make peace. Treaties of Adrianople (1829), London (1827, 1832), and Constantinople (1832) concluded the terms and established the boundaries and conditions for the existence of the new Greek state. Following the assassination in Nafplion of Ioannis Kapodistrias, Greece's first *kyvernitis* (governor) in September 1931, the Great Powers named Otto of Bavaria the king of Greece (1832). After nearly four hundred years under Ottoman Muslim rule, Greece was nominally independent though ruled by a Bavarian Catholic king.

Equestrian statue of Theodoros Kolokotronis, hero of the Greek War of Independence, in front of the neoclassical Old Parliament, now the National Historical Museum in Athens. Courtesy of Carrie Romant, May 2007.

While the Great Powers supported an independent Greece, the very small kingdom they forged, with a northern border running from Arta to Volos and cutting through Thessaly, was nearly unsustainable. The list of problems was long. The new country was deeply indebted to foreign powers, especially the British, a situation that pushed Greece to bankruptcy in 1893 and led to resentment of foreign interventions in the twentieth century. The state excluded arable lands to the north and east, where many Greek-speaking Orthodox Christians lived. Within Greece's boundaries, lands were distributed so unequally and taxed so heavily that it was impossible for peasants to break out of cycles of debt that had long ago reduced them to sharecropping for rich *tsiflikia* (land estates). Before the revolution landowners were Muslim. Now powerful Greeks took their place. For a century and a half the leaders of the country failed to address the crucial question of the distribution and use of agricultural lands. That failure forced a mass exodus of villagers to cities in Greece and to the United States and later to Canada, Germany, and Australia.

Another contentious issue was the foreign monarchy, which did not sit well with many people, as it hardly resembled the vision of independence that had inspired them to revolt. Moreover the limits and checks on the king's power remained unsettled. Unresolved constitutional issues led to numerous military coups, beginning with the "bloodless uprising" in September 1843 demanding that the king give the people a constitution. King Otto complied, and the country became a constitutional monarchy. Then came the deposal of King Otto on October 24, 1862, and the election in 1863 of King George I (formerly Prince William of Denmark). A year later a new constitution became law, redefining Greece as a crowned democracy with a single-chamber *vouli* (parliament) and prime minister as head of government. Yet the king continued to intervene in parliamentary politics, granting mandates to governments that lacked parliament's confidence. Harilaos Trikoupis, who became head of Greece's first liberal democratic party, challenged the king's authority by raising the question, "Who is to blame?" (1874) in an anonymous article criticizing the king's interventions.[39] Trikoupis became prime minister in 1880 and was in and out of power until 1895. He worked to stimulate the economy and modernize the country's infrastructure, investing in railway networks and the Corinth Canal to facilitate the transportation of agricultural and industrial goods. In foreign affairs he pursued a path of moderation and diplomacy that was not always popular. His challenge to the king's authority did not solve the thorny question of the monarchy—nor did plebiscites on the monarchy in 1924, 1935, 1946, and 1973. The issue was not settled until December 1974.

The country's serious problems—untenable agricultural policies, a weak economy dependent on foreign loans, and constitutional questions about the unchecked power of the monarchy—stayed with Greeks for a century and a half. Instead of addressing these, the state fixed its attention almost exclusively on expanding its territory. Parliamentary debate in 1844 produced the Megali Idea (Great Idea), the brainchild of Prime Minister Ioannis Kolettis, which became a popular policy motivating Greece's external affairs. Megali Idea names the irredentist vision of expanding the state's borders to incorporate territories associated with Greece's history, where Greeks still lived. From 1844 through 1922 the Greek state sought to achieve the Megali Idea's goals through diplomatic, military, and paramilitary efforts. Britain ceded the Ionian Islands in 1864. Then under pressure from foreign powers, the Ottoman Empire ceded Thessaly and the Arta region of Epirus to Greece in 1881. Crete gained autonomy in 1897 and was assigned to Greece with several other islands of the Aegean following the Balkan Wars (1912–1913), when the Treaty of London in 1913 forced Ottomans to cede the island to the Balkan allies.[40] With the Treaty of Bucharest in 1913, Greece annexed southern Epirus, southern Macedonia, Thessaloniki, Kavala, and "the Aegean littoral as far east as the Mesta [or Nestos] River"[41] thereby nearly doubling its area and population. Greece received part of Thrace west of the Evros River with the Treaty of Lausanne in 1923 and the Dodecanese Islands after World War II in 1947.

After the Balkan Wars, Greece turned its attention to Asia Minor, the west coast of Ottoman Turkey, which had a substantial Greek-speaking presence for more than 2,500 years since the archaic period in antiquity. In the early twentieth century, the Greek population around the port city of Smyrna (Izmir today) in an area "the size of Connecticut" was reportedly "about 500,000. . . . Smyrna has 375,000 people and is now the largest city in the Greek world, Athens having but 168,000."[42] Smyrna and Constantinople, the onetime capital of the Byzantine Empire, were the desired trophies of the Megali Idea. A diplomatic opening came with the outbreak of World War I. Eleftherios Venizelos, prime minister and head of the liberal party, who dominated Greek politics from 1910 to 1935, saw an opportunity to win Britain's promise of concessions in Asia Minor by supporting the Triple Entente and allowing French and British to troops to land in Macedonia in preparation for their expedition to Gallipoli. This was in open defiance to King Constantine I, who favored neutrality in the war so as not to alienate Germany. In retaliation, the king dismissed Venizelos, who responded by establishing a second, provisional government in Thessaloniki. King Constantine did not win this skirmish; the Allies forced him to abdicate the throne by threatening to invade Greece. Venizelos and the king's conflict is known as the *ethnikos dihasmos* (national schism) because it divided the nation in half between supporters of Venizelos and supporters of the monarchy. Venizelos's divergence from the king's policies had a constitutional dimension, as it challenged the monarchy's right to intervene in parliamentary politics, echoing Trikoupis's earlier challenge. Deep divisions continued for decades after Venizelos's tenure in office and bore both the acrimony and the name (*Venizelikoi kai vasilikoi*, or Venizelists and royalists) of those earlier battles.

Greece pursued the Megali Idea in earnest after World War I. When Venizelos returned to power, he lobbied at the 1918 Paris Peace Conference for Greece's expansion into Asia Minor. With British consent, he sent troops in May 1919 to Smyrna, under the pretext of protecting its Greek population there. But Venizelos's clashes with King Constantine I had divided Greece sharply, yielding more internal turmoil. In 1920 Venizelos's party lost the elections, while a plebiscite brought Constantine I back to the throne. Venizelos's fall and Constantine's return weakened allied support for Greek military ambitions. Nevertheless the Greek army pressed on. In March 1922 it turned its sights on Turkish nationalists led by Mustafa Kemal (later Atatürk) in the Ottoman hinterlands, who were fighting to replace the depleted Ottoman Empire with a Turkish nation-state. Five months later, the Greek army, routed and defeated, retreated frantically to Smyrna. Christians from the Ottoman countryside pushed desperately toward the coast, heeding news that the victorious Turkish cavalry was pursuing them. As the news spread, the initial trickle of refugees in Smyrna swelled. Turkish troops reached Smyrna on September 9 and began setting fire to Christian quarters on September 13. The Greek term *mikrasiatiki katastrofi* (Asia Minor catastrophe) or simply *katastrofi*, summarizes what followed: the massacre of Greeks and Armenians, as "more than half a million people were crammed onto the waterfront and they had no possibility of escape. Machine-gun posts at the northern and southern ends of the waterfront prevented them from fleeing, while the fire formed an impenetrable barrier on the land side,"[43] and the water offered no refuge, as Allied ships refused to evacuate refugees. The death toll according to one estimate was 100,000 dead and 160,000 deported to an almost-certain death in the interior.[44] At the very least, 190,000 people remain unaccounted for.

The Treaty of Lausanne signed in 1923 brought an end to Greek-Turkish hostilities and delimited the two countries' borders. It also called for the first compulsory exchange of populations in the twentieth century. The criterion for exchangeability was religion. All Greek Orthodox Christians in Turkish lands except for those living in Constantinople and on the islands of Imbros and Tenedos and all Muslim subjects except those in western Thrace were forced to repatriate in the neighboring nation-state. Altogether Turkey received more than 350,000 Muslims from Greece in exchange for about 1.3 million Greek Orthodox subjects sent from Turkey to Greece. Thus ended the Megali Idea.

A period of reforms, growth, and political agitation followed the Asia Minor catastrophe. A plebiscite in 1924 abolished the monarchy and created the Second Hellenic Republic (the First Republic referred to the government of Kapodistrias from 1828 to 1831). The country's immediate challenge was to find a way to absorb the refugees, who increased Greece's population by 13 percent.[45] The refugees brought with them skills, music, food, and a cosmopolitan way of thinking. They reshaped Greek culture. Their needs were enormous, however, as was their poverty. Squalid refugee housing and poorly paying jobs stirred up radical political movements, including the Communist Party. The liberal Venizelos government that returned to power in 1923 could not meet an increasingly restive labor force's demands for economic and social equality. Venizelos lost elections in 1932 and fled the country in 1935. The royal populist movement barely gained the upper hand in January 1936 elections, and the KKE (Kommounistiko Komma Elladas, Communist Party of Greece) was now holding the balance of power.[46] Responding to labor strikes in 1936, Ioannis Metaxas, leader of the royal populists, suspended parliament and key articles of the constitution and named himself dictator. Styling himself the "national father" after the model of Benito Mussolini, he outlawed communism and other political and labor movements. With strict censorship in place, he mobilized his own propaganda machine.

Metaxas faced his greatest dilemma in October 1940, when Mussolini issued an ultimatum threatening war if Greece did not allow the Italian army to occupy the country. Despite ties to Mussolini, Metaxas felt the pressure of the popular will. He answered a clear *Ohi* (no), or words to that effect. The country celebrates this *Ohi* annually on October 28. The holiday commemorates Greece's unified counteroffense, which pushed the Italians back into Albania and so humiliated a far more powerful invading army. The world took note of Greece's modern heroism. This was the first Allied victory in the war. Hitler, however, was determined to occupy Greece. His troops invaded the country early in April 1941. They entered Thessaloniki on April 9, rode into Athens on April 26, and moved on through villages, islands, and valleys. In Crete they faced mass civilian resistance to their airborne Operation Mercury on May 25, but finally took the island on June 1, 1941. The Greek king and his government retreated to Cairo, while a triple occupation of Greece under German, Italian, and Bulgarian forces settled in.

People suffered greatly under the occupation. In the first months, occupying forces requisitioned food and raw materials from Greece's countryside to prepare for their Soviet offensive, while the Allies set up a blockade. A devastated Greece faced the cold winter of 1941–1942 in resignation. According to Red Cross estimates, famine took the lives of 250,000 people between 1941 and 1945.[47] Greece's civilian casualties in the war were among the highest, despite the country's small size. In all, the war with Italy, famine under the occupation, harsh German reprisals against civilians, acts of resistance, fratricidal conflicts, and the deportation of fifty-five thousand Jews, reduced Greece's population by more than half a million people.[48]

Women standing in the graveyard of Distomo, Greece, where victims of a 1944 Nazi massacre are buried, in this undated picture. In World War II, German soldiers killed 218 people as punishment for an attack by partisans. Germany's highest criminal court, on Thursday, June 26, 2003, rejected a compensation claim by four Greeks whose relatives were among the victims. ©AP Photo.

But people did not endure the occupation without resisting. On May 30, 1941, two university students, Manolis Glezos and Apostolos Santas, climbed to the Acropolis by night through a point of entry in a cave below and tore down the swastika flag flying over the city. All of Athens observed the empty flagpole the next morning. The Nazis' threats of reprisals had the opposite of their intended effect. This small act inspired others to carry out new acts of sabotage. Soon the communist-backed National Liberation Front (Ethniko Apeleftherotiko Metopo, EAM) and its military force (Ellinikos Laikos Apeleftherotikos Stratos, ELAS), the noncommunist, British-backed National Republican Greek League (Ethnikos Dimokratikos Ellinikos Syndesmos, EDES), and other movements formed an organized resistance.

They worked together reluctantly for a time until conflicts to establish leadership and differing visions of the postoccupation order brought them to a point of civil war. EAM was by far the largest resistance movement in occupied Greece by the end of the war, with estimates of 500,000 to 2 million adherents by 1944.[49]

Political differences came to a head just as people were celebrating the Germans' withdrawal in October 1944. "The real issue for the political establishment was the transfer of power from the EAM-controlled regions to the government of Athens."[50] Power was in the hands of EAM, while the government in exile did not wish to recognize that power. As the transfer began to take the form of demobilizing the communist guerillas, the leaders of EAM, sensing that they were being closed out of government, called for a demonstration in Syntagma Square in Athens on December 3, 1944. Police shootings into the crowd, killing at least ten people and wounding more than fifty, precipitated cross fire between EAM and the Greek police.[51] Then British soldiers intervened. Following Prime Minister Winston Churchill's instructions to treat Athens as "'a captured city where a local rebellion is in progress,'"[52] they found themselves in a monthlong battle against supporters of EAM. The battle ended with EAM's defeat and the consolidation of the power of the monarchy and political right. The *Dekemvriana*, as Greeks refer to the bloody events, is fraught with irony. EAM, the most effective anti-German resistance movement, found itself attacked by Western-allied forces using Italian reinforcements to secure the reascendancy of the conservative monarchy that had fled the occupation but now promised to serve the interests of the Western block. The communist Soviet Union did not offer EAM support. A year later, the Civil War moved from city to countryside. The Greek government's pursuit of former resistance fighters, now the self-ascribed Democratic Army of Greece (DAG), found backing in President Harry S. Truman's proclamation of the Truman Doctrine (1947), which guaranteed economic and military support to Greece for the purpose of containing communism. Americans took the place of British allies of the government-backed forces, and Greece became the first theater of operations of the cold war, preceding both Korea and Vietnam. The political right used mass detentions, political imprisonment, paramilitary gang attacks, evacuations of villages suspected of harboring right-wing sympathizers, and American arms to win the war. The left used forced conscriptions and the promise of creating an independent Macedonia. Both sides placed civilians in brutal cross fire. The Greek government defeated the DAG in the mountains of northwestern Greece in October 1949.

The government's victory meant political imprisonment and exile for tens of thousands of suspected communists and communist sympathizers. Measures such as the outlawing of the KKE and repression of liberal opposition to the monarchy brought some stability to Greece after nearly a decade of war. Greece enjoyed unprecedented economic growth. New roads joined towns to cities, electrical power reached people's homes, and internal migrants created a new life. As they entered the ranks of a new urban class, migrants embraced consumer-inspired aspirations and a more liberal worldview than that of their tradition-minded, rural ancestors. Greece also strengthened its ties to the West. It joined NATO in 1951 and gained associate status in the European Common Market in 1962. The price Greeks paid for peace was a compromise of political freedoms at home and a new dependence on foreign powers, especially the United States, whose support for Greece was not straightforward. Conservative governments ruled Greece with a tight hand. The resurgence of a political center in elections of 1961 followed by the victory of the liberal George Papandreou's Center Union Party in 1963 challenged the military and monarchy, which were unprepared to surrender power. King Constantine II did all he could to bring down the Center Union government. Facing the likelihood of a renewed victory by the Center Union in elections of May 1967, he planned military intervention by the army's generals. On the morning of April 21, 1967, however, the king was as surprised as the rest of the country when a group of junior officers headed by colonels seized power in a coup d'état. Arguing that they were preempting a communist takeover, they proclaimed martial law and suspended key articles of the constitution. When a counter-coup organized by King Constantine II in December 1967 failed and the king fled the country, the junta of colonels controlling government named Giorgios Papadopoulos prime minister. Soon after the king's failed countercoup, the U.S. State Department gave its full support to the colonel's dictatorship, thereby helping it to consolidate its power.

The *diktatoria*, as Greeks refer to the dictatorship of 1967 to 1974, did not enjoy popular support. Its rhetoric of nation and religion above all else, call for a return to traditional morality, censorship of everything from books to beards and miniskirts, and torture of political opponents did not sit well with Greece's increasingly urban population. Student demonstrations began to surface. A large-scale demonstration culminated in the occupation of Athens' Polytechneio (National Polytechnic University) in November 1973. Students broadcast their opposition to the dictatorship on an amateur radio station. The effect was a mobilization of mass civilian discontent. In reaction the colonels brutally ended the demonstration by sending military tanks against the student uprising on November 16–17 and killing at least twenty-three protestors and wounding hundreds more.

Still the dictatorship did not fall. Instead it prepared a second coup d'état, this time in the independent Republic of Cyprus, an island south of Turkey with a majority Greek Orthodox population and substantial Turkish Muslim minority. Cyprus had gained independence from the United Kingdom in 1960 under a difficult, fragile power-sharing arrangement. The dictatorship in

Greece opposed Cyprus's President Archbishop Makarios III because he supported independence while the dictatorship was rallying for Cyprus's *enosis* (union) with Greece. After Makarios's reelection in 1973, the dictatorship allied itself with a right-wing movement in Cyprus that was vying for *enosis*. On July 15, 1974, it launched a military coup against Makarios. The coup failed, and Turkey responded by landing troops on the northern edge of the island as a signal that it was ready to fight to protect the island's Turkish minority. To counter the Turkish invasion, the dictatorship ordered a general mobilization, but the result was chaotic. Given the dictatorship's failure to respond to a huge international crisis of its own making, the people of Greece demanded the return to civilian rule. On July 23, 1974, General Phaidon Gizikis, commander in chief of the First Army Corps who had been appointed president of Greece in late 1973, summoned an ad hoc group of politicians to determine how to proceed. Gizikis was advocating for at least partial military control but eventually gave up this demand.[53] Under pressure from the group, he agreed to invite the conservative politician Constantine Karamanlis, prime minister of Greece from 1955 to 1963, to return from voluntary exile in Paris and head the national unity government. Karamanlis was sworn into office the next day.

To ensure a successful transition to democracy in 1974, Karamanlis dismissed collaborators of the dictatorship; legalized all political parties, including the banned KKE; and called elections for November 1974. His New Democracy Party won an overwhelming majority. In December 1974 his government oversaw the plebiscite on the monarchy, in which 69 percent voted to abolish the monarchy and 31 percent to retain it. The Constitution of Greece, drafted in 1975 by the Fifth Revisional Parliament of Hellenes to specify the terms of the new parliamentary republic, remains in place today. What was remarkable about this delicate period of *metapolitefsi* (political transition) was people's shared determination to make things work: to place the future well-being of their republic above partisan differences, which had so bitterly divided the country since the national schism.

In the midst of Karamanlis's efforts to create a transition government and in the absence of a Greek settlement with Turkey, Turkish troops invaded and occupied 36 percent of Cyprus on August 14, 1974, displacing some 170,000 Greek Cypriots before the United States imposed a cease-fire. To this day, Turkish troops remain on Cypriot soil, propping up the self-declared, largely unrecognized Turkish Republic of Northern Cyprus. The Cyprus crisis remains unresolved—a symbol of the failed politics of division.

The strain on Greek and Turkish relations created by the Turkish occupation of Cyprus seemed to worsen rather than improve over time. The two countries teetered on the brink of war on January 30, 1996, during a dispute over the unpopulated 10-acre island of Imia in the eastern Aegean. After that crisis was settled, deputies in the ministries of foreign affairs in each country agreed to take steps to ease relations by finding agreement in smaller matters before tackling the larger issues. Then in late summer 1999, major earthquakes in Turkey (August 17 and 22, 1999) and Greece (September 7, 1999) created the occasion for the two countries to reciprocate aid. The flow of goodwill from both sides was widely covered in the media and created an overwhelming sense that people wanted friendlier relations. Ministers in both countries were able to build on the initiative, which acquired the name "earthquake diplomacy." In 2000 they signed bilateral agreements aimed to improve relations despite continuing disputes in Cyprus and the Aegean.

As part of the process of shoring up Greece's still-fragile democratic institutions and strengthening its economy, Karamanlis revived Greece's application to the European Union (called the European Community at the time). He had initiated this during his earlier premiership in the late 1950s but was unable to complete the work since the dictatorship had intervened. This time he managed to bring Greece into Europe. His idea of Greece's "European Destiny" did not stand unopposed.[54] In October 1981, the year of Greece's accession, Andreas Papandreou, leader of the opposition party PASOK (Panelliniko Sosialistiko Kinima, Panhellenic Socialist Movement) and son of Karamanlis's onetime liberal opponent George Papandreou, won a landslide victory over the conservative New Democracy on a platform of *allayi* (change) from 40 years of conservative rule. Papandreou promised to stop the process of Greece's entry into the European Community, withdraw Greece from NATO, order U.S. military bases out of Greece, and generally reorient Greece away from foreign dependence.

Although Papandreou did not follow through with all his election promises, PASOK did bring about change. The fact that an explicitly left-wing political party actually won elections without interference from the radical right was change in itself, a sign that Greece's democratic institutions had matured. Moreover, PASOK's "Contract with the People" brought sweeping social reforms, some of them within the framework created by Greece's participation in an increasingly unified Europe. The revision of the family code in 1982–1983 legalized civil marriage, abolished the requirement placed on families to provide a dowry, decriminalized adultery, legitimized children born out of wedlock, eased the rules for obtaining divorce, offered generous parental leave, redefined head of household to make women and men equal partners (whereas previously men were families' all-powerful, authoritarian patriarchs), and generally brought Greece into alignment with the rest of Western Europe. These revisions, together with other laws guaranteeing women equal access and equal pay, revolutionized women's status in Greece. It is important to note here that women only gained the right to vote in 1952. Within a brief 30 years, women's position in society was radically transformed. PASOK also reformed health care, introducing a comprehensive national health-care package in 1983. Especially in its reform of agricultural policies, PASOK capitalized on resources available to Greece through its entry into the European Community. Europe's Common Agricultural Policy provided "capital to member states to address structural deficiencies," whereas its Integrated Mediterranean Programs aimed to help Mediterranean countries modernize agriculture and create manufacturing jobs in rural areas.[55] These two programs brought capital to the Greek countryside in the form of investments and subsidies. They also served to identify PASOK government as the "benign powerful state that would deliver society from economic hardship."[56] Accusations of scandals within PASOK diminished the party's grip on power during its second four-year rule and led to calls for a political "cleansing" in 1989, two deadlocked elections, and a failed coalition government. New Democracy briefly formed a government under Constantine Mitsotakis after securing a majority in 1990. PASOK returned to power under an ailing Papandreou in 1993.

Costas Simitis, Papandreou's successor as head of PASOK and prime minister of Greece from 1996 to 2004, took on the difficult task of reforming Greece's economy to meet the standards of performance required by the terms of the Maastricht treaty for full economic participation in the European Union. To accomplish this, Simitis, a professor of commercial and civil law with a detailed understanding of economics, had to reduce inflation and the national debt. This meant that he had to tame the monstrous Greek state, the product of the structural flaw of clientelism: Greek voters' and politicians' expectations of favors for votes. For the 8 years during which Simitis's government ruled, people trusted his steady, sober style. They also enjoyed his government's successes. Not only did Simitis achieve Greece's admittance into the Eurozone in 2001; his government oversaw the expansion of infrastructure in Greece—new roads, bridges, and the Attiko Metro in Athens. It assisted in dismantling November 17, a homegrown terrorist group that carried out 103 attacks and more than twenty assassinations between 1975 and 2002. Under Simitis's leadership, too, Gianna Angelopoulos-Daskalaki, chief organizer of the Athens 2004 Olympics, prepared Greece for the games. The Olympics took place 5 months after Simitis handed the leadership of PASOK to Giorgios Papandreou and saw him lose elections in March 2004 to New Democracy, led by Kostas Karamanlis, who took credit for the achievement and is currently prime minister of Greece.

Since 1974, the New Democracy Party and PASOK, two parties in the almost exclusive domain of three families, have dominated the political stage. There's the Papandreou family, with Andreas Papandreou (PASOK prime minister, 1981–1989 and 1993–1996) and his son, Giorgos Papandreou (PASOK coordinator for the bid for the 2004 Olympic Games, 1997; minister of foreign affairs, 1999–2004; and leader of the opposition party 2004 to present). There's also the Mitsotakis family, with Konstantinos Mitsotakis (New Democracy Party prime minister, 1990–1993) and his daughter Dora Bakoyanni (mayor of Athens, 2002–2006; New Democracy Party minister of foreign affairs, 2006 to present). And there's the Karamanlis family, with Constantine Karamanlis (New Democracy Party prime minister, 1974–1980), and the current prime minister of Greece, Kostas Karamanlis (New Democracy Party, 2004 to present), nephew of Constantine. Costas Simitis was the odd man out.

Integration in Europe has had far-reaching effects. The European Union gave Greece a stable framework, and EU subsidies helped Greece modernize agriculture, develop infrastructure, and raise the standard of living. Access to European institutions offered people in Greece opportunities in Europe while also making Greece an attractive destination for immigrants from other parts of the world. In fewer than 30 years Greece has been utterly transformed: from a developing country with weak public institutions and an emigrating population to a developed country with strong institutions at the European level and hundreds of thousands of immigrants. Greeks view their radically refashioned world with deep ambivalence. They regularly weigh the cost against the benefits of their new world arrangement. They complain that "European prices and Greek salaries" have reduced their buying power.[57] Seven hundred thousand resident aliens and countless illegal foreigners, totaling more than 10 percent of the population, have made their social world more complex. The deepest disillusionment is found in Greece's youth—school and university-aged young people, who call themselves the "Generation of 700-Euro" because they anticipate that years of intense schooling will yield little more than a job at €700 ($1,000) per month.[58] They regularly express their loss of faith in political and social institutions by taking to the streets in protest. An especially violent outburst, with large crowds demonstrating for weeks throughout the country, followed a police officer's unprovoked killing of a 15-year-old in the center of Athens on the night of December 6, 2008.[59] While anxious questions about Greece's social, economic, and political well-being are expressed differently now than they were 30 years ago, the sense of insecurity continues. Geopolitical fragility runs in cycles in Greece, a small country by every indicator except its cultural assets, merchant fleet, biodiversity, and long, turbulent history.[60]

Greece faces big challenges abroad and at home. Some are old, like the call to improve health care and education or the continuing necessity to smooth differences with neighbors. There are old structural problems, too: politicians

"Green City Athens 08" campaign with graffiti. Photo by author, October 2008.

have not abandoned old clientelist practices that stand in their way of governing. Perhaps no challenges are more pressing than the economy and environment. The desire for progress since World War II has made Greece a country of urban dwellers and the surrounding countryside an instrument of development. And so a gem on the face of the planet, a miracle that was millions of tumultuous years in the making, faces the real possibility of ruin.

NOTES

1. Lord Byron, *Childe Harold's Pilgrimage*, Canto II Stanza 88, in *Byron Poetical Works*, ed. Frederick Page (Oxford: Oxford University Press, 1979), 208.

2. "Archaeological Sites," Odysseus, Hellenic Ministry of Culture (accessed September 6, 2008), http://odysseus.culture.gr/h/3/eh30.jsp.

3. Lawrence Durrell and Alan G. Thomas, *Spirit of Place: Letters and Essays on Travel* (New York: Dutton, 1969), 57.

4. Efstratios D. Valakos et al., *The Amphibians and Reptiles of Greece* (Frankfurt am Main: Chimaira, 2008), 11.

5. "Greece," Encyclopaedia Britannica Online (accessed September 6, 2008), http://search.eb.com.proxy.lib.umich.edu/eb/article-9106266.

6. "Population Projections of Greece 2007–2050," General Secretariat of National Statistical Service of Greece (accessed September 6, 2008), http://www.statistics.gr/anaz_eng.asp.

7. "Olympus, Mount," Encyclopaedia Britannica Online (accessed September 6, 2008), http://search.eb.com.proxy.lib.umich.edu/eb/article-9057065.

8. "Pindus Mountains," Encyclopaedia Britannica Online (accessed September 6, 2008), http://search.eb.com.proxy.lib.umich.edu/eb/article-9060071.

9. Author's translation from Artemis Leontis, "The Bridge between the Classical and the Balkan," *South Atlantic Quarterly* 98, no. 4 (1999): 644.

10. Monteagle Sterns, "Greek Security Issues," in *The Greek Paradox*, ed. Graham T. Allison and Kalypso Nicolaidis (Cambridge, MA: MIT Press, 1997), 61. For statistics see *CIA The World Factbook* (accessed December 29, 2008), https://www.cia.gov/library/publications/the-world-factbook/index.html.

11. "Greece," *Encyclopaedia Britannica* (2008).

12. Mark Mazower, *Inside Hitler's Greece: The Experience of Occupation* (New Haven, CT: Yale University Press, 1993), 244.

13. Thanos M. Veremis and Mark Dragoumis, *Historical Dictionary of Greece* (Metuchen, NJ: Scarecrow Press, 1995), 170.

14. "Monuments," Odysseus, Hellenic Ministry of Culture (accessed January 1, 2008), http://odysseus.culture.gr/h/2/eh21.html.

15. National Statistical Service of Greece, "Greece in Figures 2008," 6; "Greece in Numbers," General Secretariat of National Statistical Service of Greece (accessed September 8, 2008), http://www.statistics.gr/main_eng.asp.

16. Nikos Kazantzakis, *Journey to the Morea*, trans. F. A. Reed (New York: Simon and Schuster, 1965), 7.

17. For a narration of the events, see Louis De Bernières, *Corelli's Mandolin* (New York: Pantheon Books, 1994).

18. "Crete," Encyclopaedia Britannica Online (accessed September 6, 2008), http://search.eb.com.proxy.lib.umich.edu/eb/article-214778.

19. "Mantinades in Crete," Explore Crete (accessed September 5, 2008), http://www.explorecrete.com/cretan-music/mantinades.html (author's translation).

20. Valakos et al., *Amphibians*, lists hundreds of species of reptiles.

21. General Secretariat of National Statistical Service of Greece (accessed September 6, 2008), http://www.statistics.gr/Main_eng.asp.

22. "Greece," Encyclopaedia Britannica Online (September 6, 2008), http://search.eb.com.proxy.lib.umich.edu/eb/article-9437852.

23. "Population Projections of Greece 2007–2050," General Secretariat of National Statistical Service of Greece (accessed September 6, 2008), http://www.statistics.gr/anaz_eng.asp.

24. John Chadwick, "Pre-Greek languages," in *Oxford Classical Dictionary*, ed. Simon Hornblower and Anthony Spawforth (Oxford: Oxford University Press 2003), available at http://www.oxfordreference.com.proxy.lib.umich.edu/views/ENTRY.html?subview=Main&entry=t111.e5318.

25. Guus Extra and Durk Gorter, eds., *The Other Languages of Europe: Demographic, Sociolinguistic, and Educational Perspectives* (Clevedon, U.K.: Multilingual Matters, 2001), 299.

26. "Foreign Population by Citizenship and Sex—2006," General Secretariat of National Statistical Service of Greece (accessed September 6, 2008), http://www.statistics.gr/anaz_eng.asp.

27. "The Roma—Europe's Largest Minority," Encyclopaedia Britannica Online (accessed September 6, 2008), http://search.eb.com.proxy.lib.umich.edu/eb/article-250269.

28. "The Muslim Minority of Greek Thrace" (1995–2008), Hellenic Resources Network (accessed September 6, 2008), http://www.hri.org/news/greek/misc/96–04–06.mgr.html.

29. K. E. Fleming, *Greece: A Jewish History* (Princeton, NJ: Princeton University Press, 2008), 210.

30. Christina Bratt Paulston and Donald Peckham, *Linguistic Minorities in Central and Eastern Europe* (Clevedon, U.K.: Multilingual Matters, 1998), 71.

31. Loring M. Danforth, *The Macedonian Conflict: Ethnic Nationalism in a Transnational World* (Princeton, NJ: Princeton University Press, 1995), 250.

32. Christopher Merrill, *Only the Nails Remain* (Lanham MD: Rowman & Littlefield, 2001), 271.

33. Matthew J. Gibney and Randall Hansen, *Immigration and Asylum: From 1900 to the Present* (Santa Barbara, CA: ABC-CLIO, 2005), 376–377, estimate 1.2 million Orthodox Christians but caution that "accurate figures of the numbers of persons involved are impossible to ascertain. Anna Triandafyllidou and Ruby Gropas, *European Immigration: A Sourcebook* (Aldershot, U.K.: Ashgate, 2007), 141, give the figure at 1.4 million.

34. Triandafyllidou and Gropas, *European Immigration*, 141.

35. "Information about Greece," Ministry of Foreign Affairs (accessed September 6, 2008), http://www.mfa.gr/www.mfa.gr/en-US/Services/Useful+Links/Greece/Information+About+Greece/INFORMATION+ABOUT+GREECE.htm.

36. Michael Llewellyn Smith, *The Great Island: A Study of Crete* (London: Longman, 1965), 117, quotes the folk song from which these lines are taken.

37. National Statistical Service of Greece, "Greece in Figures 2008," p. 6; "Greece in Numbers," General Secretariat of National Statistical Service of Greece (accessed September 8, 2008), http://www.statistics.gr/main_eng.asp.

38. Translation from Demetra Vaka Brown and Aristides Evangelus Phoutrides, *Modern Greek Stories* (New York: Duffield, 1920), 7.

39. See John S. Koliopoulos and Thanos M. Veremis, *Greece, the Modern Sequel* (London: Hurst, 2002), 64–66, on Trikoupis's political career.

40. Frank Maloy Anderson and Amos Shartle Hershey, *Handbook for Diplomatic History of Europe, Asia, and Africa, 1870–1914* (Washington, DC: Government Printing Office, 1918), 438.

41. Anderson and Hershey, *Handbook*, 440.

42. Isaiah Bowman, *The New World: Problems in Political Geography* (Yonkers-on-Hudson, NY: World Book Company, 1921), 321.

43. Giles Milton, *Paradise Lost: Smyrna 1922: The Destruction of Islam's City of Tolerance* (New York: Basic Books, 2008), 322.

44. Milton, *Paradise Lost*, 372, quoting the figures of Edward Hale Bierstadt, executive of the U.S. Emergency Committee.

45. Andrew Freris, *The Greek Economy in the Twentieth Century* (London: Croom Helm, 1986), 43.

46. Marina Petrakis, *The Metaxas Myth* (London: I. B. Tauris, 2006), 34.

47. Mark Mazower, *Inside Hitler's Greece* (New Haven, CT: Yale University Press, 1993), 41.

48. Franciszek Piper, "The Number of Victims," in *Holocaust: Critical Concepts in Historical Studies*, ed. David Cesarani and Sarah Kavanaugh (New York: Routledge, 2004), 363.

49. Richard Clogg, *A Concise History of Greece* (Cambridge: Cambridge University Press, 2006), 126.

50. Polymeris Voglis, *Becoming a Subject: Political Prisoners during the Greek Civil War* (Oxford, U.K.: Berghahn Books, 2002), 52.

51. Mark Mazower, "Policing the Anti-Communist State in Greece, 1922–1974," in *The Policing of Politics in the Twentieth Century: Historical Perspectives*, ed. Mark Mazower (Oxford, U.K.: Berghahn Books, 1997), 130.

52. Mazower, "Policing," 131.

53. Richard Clogg, "General Phaedon Gizikis Obituary," *Independent*, August 5, 1999, BNET Business Nework (accessed September 9, 2008), http://findarticles .com/p/articles/mi_qn4158/is_19990805/ai_n14249713.

54. Christopher Montague Woodhouse, *Karamanlis, the Restorer of Greek Democracy* (Oxford, U.K.: Clarendon Press, 1982), 274.

55. Thomas W. Gallant, *Modern Greece* (London: Arnold, 2001), 215.

56. Koliopoulos and Veremis, *Greece*, 177.

57. Nikos Konstandaras, "Blame It All on the Euro," *Kathimerini*, June 2, 2008 (accessed December 30, 2008), http://www.ekathimerini.com/4dcgi/ _w_articles_columns_2_02/06/2008_97295.

58. "Generation €700 is the silent majority of young Greeks, aged between 25 and 35, who are overworked, underpaid, debt ridden and insecure." For a definition and regular postings see "Generation €700" (accessed January 1, 2008), http://g700 .blogspot.com/.

59. Events have received extensive coverage. See for example Malcolm Brabant, "Riots Push Greece to the Edge," December 25, 2008, BBC World News America (accessed January 1, 2009), http://news.bbc.co.uk/2/hi/europe/7798056.stm and Valia Kaimaki, "Mass Uprising of Greece's Youth," *Le Monde Diplomatique* (accessed January 1, 2009), http://mondediplo.com/2009/01/06greece.

60. The fleet of 3,084 ships is the largest in the world, according to the U.N. Conference on Trade and Development, "Review of Maritime Transport," 2007, Chapter 2, "Structure, Ownership, and Registration of the World Fleet," 31 (accessed September 8, 2008), http://www.unctad.org/Templates/webflyer.asp?docid= 9248&intItemID=4398&lang=1&mode=toc.

2

Religion

WHETHER PRACTICING or not, reverent or resistant to the Greek Orthodox Church's deep influence, for more than 97 percent of Greek citizens, to be Greek is to be Christian and Orthodox. Greek Orthodoxy (*ortho* means "correct," and *doxa* means "belief"),[1] the common and official name used by the Greek Eastern Orthodox Christian Church, is the state religion. While the constitution of Greece guarantees all people living in Greece full protection of life, honor, and liberty irrespective of religion, section 2, article 3, confirms that the "prevailing religion of Greece is that of the Eastern Orthodox Church of Christ."[2] It recognizes the church's canon law, maintains that the text of the Holy Scripture shall remain unaltered, and gives the church special privileges. When Archbishop Christodoulos (1939–2008) died on January 27, 2008, bells tolled, cannon were fired, and tens of thousands followed a state-sponsored funeral fit for a head of state on a national day of mourning.[3] The state pays the church's hierarchy and clergy and supervises its property. It supports the teaching of Greek Orthodox theology in public schools and universities. Greece is now part of the European Union and so technically surrenders old, noncompliant laws to EU laws. Yet even those Greeks who rarely attend church firmly resist changes that would diminish the historical ties between the Greek nation and Orthodox religion. When in 2000 Prime Minister Costas Simitis, following EU rules, announced that religion would not appear as a rubric on national identity cards, a crisis ensued as then archbishop Christodoulos mobilized 3 million people to sign a petition calling for a referendum on the optional inclusion of religion. The archbishop lost the fight and protests quickly subsided. But feelings that Greek and Orthodox are one and the same persist.

Religion is embedded in Greek life in ways too numerous to count. Orthodox churches fill the landscape, giving form to Orthodox theology through their architecture, services, archaic language, and recollection of history. The church calendar orders peoples' lives by defining holidays and fasts. Religion takes its most familiar form in icons, which represent in living color a central tenet of Orthodox theology: the humanity of God and his divine promise that salvation begins in living matter. It is found in monasteries where people live in retreat but also in the everyday practices where God and the saints seem close at hand. A popular saying suggests that God might be as near to everyday life as a receptive ear is to a wishful mouth: *Apo to stoma sou kai stou Theou t'auti* (From your mouth to God's ear). Religion enters so many material aspects of people's lives: the water they drink, their good and bad health, the foundations of buildings they build, how they bring into the world the young, how they remember the dead, how they avert an envious eye, or just how they spend their evenings, walking, sitting, or playing in a church square. Even Greeks' strong tendency to resist authority, especially to a perceived domination by the West or by foreign forces that assert themselves from within, owes something to the history and spirit of Greek Orthodoxy.[4]

Perhaps the event that best summarizes how Greeks experience religion is the *panigyri*, the celebration of a patron saint or feast day that encompasses almost every aspect of the Greek Orthodox religion. The *panigyri* offers itself for an anatomical study of key elements of religion as they make their presence felt in Greek culture.

PANIGYRI

The *panigyri* begins on the eve of the feast day of a saint or a major religious holiday. *Panigyri* (plural *panigyria*, from *pan*, "all," and *agora*, "a gathering of people") is the word Greeks have been using since medieval times to name a community's feast day celebration. Like its medieval predecessors, today's *panigyri* combines rituals, prayers, and processions with feasting, singing, and dancing with abandon.

A Greek village can be a dark, silent place. Its population may diminish to a handful of octogenarians in winter. But around the time of a summer *panigyri*, people arrive in droves. The population may swell to several thousand, and the noise level rises radically.

Anticipating a great gathering from the surrounding villages and distant cities where the village's emigrants live, shop owners and village authorities set up rows of long tables and chairs across the town square, leaving room at the center for the dancing around the stage. The smell of roasting lamb fills the air. When they encounter strangers arriving early, villagers return hard, unrelenting stares. A Greek's gaze can be unyielding.

Traffic starts to jam on the few roads leading to the village from the four compass points as evening arrives. On the roadside, peddlers set up booths to sell their roasted seeds and nuts, cotton candy, *halva Farsalon* (a buttery sweet made from rice flour and burnt sugar), plastic toys, Philips electronics and Louis Vuitton handbag knockoffs, pirated CDs and DVDs with the summer's greatest hits, silver jewelry, antique lighters and coins, old stamps, tablecloths, towels, doilies, religious items, and even precious heirloom handicrafts from a destitute person's hope chest. An old man walks toward town with a bundle of helium-filled balloons shaped like unicorns and elephants. People abandon their cars and begin to walk while browsing the merchandise.

In the late afternoon, clergy, acolytes, and villagers parade the flower-decorated icon of the patron saint around the square. They return to the Byzantine-style Greek Orthodox church that dominates the square to complete the vespers service. In the square the scent of incense lingers.

As dusk arrives emotions rise. Shouts of joy, questions of "Where have you been?" and "When did you arrive?" accompany unexpected reunions. Baskets of lamb ribs, shoulders, legs, and an occasional head with glaring eyeballs, breads, salads, and liters of wine make their way down the tables. The band imposes its sound above all others, superimposing a strong club beat to the 7/8 rhythm of the traditional dance called *kalamatianos syrtos*. The singer's flat, distorted voice and the wildly amplified bouzouki compete with a happy mix of human exclamations. In no time a long sinuous line fills the dance floor. It will continue to swell and meander until late night, when the slow songs of abandonment, unrequited love, and bitter defiance take the place of peppy line dances. Now a few lingering men, decidedly drunk, take turns improvising heavy jumps and turns of the *zeibekiko*. The store owners begin to break down tables and chairs.

Morning comes. The loudspeakers in the square broadcast the Divine Liturgy. Villagers and guests now follow the procession of clergy, acolytes, and icons around the entire village. After church the square's coffee shops fill with name-day celebrants and their guests. Eyes locking in warm embrace, friends and strangers wish one another *hronia polla* (may you live many years), then crisscross the square to pay their feast day visits.

Throughout Greece this scene recurs in endless variations. Every village or neighborhood has its special saint's or feast day: St. Basil on New Year's Day, Theofania (Epiphany), Evangelismos (the Annunciation), St. George,

Church of Panayia Paraportiani, Mykonos. Photo by author, September 2008.

St. Thomas, St. Irene, Sts. Constantine and Helen, the Ascension, Pentecost, Sts. Peter and Paul, the Nativity of St. John the Baptist, St. Marina, the prophet Elijah, St. Paraskevi, St. Panteleimon, Metamorphosis tou Sotiros (the Transfiguration), the Koimisis (Dormition or Repose of the Virgin Mary), Tou Stavrou (the Elevation of the Cross), St. Dionysios, St. Demetrios, the archangels Michael and Gabriel, St. Andrew, and St. Nicholas are just some of the feast days celebrated with abandon in Greece. Especially during the warm spring and summer months, *panigyria* fill the countryside. Local musicians play traditional and contemporary tunes and rhythms.

Everywhere the same elements combine: chants, rituals, liturgy, hierarchy, icons, processions, burning candles, and the community of faithful, on the one hand, and loud instrumental music and singing, food, drink, dance, the wares of a county fare, and the high spirits of enthusiastic crowds, on the other hand. The Holy Spirit and high spirits, sacred and secular intertwine so seamlessly that it is hard to grasp where the one begins and the other ends, even though some celebrants' scant dress seems hardly compatible with church models of modesty.

The integration of material and spiritual, and the emphasis on sensory pleasure as an essential approach to divinity, are deeply embedded not just in popular practices but also in the Greek Orthodox Church and its rites. Those rites seem somber and severe at first glance but contain the theological germ of Greece's earthy, material celebrations and a belief that Divinity is not far from the realm of the human.

IN CHURCH

The church that dominates a particular village square and becomes the focal point during its feast day services is a variation on a theme in Greece. Byzantine-style churches, chapels, and shrines grace the Greek landscape. In cities there are few non-Orthodox houses of worship. A few synagogues are still functioning in Greece: two each in Athens and Thessaloniki, and one each in Chalkida, Larissa, Kos, Chania in Crete, and Rhodes. Remains of nonfunctioning synagogues exist in Veroia, Ioannina, Kerkyra, and Zakynthos.[5] Ioannina's Kehila Kedosha Yashan Synagogue opens very rarely for a community event. St. Dionysios Catholic Church stands in the center of Athens, with others in Athens's surrounding neighborhoods and suburbs, Thessaloniki, Kerkyra, Crete, and on peaks of the Aegean Islands. On some Cycladic islands, Syros for instance, more than half the island's population was once Roman Catholic. Today Tinos has the largest Catholic population in Greece.

St. Paul's Anglican Church is another Athenian landmark, designed by Christian Hansen in a neo-Gothic style,[6] while other Protestant and Evangelical churches do not advertise their presence. The Armenians of Greece have their own Catholic, Apostolic, and Evangelical churches. Some three hundred mosques exist, mainly serving the Muslim minorities (50 percent of Turkish origin, 35 percent Pomaks, and 15 percent Roma) in Thrace. Plans for a new mosque in Athens have gone through several phases of controversy. A converted factory in the city's southern outskirts functions as a temporary place of worship for the city's sizable Muslim immigrant population, estimated by some to be five hundred thousand.[7] There are also a handful of Baptist, Evangelical, Pentecostal, Jehovah's Witness, Mormon, and other Protestant churches, as well as Muslim, Catholic, and non–Greek Orthodox meeting places for immigrant groups from Eastern Europe, the Philippines, the Middle East, and Africa. But mostly there are Greek Orthodox churches, which serve more than 90 percent of the population. Many are small and intimate. A few are grand. All of them keep the Orthodox religion's presence clearly in view.

While domed churches of luminous white stucco have become tourist icons, Byzantine buildings from the seventh to the early fifteenth centuries work on the imagination in more muted ways.[8] Their earthy tones complement the environment, and intricate brick- and stonework creates complex zigzag, tooth-shaped, and Kufic patterns. Sometimes a building's surface reveals *spolia* (reused materials or art) from ancient temples. Byzantine-style churches commonly have a cruciform, or cross-shaped, plan topped with a hemispheric, cylindrical, or octagonal dome or set of domes. From the outside, it's only the dome that stands out.

To enter a Greek Orthodox church is to pass into a universe of quiet mystery, illuminated darkly by small, circular windows of colored glass above and slow-burning beeswax candles or olive-oil-filled vigil lamps at eye level. If the ancient Greek temple revealed its sculptured exterior splendor under the bright Mediterranean sun, the Byzantine-style church yields its beauty slowly from within. Its interior consists of three main sections, each less accessible than the previous one. The western-facing doors, the back of the church, open into the narthex, where people light candles, leave *tamata* (votive offerings), whisper their petitions, cross themselves, and venerate icons. Historically the narthex was the place where nonfaithful, catechumens, and penitents stood after the priest announced, "The doors, the doors!" to close the nave just before the recitation of the Nicene Creed. Today faithful and nonfaithful can enter both narthex and nave but are reminded to show reverence as they approach the eastern face of the church.

Over the nave, the main part of the church, a dome usually hovers, decorated with a mural or mosaic of the Pantokrator (ruler of all). Here the *ekklisia* (from the ancient Greek, meaning "assembly") or *laos* (people), the "community of common worship,"[9] gathers to take part in services. People face east in the direction of the rising sun, a daily reminder of resurrection. During prescribed sections, they may sit in chairs set up in two sets of rows on either side of a central aisle, though standing or kneeling is the traditional posture of worship. Yet many people wander, shuffling their feet on marble-decorated floors as they move from one icon station to another, restating their petitions. Before them is the *soleas*, a raised platform extending outward from the sanctuary, where the sacraments and many other rituals take place. To their right is the bishop's throne and to the left an elevated pulpit. From there the clergy read the Gospel and preach the homily.

The apse on the eastern end of the church houses the *iero* (sanctuary and holy of holies). The Platytera (from the Greek phrase, *platytera ton ouranon*, "wider than the heavens"), a tall mural of the Theotokos (birth giver of God) holding the Christ child in her lap and extending her arms wide stands as a bridge between church floor and roof, earth and heaven. At the center of the sanctuary is the altar table containing the relic of a saint placed there during the church's consecration.

Between the sanctuary and the nave stands an elaborately decorated iconostasis, an icon screen of wood or stone. While the iconostasis separates the laity from clergy and the mysteries of the service, theologically it is said to bridge, and thus unify, the human and the divine. At the center of the iconostasis is an opening, called the royal doors, leading to the altar table, where only ordained bishops, priests, or deacons may pass. Icons cover the iconostasis on its western side facing the nave in several tiers. They follow prescribed guidelines, though there is room for some variation. Flanking the royal doors on the first, or sovereign tier, to the right are the icon of Christ representing his second coming, followed by St. John the Baptist, the forerunner, while to the left are the icon of the Theotokos, Virgin Mary, and Child representing the Incarnation, followed by the patron saint or feast to which the church is dedicated. Third in line on either side of the royal doors are the north and south doors, also called the deacons' doors because they serve as exits and entrances for deacons and acolytes. The archangels Michael and Gabriel traditionally stand on these doors, followed by Sts. Peter and Paul or other important saints. On a second tier above these icons are images of the twelve great feasts, representing the most theologically significant scenes from the life of Christ, with the Last Supper at the center. Another tier may represent the prophets and patriarchs of the Hebrew Bible.

MUSIC, LANGUAGE, AND SERVICES

The visitor to a Greek Orthodox church service will take note of the chanting, especially during the glorious feast day vespers offered for the church's patron saint, when bishops and priests from other churches all celebrate the occasion with enthusiastic male unison singing. Chanting is the vocal ornamentation indispensable to all Greek Orthodox services. The chanting during the vespers service, however, is itself a feast, though it requires an unhurried approach.

Almost every word pronounced in Greek Orthodox services is chanted. Chanters surround the *psalteri* or *analogion* (chanters' stand) to the far right and left before the iconostasis. They sing a capella following a Byzantine style developed from a series of influences: Jewish sacred music, early Middle Eastern Christian music, and the music of Byzantium as it evolved over the centuries in schools in Constantinople and other large cities of the Byzantine world. The very difficult, complex tradition of chanting was transmitted through generations of oral instructions, with some help from Byzantine music notation invented around A.D. 950, and is learned today in much the same way.

The singing is monophonic, which means that it emphasizes melody over harmony. Like Western music, it is based on a seven-note diatonic scale; but it adds microtones and odd accidentals that do not exist in tempered Western scales. A *protopsaltis*, or lead chanter, illustrates the meaning of the religious text as tradition has prescribed it, by elaborating on the *echos*, the tone or melodic line of a hymn. To develop the melodic line the chanter adds *melisma*, long vocal runs on a single syllable. In certain longer hymns he postpones the melodic climax indefinitely as he takes ornamental turns that seem to walk in place. The chorus of voices has the difficult task of holding steadily and in unison the base *ison* (drone). This anchors the tonality and mode of a melody while also introducing an occasional dissonance. The chorus sometimes joins the lead chanter with unison singing.

Music sets the tone of worship. While it is meant to draw out the inner meaning of the poetry and heighten the significance of services, mostly it deepens the feeling of mystery. The music sounds Eastern, modal, untempered—decidedly strange to the ear trained in Western, polyphonic, tempered sounds. It emphasizes syllables while elongating words and phrases to the degree that they lose their audible meaning. In any case the language of the hymns, petitions, and prayers, liturgical Greek, is archaic: it is based on the Greek of the New Testament and even on older, poetic forms of Greek. Today's Greek speakers don't automatically understand liturgical Greek unless they possess a deep knowledge of ancient Greek or have lifetime familiarity with the services. Yet Greeks insist that the language of the services speaks to them. They are accustomed not to understand each word or automatically grasp the meaning of each sentence. Instead they enjoy the antiquity, the layered meanings, and the otherworldly feeling of words.

Every service follows a clear, prescribed order according to the kind of service, the time of day, and calendar date. Evenings bring vespers with prayers and hymns to the honored saint. Matins precede the Divine Liturgy, or Mass. This is celebrated on Sundays and major saint's days or feast days. It culminates in the sacrament of Eucharist, or Communion shared in remembrance of the Last Supper, and shares the structure, though not exactly the tone, of the Roman Catholic, Anglican, or Episcopalian Mass.

There are many other kinds of services, each specified by the church calendar and, occasionally, the special needs of a parish. The Paraklisis, or prayer of supplication to the Virgin Mary, is recited on specified days and whenever the community has a special need. Preparation for Easter brings a set of services: Saturday of Souls honoring the dead, the Compline, Presanctified Liturgy, and Hairetismoi, Salutations to the Virgin Mary. The high point is Megali Evdomada, or Holy Week, with a total of sixteen services in nine days that distill the message, meaning, expressive potential, theology, and poetic grandeur of Greek Orthodoxy through glorious rituals, hymns, and processions. The week recalls, rehearses, and reenacts the last days or Jesus' life—raising Lazarus, entering Jerusalem in triumph, meeting with his disciples, undergoing trial and crucifixion. On Good Friday Greek Orthodox offer the service of Lamentation, a kind of funeral for Jesus recalling the rites of burial: anointing, sprinkling with rose water, and lamentations. Women decorate with flowers the *kouvouklion*, a wooden canopy representing the bier. It holds the Epitaphios, an elaborately embroidered icon depicting the supine body of Christ as it was prepared for burial. During the vespers service of the Epitaphios, people join together in communal singing of three long hymns of lamentation and process around the church, neighborhood, or village.[10] As a measure of good luck for blessings in the coming year, the entire community, animals and all, passes under the Epitaphios before it reenters the church. The Pascha (Easter) service begins dramatically at midnight on Saturday in complete darkness, which gives way to candlelight as the clergy emerges from the altar with a lit candle and passes the burning light, flame by flame, to the entire *laos* while chanting, "Defte lavete phos" ("Come Receive Light"). The flame taken from the tomb of Christ at the Holy Sepulchre in Jerusalem, where the Greek Orthodox patriarch receives it miraculously during the annual "miracle of the holy fire,"[11] has reached churches earlier that evening from a small chapel high in the Plaka of Athens, an outpost of the Church of the Holy Sepulchre. Outside churches everywhere in Greece almost the entire country attends the Gospel reading of the Resurrection and sings the beloved Easter hymn, "Christos Anesti" ("Christ Is Risen") over and over again. The throngs celebrate the message by setting off fireworks, embracing one another warmly, cracking red-dyed Easter eggs, and then returning home to a midnight meal of *mayiritsa* (tripe soup) or some other delicacy, where they continue to share the unalloyed joy of the holiday until early morning, then feast on roasted lamb the next day.

Although Divine Liturgy immediately follows the Resurrection service, most Greeks do not remain, just as they do not regularly attend church on Sundays. They are more likely to drop by momentarily any day of the week to light a candle and say a quick prayer. They are Christmas, Easter, and *panigyri* Greeks, happy to take part in celebrations without enduring long traditional services.

MONASTIRIA (MONASTERIES)

Alongside Greece's many nonpracticing Orthodox Christians is the *mon-ahos* (from Greek *monos*, which means "alone") or *kalogria* (nun) who elects to dedicate him- or herself completely to God by retreating to a *monastiri* (monastery, literally "a place of solitude"). Monks and nuns are not visible in a *panigyri*, though their manual work may be evident in the religious articles vendors sell: icons, incense, prayer ropes. Monks and nuns reject the worldly life. They take vows of celibacy and live in single-sex communities, large or small, next to towns or worlds apart.

Monasteries occupy some of the most beautiful locations in Greece. The pristine peninsula of Mt. Athos and the limestone peaks of Meteora are the two best known. Mt. Athos is also known as the *perivoli tis Panayias* (Garden of the Virgin Mary) because tradition has it that Panayia and John the

Evangelist found refuge there when traveling on stormy seas and, admiring its natural beauty, asked that it be made her rufuge. It is forested, mountainous environmental haven of unparalleled beauty, with seventeen Greek and three Slavic monasteries, all self-governing but lying within the sovereignty of the Hellenic Republic. The peninsula is *avaton*, meaning it bans access to anyone of the opposite sex (female in this case). Athos restricts all human traffic by requiring special permission for entrance and limiting the amount of time visitors can spend.

Monasticism and asceticism have been part of Eastern Christianity from the earliest years of the church, when people like St. Anthony retreated into the desert of Egypt and St. Simeon in Syria climbed up a freestanding column fifteen meters high to live a life of contemplation for more than thirty years. These are eremitic monks, hermits living a solitary life of denial in complete, almost self-punishing retreat. There are also coenobitic (Greek *koinovion*, or "life in common") monks, people of one sex, female or male, living as a community together. And there is a third order, idiorhythmic (having their own rhythm or style), people who share Divine Liturgy and a few communal services but live alone or in small groups. St. Basil, the Athenian-educated bishop of Caesarea who brings gifts to children each year on New Year's Day, gave coenobitic monasticism structure and defined its calling: to live a continuous life of prayer and fasting, to seek personal repentance, and to pray unceasingly for the salvation of the world. This calling continues to motivate people from within Greece and outside to retreat to the monasteries of Greece.

Coenobitic is the most common order of monasticism. People live together and participate together in a life of prayer, study, and contemplation, but they also work to sustain their community by attending to the everyday tasks of farming, cooking, and cleaning. In addition to these activities, monks and nuns can be quite enterprising. They make icons and other home-altar items, or wood- or metalwork ritual vessels for churches and sell these to maintain their buildings. An important source of income but also a distraction is tourism, especially spiritual tourism. Places like Mt. Athos and Meteora attract a large number of tourists. While location itself is an attraction, a single monk attaining a reputation for great wisdom and insight may draw visitors. People from all over the world visit monasteries as places of retreat. They attend services and venerate a particular icon. They may also ask a wise monk dedicated to the life of the soul to help them find healing from some trauma or weariness of the soul.

ICONS

Icons are everywhere present in the intensely social world of the *panigyri* and in most other arenas of Greek life. They take center stage in the vespers

Roadside shrine with icons and olive oil for votive lamp, marking place of car accident at a bend in the road to Lake Stymphalia near Corinth. Photo by author, May 2008.

service procession. Vendors sell them in their booths, together with blue-eyed amulets to ward off the evil eye. Icons seem to look down from every niche and corner. They fill walls everywhere with images of Christ, the Virgin Mary, the prophets, apostles, martyrs, saints, mothers and fathers of the church. Their eyes stare back from dark corners of apartments, shop windows, and roadside shrines. They express the feelings of someone who has lived in the world and seen through it. Day to day, Greeks subconsciously register the presence of icons in their lives. They have grown up with icons in their homes and so give them little thought. But when they turn their attention to an icon, they approach it reverently and lock eyes, as they might approach the faded photograph of a revered ancestor.[12]

Icons are images of sacred people and scenes. They are freestanding or murals, painted or mosaic, or made of a variety of materials. Although figurative, they do not depict people realistically as they exist in the material world but are intended to capture a spiritual expression that opens up a window to heaven. Human features are elongated, facial expression serious, and eyes warm but severe. The background is usually gold, a sign of the figures' existing in timeless infinity.

Most icons establish strong eye contact. They seem to observe their viewers from all angles, fulfilling a sense that they are ever present and quick to hear the living's heartfelt prayers. They offer themselves for dialogue, as they impress upon a viewer the memory of their presence, not unlike an ancestor who stares from a photograph. They require not worship but veneration. This veneration involves kissing, burning incense, lighting a candle, decorating an icon with flowers, and surrounding it with votive offerings. According to Greek Ortho-dox theology, veneration is paid not to the image but to the prototype, the eternal human soul represented by the icon. In practice, though, people grow quite attached to particular icons.

While the Greek Orthodox hold all icons to be instruments of intervention in human communication with the divine, they believe some are especially miraculous. Deeply revered icons are those connected to revelation or mirac-ulous healing. The Axion Esti (truly worthy) icon on Mt. Athos has special significance because more than one thousand years ago a small group of monks saw the archangel Gabriel visit it and sing the "Axion Esti," a hymn of praise dedicated to the Virgin Mary. The monks introduced the hymn to the Divine Liturgy. Another deeply revered icon, perhaps the most visited in Greece, is the Panayia Evangelistria (Annunciation of the Virgin Mary) found on the island of Tinos. Tradition renders it a long-lost work of St. Luke the Apostle, held to be the first painter of Christian icons. A nun named Pelagia dreamed of the icon in 1822 and led neighbors to its buried site next to a ruined Byzantine church. Today thousands of people visit the church of Panayia Evangelistria each year on August 15, the feast day of the Dormition of the Virgin Mary, to venerate the icon, now lavishly decorated with votive offerings of silver or gold or precious stones depicting a hand, a foot, an eye, an ear, a house, a car. Votives as well as crutches left by the side of the church represent the petitions people have made or thanks they have given for a miraculous cure. The jour-ney can be hard, especially when made crawling on the knees over the one-kilometer distance from the dock to the church, an expression of deep devotion.

A second class of miraculous icons, the *acheiropoieton* (not made by hu-man hands), is theologically the most significant because it is the prototype of all other icons. The icon depicts the face of Christ on a piece of cloth. Tradition tells the story of King Abgar of Edessa. Having fallen sick, he dis-patched a message asking Christ to visit him. Instead Christ wiped his face on a *mandylion* (handkerchief) and sent it. Christ's image revealed itself miracu-lously on it and cured Abgar upon arrival. The *mandylion* became not just a holy relic but an image to be copied, either as textile or as iconographic type on a hard surface: a painted icon of a *mandylion* with Christ's face on it. Fur-thermore it became a theological prototype. Just as the *mandylion* bore the impression of the incarnate God on its surface and became a vessel of divine healing, so all icons bear witness to the power of matter to reveal divinity and of revealed divinity to effect eternal salvation.

Icons were a controversial part of Christian worship from its early beginnings, perhaps as early as the time when St. Luke the apostle reportedly picked up a paintbrush and recorded events he had witnessed. In his time, icon painters could credibly claim that they were close enough to the subject to give a reliable biographical record. Almost as soon as icons were put to religious use, however, they faced the charge of being graven images. The charge struck in two directions. It stated that, because icons were created material, their religious use amounted to idolatrous worship of created matter. It also argued that icons aggrandized the human side of Christ's incarnation at the expense of his divinity. For more than one hundred years from 725 to 842 a powerful group known as iconoclasts, or image breakers, opposed icons forcefully. So effective was the iconoclast movement in eliminating icons that very few pre–ninth-century icons survive. Yet *iconophiles* (supporters of icons, also know as *iconodules*) were a strong presence too, especially in the monasteries and among the masses. They eventually found a powerful supporter in the Empress Irene, an Athenian and the first woman to rule Byzantium alone (from 797 to 802). She rejected iconoclasm from her position of authority. No doubt the veneration of icons was itself a survival of sorts from pre-Christian religion, especially in a place like Athens, where people loved to represent gods in human form. Yet theological arguments supporting the use of icons turned on the Christian doctrine of the nature of Christ as equally human and divine. Just as the Son's incarnation had effected human salvation, so icons, material signs animating the faith of the illiterate masses, directed the faithful to a transcendent universe. John of Damascus's famous *Apology of Icons* summarizes the position that finally prevailed: "I do not worship matter but I worship the Creator of matter, who for my sake became material and deigned to dwell in matter, who through matter effected my salvation. I will not cease from worshipping the matter through whom my salvation has been effected."[13]

Icons follow established prototypes. Yet iconography reveals the subtle dialogue of its makers with the spirit of each era. Today's icons are painted in a decidedly Byzantine style that avoids the illusion of three-dimensionality. They make use of abstraction and antirealist techniques in their attempt to present a transfigured humanity, reality from the point of view of eternity. They embrace Eastern, Byzantine over the once-more-popular Western, Renaissance-inspired prototypes. To achieve their end of transforming matter into a spiritual language, icon painters fast before participating in the sacraments of confession and communion. They also consecrate their brushes, paints, and surfaces. When working in groups, as monks or nuns do in their monastic studies, they each take on a particular task. Each artist paints a piece of the icon: one outlines the human figure, another paints the facial features, another renders the shape of the face, another the feet or hands or the folds in the clothing, another applies the gold-leaf background—each according to his or her own gifts.

MATTER AND SPIRIT IN PRACTICES AND BELIEFS

Icons are just one sign of a Greek worldview that sees the material and spiritual in close proximity. Other material objects, too, and the senses they appeal to, work to bridge the distance between the material and otherworldly. They are everywhere in Greece. They are even present in the *panigyri*.

In church burning incense fills the senses, representing the sweetness of prayers rising up to God. Candles of beeswax add their luscious scent and tiny light as they melt gradually into oblivion. They are votive offerings, signs of the small flame that burns inside everyone, of the day when it will disappear, and of the hope in eternity. Artoklasia (breaking of bread), a service blessing and sharing five sweet breads, comes at the end of a great vespers. The service of blessing recalls the five loaves of bread that reportedly fed the thousands. There may also be an offering of Fanouropita (cake of discovery) as thanks for finding something desperately lost. The cake thanks St. Fanourios, about whom nothing is known except the name found on a buried icon discovered by serendipity. Gifts of bread and wine are made to the church and returned to the people in the Eucharist offered during the Divine Liturgy. *Kolyva*, boiled wheat mixed with seeds of pomegranate, nuts, raisins, and parsley and decorated on a platter with a sugar covering, candied beads, and Jordan almonds, may be shared after the memorial service to the dead that follows the liturgy, the wheat serving as a symbol of resurrection. Flowers used to decorate the icon of the patron saint or other items in the church may be collected when they wither and placed inside tiny *fylakta* (protectors), square pouches pinned to underclothing and worn for their miraculous protecting powers.

The procession of the decorated saint's icon follows a path around the village. At the village's edge it passes the cemetery, a lovely area of cypress trees and family tombs marked with marble crosses. Contemporary Greek burial practices do not hide the fact that the body decays but instead keep within view its material remains.[14] Due to the scarcity of land, Greeks bury their dead above ground. Three years later they exhume the bones and place them in a tin box in an ossuary. In monasteries and mass graves, such as the one for thirty thousand massacred on the island of Chios by the Ottomans in 1822, human skulls are displayed for people to contemplate not just their history but their ultimate destination.

Every moment spent in the *panigyri* involves an exchange of glances: unapologetic stares, a reciprocated gaze. Like other peoples of the Mediterranean and Near East, Greeks believe that eyes can emit uncontrollably

Mati (eye) charms for sale to guard against *kako mati* (evil eye). Photo by author, October 2008.

negative energy. The emotional source of the *kako mati* (evil eye) is envy, a human response, Greeks believe, to the observation, whether consciously or unconsciously made, that someone or something is richly endowed with a scarce resource. Especially vulnerable to the *kako mati* are young children, beautiful girls with unusual features, people who flaunt their wealth, and plants or animals that visibly stir envy. The eye can penetrate any point in social life. It can affect humans, animals, and material property. Its symptoms are physical—usually an inexplicable headache, nausea, or dizziness. The church calls the evil eye *vaskania* and offers prayers to cure its symptoms. It does not object to other forms of intervention: hanging a blue-glass, eye-shaped charm or garlic to ward off the eye, or dripping a few drops of oil in a cup of water, uttering incantations, and making the sign of the cross.

At the heart of these and other practices lie old habits, some of them reaching back to pre-Christian times. Central to the Greek Orthodoxy is the story of resurrection and victory over death. Here we see its peculiarly Christian orientation, the aspect of religion that entered Greece from the East, especially with the preaching of St. Paul and others who followed. But Greek Orthodoxy spins the Christian story of resurrection in its own direction, one compatible with the Greek impulse to squeeze the joy out of every living moment, on the one hand, and the persistent belief that humanity and divinity occupy the same space. Greek religion emphasizes the resurrection of Christ over his crucifixion, the promise of salvation over the condemnation of the world for its hard-heartedness, the humanity of Christ and the potential of humans to partake of divine nature. Although sin is a strong theme, Orthodoxy defines sin as anything that separates humans from God. The church accepts a rather mild doctrine of original sin, a notion of humanity not wholly depraved and cut off from God by Adam and Eve's transgressions but wounded by sin. "The image of God is distorted by sin, but never destroyed; in the words of a hymn sung by Orthodox at the Funeral service, ... 'I am the image of Thine inexpressible glory, even though I bear the wounds of sin.'"[15] Humans retain their potential for *theosis* (becoming like God). The church offers the Virgin Mary and saints as approachable, human examples to be emulated for their ascent toward God. It puts human beings and the material world that is their playground at the center of the universe and promises nothing less than spiritual perfection and a bodily, material resurrection at the end of time.

At every turn religious practices bring into consciousness the powerful presence of material creation and the joy it offers. Religion in Greece does not condemn people for seeking pleasure. Instead it reminds them that as they embrace the material world they should also look for the bridge to spiritual perfection.

ORTHODOX AND GREEK

Most Greeks are neither theologians with great spiritual stamina nor regular churchgoers. At the *panigyri* they may criticize the church, especially its hierarchy. They do not follow its requirements—even the fast from dairy and meat on the evening before a feast day is more than they sometimes aspire to. Yet there has been no organized cry for the elimination of the Orthodox element of Greek national identity. There has instead been a revival of interest in the Byzantine component of modern Greek identity, including an increase in the number of young people and professionals entering monasteries. Many nonreligious Greeks embrace the identification of the Greek nation with Orthodoxy and take pride in the deep influence Greek had on early and medieval Christianity. The roots of their deeply held beliefs lie in church history as they understand it.

According to the New Testament book of Acts, Christianity reached Europe by way of the Greek peninsula when St. Paul preached in Philippi of Macedonia in A.D. 44. Moving on to Athens, he reasoned with Jews and Gentiles, Epicureans and Stoics. He introduced to them the idea that they "worship without knowing" the "unknown God" Jesus Christ (Acts 17:13). Of course, the language of Paul's missionary work and dispatches was Greek. This fact touches the Greek imagination. Here as in so many dimensions of Greek life, the antiquity and authority of Greek plays a profound role in Greek self-understanding.

Greek Orthodoxy is the religious and cultural inheritance of the Byzantine Empire, the Greek-speaking eastern part of the Roman Empire that continued until 1453. The religion evolved from the early Christian churches. It gradually took its liturgical, cultural, and theological shape after Roman Emperor Constantine the Great legalized Christianity and transferred the imperial residence and administration from Rome to Byzantium, which he renamed Constantinople (*polis* of Constantine). In the eastern provinces surrounding Constantinople, which included all of what is Greece today, Greek was the primary language, a lingua franca, so to speak. As it was also the language of the New Testament, Greek became the language of the church, the liturgy, theological debate, religious poetry, and eventually, after the fall of Rome in 476, of the Roman imperial administration in the East, while Latin was the language of the church in the West.

Two disruptive events gave ethno-symbolic weight to the Eastern church and later fed Greek nationalist sentiments. The first was the Great Schism of 1054, the major theological break that severed relations between the Orthodox East and Catholic West and created two separate Christian churches. The break deepened cultural and social differences between the Greek East and Latin West and created a symbolic divide. The Orthodox Church became the church of Greek, in contrast to Latin—the church of Constantinople separate from Rome. More than the theological disagreement over the nature of the Trinity, which was the prima facie cause of mutual excommunication,[16] it was the cultural distinctions that weighed on people's minds: distinctions such as the fact that in the Eastern church priests marry and don't take vows of celibacy, or that the people receive the Eucharist as both leavened bread and wine and not just unleavened bread, or that religious images take the form of icons and frescoes and not three-dimensional statues as in the Catholic West.

The second event was the fall of the Byzantine Empire to the Ottomans in 1453, leading to four centuries of Ottoman Muslim rule over the Greek Orthodox population. Greeks remember this as a period of captivity, because many Greek Orthodox churches, most significantly the Hagia Sophia in Constantinople, were converted to mosques. Yet the Ottoman sultan assigned to the Greek Orthodox Patriarch of Constantinople the role of *ethnarch* (head of the *ethnos* or nation) with civil and ecclesiastical power over the entire Orthodox population in the empire, and so strengthened the hierarchy's position and increased the church's power. More important, the sultan's move made Greek Orthodoxy the primary marker of identity for this group of subjects.

Today's Greeks cling to their religious difference from other Christians and from Islam, even if the particulars of Greek Orthodoxy do not speak to them. It matters to them that they do not belong to the Protestant West or Muslim East. They embrace the linguistic and geographical markers of their Greek Orthodox distinction. They are keenly attuned to the symbolic significance that Greek, the historical language of Christianity as well as the language of classical antiquity, gives to their national self-definition. Orthodoxy and Greekness are two sides of a coin, embraced as a sine qua non of identity, whether people attend church or stay up until four in the morning dancing.

The church's influence appears diminished as people go about their business every day. Their lives are increasingly removed from the cycles of the seasons, the plantings and harvests, the insecurities of agricultural or sea livelihoods. With contagious and childhood diseases in retreat, Charos—the ancient ferryman of Hades whose name Greeks still use to refer to the angel of death— no longer looms around the corner. People find fewer reasons to retreat into mysticism or fatalism, as they have some measure of control over their lives. They may have enough money to help them pursue new pleasures rather than contemplate the lessons of a monastic ossuary or seek out the countryside shrine, whose small universe of mystery might direct their thoughts to a parallel, more perfect world on another plane. Matters of faith rarely come up in conversations.

Yet a system of belief that places divinity close at hand permeates expressions people utter daily: "If God wills," "God forbid," "God knows," "From your mouth to God's ear," "God takes his time but he doesn't forget," "By your saint," "That man wouldn't give even his own saint water," "Even the saint requires threats," "Whatever God owes you, he'll give," "God is up high, but he sees down below," "Panayia, help me!" People are still drawn to the Greek Orthodox Church as a repository of tradition, a place of continuity, a quiet retreat where they can empty themselves of life's turmoil and seek a temporary peace. Eurostat, the Eurobarometer poll, reported in 2005 that 81 percent of Greeks, more than most other Europeans, believe in God.[17] Also, 95 percent of marriages still take place in church, even though the state legalized civil marriages with Greek Law No. 1250 of 1982.

Summer evenings keep calling people back to the church square. The *panigyri* is now a sweet memory. The tables and chairs are gone. Visitors are traveling to their next destination. Old people sit on benches around the church while the young play their childhood games. Children's voices penetrate the church's entrance, where someone has stopped to light a candle and make a special deal with God. Later in the evening the candles are extinguished and doors locked, while oil lamps burn, reflecting dimly in a saint's eyes. For much of their day Greeks are indifferent to religion. Some are downright hostile to it, while a few seek spiritual alternatives: Buddhism, paganism, Evangelical Christianity. Immigrants from other lands, a growing population, do not share with Greeks their sense of the past or the same history of beliefs and practice. Demographics may eventually affect the place of Orthodoxy in Greece. For now, the church square resonates with familiar sounds and emotions.

NOTES

1. "[Orthodoxy] is applied to the Eastern Church because it has attempted to keep its beliefs and practices unchanged." *The New York Times Guide to Essential Knowledge*, contributor William Safire (New York: Macmillan, 2007), 699.

2. "The Constitution of Greece," Hellenic Resources Network Documents (accessed January 1, 2008), http://www.hri.org/docs/syntagma/artcl25.html. Bert Groen, "Dominant Orthodoxy, Religious Minorities, and Human Rights in Greece," in *Orthodox Christianity and Contemporary Europe*, ed. Jonathan Sutton and William Peter van den Bercken (Wilsele, Belgium: Peeters Publishers, 2003), 439–454, gives an account of the place of non-Orthodox minorities in Greece.

3. Ieronymous II was named Archbishop of Athens and All Greece and Primate of the Autocephalous Orthodox Church of Greece on February 7, 2008.

4. Carl S. Tyneh, *Orthodox Christianity* (Hauppauge, NY: Nova, 2002), 150–308, offers a comprehensive, up-to-date, annotated bibliography of English titles on Orthodoxy.

5. Shira Schoenberg, "The Virtual Jewish History Tour, Greece," Jewish Virtual Library (accessed January 1, 2008), http://www.jewishvirtuallibrary.org/jsource/vjw/Greece.html.

6. John Freely, *Strolling through Athens* (London: Tauris Parke Paperbacks, 2004), 239.

7. Niki Kitsantonis, "Muslims in Athens Build Their Own Mosque," *International Herald Tribune*, July 6, 2007, archived at http://www.iht.com/articles/2007/07/05/news/greek.php.

8. Timothy Ware, *The Orthodox Church* (London: Penguin, 1964), 275–280, describes the interior of Orthodox churches in detail.

9. John Campbell and Philip Sherrard, *Modern Greece* (New York: Praeger, 1968), 199.

10. Margaret Alexiou, *The Ritual Lament in Greek Tradition*, ed. Dimitrios Yatromanolakis and Panagiotis Roilos (1974; repr., Lanham, MD: Rowman and Littlefield, 2002), 62–77, analyzes the service of the Epitaphios in the broader context of ancient rituals of lament in the eastern Mediterranean.

11. See "Description of the Miracle of Holy Fire," Holy Fire (accessed January 1, 2008), http://www.holyfire.org/eng/.

12. Kyriacos C. Markides, *The Mountain of Silence* (New York: Doubleday, 2001), 67–77, draws this analogy.

13. St. John of Damascus, "Apologia against Those Who Decry Holy Images," Internet Medieval Sourcebook (accessed January 1, 2008), http://www.fordham.edu/halsall/basis/johndamascus-images.html.

14. Neni Panourgiá, *Fragments of Death, Fables of Identity: An Athenian Anthropography* (Madison: University of Wisconsin Press, 1995), discusses graves and burial practices in Greece.

15. Ware, *Orthodox Church*, 229. See also Barry Baldwin, "Cappadocian Fathers," *The Oxford Dictionary of Byzantium*, ed. Alexander P. Kazhdan (Oxford: Oxford University Press, 1991), available at http://www.oxfordreference.com.proxy.lib.umich.edu/views/ENTRY.html?subview=Main&entry=t174.e0902.

16. See Ware, *Orthodox Church*, 58–59, on the Trinitarian dispute. It hinged on the *filioque* (from Latin "and the Son"), a phrase the Spanish church first inserted into the Nicene Creed in 589 and Charlemagne then made an issue of contention in the ninth century.

17. Eurobarometer "Social Values, Science and Technology," (Fieldwork: January–February 2005, Publication: June 2005), 11, archived at European Commission Public Opinion (accessed January 1, 2008), http://ec.europa.eu/public_opinion/archives/eb_special_en.htm.

3

Society

A CAREFUL LOOK at a scene from everyday life, the prose of the world, as it has been called, can offer insights into many facets of Greek society. Insiders might not give special notice to an event such as the purchase of a *karpouzi* (watermelon) at an urban neighborhood's *laiki agora* (farmer's market). If asked to think about it, Greeks would find it familiar. Subconsciously, without reflection, they would understand how it took shape. Perhaps the scene would have played out differently in their lives, but the behavior would make sense to them. To eyes and ears unfamiliar with the spaces and forms of social interaction in Greece, however, the scene presents a set of puzzles, which, through careful inquiry into its constituent elements, can "elucidate the network of situations making up the practical sphere" and expose the "ground rules and background expectancies that are constitutive elements" of Greek society.[1]

The purchase of the watermelon is surprisingly comprehensive in the number of spaces, the kinds of relations, and the social values it draws into its sphere. The event moves between an apartment building and the *laiki* on a city street. Along the way it engages the transitional space of a balcony and the *kafeneio* (coffeehouse), a business designed to encourage mingling. It puts on display family dynamics, neighborly interactions, and relations between people on the street. At the *laiki*, there is a purchase—euros for produce—but also something more: negotiation over the terms of purchase. Because farmers' markets are weekly events in most neighborhoods and towns in Greece, they regularly bring the same shoppers and producers face to face, with each side taking advantage of familiarity to create a more profitable exchange. The

Producer selling *karpouzia* (watermelons) at the *laiki* (farmer's market) in an Athens neighborhood. Photo by author, October 2008.

scene is ethnically mixed, as people who immigrated in the 1990s are now raising families here. At the scene's edges, Greece's most recent illegal immigrants linger in the market's shadows behind vendor's stalls as they wait for a gofer job to come their way.

In this and other daily incidents, forces are at work reinforcing ties while others are cutting them loose. One important reason why people come together is that appearances matter in Greece. People deploy social values to shore up appearances. In this scene the values put into play are reciprocity, care for elderly parents, esteem for education and success, suspicion and trust, ambivalence toward the *xenos* (stranger), and some notion of *timi* (integrity, honor), *filotimo* (literally "love of honor"), and *dropi* (shame).[2] Yet the social realities setting the incident in motion and bringing it to a conclusion—the fact that Greece is a developed, urbanized country of emigrants and immigrants—threaten cohesion. People's lives are far removed from the tight circles of association identified with Greek village life, at least as anthropologists described it when they roamed Greece's countryside in the decades after World War II. Perhaps what is most important to recognize is that people are alert to social fragility, readjusting older tools of association to help them hold things together in the present day.

THE SCENE

It is the heart of summer. The *laiki*, a weekly farmers' market, is in full swing on the street below, and a woman has a taste for watermelon. But she is aged and unable to walk down and carry it back to her second-floor apartment.[3] Besides, a whole watermelon will not fit in her narrow refrigerator unless she has hungry mouths to consume a good part of it. And, for reasons of her own she won't share, she doesn't want to involve her husband. So one morning when the husband has gone out for errands and coffee, she approaches her grown son and his foreign wife, who are visiting from abroad. She asks them obliquely, "Is it a good day to buy a watermelon?" Her small-town upbringing long ago taught her that a woman frames her wishes as questions and expresses them politely in the absence of her husband.

The couple plays along by studying the matter from all sides, knowing well that the decision is already made. Do the watermelons look good today? Can they carry one up the stairs? Will they be staying for lunch and dinner? How quickly will they eat the watermelon? Will the remainder fit into the refrigerator when cut up?

After careful deliberation, the son and daughter-in-law head for a particular vendor following the mother's advice—"Buy from the really short man on the corner: he is *dhikos mas* [one of ours]." As they study the fruit, half a dozen acquaintances greet them and freely share their opinions on how to choose a watermelon: by its color (bright green), its underbelly (buttery yellow with minor blemishes but no soft spots), and the sheen and hollow sound of its rind. One even expounds on the dangers of genetically engineered, seedless watermelons. The vendor stands tall on a crate and offers to cut any specimen to prove all his watermelons are beautifully ripe: "*Ola ta sfazo, ola ta mahairono!*" ("I slaughter them; I knife them all!"). As the couple studies one shiny watermelon on the underside, a tall woman decisively hands over another fruit and utters in broken Greek, "*Pairne*" ("Be taking"). The son and daughter-in-law recognize her as a newly arrived immigrant, sister of the woman who manages the *kafeneio* where their father drinks his coffee. They obediently comply.

A neighbor observing the entire scene from her ground-floor balcony praises the couple upon their return. "Most young people today have abandoned their responsibilities." She's especially pleased to accept an invitation for ice-cold watermelon later that afternoon. She regularly brings their mother cheese from her village.

Heading home from the *kafeneio*, the father catches up with his son and daughter-in-law as they are entering the apartment building. He grabs the watermelon and carries it upstairs.

The incident, the act of buying a watermelon, in no time develops into a complex act with several interrelated scenes. To anyone unaccustomed to the shape of human interactions in Greece, the complexity stands out. Several things are puzzling. First, why does the mother pursue her wishes obliquely? Why does she use her son to circumvent her husband, who in the end has no problem carrying the watermelon upstairs? Second, why do so many people involve themselves in the act? In this and many other scenes in Greece, people seem to get into one another's business. Here almost a dozen superfluous souls are drawn into the drama of a simple domestic task. It could almost be a joke. How many Greeks does it take to buy a watermelon: one to place the order, two to interpret the buyer's desires, six to offer advice, another to pick it out, one to sell it, several neighbors to observe and comment, and one to carry it upstairs. Third, why is so much discourse indirect? Why don't people say what they mean? Fourth, how do people choose their vendors, acquaintances, and friends. Last, what kind of clout does a complete stranger have, and an illegal immigrant no less? Questions similar to these come up in careful observations of many social interactions in Greece from an outsider's vantage point.

LAIKI, A FARMERS' MARKET

Like many scenes from everyday life in Greece, the task of acquiring a watermelon invariably moves outdoors. The social space that gives occasion to the old woman's desire for watermelon is the *laiki*, literally the "popular" market, Greece's version of a large, traveling farmers' market, which, every Wednesday in this particular neighborhood, fills several blocks along a street not far from the heart of Athens.

The *laiki* is a weekly, year-round event in most urban neighborhoods, suburbs, towns, and villages of more than five hundred residents. In large cities farmers' markets take place in more than one neighborhood each day. Municipal Athens holds about thirty-seven from Monday through Saturday.[4] Altogether hundreds of markets reach every corner of Greece in the cycle of a week.

Each weekday hundreds of separate streets cut off traffic and open up to local vendors. And the municipal authorities oblige. This in itself is a testament to the will power of farmers who take their produce to market and managers and buyers who support the event often against difficult odds. For producers and distributors, the day begins early in the morning, hours before the customers arrive, when they set out with their goods for the market area to find their choice vending spot and neatly arrange their produce. For the managers of the *laiki*, too, the hours are long, as they have to block traffic, move parked cars, and oversee the setup, breakdown, and cleanup. For shoppers, the *laiki* can take up the better part of a morning. No one questions the time commitment. No one argues that it is too much trouble. People continue to support their farmers' markets despite the effort, for they benefit both farmers, who make a better profit by selling directly, and customers, who purchase fresher produce at a good price. It's likely, too, that they help urban Greeks remember their rural roots—since most city dwellers in Greece today are just one or two generations removed from agricultural life.

The quality, color, sight, and smell, and the variety of produce are memorable. Potatoes, onions, and garlic descend from different regions of Greece, each regional kind known for its special qualities and flavors. Piles of herbs and greens send their aroma down the street: dill, parsley, sage, lettuce, Mediterranean arugula, spinach, cabbage, leeks, dandelions, chicory, Swiss chard, amaranth, chickweed, beet greens, radish greens, among others. Only fruit in season will appears in the market: oranges, nectarines, kiwi, bananas in the winter and spring, strawberries, peaches, nectarines, apricots, plums, melons, watermelons, cherries, and varieties of figs through the summer months, and grapes, apples, and pears in the fall. Tomatoes of different shapes and colors, cucumbers long and short, and string beans narrow and wide may form a separate display or combine with peppers, zucchini, other squash, and eggplant of every variety. Fresh or dried legumes, an important element of the diet, occupy another space, as do olives, dried fruit and nuts, and fresh, free-range farm eggs, and cheese. Grouped together are the fishmongers, competing noisily with one another.

At both ends of the market one finds underwear, clothing, socks, stockings, and inexpensive shoes, china and silverware, plastic and metal vessels and tools for the home, toilet paper and paper towels, bolts of fabrics, embroideries that are usually machine made but for brief periods may be originals of exceptional quality, linens, towels, blankets, knickknacks, and plastic toys.

People saunter purposefully up and down the street with their small, portable shopping carts, or they load themselves with as many bags as they can carry and make several trips back and forth. Today's shoppers cover the spectrum of Greek society. There are Muslim women wearing head scarves, most of Albanian descent; old people bent with age and the weight of their produce; young Greek or non-Greek women dressed in the latest styles, or in classic designs, or in tight jeans with revealing tops; and men in freshly ironed cotton shirts, which they leave hanging in summer but tuck in and cover with fashionable jackets in winter.

At the edges of the markets, standing almost invisibly behind vendors or on the market's far ends, groups of men loiter. Their darker skin and shiny black hair betray their origins from northern Pakistan, Bangladesh, India, Syria, Egypt, or Iraq. They cluster together for security and move as a group, eyes alert for signs of the police, yet ready to work for little if asked. They are some of Greece's many undocumented laborers.

Apart from a few harried customers who are especially pressed for time, people move unhurriedly. Their relatively slow gait signifies not just their effort to find the freshest goods at the best price but their desire to greet others and be greeted, to see others and be seen. In the market women especially put on display the fact that they are fulfilling their domestic duties in ways that benefit their family's health and finances. In this way they are maintaining their reputation as good managers of the home. If hired household help is their proxy, good behavior and sound choices reflect well on the family. Appearances matter a great deal in a society where people's eyes are turned on one another and where talk precedes and follows every social exchange.

DHIKOS

The words people use to talk about one another matter. Notable is the term the mother uses to name the family's relationship with the vendor: he is *dhikos mas*, "one of ours." Anthropologists have singled out the possessive adjective *dhikos* as the term for an insider, with *xenos* as the opposite, the outsider, the stranger, the one who is not ours.[5] *Dhikos* indicates a bond holding people together. The bond derives from the reciprocation of obligations and sentiment. It translates into loyalty. In rarer instances, it becomes *embistosini* (trust), a hard-won feeling.[6] In smaller or larger ways, *dhikos* is a person who meets another's needs—hence the mother's recommendation.

Greeks see themselves connected to one another through webs of reciprocity. Like a spider's web, social relations are a work in progress. Wherever people gather they are spinning their social web. In the neighborhood or square, in a coffee shop, in a shared hospital room, on the beach, at a restaurant or club, at work, at the airport gate awaiting the return of a beloved friend or relative. Wherever they share circumstances, they may exchange greetings first, then good wishes, then personal information and promises. At some moment, the feeling of connection may motivate one person to act beyond expectations. When renting a beachside apartment, for example, renters and a landlord may enter a relationship of reciprocity exceeding the economic one. If a landlord treats the renters to a homemade meal or invites them to an *onomastiki yiorti* (name-day celebration on the feast day of a patron saint with the same name as the person), the renters will care for the property as if it were their own and accept an increase in rent. In the process the bond of *dhikos* will have formed. The connections grow outwardly from the center, where the closest of friends and family stand. Wherever ties are strongest, people will overlook the other's faults and overcome obstacles to offer assistance.

A close constellation of *dhikos* is a *parea* (group of friends), whose members share good times and bad over the long stretch of life. An impulse prevails to form and keep such groups wherever Greek communities exist—whether in Greece or abroad. In cases where family controls are strict, which are more rare today than they were in the not-so-distant past, people find in *parea* the comfort of an egalitarian space in contrast to authoritative family relations.[7] Today's *parea* can be an antidote to the workplace, where people often feel overlooked, or to the anonymous state, which people generally do not believe is working to serve their interests. *Parees* (plural of *parea*) may form rather spontaneously when a group of people (from a neighborhood, school, university, work, a common cause such as a political party or religious beliefs) decide jointly to socialize. The *parea* with longevity is the one whose relationships have been tested individually and collectively over time. Singer-songwriter Dionysis Savvopoulos captures the process by which "Greeks create *networks,* / parees make history" in his very popular song, "As kratisoun oi horoi" ("May the Dances Go On").[8] The song describes how an intergenerational group coalesces around music, as one person takes the leads in song and others form the traditional circle dance. The gravitational center of this "old, lit orbit" is a shared sense of history and beliefs, but also the prospect of increasingly warm bonds of friendship in future gatherings. Savvopoulos idealizes the *parea* as *the* quintessential Greek community: a quasi-religious congregation dedicated to song and dance.

People tend to create regular occasions for their *parea* gatherings. They meet often to enjoy food and drink in a favorite setting. Once together, they seize the present moment. They may recall their troubles momentarily but quickly forget them by affirming the joy of togetherness. Lively conversation, music, and dance are the key to their life affirmation. So is the follow-up. The next day telephones ring, text messages fly, as two by two people analyze who said what to whom and what it all meant. Despite the strong, almost-erotic emotions that develop in a *parea*, despite the intense scrutiny, despite tests of time, high expectations, and even distance, a *parea* from as early as grade school can cohere for a lifetime.

Dhikos is a conditional relationship. Bonds are weaker or stronger depending on time, reciprocity, emotions, and trust. Relations are weakest around the edges and strongest near the center. Loose relationships of *dhikos* form when people find they are in agreement or share a single evening. Deeper relations develop more slowly, through long hours on the job, for example, or cohabitation in an apartment building, when one person runs errands at a time of need and the recipient of goodwill reciprocates. The strongest tie is *filia* (friendship), an emotional alliance perceived as standing on its own ground, without obligation as a motivation for association. The most cohesive *filia* is "characterized by the absence of significant economic functions."[9] The sense that someone is *dhikos* may strengthen with time as positive feelings grow. Or it may weaken where there are fewer opportunities to offer and receive. Or it may end suddenly through betrayal.

The web of relations is strong but not impregnable. A thread connecting two people can gain or lose strength through a series of tests life may provide, as the relationship faces complications caused by group dynamics, emotional distress, hardship, illness, or physical distance. Lines of connection can become stretched when challenged by overpowering circumstances: living in too-close quarters, going into business together, competing for a rare promotion, introducing a new liaison or spouse to a close friendship, facing financial or other undisclosed troubles that alter behaviors. A sharp break at the center of one's social web is particularly destructive.

What lies beyond relations of *dhikos*? As a general rule, a relationship in Greece implies some level of reciprocity, so a lack of relationship means people owe nothing to one another. While people may keep looking to bring others into their circle, they also remain indifferent to those outside their sphere. Still the cutoff line is never entirely clear. *Xenos*, the opposite of *dhikos*, refers to the foreigner or stranger to whom one has no obligation. In between is *allos* (other), a person or group that is not *dhikos*. There are degrees of *xenos*, just as there are of *dhikos*. The nearest *xenos* is the houseguest. This sense of *xenos* is connected etymologically to *filoxenia* (hospitality), which means extending treatment worthy of friendship to a *xenos*. Thus the *xenos* may lie at the doorstep not just of *filoxenia* but of *filia* (friendship). The *xenos* may also refer to acquaintances who exchange greetings but do not expect future positive actions. Further afield lies unfamiliar social ground. Because *xenos* in Greek means both stranger and foreigner, *xenophobia* can refer to fear of the stranger or intolerance of the foreigner. The stranger or foreigner usually lies outside people's frame of reference. Yet in a gesture of spontaneous delight, a person may show *filoxenia* to the *xenos* with no expectation of return—whether from a strong sense of ethnic pride or a desire to increase one's sphere of influence.[10] One last fated relationship lies on the outer rim of Greek sociability, beyond the *xenos*. Here is the *ehthros* (enemy), the estranged friend or relative or inherited foe who used to be *dhikos* but betrayed the relationship.

How exactly does a farmers' market vendor become *dhikos*? The *laiki* is cyclical but short lived. Vendors appear weekly at best. Consumers see them in passing. Relations of shoppers with vendors do not evolve personally to the degree that they would with a storekeeper in the neighborhood, where people pass regularly, address one another by first name, offer greetings on holidays and name days, barter heavily on lucky days such as the first of the month, and ask about children and other relatives. Still haggling, flirting, manipulating, complimenting, praising, and blaming enter the give and take in the market. On both sides of the exchange, people seek out proven familiarity, though this does not translate into proven trustworthiness.[11] People regularly suspect that they have been cheated, whether or not this is true. As familiarity grows, people may divulge bits of personal information. They use this information to confirm—and keep testing—the other's trustworthiness. Somewhere in the long sequence of interactions, when there is sufficient evidence that the other person plays more fairly than expected, the one may begin to consider the other *dhikos*.

On the occasion described, a successful son from abroad descends upon the market, sent there by his mother, to confirm the family's trust in the vendor and show off the son's success. The vendor remembers the parents' nostalgia for the absent son and celebrates his return by rounding down the price. Each side dispenses small scraps of trust before moving on to the next exchange.

THE EYES OF THE WORLD

In the gestures and facial expressions of the couple as they pay the vendor, part with the acquaintances who offered them advice, thank the immigrant woman who selected their watermelon, or stop to greet Panayota, their nosy neighbor, there are expressions of great warmth but limited trust.

Here is Panayota observing everyone from her ground-floor balcony. "Most young people today have abandoned their responsibilities, especially when they live abroad—but not you," she clucks as the son and daughter-in-law round the corner into the apartment building. The son replies tactfully, "It's nice to see you, Mrs. Panayota! Isn't this the perfect watermelon?" But Panayota would like to steer the conversation in another direction, to find out more about his living so far from his parents, "I don't suppose you find watermelons like these in America? Good that you can buy one for your parents when you're here," she says. The son keeps his talk strictly fixed on watermelon. "Yes, it's a beauty! Won't you share it with us this afternoon?" He knows this conversation is really about his eleven-month absence, but he won't reveal any information about the family's difficulties balancing his absence with his aging parents' growing needs.

Trust is the hardest-earned of relations in Greece and the most easily broken. People may drink coffee together regularly. They may share emotional moments. They may run to the other's assistance. They may consider one another *dhikos*. Yet they are slow to reach a point of speaking spontaneously, without checking their words to consider how another might receive or use them. They will not completely trust the other person's intentions.

Greeks often refer to their lack of trust in systems, institutions, the state, and strangers. They believe that systems are rigged against them. Institutions exploit. The media manipulate. Industries profit. The state is impersonal. Politicians, their personal representatives, line their pockets with taxpayers' money and do no good. Greeks suspect that foreign powers are conspiring day and night to undermine their country. They doubt that anyone in the world has their best interests at heart. These suspicions they justify in terms of Greece's dark modern history, whose harshest events they enumerate from the beginning of Ottoman rule in 1453 through the seven-year military dictatorship, the Turkish invasion of Cyprus, the American stand on Macedonia, or the latest public scandal. They recall years of occupation and enslavement, war and hunger, impoverishment and emigration, foreign intervention and political corruption. In their discourse, the competition for scarce resources seems almost palpable, even though Greece enjoys benefits from its entry into the European Union. People older than 70 years vividly recall their sufferings during the Nazi occupation and Civil War. But even their children and grandchildren speak of these as if from personal experience. They have adopted earlier generations' memory as a kind of cultural experience. Brutality and scarcity have become part of a collective memory defining a people.

The same narrative is used sometimes to explain the mistrust people reveal in their close associations, where they also behave as if others do not have their best interests at heart. In face-to-face relations, however, something else is also at issue: the power of one's neighbor, acquaintance, relative, even *dhikos* to harm one's reputation. Why do people expect from others ungenerous scrutiny in the form of harsh tongues and the covetous *kako mati* (evil eye)?

A partial answer to this question lies in the high level of public exposure in Greek society. Anonymity is not a feature of life even in most city neighborhoods. Hypothetically one might remain anonymous in a neighborhood where there is no public square, people drive everywhere, windows and balconies are never open, houses and stores are turned inward, and populations are transitional. This may describe a few upper-class neighborhoods in the northern suburbs of Athens but not most of the city. Even in this metropolitan area of almost 4 million people one sees holdovers of face-to-face communities, where social surveillance serves as a means of social control. Almost anywhere in Greece a stranger can appear and be noticed. Foreigners will feel lonely and forgotten, but they will not have gone unobserved.

The architecture of the social world in Greece leaves people endlessly vulnerable to the eyes of others. Greece enjoys many months of good weather, so people conduct their business and enjoy their leisure outdoors, where they meet and deliberate. Shops face streets with doors and windows wide open through the spring, summer, and fall. They tend to spill their wares onto sidewalks. Apartments have balconies on the backs as well as the fronts of buildings—on the *akalyptos horos* (uncovered space) in the center of a block, where people air their laundry. Private homes stand close to the road. Interior courtyards and balconies face the inner balconies of others. Whether they reside in cities, towns, or villages, people live together in close quarters that open onto public spaces and leave little room for privacy. Indeed, the Greek language lacks a word for and even the concept of privacy. Perhaps it is no accident that *idiotes*, the word for a private person as opposed to a public official, yields *idiosyncrasy* and *idiot* in English. People in Greece do not consider keeping to oneself to be conventional behavior.

Moreover, people talk. Every dimension of human activity is fair game: what people eat, what they wear, when they go in and out, where they work, their children, their relations, their marriages, their friends, their health, their affairs, their drinking habits, their obligations and whether they fulfill them, how food enters their home. The watermelon-buying scene gives evidence of people's chatty involvement in every aspect of even the most trivial pursuit. Acquaintances both take the time to declare what they know about watermelons and to find out what they can about sons who live abroad and visit their parents when they return.

A fuller answer to the question of why trust is so hard earned, however, must take into account deeply entrenched communicative codes, which for generations have kept in a functional balance opposing principles such as sociability and autonomy, collaboration and antagonism, sharing and thinking of oneself first, conforming and putting oneself on display. Individuals find themselves in a kind of contest with one another while also fragilely invested in the collective good. On the one hand, in times of scarce resources people in Greece learned to pursue their self-interest. On the other hand, under those same conditions, they saw that collaboration was essential to group survival. Thus, for generations Greek society has functioned under a set of social restraints affecting both individual and group behavior. Individuals strive to improve their condition while never appearing to differentiate themselves from the group. The group, in turn, works to expose excess while also appearing to accommodate individual needs. All eyes are turned on one another in a kind of battleground of social self-regulation. This contest and its occasionally brutal effects is succinctly summarized in the lyrics of a traditional folk song, "Whoever saw such a war of eyes, things coming apart without swords or knives?"[12]

No one who travels to Greece will fail to notice the omnipresent blue-eyed charms known as *matia* (eyes). From tourist kiosks to jewelry shops, these are as symbolic of Greece's charming exoticism as the *komboloi* (worry beads). Although people buy *matia* as decorative items, they are apotropaic objects intended to protect children, domestic animals, plants, houses, and all kinds of human possessions from the effects of the *kako mati*. Not every person in Greece wears a *mati* (eye), just as not everyone confesses belief in the *kako mati* or is willing to undergo the rituals of *xematiasma* to undo the eye's evil effects. But the internalization of the beliefs runs very deep, without clear distinctions of gender or class.

In a system of social restraint where the human gaze features so prominently, common belief holds that eyes contain within them a negative as well as a positive force. The negative energy derives from covetous feelings. The bearer of the *kako mati* may remain unconscious of those feelings or of his or her power to inflict harm. Whatever the intentions, the gaze attaches itself to that which inspires envy: something of exceptional beauty, an excess of wealth, a remarkable achievement, unconventional behavior, looks, or dress, an unexpected action. The short-term affects of the *kako mati* are negative. A person may develop a headache, an animal become sick and die, a plant wither, a home catch on fire. In the long run, however, the evil eye functions to protect a social environment marked with scarce resources by restraining individuals from acquiring things in excess and so promoting themselves at the expense of the group.

Like many communities in the world, Greek society stands at a kind of tipping point between older and newer codes of communication introduced by modern forms of social mediation such as the mass media. The newer codes support commodity capitalism and therefore value the kind of social competition that encourages people to buy and display new things. Yet society keeps sounding old warnings against overstepping one's place while complaining that today's excesses sacrifice time-honored feelings of togetherness. More than ever, the social world in Greece stands in a contest with itself, with individuals pursuing every avenue for achievement under the watchful eye of the collective that works to maintain its old, delicate balance.

AT THE *KAFENEIO*

The father's whereabouts during the negotiation of the watermelon's purchase need to be traced so as to prepare for his return in the closing scene. His morning errands have taken him through the neighborhood, then deposited him at Kafeneio Rosa, the coffee shop of his choice in the *plateia* (city square).

This particular square offers five coffee shops to choose from, something not especially unusual in Greece, a country where eateries abound and people carefully choose their regular place of gathering. Two coffee shops stand to the left of the church. These cater to a younger crowd of college-aged kids, who spend their days playing *tavli* (backgammon). They drink cappuccino, frappuccino, freddo, or, more likely, frappé: a Greek-invented, frothy, thick, ice coffee made from low-quality instant Nescafé, sugar, and optional milk. The mixture is shaken or beaten and served in a tall, narrow glass with ice. A *kalamaki* (straw) is a fixture of frappé, used to drink from but also to keep mixing the froth in the prolonged process of consuming the drink down to its last syrupy bubble. Frappé is the beverage of choice for people 55 years and younger. In the first decade of the twenty-first century, Starbucks coffee shops have tried to cut into market share by converting the newest generation of coffee drinkers to their multiple brews and blends. The success has been mixed; many young people still prefer frappé in their favorite outdoor café.

To the right of the church on the corner is an old-fashioned *kafeneio*, a social hub, sometimes identified with a political *komma* (party), where men of working or retirement age spend their days. They sit for hours from morning to night, smoking, drinking coffee or ouzo, playing *tavli* or cards, tossing their *komboloi*, reading newspapers, watching soccer matches, and fervently arguing—about politicians, political parties, foreign governments, American international policies, and soccer.

Although the father is as passionate about politics as any man of his generation, his version of politics is a bit out of fashion, and he has not learned to argue in any other way. Besides he does not like to waste his time sitting in the *kafeneio* all day. So he stays out of the fray, preferring to drink a morning coffee at Rosa, a modern *kafeneio* in the style of a café-bar, where women and men stop to socialize. His regular choice is *ellinikos kafes varyglykos* (heavily sweetened Greek coffee) with two heaping teaspoons of sugar. *Ellinikos kafes* (also known as *vyzantinos*, Byzantine, or *turkikos*, Turkish) is made with a demitasse of water and a teaspoon each of sugar and finely ground coffee. The mixture is heated just to the point of boiling in a small, narrow pot called a *briki*, so that a *kaimaki* (thick foam) rises to the surface. Poured into a demitasse immediately, the coffee keeps its foam on top while the grinds settle to the bottom, inviting people to drink slowly, then read their fortunes in the patterns that form below the rim.

During his half hour at the *kafeneio*, the husband trades gibes with other regulars. His endless teasing never reaches a point of insult. Today he calls out his neighbor Andreas playfully, "Mr. President from Leivadia," referring to Andreas's place of origins and his role managing the old man's apartment building as supervisor. Andreas tugs at his shirt just above the chest in a gesture of fond disgust. He shakes his head disapprovingly but smiles. "May the Peloponnese sink and disappear!" It is all in jest, though based on generations of strong regional loyalties. Today the old man treats Andreas in celebration of his son's return. Andreas offers cheers: "*Kalos tous dechtikate!*" ("May you have received them well!"). The husband's face is aglow as he heads home.

Outside the apartment building he finds his neighbor Panayota on her ground-floor balcony chatting with his son and daughter-in-law, ostensibly about watermelon. He observes Panayota's gaze and understands that this conversation is really about his son's distance from home. This is something people talk about often, especially when a son or daughter are living abroad. People in Greece assume that children should care for aging parents and that they are delinquent if they don't. It's a matter of *filotimo*. Rumor mills churn both when children return and when they stay away, so it is always a good idea for anyone who has returned home to make a bold appearance before neighbors and friends.

EDUCATION AND *XENITIA*

Everyone is celebrating the son's visit to his native home. People welcome him and his wife. They congratulate the parents. But why is the son living abroad? Like every other detail, this one has significance for Greek society at large.

Sons and daughters living outside Greece are a fact of life for many families. An estimated 3 to 4 million and perhaps as many as 6 million Greeks live in more than one hundred countries outside Greece and Cyprus.[13] Even the conservative figure of 3 million gives an astonishing ratio of more than one person abroad for every four who live in Greece. Greek emigration has a long history. The ancient word *xeniteia*, which means "living in a foreign place," suggests profound alienation and rings with nostalgia for the distant homeland. In the modern era, *xenitia* became a reality for mass numbers of emigrants in the twentieth century. The first wave of emigration took place from 1899 to 1924 after several decades of inward migration and a "high-growth demographic regime" yielded more people than Greece could sustain.[14] At a time when Greece's population was less than 3 million, about 500,000 left their rural homes for the United States.[15] From 1950 to 1980 a second wave of 1 million people, again mostly from rural communities, emigrated to Australia, Canada, Germany, and the United States.[16]

Since Greece's entry into the European Union, the numbers of emigrants have diminished. Yet the outflow is significant because the emigrating population is educated or pursuing higher education. *Xenitia* today is the drama of Greece's most ambitious youth.

Education is compulsory for all children ages 6 to 15. Children attend six years of *dimotiko* (elementary school) and three years of *gymnasio* (middle school). After *gymnasio* they may attend three years of either *lykeio* (high school) or *epangelmatiko lykeio* (vocational high school). Students completing *lykeio* receive an *apolyterio* (degree). The Greek Ministry of Education and Religious Affairs supervises the public system of primary and secondary education. It also recognizes private schools and the degrees they offer at these two levels.

Higher education is another matter. The Greek constitution (article 16) recognizes only public institutions at the tertiary level, though a recent proposal for *anagnorisi* (recognition) of private, nonprofit colleges and universities is under discussion, generating heated debate. Public tertiary institutions in Greece are free. Although self-administered, they are supervised and

Student demonstration against proposed governmental reform of higher education.
Photo by author, February 2006.

funded by the Ministry of Education. They consist of *panestimio* (university),
or Anotata Ekpaideftika Idrymata (AEI), higher educational institutions, and
Tehnika Ekpaideftika Idrymata (TEI), technological educational institutions.
They do not offer a general liberal arts education but a specialized course of
study in a subject (e.g., philology, chemistry, mathematics, political science)
or a profession (e.g., law, architecture, engineering, medicine).

Admission to public universities and technical institutions is restricted by
state-administered *Panelladikes exetaseis* (Panhellenic exams), which are offered at the end of the third year of upper secondary education. The majority
of students elect to take these exams. Greece's educated population is growing. Its secondary graduation rates exceeded 90 percent in 2002.[17] In 2003,
16 percent of people ages forty-five to fifty-four and 25 percent of people
ages twenty-five to thirty-four had attained tertiary education.[18] People consider a university degree desirable, if not essential, perhaps because they can
no longer imagine working in jobs that do not require a degree. Additionally, success (and failure) on entrance exams has social status implications. So
parents make sacrifices to prepare their children, and children comply with
the demands placed on them. From an early age children attend *frontistirio*

(private-sector tutoring schools designed to supplement the state system) in at least one foreign language (usually English) and often a second. In the last years of high school, they attend *frontistirio* and sometimes *idiaitera* (private lessons) to prepare them for the exams. Parents spend a high percentage of their wages or salaries on tutorials and, increasingly in the past two decades, private schools. "According to even the most conservative estimates, Greece appears to spend more on education—2.4 percent of [gross domestic product (GDP)]—than any other EU country," compared to 0.1 percent of GDP for Spain, 1.3 percent for Portugal, 1.4 percent for Ireland, and 0.5 percent for Germany and France.[19]

Depending on their performance on *Panelladikes* and on a set of high school exams, students may find a place in the program or school matching their scores, although not necessarily their ambitions. Although three out of four students gain admission to a public Greek university or technical educational institution—and according to 2006–2007 statistics, 314,111 students are currently registered in Greece's public tertiary schools—many students do not gain admission to their desired course of study.[20]

Because public universities fail to meet the population's very high demand for entrance to a limited number of schools, families look elsewhere for higher education. Some students attend private franchises of European and American universities or nonprofit accredited institutions in Greece, which operate legally as *ergastiria eleftheron spoudon* (laboratories of free study). More often they study abroad at universities in countries such as Britain, France, Germany, Italy, and the United States. In fact, "Greece sends more students on a per-capita basis to universities abroad (especially Britain) than any other country in the world."[21] Students who complete a bachelor's degree in a foreign institution face additional hurdles if they return. The Greek state does not automatically recognize many foreign degrees but requires graduates of foreign universities to apply to the Hellenic National Academic Recognition and Information Center (DOATAP, formerly DIKATSA) for *anagnorisi* (recognition). Furthermore, it excludes candidates with such degrees from the public sector. And it requires that doctors and lawyers trained abroad must undergo additional training and testing in order to practice in Greece.

Thus many young people elect not to return home but instead pursue advanced degrees abroad and remain there for work. Their *xenitia* contributes to Greece's significant brain drain, the outflow of Greece's highly trained young people to larger, richer countries in the West.

Education, work opportunities, personal attachments, and decisions to marry, buy a home, have a family, make close friends, and generally put down roots—all these things have drawn the son, like so many other sons and daughters, to live his adult life outside Greece. At the same time, a highly developed sense of responsibility to family and country leads him to make regular summer visits to his parents' home.

SPITI, HOME

Spiti (house or home) is one of few social spaces in Greece facing inward, away from the rest of society. In traditional town and country homes, this is literally the case, with courtyards built behind houses or protected from view from the street by high walls, just as John Campbell and Philip Sherrard observed forty years ago: "Every family, in its domestic life, wishes to live to itself closely and secretly."[22] In their homes Greeks remain vulnerable to public scrutiny, to the degree that the eyes and ears of the world are able to penetrate that space and, especially in villages, acquaintances drop by and let themselves in without notice. Yet members of a well-functioning family manage to create a place of retreat where they withdraw from Greece's relentless sociability and consult one another, tacitly or explicitly, on how to deal with the rest of the world. In the tight embrace of a well-functioning Greek family, an individual will surrender part of the "struggle for individuality" to the family in order to find "emotional support."[23]

Observers of Greece have called the home of the recent past and the family residing within "a domestic fortress."[24] Greeks today sometimes wonder how solidly the family's foundations are standing. Relations within families are in a perpetual state of stress as the individual will of younger members, who accept advice from the increasingly powerful media and their peers, collides with the authority of those who hold the power of the purse. As family expenses grow so do the working hours of mothers and fathers, while their influence on children diminishes proportionally. And parents' dedication to educating their children and seeing them advance socially has the effect of increasing the chances that children will move far away. The home today seems quite porous.

Yet it is worth noting the number of ways Greeks express their commitment to close family relations. In Greece the majority of patients in hospitals count on family members to attend to their needs. Working children will oversee—if not always tend to every minute of—their aging parents' care; aunts and uncles of children with parents who abandon or abuse them or are otherwise unable to raise them will take on huge responsibilities. Grandparents, who proverbially believe that "my child's child is twice my own child," will help their working children by caring for grandchildren after school and during the summer months. Husbands and wives find themselves married not just to their spouses but also to their spouses' families. Finally, parents do not relinquish financial responsibility for their children when they complete their studies but do everything they can to set up the next generation for life: to the degree that they are able, they provide their children with a house or apartment, furniture, and a reserve of cash. Although a growing if still small proportion of Greeks find identification and moral approval outside traditional family relations, people continue the tradition of making deep personal sacrifices to hold together the family's system of support.

The watermelon-buying incident shows individuals in the family surrendering their will, working as a unit to perform some rather old-fashioned roles tied to the family's survival. One element highlighted is the primary task of managing the food supply. The scene shows the mother playing a central role in food management. This is a key role for the *noikokyra* (female manager of the *oikos*, another word for home or house), under long-standing, traditional arrangements, together with managing the cleanliness, arrangement of interior spaces, and the care and placement of a family's belongings within those spaces. She determines what to buy and how to use it properly without waste. In the role she plays it is possible to recognize the traditional division of labor along gender lines, which gives women the central place in reproducing, nourishing, and caring for the family and home.

By sending her son and daughter-in-law to market with clear instructions on how to negotiate the exchange, the mother is also handling a second, major responsibility: behind-the-scenes management of the social stage where the family's reputation circulates. It is evident that the mother is not comfortable involving her husband in the decision to buy a watermelon, or at least that she would rather engage her son in the activity. Perhaps she is protecting her space from her husband's authority, not wishing to introduce him to making a decision about food. Quite possibly she is renegotiating the balance of power and dependence between herself and her spouse. Even more likely, however, she has determined that the family's reputation has the most to gain by exhibiting the returning son and daughter-in-law on the street. And it has the least to lose by sidelining the father.

The father's role is harder to grasp. As a general rule the family involvement of the *noikokyris* (male manager of the house) is harder to pin down, perhaps because it happens largely outside the home. Men tend to be at loose ends in the interior aspects of family life. But they play a powerful role representing the family in public spaces. Part of their job is to uphold the family's public face. Men are expected to fulfill a family's financial obligations, even when both men and women in a family work outside the home, as most do today. They manage the inflow of money. They also keep track of what is happening in the larger social world that might affect the family's survival. They seek to create good family alliances through ties of friendship or *koumbaria* (sponsorship of a wedding or baptism). They tend to read newspapers, watch news shows with a high political content, and pay close attention to current events. They are known for their heated debates in politics and involvement in political parties, and they pursue promises of favors in return. The father here concerns himself with informing the *kafeneio*'s regulars that his son has arrived, initiating a round of coffee drinks, and generally asserting his authority as the family's representative in public. His carrying the watermelon into the apartment is a kind of postscript: an acceptance of his limited role in managing the home. For this particular scene shows the woman of the house having greater authority in directing family activities, even though her public presence is limited.

Social scientists have debated the relative power of women and men in Greek society and especially the degree of isolation women's traditional role in the family subjected them to. Whether they find power or weakness in women's reproductive dominance, however, they agree that legal inequalities existed for a long time in men's favor. Women in Greece, who could not vote until 1952, traditionally had very little legal power. A wife was subjected to her husband's will in the handling of her own financial affairs, decisions about her children's fate, complaints she may have had about his treatment of her in the marriage. Revisions in Greece's family law code in 1982 and 1983 and thereafter addressed these issues. The revised code of law named as joint heads of household mothers and fathers—rather than just fathers, as the old law stated. It abolished the family's obligation to provide a dowry as a legal requirement for marriage, decriminalized adultery, legalized divorce by consent, and offered couples the option of a civil marriage ceremony rather than the once-required religious service. It allowed a married woman to preserve her family name after marriage and even to give it to her children. It addressed matters of access to education and made provisions for generous maternity and parental leave. And it tried to correct inequalities in compensation for labor that had left women economically disadvantaged.

Over time, legal changes, reinforced by social, political, and economic transformations of the past thirty years, have had their structural effects. Well-educated women have taken on more work in the public sphere, in addition to their domestic and social responsibilities inside the home, which they have not relinquished. Thus, a young mother today is as likely as a man to be educated and working. Yet she still has as much responsibility in maintaining the home as her mother's and grandmother's generation did. At the same time, "neolocality," a pattern of settling in which young couples make their home away from their parents, has become the norm; it has replaced "virilocality" (settling near husband's family), which was the most common practice, and "uxorilocality" (settling near the wife's family), an arrangement found in communities where men spent months or even years away from home. Thus, the family elders are as likely to require as much care as they did in previous generation, but their children are less likely to live next door.

IMMIGRANTS

The climax of the scene comes when the foreign woman appears, like a deus ex machina, and places the perfect watermelon in the couple's hands. While many other actors in the incident make their presence felt, this illegal immigrant from Romania intervenes at just the right moment to solve a larger problem. Her intercession speaks to the transformative power of immigrants in Greek society, not because she selects the perfect watermelon but because she captures the couple's attention on a day when they are asking themselves a hard question: who will care for our parents when we leave? For they have recognized their mother's growing need for daily assistance and their own powerlessness to meet that need. The incident has a sequel. After three weeks in Greece, the couple manages to convince the father that his wife needs hired help. The Greek family turns to a Romanian woman, who was sitting in the shadows of the market waiting for an opportunity to make her services available. The husband already knows her from the *kafeneio*, for she is the newly arrived sister of his favorite waitress there. The woman takes the job willingly. She has a daughter back home whose expenses for education she must pay.

There are 761,813 permanent residents in Greece and countless illegal immigrants working illegally or with a recently gained work permit, totaling more than 1 million non-Greek *metanastes* (immigrants).[25] They occupy themselves with an array of rural and urban jobs. Many with permanent residence are moving toward fuller integration in Greece's economic and social life, although the absence of a process for naturalized citizenship—even for immigrants' children born in Greece—stands as a hard barrier to full integration. Others move completely in illegal circles. African and Asian men and women—many are certainly minors—line streets everywhere in Greece, selling their bodies, drugs, and knockoffs or pirated products. The Greek state has shown an inexplicable tolerance for their illegal entrance into the country and even greater indifference to their illegal activities. Greek society is at best ambivalent. People are happy to hire them but fearful that impoverished foreigners with undetermined loyalties are in their midst.

Women from the Philippines were the first to enter Greece as housekeepers and nannies. To this day they are the most desirable immigrant workers for the upper classes and have their own well-organized communities, for example, in the Athenian neighborhood of Ambelokipi. Women from Albania, Bulgaria, Romania, Russia, and the Ukraine do the work of caring for Greece's aged in their homes. In a sense they hold the most vulnerable position of

Immigrants line up outside orientation center for *allodapoi* (foreigners). Photo by author, October 2008.

all immigrants because they find themselves inside the "domestic fortress" of the Greek *spiti*. A foreigner who enters a Greek home has few weapons at her disposal if family members turn on her. She speaks fractured Greek. When she accompanies her ailing employers to a public setting such as a hospital, authorities treat her without deference. Her work status is dependent on the goodwill of her employers and the whims of officials. Yet because her employment brings her into the intimate setting of the *spiti*, where her handling of the job can have life-or-death consequences, her employers grow dependent on her. They may show gratitude and generosity for a job well done. They may begin to consider her *dhikos*—even to take an interest in the family she left behind. The immigrant caregiver will not necessarily reciprocate the feelings. People whose legal status is unsettled do not stand on ground they trust.

Emigration and immigration in Greece are closely linked but asymmetrical in their relations to the Greek state. Emigrants leave Greece because they are unsatisfied with opportunities at home. Immigrants do the work that emigrants or people who have raised their social status through education leave behind. In the past two decades the Greek state has formalized its belated sense of obligation to Greeks abroad, creating the Symvoulio Apodemou Ellinismou (SAE, World Council of Greeks Abroad) aimed to support the cultural and educational needs of more than 3 million emigrants and their descendents living abroad and, most recently, taking steps toward "approval of legislation that will allow overseas Greeks to vote in Greek national elections."[26] During the same period it has inadequately dealt with the question of its obligation to the more than 1 million immigrants living in Greece, 10 percent of its population, who load cargo, work on ships, tend flocks, harvest crops, build roads, run errands, care for children and the elderly, clean streets, businesses, and homes, and do a lot of other unspecified dirty work.

The end of the twentieth century brought irreversible change to Greek society. Internal migration and emigration, constitutional restructuring after the fall of the dictatorship in1974, economic growth following Greece's entrance into the European Union, revision of the family law, and mass immigration altered the social order within which women and men create bonds of association. The sense of obligation to a small circle of kin, once a mainstay of rural social units, loosened as the country become more urban. Today's continuing exodus of educated Greeks and inflow of immigrants from three continents is greatly expanding the horizon of obligations. Sensing the potential for social dissolution—and often feeling overwhelmed by the difficulty of holding things together—people are deploying old and new tools to sustain the web of reciprocal relations across a broader, more complex horizon.

NOTES

1. Mary F. Rogers, "Everyday Life and Text," *Sociological Theory* 2 (1984): 169.

2. John Campbell and Philip Sherrard, *Modern Greece* (New York: Praeger, 1968), 44, provide definitions for values anthropologists once saw as pervasive in Greek society: "Subjectively [*timi*] is the sense of integrity, of not being touched, or humiliated before others, or oneself, through particular kinds of failure. Outwardly *timi* is the recognition of social worth which is conceded grudgingly by the community." *Filotimo*, "'love of honor' ... encourages a man to act rightly, and therefore is particularly sensitive to any suggestion that he has not done so; and *dropi*, shame, which is the fear of failure that prevents wrong actions, or a sense of acute discomfort which follows after them."

3. This is equivalent to a third floor in America. In Greece the ground floor is the entry floor, the floor above that is the first floor, and so on.

4. "Weekly program of farmers' markets in municipal Athens" (in Greek), City of Athens (accessed September 13, 2008), http://www.cityofathens.gr/ebdomadiaia-katastasi-laikon-agoron-sta-oria-toy-dimoy-athinaion.

5. See E. Neni K. Panourgia, *Fragments of Death, Fables of Identity: An Athenian Anthropography* (Madison: University of Wisconsin Press, 1995), 17, for definitions of *dhikos* (plural: *dhikoi*) and *xenos*. See Harry C. Triandis, "Education of Greek Americans for a Pluralistic Society," in *Education and Greek Americans: Process and Prospects*, ed. Spyros D. Orfanos, Harry J. Psomiades, and John Spiridakis (New York: Pella, 1987), 19–34, on insiders and outsiders in Greek social groups.

6. Keith R. Legg, *Politics in Greece* (Stanford University Press, 1969), chap. 1, "The Character of Greek Society," 31–40, discusses loyalty, mistrust, and trust in the

context of political relations. Paul Sant Cassia and Constantina Bada, *The Making of the Modern Greek Family* (Cambridge University Press, 1992), 251, observe: "In the city, or rather in the image of the city (largely manufactured by peasants who brought their own culture with them), the potential absence of trust is even greater" than in the countryside.

7. Peter Loizos and Evthymios Papataxiarchis, "Gender and Kinship in Marriage and Alternative Contexts," in *Contested Identities: Gender and Kinship in Modern Greece*, ed. Peter Loizos and Evthymios Papataxiarchis (Princeton, NJ: Princeton University Press, 1991), 3–25, compare patterns of relations in kinship and in friendship.

8. Dionysis Savvopoulos, "As kratisoun oi horoi," *Trapezakia exo* (Lyra 1983), author's translation. The song is ubiquitous in Greece and was sung in the closing ceremonies of the Athens 2004 Olympics.

9. Evthymios Papataxiarchis, "Friends of the Heart: Male Commensal Solidarity, Gender, and Kinship in Aegean Greece," in *Contested Identities*, ed. Peter Loizos and Evthymios Papataxiarchis (Princeton, NJ: Princeton University Press, 1991), 156.

10. "Hospitality," in *Greece: Insight Guides*, ed. Karen Van Dyck and Hans Hoefer (Singapore: Apa Productions, 1988), 280–281, comments on hospitality as a complex play of power relations.

11. See Michael Herzfeld, *A Place in History: Social and Monumental Time in a Cretan Town* (Princeton, NJ: Princeton University Press, 1991), 151 on the "brittle and unstable" degrees of trust between sellers and buyers.

12. Author's translation.

13. Victor Roudometof and Anna Karpathakis, "Greek Americans and Transnationalism: Religion, Class, and Community," in *Communities across Borders: New Immigrants and Transnational Cultures*, ed. Paul T. Kennedy and Victor Roudometof (New York: Routledge, 2002) 41, quote the lower figure. *About Greece* (Athens: Ministry of Press and Mass Media, Secretariat General of Information, 2007), 171, quotes 6 million, in which it includes estimates of people of Greek descent living in states that do not count Greek ethnicity.

14. Thomas W. Gallant, *Modern Greece* (London: Arnold, 2001), 79.

15. Charles C. Moskos, *Greek Americans, Struggle and Success* (New Brunswick, NJ: Transaction Publishers, 1989), 11.

16. Moskos, *Greek Americans*, 11, gives a breakdown of figures.

17. Organisation for Economic Co-operation and Development, *Education at a Glance: OECD Indicators 2005* (Paris: OECD Publishing, 2006), 40.

18. OECD, *Education at a Glance*, 32.

19. "Real Costs Are 1.5 Billion a Year," *Kathimerini English Edition*, February 5, 2004, http://www.ekathimerini.com/4dcgi/_w_articles_ell_2_05/02/2004_39254.

20. National Statistical Service of Greece, "Greece in Figures 2008," 10, General Secretariat of National Statistical Service of Greece, "Greece in Numbers" (accessed September 8, 2008), http://www.statistics.gr/main_eng.asp.

21. Anastasios Giamouridis and Carl Bagley, "Policy, Politics, and Social Inequality in the Educational System" *Journal of Modern Greek Studies* 24, no. 1 (May 2006): 9.

22. Campbell and Sherrard, *Modern Greece*, 334.

23. Neni Panourgia, *Fragments of Death*, 72.

24. James Pettifer, *Greece: The Land and People since the War* (London: Viking, 1993) 149.

25. "Population Projections of Greece 2007–2050," General Secretariat of National Statistical Service of Greece (accessed September 6, 2008), http://www.statistics.gr/anaz_eng.asp. Note that Greeks use the word *metanastes* for immigrants, emigrants, and internal migrants.

26. SAE homepage (accessed September 15, 2008), http://en.sae.gr/.

4

Leisure, Holidays, and the Greek Table

LEISURE IS TIME not dedicated to labor, while labor is time not given to leisure. Human groups imagine the relationship of these two categories in different ways. The words they use may indicate which idea holds priority. In Greek, *ascholia* and *apascholisi*, words associated with labor (*apascholisi* officially designates labor, as in Ypourgeio Apascholisis, Department of Labor), derive from the ancient Greek word *schole*, free time, and the privative *a-* (un-). So Greek labor is the lack of leisure. The verb *scholao* means to get off work: to leave the place where one is deprived of time to pursue what one likes. The root *schol-* is also linked to learning (hence the English derivatives *school* and *scholar*), so leisure in Greek means making good use of free time. The Greek language gives the arts of leisure logical precedence over the necessity of labor.

To understand Greece is to sense the value people give to time away from work and the resentment they sometimes feel when work ties them down. Even while working, people dedicate time to choreographing the rest of their day. They may discuss the passive entertainment they will pursue after work, such as a televised soccer match or endless hours of *tavli* (backgammon) or card playing,[1] or a growing but still limited preoccupation, the Internet.[2] They will share countless ideas for weekend excursions—to an ancestral home or a picturesque town for a holiday, or to the nearby *paralia* (waterfront) for a weekend. Casinos feed on people's appetite for risk.[3] The casino at Loutraki and the Regency Casino in Thessaloniki both claim to be the largest in Greece and even Europe, while Casino Rio near Patras has forty tables and 200 slot machines. Arahova, a base for skiing on Mt. Parnassus, is known as the

"Mykonos of winter." A simpler option is an evening *volta* (stroll) or a neighborhood *panigyri* (fair) or just sitting at a *kafeneio* (coffee shop) fidgeting with an amber *komboloi* (worry beads). And a key question is what to eat and with whom to share the meal.

Always the day's leisure activities are sensitive to the arc of the sun's rise and fall. Thus the subject of leisure opens a window onto Greek time, the Greek calendar, holidays, customs, outdoor recreational spaces, and the Greek table. (Of course, leisure is inextricably connected with music, cinema, theater, and the media, cultural forms explored in later chapters.) It raises the question of what old practices mean to people who are vying each day to become more *monternoi* (modern) even as they struggle to "make sense of their place and identity amid rapid change."[4] For although Greek society has grown more distant from its agrarian roots, the rhythms of life are still very closely attuned to the sun and the weather. People are still closely attuned to the rhythms of the year as marked by religious and national holidays, by the August vacation period, to a lesser extent by national sports events, and certainly by the Greek table: by shopping for, preparing, and sharing meals.

GREEK TIME

Visitors to Greece seek out the sovereign sun in the months of endless sunshine from late May through October.[5] Their days orbit around the sun. They pursue the long hours of peak sunlight for swimming, sunbathing, and sightseeing. Dusk finds them in restaurants with a view of the sunset over water. The few hours of darkness inspire a frenzy of activity in beautifully lit bars on the narrow streets of a picturesque town or in loud clubs along a waterfront. Then just a few hours of sleep herald the coming of a new sunny day and their return to a coveted spot under its direct rays.

Of course the sun does not rise in Greece just to give visiting hyperboreans their desired tan. Greeks know the sun in a different way. It gives order to the day and shapes a way of life over the course of the year. Greeks divide the day in relation to the presence or absence of sunlight rather than to fixed hours of the day. *Proí* (morning) comes with the sunrise and *mesimeri* (midday) at its peak hours from noon until the midday meal is set aside. *Apogevma* (afternoon) is the period after the midday meal until the warmest hours of days recede. Throughout the year the hours from 3 to 5 P.M. are set aside for a midday rest, something like the Spanish siesta. Shops, banks, and government offices open Monday through Saturday from 8 or 8:30 A.M. to 2 or 2:30 P.M.; shops reopen from 5 to 8 P.M. on Tuesdays, Thursdays, and Fridays, giving their workers a break in the midafternoon. Private companies and supermarkets keep longer hours. Sundays are days of rest for all except certain restaurants, cafés, and businesses catering to tourists. Restaurants serve food through the midday hours and again in the evenings. *Vradi* begins when night falls and lights turn on—bright spotlights on Greece's monuments, streetlights at every corner, chandeliers in living rooms, streams of lights under awnings. Evening lasts through the second main meal, which is rarely earlier than 9 P.M. As *nychta* (nighttime) settles in, people do whatever they do during the day's darkest hours.

The changing length of the sun's graceful path from dawn to dusk carves out the pattern of seasonal activities. Changes in the average hours of direct, cloudless sunshine from December (fewer than four hours) to July (more than twelve hours) are more pronounced than changes in temperatures in Greece's Mediterranean climate. The Greek language names four seasons: *fthinoporo* (fall), *heimonas* (winter), *anoixi* (spring), and *kalokairi* (summer). Four seasons make their presence felt in the continental north. Some mountains are snow covered most of the year. But the subtropical climate in southern Crete and temperate, dry Mediterranean climate in much of the rest of Greece yields long, dry, hot summers and short, mildly wet winters, with short transitions of fall and spring in between. Winter's beauty is the long night. Summer's gifts are its unyielding sunshine and long day. Greek life is different in the winter and summer.

In winter, Greeks orient their lives inward. Farmers recover from the hard work of the summer harvest and turn their attention to preserving the fall produce, planting winter wheat, trimming vines, and organizing themselves for the next planting season. Shepherds move their flocks downhill from mountainous pastures and settle into their winter homes. Urban dwellers rediscover their city streets. They take over the establishments crowded by tourists in the summer. The Plaka fills with strolling Athenians, island and coastline establishments known for their tourist trade become attractive again to Greeks. Restaurants move their tables inside, close their sliding doors, and light the winter hearth. Theaters and concert halls come to life. In their homes people cover their floors with warm area rugs. They turn their balconies into storage areas. They attend to their children's schooling and after school tutoring. They spend long nights in taverns, restaurants, and bars, or at home, eating, drinking, and talking. Occasionally, when the weather is convincingly warm, a few people break out to sit outdoors in the middle of the day.

Spring may continue the rainy pattern of winter or bring sudden warmth, or it may move undecidedly between extremes. Whatever the temperature, people wear long sleeves and excess layers until mid-May, at which point they peel them off and turn their attention to the world outside. They start planning their days around the intense presence of the sun. For a few weeks before the sun really begins to burn, they may bask in it.

But when the summer heat arrives people try to avoid the sun's direct rays. Laborers set out early in the morning. If they work close enough to home, they return at midday to eat a complete meal and catch an afternoon nap during the warmest hours, a practice that persists in Greece (even though it is disappearing in other parts of southern Europe). When the day shows signs of cooling, they either return to work or enjoy the hours of leisure. They drink their coffee on a balcony or porch, or they visit a neighborhood café. Another full meal comes late—for many people even 10 P.M. is too early. Summer's night birds seek outdoor taverns, bars, and clubs in places invisible to tourists. Summer doesn't end when the first whiff of rain blows in from the north in late August. There are the hot days in September and beautiful days in October, when the sea's waters reach their warmest temperatures. While people continue to enjoy the blessings of Greece's long summer, the days lose their leisurely ease as families turn their attention to the demands of another school year.

THE CALENDAR

Greece follows the Roman calendar. Greece also recognizes most of the Gregorian reforms of 1582 accepted by the West, unlike Mt. Athos and the Orthodox Churches of Jerusalem, Russia, Serbia, Georgia, the Ukraine, and a small group of Greek Old Calendarists, who follow the old Julian Calendar. Greece's "reformed Julian" calendar is synchronized with the calendar in the West in establishing most religious holidays except Easter. Still Greeks mark time in their own ways. Like people everywhere, they offer the greeting, *kali hronia* (blessed year), on January 1. But they also wish one another *kalo mina* (blessed month) as the first day of each month rolls around, *kali evdomada* (blessed week) on Mondays, *kalo heimona* (blessed winter) upon their return from an almost universally observed August holiday (even though sultry, windless September days lie ahead), and *kali hronia* on September 1, when religious, educational, and agricultural time renews itself after the summer harvest.

The seasons together with Orthodox Christianity determine the procession of countless *yortes* (holidays), giving the Greek calendar its rhythm.[6] Schools open around the Feast of the Cross (September 14), a celebration of the Byzantine emperor's recovery of the cross of crucifixion from the Persians in the seventh century. Fall brings the Feast of St. Demetrios (October 26), whose name is etymologically linked with Demeter, ancient goddess of wheat and the harvest, and with *dimitriaka* (grains). The day coincides with preparations for planting winter wheat. On the island of Lesvos people slaughter a bull and boil it with *kiskesi* (couscous). The twelve days from Christmas to Epiphany follow the winter solstice, while Carnival, Lent, and Easter herald spring. St. George's Day (April 23 or the first Tuesday after Easter) is the agricultural bookmark opposite St. Demetrios. George, slayer of a dragon guarding a spring where he would not allow people to drink, is etymologically connected with *georgia* (agriculture). He is the patron saint of the countryside, springs, and wells. The end of the school year coincides with the arrival of the summer solstice and celebration of the Nativity of St. John the Baptist (June 24), with its midsummer rite, perhaps with pre-Christian roots, of lighting bonfires and hurdling them. Koimisis (the Dormition or Assumption of the Virgin Mary, August 15) is both the culmination of summer and a reminder of its approaching end.

Two temporal systems are at play in the Greek calendar. The one draws on old roots fashioned by agricultural practices and propped up by the church's conservative tendencies and the national idea that Greeks share a history, language, and time-honored *ethima* (customs) and *paradosi* (tradition). Urban dwellers' regular visits to the countryside renew old rituals by giving them folkloric prestige and financial incentive. A newer layer signifies Greece's place as a modern, independent European nation-state. The two coexisting systems are representative of the amalgamations of old and new that give Greek culture its rich surface and many tensions.[7]

The systems overlap in the holidays the state officially recognizes. The public holidays are October 28 (Ohi, or No Day), Hristougena (Christmas, December 25–26), Protohronia (New Year's Day, January 1), Theofania (Epiphany, January 6), Kathara Deftera (Clean Monday, the first day of Lent), March 25 (Independence Day), Megali Paraskevi (Good Friday), Pascha (Easter), Protomayia (May 1), and Koimisis (August 15). On religious and nonreligious holidays, all government offices, schools, banks, and most businesses, museums, and archaeological sites are closed. In addition there are two school holidays, one religious and one national. January 30 is the commemoration of the Treis Ierarches (Three Hierarchs), patron saints of Greek education Basil the Great, Gregory the Theologian, and John Chrysostom. On November 17, the anniversary of the 1973 Athens Polytechnic uprising against the dictatorship, schools close and students, politicians, and civilians gather to lay wreaths on a monument at the Polytechneio dedicated to those killed in the 1973 event, then march several miles through the center of Athens to the U.S. embassy to demonstrate their protest of U.S. support for the dictatorship and other unpopular American policies.

NATIONAL AND INTERNATIONAL PUBLIC HOLIDAYS

Of the public holidays, three are national and one international. Two national holidays involve government-led celebrations on all levels. The media feature speeches and programs on Greece's music, history, and national heroes.

Evzones, dressed in the traditional vest and skirt with four hundred pleats, change guard at the Tomb of the Unknown Soldier on Syntagma Square every Sunday at 11 A.M. Photo by author, May 2008.

Schoolchildren take part in celebrations by reciting poetry, wearing tradition-al costumes, and exhibiting traditional dances. Top students carry the Greek flag at the head of a parade. October 28 recalls Dictator Ioannis Metaxas's response of *Ohi!* (No) to Mussolini's demand that Greece allow the Axis pow-ers to occupy Greece on October 28, 1940. Celebrations emphasize not just Greece's refusal to yield to the Axis powers but also victory over the Italians on the Albanian front (1940) and resistance to the joint German-Italian-Bulgarian occupation (1941–1944). The day becomes an occasion for elo-quent pronouncements about the small country's resistance to unjust, foreign interventions. March 25 Greek Independence Day has both national and re-ligious resonance, as the holiday commemorates the declaration of indepen-dence, symbolized by Bishop Germanos's raising of the flag of revolt against the Ottomans in March 1821, and the angel Gabriel's announcement to the Virgin Mary that she would bear a Savior. These two sides of the day merge into one as the message of freedom is conflated with the message of divine salvation.

In the twenty-first century, controversy has entered the selection process by which flag bearers are chosen for these two celebrations. The controversy began in October 2000, when Odysseas Tsenái received that honor in his *gymnasio* (junior high school) in a town near Thessaloniki, with strong support from teachers and fellow classmates. But the local parent organization opposed his selection, referring to a Greek law prohibiting noncitizens from carrying the flag. Odysseas, the son of Albanian immigrants, had no legal status in Greece—like all children of immigrants who enter the country illegally. When the Greek Minister of Education Petros Efthymiou and even President Kostas Stephanopoulos intervened to modify the law and reinstate Odysseas, some citizens of the town protested by announcing they would not allow their children to take part in the ceremony if Odysseas carried the flag. At issue for them was the national dimension of the holiday, which they felt would be compromised if an Albanian had a leading role. Responding to the protests, Odysseas handed the flag to Katerina Kalfaki, who had the second-highest grades. The story had a sequel three years later, when Odysseas was again the top student of his class and again gave up the honor, although students occupied the school on his behalf and a powerful politician sought to give him citizenship. Since then there have been other related disagreements about the ownership and meaning of Greek history and its holidays.[8] Many ethnic Greeks are adapting to the changing demographic makeup of their country. But there is an overwhelming feeling that Greece still belongs to a nation that defines itself culturally, historically, linguistically, and religiously as Greek. The fissures appearing in the twenty-first century represent an overarching fear that demographic changes are diminishing Greeks' claim on their state, on the one hand, and that international investment in Greece is making those claims irrelevant, on the other hand.

One public holiday, Protomayia (May 1), is the internationally observed workers day inspired by a three-day strike in Chicago in 1886. Commemorating the agitation that led to the recognition of the eight-hour workday, May Day becomes an occasion for political demonstrations against inequalities. May Day also has traditional roots as a day when people celebrate the midpoint between the vernal equinox and summer solstice, the heart of spring. There is no maypole, but certain villages on the island of Euboia decorate a *pípero* ("pepper," here a young man) with flowers and parade him through the village to collect money for an evening celebration. Elsewhere people make a crown of flowers and use it to decorate their doors and balconies.

RELIGIOUS HOLIDAYS

Religion's strong presence on the national calendar indicates just how inextricably the history of modern Greece is interwoven with the history of Greek Orthodoxy.[9] People's sense of the inevitable entwinement of religion in definitions of Greekness looks back to the Ottoman Empire, when Greek

Orthodoxy rather than ethnicity distinguished a person from the ruling Muslim or member of another group. Or it may look further back to early Christianity's adoption of Greek as the language of the New Testament. It should be noted that the strong link of Greekness with Orthodox Christianity leaves out the very small but important Jewish minority in Greece, particularly Romaniotes, who have lived in Greece's territory for more than two thousand years and feel fully Greek.

Hristougenna (*Hristos + genna*, Christ's birth or Christmas) is the holiday of the winter solstice. Christmas in Greece has come to resemble the holiday commercialized everywhere in the world. The religious focus of the day has diminished, the Advent all but ignored, and many local traditions have weakened their hold on people's imagination. People decorate their houses with lights and Christmas trees, as they have for many decades, though the tradition is probably an imported one. In the past it was more common for seafarers to hang Christmas boats on their windows. People today no longer concern themselves seriously with *kalikantzaroi*, demons that used to be seen lurking in dark places, polluting the home and causing mischief. They emerged from their underground homes during the twelve days between Christmas and Epiphany. Underground their work was to chop down the tree of life, but they abandoned that work just as it was almost complete so they could disturb life above ground on Christmas. People would burn a *skarkantzalos* (Christmas log) for the twelve days to scare the *kalikantzaroi* away. The waters blessed during Epiphany would finally banish the spirits.[10]

Although celebrations of Christmas have lost some of their local color and religious significance, certain customs and ideas persist. People associate the holiday with a full twelve days of *yortes* (holidays) from Christmas to Epiphany. December 25 and 26, January 1, and January 6 are public holidays, but schools are closed for the entire stretch. These days represent the birth and maturation of Jesus, on the one hand, and good cheer and generosity in the darkest days of winter, on the other. Religion and culture are inextricably intertwined, whether or not people view themselves as devout. Greeks feel the spirit of the holidays building through a procession of important saints' days in late November and December: Katherine (November 25), Andrew (November 30), Barbara (December 4), Nicholas (December 6), Spyridon (December 12), Christina (December 25), Emmanuel (December 26), and Stephen (December 27). For more than a month, text messages, phone calls, and visitors cross the country with wishes of *hronia polla* (may you live many years) to anyone celebrating an *onomastiki yiorti* (name day), the saint or feast day associated with a person's given name. It should be noted that for many people name days are more self-defining than a birthdays. People celebrating name days fill their homes with sweets to treat anticipated visitors. During this period, the media run special television programs of vespers and liturgical services, documentaries about local traditions, and presentations of traditional music and dance.

With Christmas's approach, lights glow, stores push their merchandise, and people greet one another, *kala Hristougena!* (merry Christmas) and *kales yortes* (happy holidays). On Christmas Eve children go from house to house singing *kalanda*, a traditional Christmas carol, accompanied by a metal triangle, and expecting a gift of money and sweets in return. It's interesting that caroling persists today, spurred perhaps a bit at least by the financial motive (kids pocket the money they are given). What's more interesting is that immigrants' children have taken up the practices, traveling together or in groups with their Greek friends. In the countryside there is a strong effort to sing carols of local distinction. The traditional Christmas carol offers good wishes to the masters of the household as it tells the Christmas story, then recommends a good nap before the Christmas service late on Christmas Eve. Families share the Christmas meal of stuffed turkey or pork late that night or on Christmas Day. Some homes still prepare the sculpted *Hristopsomo* (Christ's bread) decorated with a cross or a symbol depicting the family's occupation, for example, a harness, a plow and ox, or a wine barrel.

The Greek Orthodox calendar dedicates New Years' Day to Agios Vasilis (St. Basil) who, like St. Nicholas, is remembered for his generosity. So Greeks exchange presents on New Year's Day rather than Christmas and attribute these to Agios Vasilis rather than Santa Claus. "Ti sou efere o Agios Vasilis?" ("What did St. Basil give you?"), they ask. New Year's Eve parties are part of celebrations. But the emphasis falls on the dawning day, when it's preferable for a child to be the first to enter the front door, and a pomegranate smashed on the floor of a home brings good luck. There's another set of *kalanda* (carols) narrating the life of the learned St. Basil, books and pen in hand, attending to his lessons. He's invited to teach the family the alphabet and cut the *pita* (pie or bread). The song's reference is to the *Vasilopita* (St. Basil's *pita*) shared on this day. Recipes for the *pita* vary. Some regions make a savory pie, though the sweet, leavened bread flavored with orange and lemon or anise has become mainstream. The *pita* always hides a coin to recall the legend of St. Basil, who baked coins into bread in order to redistribute excess money amassed by an unscrupulous tax collector. There's a delightful ritual of cutting the *Vasilopita* while naming the recipient of each piece: first Christ, then the heads of the household, then individuals present or absent in the group. The coveted piece with the coin offers the promise of good luck in the coming year.

Epiphany on January 6 closes the cycle of Christmas's twelve days. The holiday recalls the baptism of Jesus in his thirtieth year, the revelatory event that marked the beginning of his ministry. Epiphany is theologically important in

Orthodoxy, a second Christmas. Yet as in so many Greek Orthodox religious celebrations, the theology takes a less active role in people's imaginations than the ritual. Ritual rather than systematic theology or even a clear idea of what one actually believes marks religious practice. The service of Epiphany contains an *Agiasmos* (blessing) of water, with a long litany of prayers followed by the sprinkling of the space of the church with water using a sprig of basil and a distribution of the blessed waters in plastic bottles. The *Agiasmos* serves as an important reminder that water is a blessing in the eastern Mediterranean, where it is an increasingly limited resource. The blessed water is later sprinkled on people's heads, their possessions, their animals, their living and working spaces. Because the line separating church and state in Greece is not solid, and because people broadly accept this permeability without protest, the rituals of sprinkling waters and cutting the *Vasilopita* happen again on school grounds and in governmental offices. A dramatic ritual associated with the Epiphany is the throwing of a cross into the cold waters of a river or the sea. Young people compete to recover the cross.

Some customs associated with the days of Christmas are local. In Evros, the northeastern corner of Greece, people create a *kamila* (camel effigy) out of mulberry branches, blankets, and the skin of a hare. They give it marble eyes and a red pepper tongue. Then a *kamilieris* (camel driver) drives it through town, accompanied by the men carrying the effigy and a bagpipe player. At each house, the *kamilieris* strikes the *kamila* with switches and orders it to dance. Members of the household treat the group to wine and gifts. The tradition may be connected with the arrival of St. Basil on New Year's Day or with the camel-riding magi.[11] On January 8 in a village in eastern Macedonia people celebrate the day of Gynaikokratia (women's rule) with women and men switching roles in their customary activities.

A second set of religious holidays aligns with spring. These are the movable feasts connected with Greek Orthodox Pascha (Easter). The exact dates of Clean Monday, Good Friday, Pentecost, and Pentecost Monday all depend on the calculation of Easter, which follows a formula involving the cycle of the moon, vernal equinox, and Jewish Passover, and is complicated by unexpelled vestiges of the Julian calendar. The Greek Orthodox Church shares Easter holidays with *palaioimerologites* (old calendarists). The Greek Orthodox Easter falls on or, more often, after Easter in the West: somewhere between mid-April and the first week of May. This makes the beginning of Lent fall near the spring equinox and Pentecost near the summer solstice. Thus Easter, the most joyous holiday in Greece, is also a celebration of spring. The holiday's promise of a victory over death finds its correlative in the natural world's rebirth.

Apokries (Carnival or Mardi Gras) runs for eleven days from Tsiknopempti ("Thursday when people eat grilled meat," the equivalent of Fat Tuesday) through the weekends of "Meat Fare" and "Cheese Fare" and ends just before Kathara Deftera. It gives people the opportunity to enjoy an "inversion of social life" before they face the prohibitions of Lent.[12] Carnival offers variations on the general theme of masquerade, satire, and excess.[13] Patras hosts the biggest Carnival in Greece, Rethymno the biggest on the island of Crete. In Rethymno more than four thousand people dress in masquerade to share in *cantades* (choral songs), search for a buried treasure, and dance to live music. Groups of masqueraders present satirical skits and a staged "stealing of a bride." Sohos in Macedonia is well known for its *koudounoforoi tragoi*, people in goatskins and large bells, who jump, jiggle, sing, and perform symbolic acts throughout the town. Prostavani, another part of Sohos's Apokries celebrations, is a day of forgiveness when younger people apologize to elders.[14] The island of Skyros has a rite involving young men who mask their faces in young goatskins and dance about with metal goat bells that weigh about one hundred pounds.[15]

Following the excesses of Apokries, Kathara Deftera begins Sarakosti (Lent, literally), a period of fasting that leads up to Easter. *Lagana*, unleavened bread, is a traditional food and kite flying the traditional activity in places such as Philopappos Hill in Athens. While Greeks turn their attention to Lent, the wind spends the next forty days disentangling kites from power lines and tree limbs. The Lenten fast specifies that no meat, fish, or dairy products are to be consumed. It finds a few conscientious observers, though more people try to limit their intake of rich foods, especially during the week before Easter.

Orthodox Christians, whether observant or not, take pleasure and pride in the poetry, chanting, and drama of the religious services of Holy Week.[16] The services and processions are the same throughout Greece, though certain places embellish them with a special flare. Kerkyra (Corfu) has a reputation for its Holy Week services. On Palm Sunday people process around town with the relics of St. Spyridon and cook the ritual *kolobina*, a bread shaped like a bird. On Holy Thursday during the service of the Twelve Gospels of the Passion, twelve lit candles are blown out one by one after each Gospel reading—an inversion of the usual practice of lighting a candle after each reading. Good Friday services culminate in the procession of the Epitaphios, an image of the supine Christ who lies ready for burial. The image is embroidered on a ritual cloth, which is then placed on a *kouvouklion*, a wooden frame decorated with flowers. A ritual procession in the streets around the church has hundreds and even thousands of reverent and irreverent followers. Towns with more than one church have processions crossing paths. Kerkyra's Epitaphios is famous for its three processions with three different philharmonic orchestras. One orchestra plays the "Adagio" of Albinoni, a second Verdi's "Marcia Funebre," and a third Chopin's "Funeral March" from the third movement of the Piano

Sonata no. 2. On the following day, Holy Saturday, people throw clay pitchers full of water from their balconies, signifying Christ's breaking the chains of death.

The midnight service of the Anastasis (Resurrection) is shared by almost everyone. The sheer spectacle of the evening is too great to resist. People come out to enjoy the strong communal celebration. They show up in church squares holding unlit candles, regardless of their religious beliefs. A mixture of deep piety and high-spirited irreverence is in the air. A witness to the scene senses that religion in Greece is really about spectacle and high community spirits, while dogma occupies people vaguely at a subconscious level. Just before midnight all lights go out. Then a bishop or priest emerges from a pitch-black altar carrying a lit candle and chanting, "Defte lavete fos" ("Come, receive the light"). The acolytes pass the flame, candle by candle. As the square fills with candlelight and the clergy start reading the Gospel of the Resurrection, a contest of fireworks (or dynamite in places with a more explosive sense of adventure) adds excitement to the scene. The atmosphere is dangerous but triumphant. The most famous Easter rocket war takes place between gangs from two churches in Vrontados on the island of Chios: Agios Markos and Panayia Eridiani. About 150 people are involved in firing twenty-five thousand rockets at the opposite church while the Anastasis service is taking place. The churches are boarded up with wood and wire as protection, and local residents stand by to prevent fire from spreading.[17] Here is a description of a related scene as it evolved one year in Kalymnos:

Midnight is . . . the signal for a barrage of dynamite to be thrown from the courtyards of the churches throughout Kalymnos. . . . The priest who came out after midnight to read the liturgy from the second floor of the church went back inside, visibly shaken, after two or three rounds of explosions. This was considered the dynamiters' victory over the priest and the church authority he represents. The bombing went on for about forty-five minutes until the police showed up. Their presence seemed to quiet things down.[18]

Most people retreat from the public square as soon as the fireworks begin, even though the Resurrection service continues for another hour and a half. They break the fast after a contest of cracking red-dyed eggs and exchanging the words *Hristos anesti* (Christ is risen) and the response *Alithos anesti* (Truly he is risen), or, occasionally as a joke, the street-smart *Mangia tou!* The tone of this second phrase is affirmative: "Really tough guy!" Translated more loosely, it means, "Bet you can't do it!" *Mayiritsa*, a rich soup of lamb offal and intestines, green onions, dill, and egg-lemon sauce, has become the national midnight meal. If they can get away, urban Greeks try to spend Easter with family and friends in the countryside, whether in their villages of origins or in a second home in the mountains or near water. Lamb roasted on a spit is the traditional Easter Sunday meal. It is served with a rich spread of *pites* (savory pies) of cheese, greens, or spinach, green salad, and *tsoureki* (braided sweet bread flavored with *mastiha* and *maglepi* or *mahlepi*[19] and decorated with a red egg). The Easter holiday continues for the entire week following Easter, which is known as Lambri (Bright Week) and really does not come to an end until Pentecost, which falls close to the summer solstice more than one hundred days after the first day of Carnival.

August 15 is the feast day of the Dormition of Mary Mother of God. A popular name for the day, Tis Panayias (Day of the All Holy One), uses the familiar name for Mary in Greece. The theological visualization of Mary's "translation" appears in the feast day icon: it shows her supine, surrounded by the mourning apostles, while an airborne Jesus lifts a much smaller image of her into the clouds. Mary plays a practical role in people's lives in Greece, whether they are consciously pious or Orthodox Christians by habit. She is the intercessor: a kind of deputy entrusted with the work of conveying people's wishes, desires, and needs to more distant authorities. That is to say, people appeal to her in spiritual and personal matters as they might appeal to a local representative in Parliament to help them work the political system. August 15 is universally celebrated in Greece with *panigyria* (festivals or fairs), name-day celebrations for those called Maria, Marios, Panayota, Panayotis, and Despoina (which means "lady" or "mistress" and is an epithet for goddesses transferred to the Virgin Mary), family reunions in ancestral homes, and home-cooked meals with the freshest flavors of the year.

THE BEACH AND OTHER PLACES OF RECREATION

A story is told about a father with two sons, one industrious and the other prodigal.[20] One day the father considered how to allot his lands. He took into account the sons' proclivities and the potential of each piece of property. After some deliberation, he decided to offer the fertile, agricultural ground in the plains, full of well-tended vineyards and silver olive groves, to his favored hardworking son. To the lazy one he gave the worthless marshlands along the coast. This seemed like a fair distribution some sixty years ago. Today the family of the industrious son hires foreign hands to harvest the grapes and olives. The family of the prodigal son has made a fortune selling beachside properties.[21]

This anecdote about capricious fortunes and unintended consequences registers with people who have observed changing property values in Greece since World War II. Perhaps the greatest change is the meteoric rise land values along the coastline. As hard as it may be to imagine at a time when Greece's name brings to mind beautiful beaches under a glorious sun, the coast of Greece before 1950 was no place to own a piece of land. Places such as Vouliagmeni, an exclusive seaside suburb 12 miles southeast of Athens with some of the most expensive real estate in Europe today, had a nautical club and a few summer huts but no expensive condominiums or developed beaches. The coastal lands on Aegean islands such as Mykonos were undesirable. Beaten by waves, battered by the wind, haunted by the specter of pirates from centuries past, threatened by damp salty air and malarial mosquitoes, they offered people few reasons to invest in their infertile ground.[22]

The story also records a cultural reorientation in the years since the war, as people left villages with their surrounding farmlands to remake their lives in cities. As city dwellers, their needs changed with their perceptions of leisure. Foreign tourists' discovery of beaches, which has transformed Greek society in so many ways, also introduced newly urbanized Greeks to new ideas about how to enjoy their holidays. Ownership of *I.X.* (private use vehicles), as Greeks refer to the automobile, altered perceptions of distance, bringing clean beaches closer to city dwellers. Gradually Greeks turned their attention from ancestral villages on mountainsides to the waterfront. Developers carved up coastal lands nearest Greece's large cities—Halkidiki east of Thessaloniki, the coastline between Corinth and Patras, the beaches of Attica—and built first summer huts, then condominiums, houses, and villas.

People also learned to swim. Before the 1960s, generations of Greeks had grown up with a view of the sea and fearful respect for the destructive potential of its waters. Few people who came of age before the war know how to swim. One sees them sitting at the water's edge during the morning hours before the sun begins to burn, bobbing up and down in shallow waters, conversing about the luncheon meal they have prepared. Later in the day their grandchildren or great-grandchildren, who slept in until noon, can be seen sunning themselves like foreign tourists, playing beachside racquetball, and diving fearlessly in deep waters. Meanwhile baby boomers, the parents and grandparents of today's fearless swimmers, have already enjoyed their swim and are ordering *mezedes* (appetizers) with ouzo to inspire passionate conversations about the day's news.

Thus Greece filled with noisy beachside resorts offering natives waterfront escapes from the urban din. Porto Rafti, officially known as Limani Mesogeas, the port of Mesogea in eastern Attica just twenty miles from Athens's city center, can serve as a case study. Within a few decades, this onetime fishing village has become a coastal destination for all classes of Athenians. The population of the area more than doubled from 3,292 in 1991 to 7,131 in 2001.[23] Condominiums and villas now fill the natural amphitheater overlooking the beach up

Harbor of Chania, Crete. Photo courtesy of Daniel Loumpouridis, July 2007.

to the peaks of the steep hillside. In addition to the homeowners and renters who descend on the waterfront, dozens of buses bring bathers from Athens twice a day. In the morning and late afternoon hours, Porto Rafti's long beach, Avlaki, fills with flocking hordes. The beach's supermarkets, its comprehensive beachside *periptero* (kiosk), three outdoor cinemas, bars, restaurants, and taverns do enough business between late May and early October to more than make up for winter's repose. On weekends, traffic builds along the two-lane road for several miles from the nearby town of Markopoulo, with its popular Darama bakery, to the athletic center with its tennis and volleyball courts, and from there all the way to the noisy club Kalua at the end of the long beach. People have learned to anticipate traffic jams at 2 A.M. on Saturday nights.

The presence of organized athletic facilities in Porto Rafti indicates another area of development. Porto Rafti has a municipal athletic center. There are soccer fields and basketball and volleyball courts, an athletic club, and two nautical sports clubs. Schools offer lessons in sailing and water skiing. These opportunities are representative samples of the kinds of active recreation people are now seeking out as they try to figure out what to do at the beach all day.

Spectatorship remains more popular than active participation in sports.[24] Greek males have been spectators for many decades. Soccer has the longest history as an organized sport with a Greek following. It reaches back to the turn of the twentieth century, when Greek clubs formed in the port cities of Piraeus, Patras, Thessaloniki, Constantinople, and Smyrna. Today Greece has sixteen clubs in its super league and three more tiers of clubs (Beta, Gamma, Delta) with hundreds of teams competing. Teams have devoted followings from passionate fans. But the country has also been building other sports programs. The General Secretariat of Sports, a branch of the Ministry of Culture, implements the government's policy on sports. It subsidizes Greece's most popular sports, including basketball, volleyball, swimming, water polo, soccer, gymnastics, wrestling, weightlifting, and track and field. Greece has seen important victories in these and other areas, including Olympic medals in gymnastics, weightlifting, wrestling, track and field, diving, judo, and tae kwondo, though the victories have been tarnished by recent revelations of widespread doping. Greece's men's national basketball team has developed an international reputation. It won Eurobasket Championships in 1987 and 2005 and reached the Final Four in International Basketball Federation (FIBA) World Championships in 1994, 1998, and 2004. The junior basketball team won the World Junior Championship in Athens in 1995.

In important ways, the ups and downs of Greece's national soccer team in 2004 and 2008 serves as a barometer of national feeling and indicates something of Greece's comfort level in organized leisure activities on the world stage. In 2004 in Portugal, the team, coached by Otto Rehhagel, achieved its greatest, most unexpected victory in the Euro Cup Championships, overcoming bookmakers' 100–1 odds against Greece to become the final champions. The team used a favorite underdog strategy of minimizing opponents' talent rather than trying to outplay them. It also took advantage of the surprise factor: nobody imagined that the Greek squad would win the tournament. "The Greeks were able to muck up each match so badly that their opponents would suddenly look up and realize they were at the sixty-minute mark of a 0–0 match. At that point, one mistake will lose you the game, and the Greeks were simply the team that cashed in on those mistakes."[25] After each win in the semifinals and finals, there was national jubilation in the streets of Greece, as people expressed their own utter astonishment that victory actually belonged to them. According to Stathis Gourgouris, Greeks found the victory miraculous, almost too good to be true: "What fortified our sense of wonder was that we achieved this victory because in the end we . . . gave the best performance. This realization does not come often to Greeks. The sheer fact of superior achievement without anybody else's help and without bending the rules has a sense of the miraculous in the Greek experience, and it registered

Greece 2004 Euro Cup Homecoming, July 5, 2004. Greece striker Angelos Charisteas lifts the Euro 2004 Cup at the all-marble Panathenian stadium, where the first modern Olympics were held in 1896, during celebrations in Athens on July 5, 2004. Charisteas, who scored the winning goal against host Portugal in the Euro finals, was honored together with his teammates by hundreds of thousands of Greeks in a homecoming celebration. ©AP Photo/Thanassis Stavrakis.

all the more as miraculous because it was indeed a fact."[26] Greeks were willing to suspend their disbelief, as the national team's victory augured well for the Athens 2004 Olympics. There Greeks again faced the world's and their own uncensored doubts that they were not capable of succeeding as hosts. They held onto their sense of the miraculous for the entire event as they witnessed a spectacular opening ceremony on August 13 and two nearly flawless weeks of games. Through countless happenings on their streets, too, in which they participated as enthusiastic hosts, they created for guests attending the games a memorable atmosphere of hospitality and celebration, leading Jacques Rogge, president of the International Olympic Committee, to conclude before the closing ceremony on August 29 that the Athens 2004 Olympics were "unforgettable, dream Games."[27] Just four years later, the dream gave way to gnawing doubts and a stinging new pronouncement by Rogge. The same soccer team played indifferently in the 2008 Euro Cup competition in Austria and Switzerland, losing three successive games. Greece won just four medals in the 2008 Olympics (compared to sixteen in the 2004 Olympics), and several athletes failed to pass drug tests, with Rogge declaring that they had won the gold in doping.[28] The humiliations of 2008 may have born out Greeks' deeply held belief that their country's superior achievement in world events is a rare miracle. In the arena of organized sports, at least, Greeks are not convinced they can be good team players.

THE GREEK TABLE

Greeks' faith in the miraculous, specifically the miracle of turning labor into a kind of "communion" of shared good feelings, remains vital on more intimate ground, especially in the Greek kitchen.[29] Patricia Storace lists the "appetite for the miraculous" as a principle of Greek cooking.[30] Certainly Greeks' faith in homemade cooking persists, as "ready-made meals and frozen foods have failed to achieve the prominence they now hold in Western Europe."[31] Despite women's entrance into the workforce in large numbers, the kitchen remains an outlet for creativity and a source of power for women. According to Diane Kochilas, women's ability to cook well, "to nourish and please, is . . . part and parcel of their ability to control a large part of family life, to draw the family in, to keep the children, young and old alike, in tow, to keep their husbands close."[32] Women are still willing to dedicate precious hours of their leisure time to preparing the Greek table even after they return home from a day's work. And both sexes seem ready to give themselves over to the spell of the Greek table, the social space where Greeks are readiest to affirm their faith in one another and shore up their sense of self-worth.[33]

The miracle of Greek food begins with the sun. Besides regulating the Greek day and its seasons, the sun also penetrates the thick canopy of coniferous and deciduous forests to create a rich habitat for wild flora and fauna. On hillsides and plains it ripens olives, fruit, and nuts. It encourages wild greens to take root in rocky crevices. It gives wheat and other grains their golden hue and stimulates grasses and shrubs to feed chickens, sheep, and goats. It helps bees navigate. It reaches down into the topsoil of gardens to give bulbous vegetables and vine plants—from potatoes to tomatoes to eggplant to grapes—their concentrated flavors and colors. On the Mediterranean *phrygana* (scrubland) the sun dries out aromatic shrubs and flowers. Anyone walking off road near Greece's shoreline will kick up a rich potpourri of thyme, sage, oregano, and lavender.

Greece's compact, diverse geography continues the sun's miracle by yielding a rich array of fruits, vegetables, nuts, oils, legumes, grains, dairy, greens, and herbs and making these available throughout the country. Farmer's markets, cities' central markets, roadside stands, and family-run stores have a built-in freshness factor, because food does not have to travel far to reach them and customers keep turning over the supply. People also grow their own produce and herbs and transfer them directly to the boiling pot—not just in country homes but in villages or suburbs or even on the terraces of urban apartments.

In the past fresh produce was distributed unevenly across Greece. Even today different locations have their specialties, for example, Aegina pistachios; Arcadian chestnuts; Amphissa, Attica, Cretan, and Kalamata olives; Argos melons; Thessaly grains; and so on. Different regions also display influences from empires that once occupied them, for example, the Venetian, French, and British in the Ionian Islands. All this distinctiveness once contributed to clear lines of regional diversity.[34] Different environments produced distinct "arteries" in Greek cooking: "the shepherd's traditions, the laconic cooking of the Aegean Islands, and the urbane, fragrant cuisine of the Asia Minor Greeks."[35]

For a while there were forces pushing toward the definition of a national Greek cuisine. Nicholas Tselementes, an internationally trained chef, was one such force. His widely influential cookbook, first published in 1910, removed improvised variations and exotic flavors as it also "upgraded" recipes by adding French culinary techniques to create a reproducible set of recipes. For example, Tselementes standardized the layers of pastitsio and moussaka, two casseroles that were typically prepared in a more improvised way, and topped them with a thick layer of béchamel. His recipes offered to the world an idea of a unified but distinctive Greek cuisine. They also gave Greeks an upwardly mobile sense of their kitchens' potential. Tselementes's cookbook has gone through numerous editions. To this day people still call any cookbook "Tselementes" and follow many of his procedures. Refrigerated trucks and improved roads and ferries after World War II were another unifying force, since they made ingredients from the far ends of the country available to more Greeks. The migration of people to centrally located cities from those same distant corners brought them into closer alliance with an urbanized code of eating.

Tselementes's extended hold on people's imagination broke in the last two decades of the twentieth century as Greeks developed a growing sense of their own plurality. This included an appreciation for the cultural contributions of Asia Minor refugees, who introduced to Greece rich cooking from Constantinople, Smyrna, and Anatolia with some of the exotic "Turkish" spices Tselementes sought to expunge.[36] More important still, a new generation of food experts appeared with cookbooks, restaurants, newspaper columns, books, and television shows, including Soula Bozi, Vefa Alexiadou, Diane Kochilas, Aglaia Kremezi, Epikouros, and Ilias Mamalakis.[37] Their ethnographic approach to cooking has expanded Greeks' imaginative grasp of what they can do with basic, seasonally fresh ingredients, time-tested techniques, and their own creative engagement with the contemporary world of food.

Greek cooking today is still urban centered, and occasionally patriotically stirred, but it has an enriched sense of its own possibilities.

Foundational ingredients of Greek cooking are really good olive oil and lemon juice or wine vinegar. The first supplies the fat, and the other two the acid. Beer, wine, and retsina (resinated wine), as well as distilled products of wine such as cognac, ouzo (with its anise flavor), *raki*, *tsikoudia*, and home-made liqueurs from cognac and fruit have a long history of enlivening the Greek table. Other drinks are coffee, tea, and infusions of *faskomilo* (sage), *tilio* (lime blossom), *hamomili* (chamomile), and *diosmo* (mint). Carbohydrate sources are grains and legumes. Cheeses, eggs, yogurt, legumes, fish, shellfish, octopus, calamari, poultry and game birds, and meat are sources of protein. Cheese making has a long history in Greece, following a trail from the East to Neolithic Crete before it reached the Greek mainland.[38] Meat used to be a limited resource, but since World War II Greeks have become dedicated carnivores. Ubiquitous vegetables are beans, cucumbers, eggplant, onions, peppers, potatoes, tomatoes, zucchini, and *horta*, a mixture of wild and cultivated greens. Walnuts, pine nuts, chestnuts, almonds, and sesame seeds find their way into savory or sweetened foods as stuffing or toppings, or they play in people's fingers in combination with dried fruit. Fresh fruit is the preferred dessert. Sugar is a popular ingredient in sweets or fruit preserves served to accompany coffee, but the traditional sweetener is honey from thyme, lavender, rosemary, and orange blossoms and conifers.

Flavors for savory foods are bay leaf (called by its mythical name, *daphne*), dill, garlic, mint, oregano, parsley, pepper, salt, and thyme, all of them widely used. There is also the caper, the bud of a humble, spiny shrub, which Greeks pickle and add to salads. Favored spices in savory and sweetened foods are allspice, cinnamon, cloves, cumin, nutmeg, and vanilla. Other flavorings are anise, orange and lemon zest, fennel, currants, *mahlepi*, and *mastiha*—the peculiarly flavored resin of a subspecies of the evergreen *Pistacia lentiscus* produced only in the southern part of Chios. Greeks love to pair these in certain combinations: lemon and dill, lemon and olive oil, vinegar and olive oil, vinegar and honey, vinegar and garlic, garlic and oregano, garlic and mint, tomatoes and cinnamon, tomatoes and capers, anise (or ouzo) and pepper, orange and fennel, allspice and cloves, pine nuts and currants, *mahlepi* and *mastiha*.[39] Although basil plants are ubiquitous in Greece and highly revered—people will decorate them with amulets to ward away the evil eye—fragrant basil leaves, typically used in special religious ceremonies, had until recently a limited place in Greek food.

Traditional procedures continue to inspire Greek cooks. One is the practice of filling vegetables with grains, meats, or cheeses. *Dolmades* (stuffed grape leaves) and *yemistes* (stuffed vegetables) are the most common, though they are by no means simple, effortless foods. But the most divinely ephemeral dish is the zucchini blossom filled with a cheese mixture, battered and fried. Another technique is to build a *pita* (pie) from kneaded, stretched, oiled, and layered *filo* dough, its architectural building block, by filling it with a savory mixture of greens, meats, and/or cheeses, or a sweet mixture of nuts and/or fruit, and baking it slowly in an oven. A third is to top boiled meat with a delicate *avgolemono* sauce of beaten eggs mixed with lemon juice and combined with a warm broth, which is then heated to the point of thickening but not curdling. *Avgolemono* is best known as the sauce that thickens chicken soup or is poured over *dolmades*, but it also combines delicately with lamb and other meat dishes prepared on the stove. *Paximadia* (rusks, or twice-baked breads and cookies), are another traditional element of the Greek kitchen, invented by the necessity to preserve bread. Barley rusks take a deliciously edible form when wetted with oil and something acidic. The Cretan *dakos* salad tops barley *paximadi* with olive oil, grated tomato, and oregano. Sweetened *paximadia*, the Greek version of biscotti, release their flavors with coffee or tea. Traditional cooking also encourages inventiveness in creating one-pot vegetarian meals called *ladera* (oily food), combinations of vegetables, grains, or legumes and ample olive oil cooked slowly in their own juices, perhaps with a little water. This is Greek cooking at its simplest, healthiest, and most economical. A richer dish will add meat, possibly tomato (depending on the accompanying vegetable), and other flavorings to the same pot. Grilling meat or fish over charcoal and flavoring it with a suspension of garlic, oregano, and salt and pepper in olive oil mixed with lemon has a very long history.[40] Whether swiftly cooking a tender cut on a grill or slowly turning a whole animal on a *souvla* (a long skewer), grilling, a procedure favored in taverns but also at spring and summer gatherings, has a special resonance for Greeks, conjuring up images of the wandering Odysseus or their wartime starved ancestors breaking a life-threatening fast.

The Greek table "has absorbed and co-opted and shunned and embraced three thousand years of people's fortunes and follies."[41] Today the Greek table serves as a kind of metaphor for Greeks' mixed investment in the modern world. It stands at a place between leisure and labor, tradition and innovation, men and women, hunger and excess, where opposites find themselves inextricably intertwined. Good food cannot reach the table without labor, though it requires leisure for its enjoyment. And the pain of its preparation, which still mainly falls on the backs of women, seems to evaporate once a crowd of friends sits at the table. Meals may vary widely in the effort expended and amount and variety of food produced. One day a table may be filled with a rich repast of many small dishes combining exotic flavors in the most creative ways. Another day the offering may be a house wine, bread, a sparse salad of confetti-cut lettuce, dill, green onion, and lemon and olive oil dressing, and a one-pot meal of octopus cooked slowly in its own juices over a stove-top fire, dressed at the last moment with a spray of vinegar. Or there may be poached fish and a salad of potatoes, lemon, parsley, and oil. The simpler meal will likely trump the richer, fancier one in the pleasure it brings as it makes those sitting at the table feel closer to their ever-receding traditional roots. People in Greece will say—and they will be utterly sincere, though they may have traveled in an expensive new car to experience this pleasure—that nothing makes them happier than just sitting with beloved friends, dipping bread in olive oil, sharing nonsense and complaints, diagnosing all that is wrong in today's working world.

NOTES

1. Evthymios Papataxiarchis, "Friends of the Heart: Male Commensal Solidarity, Gender, and Kinship in Aegean Greece," in *Contested Identities: Gender and Kinship in Modern Greece*, ed. Peter Loizos and Evthymios Papataxiarchis (Princeton, NJ: Princeton University Press, 1991), 166–167, discusses card playing as an after-work activity in the Greek *kafeneion*.

2. The Special Eurobarometer No. 293, "E-Communications Household Survey" (Fieldwork November 9–December 14, 2007), ec.europa.eu/information_society/policy/ecomm/doc/library/ext_studies/household_07/el-2.pdf, reports that 22 percent of Greek households had Internet connections, the second-lowest figure in the European Union in 2007.

3. Thomas M. Malaby, *Gambling Life: Dealing in Contingency in a Greek City* (Urbana: University of Illinois Press, 2003), explores people's exposure to risk in Chania's gambling practices.

4. David Sutton, "Explosive Debates: Dynamite, Tradition, and the State," *Anthropological Quarterly* 69, no. 2 (April 1996): 66.

5. Greek National Tourism Organization (accessed June 23, 2008), http://www.gnto.gr/pages.php?pageID=20&langID=2, reports average temperature, rainfall, humidity, and hours of sunshine.

6. Photis K. Litsas, *Our Roots: Holidays and Customs* (New York: Greek Orthodox Archidiocese of North and South America, 1982), Marilyn Rouvelas, *Guide to Greek Traditions and Customs in America* (Brookline, MA: Holy Cross Bookstore, 2004), and Vefa Alexiadou, "Greek Feasts, Anniversaries, Customs" (accessed June 30, 2008), http://www.greek-recipe.com/modules.php?name=News&file=article228, are English-language sources describing the procession of Greek Orthodox religious holidays and their celebrations.

7. Charles Stewart *Demons and the Devil* (Princeton, NJ: Princeton University Press, 1991), 116–134, explores the interaction of Greek modernity and folk practices.

8. "History Book Divides Public Opinion," *Kathimerini*, March 6, 2007, details a controversy that erupted in 2007 over a revised sixth-grade Greek history textbook

issued by the Ministry of Education and then withdrawn under pressure from people who argued that it sacrificed national consciousness to a dangerous political correctness.

9. A. Marina Iossifides, "Wine: Life's Blood and Spiritual Essence in an Orthodox convent," in *Alcohol, Gender and Culture: 1st Conference, Papers*, ed. Dimitra Gefou-Madianou (London: Routledge, 1992), 81. See also Victor Roudometof and Anna Karpathakis, "Greek Americans and Transnationalism: Religion, Class, and Community," in *Communities across Borders: New Immigrants and Transnational Cultures*, ed. Paul T. Kennedy and Victor Roudometof (New York: Routledge, 2002), 45–48, on the secular and religious roles of the church.

10. Stewart, *Demons and the Devil*, 51, discusses practices associated with the exorcism of *kalikantzaroi*.

11. The Web site Agrotravel.gr (accessed June 21, 2008), http://www.agrotravel. gr/agro/site/AgroTravel/t_docpage?sparam=thraki&doc=/Documents/Agrotravel/ event/Evros/kamila&sub_nav=Lodgings, suggests that the event satirizes the role of the tax collector under Ottoman rule.

12. C. Nadia Serematakis, *The Last Word: Women, Death, and Divination in Inner Mani* (Chicago: University of Chicago Press, 1991), 61.

13. Christophoros Milionis, "Carnival" (Apokries), in *Greece: A Traveler's Literary Companion*, ed. Artemis Leontis (San Francisco: Whereabouts Press, 1998), 135–149, explores the intersection of Carnival with more violent forms of excess during the Greek Civil War.

14. Yiorgos N. Aikaterinidis, "Ta karnavalia ston Soho," in *Epta imeres: Apokria: Agrotika dromena* (the Sunday magazine of the newspaper *Kathimerini* published on March 1, 1998), 9–12, and "Apokries sto Soho" on Agrotravel.gr (accessed June 21, 2008), http://www.agrotravel.gr/agro/site/AgroTravel/t_docpage?doc=/ Documents/Agrotravel/event/Thessaloniki/karnavalisoxos.

15. David Dean Schulman and Guy G. Stroumas, *Self and Self-transformation in the History of Religions* (New York: Oxford, 2002), 7, comment on this rite.

16. Neni Panourgiá, *Fragments of Death, Fables of Identity: An Athenian Anthropography* (Madison: University of Wisconsin Press, 1995), 151–160, writes of the entwinement of her family drama, city life, and the rituals of Holy Week.

17. "Rocket War" (accessed October 15, 2008), http://www.rocketwar.gr/index. php.

18. Sutton, "Explosive Practices," 68.

19. *Mastiha* is a resin from the Chia variety of Pistacia lentiscus, an evergreen tree that grows almost exclusively in Chios. Dried into nuggets it is used for its flavor and healing properties. *Mahlepi* is a spice from ground pits of the prunus mahaleb or St. Lucie cherry.

20. The author heard this story narrated in Porto Rafti in July 2000.

21. On the changing conditions of working the land in Greece, see David Holden, *Greece without Columns* (Philadelphia: J. B. Lippincott Co., 1972), chap. 19, "The Dying Olive Tree," 302–318; James Pettifer, *The Greeks: The Land and People since the War* (London: Viking, 1993), chap. 9, "Agriculture," 102–112; David H. Close,

Greece since 1945 (London: Pearson Education, 2002), chap. 9 "Restructuring the Economy, 1974–2000," 168–194; and Thomas Gallant, *Modern Greece* (London: Arnold, 2001), 212–217.

22. The Travel Medicine Web site (accessed June 19, 2008), http://www.travmed. com/maps/country.epl?c=Greece, states that Greece was declared malaria free in 1986.

23. Population statistics from "Porto Rafti" on Wikipedia (accessed June 28, 2008), http://en.wikipedia.org/wiki/Porto_Rafti.

24. Iakovos Filipoussis, "Sports," in *About Greece* (Athens: Ministry of Press and Mass Media, Secretariat General of Information, 2007), 409–418, describes organized sports in Greece.

25. Mohit Arora, "Euro Cup: How the Hellas Did Greece win?" *McGill Tribune* (accessed June 20, 2008), http://media.www.mcgilltribune.com/media/storage/ paper234/news/2004/09/01/Sports/Euro-Cup.How.The.Hellas.Did.Greece.Win- 708096.shtml.

26. Stathis Gourgouris, "Euro-Soccer and Hellenomania," University of Michigan Modern Greek Web site (accessed June 26, 2008), http://www.lsa.umich.edu/ modgreek/wtgc/culture.

27. "Rogge, 'Unforgettable Dream Games'" (August 29, 2004), ESPN.com (accessed December 30, 2008), http://sports.espn.go.com/oly/summer04/gen/news/ story?id=1870458.

28. "Greece, Bulgaria, and Russia in the Pit of Doping" (in Greek), *To Vima Online* (accessed August 25, 2008), http://www.tovimadaily.gr/Article.aspx?d= 20080822&nid=9555095&sn=&spid=.

29. Emily Hiestand, "Lessons from the Taverna" in *Travelers' Tales Greece*, ed. Larry Habegger et al. (San Francisco: Travelers' Tales, 2003), 67, describes the "communion that occurs…in the great ritual of the village tavern."

30. Patricia Storace, "God as Pâtissier," in *Travelers' Tales Greece*, 101.

31. "Greece Food and Drink Report" *Business Monitor International*, June 2008, summarized on Researchandmarkets.com (accessed June 30, 2008), http:// www.researchandmarkets.com/reports/612733/greece_food_and_drink_report_q2_ 2008.pdf.

32. Diane Kochilas, *Glorious Foods of Greece* (New York: Harper Collins, 2001), xiv.

33. Nicholas Gage, *Portrait of Greece* (New York: New York Times Books, 1971), 130, brings out Greeks' proverbial faith in food's unifying power. Pettifer, "Food, Drink, and Material Life" in *The Greeks*, 125–135, describes other aspects of food, such as taverna culture, the food industry, wine production, and tobacco.

34. "The Greek Way of Life," *Insight Guides: Greece*, ed. Karen Van Dyck (New York: Houghton Mifflin, 1993), 61–83, discusses regionalism in Greek culture.

35. Kochilas, *Glorious Foods of Greece*, 2.

36. *Politiki Kouzina* (A Touch of Spice), a film from 2003, features foods and spices of Greeks from Istanbul. Soula Bozi's ethnographic study, *Mikrasiatiki Kouzina* [Asia Minor Cooking] (Athens: Ellinika Grammata, 2005), extends the lessons to central Turkey.

37. For an analysis of this phenomenon, see Vassiliki Yiakoumaki, "'Local,' 'Ethnic,' and 'Rural' Food: On the Emergence of 'Cultural Diversity' in Greece since its Integration in the European Union," *Journal of Modern Greek Studies* 24, no. 2 (October 2006): 415–445.

38. Diane Kochilas, *The Food and Wine of Greece* (New York: Macmillan, 1993), 29.

39. Diane Kochilas, *The Greek Vegetarian* (New York: St. Martin's Griffin, 1999), 21–22.

40. Pettifer, *The Greeks*, 135, and the introduction to Diane Kochilas, *Mediterranean Grilling: More Than 100 Recipes from across the Mediterranean* (New York: Macmillan, 2007), touch on the longevity of cooking practices in the region.

41. Kochilas, *Glorious Foods of Greece*, xiv.

5

Language and Literature

GREEK WRITERS WRITE Greek. As obvious as this seems, it is no simple matter. For nearly 150 years from the foundation of the Greek state to 1976, people debated the *glossiko zitima* (language question): what form standard Greek should take—an archaizing *katharevousa* (purified) version imitating ancient Greek or *dimotiki* (demotic), a vernacular closer to people's everyday speech. In the past three decades since *dimotiki* prevailed, the category of Greek writing has become all encompassing, including not just works by a growing number of women writers and a reserve of forgotten texts in *dimotiki* and *katharevousa* but also foreign immigrant writing in Greek and works in other languages by people of Greek descent. As the literary canon has expanded, the task of summarizing what it includes and finding meaningful patterns has become all but impossible. It's easy to say that poetry has traditionally occupied a more important place than prose. It's important to recognize that prose today has a bigger audience than poetry does. Poetry takes lyric, epic, and satiric forms to explore the nature of the national body, and it follows a trajectory toward greater reflexivity and skepticism over time. Prose concerns itself with complications in the individual's dealings with the nation and other—family, ethnic, religious, class, gender, ideological, and geographic—alliances. Yet no discussion, and certainly none this brief, can possibly do justice to the multitude of exceptional writers or the interesting counterexamples and crosscurrents. What may be useful for an English-speaking readership is to highlight a few trends in poetry and prose, beginning with the passionate relationship between Greek ascription and Greek writing, and giving some priority to works that have appeared in English translation.

GREEK

Greek is old. A spoken language since the second millennium B.C., it was written first in Linear B[1] around 1200 B.C., then in the Phoenician-derived alphabet of twenty-four letters from about 800 B.C. to the present day. Its alphabet is the oldest in continuous usage. Thus, today's users of Greek have access to a rich treasure trove of more than 2,700 years of written texts. As delightful as it may be to feed on the words of Homer, Plato, and Callimachus, people grow weary of having to compete with their glorious ancestors whenever they try to write something new in the same language. They have a hard time escaping the influence, prestige, and weightiness of ancient Greek and Koine Greek of the New Testament. In the words of Odysseus Elytis, a Greek writer's difficulties begin "when he must make use, to name the things dearest to him, of the same words as did Sappho, for example, or Pindar, while being deprived of the audience they had and which then extended to all of human civilization."[2]

Greek is spoken by approximately 13 million people worldwide.[3] Apart from a handful of well-known authors whose work circulates in multiple translations (the poet Constantine Cavafy ranks as the most translated Greek author in modern times), Greek writing does not reach many people outside Greece or Cyprus. Most people in the world do not have a firsthand or even secondhand access to Greek writers. And Greek literature, with its many linguistic registers, layered meanings, and rhyming schemes, is notoriously difficult to translate. Writers of Greek risk confining themselves to a small audience in Greece.

Greek exists in a variety of forms. Today older texts bear witness to the babel of Greek dialects before mass media began exerting its homogenizing force. As recently as the early twentieth century, there were many vernacular dialects. People also mixed Greek with other contact languages: Turkish, Bulgarian, Ladino, and Italian, just to name a few. And diglossia, the coexistence of a learned, archaizing *katharevousa* imitating classical Greek and an evolving Greek *dimotiki* used in everyday communication, was a fact of life. The two forms, *katharevousa* and *dimotiki*, collided repeatedly in language battles lasting from the early 1800s until the 1970s and even included bloody riots in Athens over Alexandros Pallis's translation of the Gospels into *dimotiki* in 1901 and the performance of Aeschylus's *Oresteia* in *dimotiki* in 1903. Writers ran against the course not just of convention but sometimes even of the constitution when they wrote in *dimotiki*, or they risked being classified as hopelessly conservative when they wrote in *katharevousa*. As they placed their bets on one or the other form, they hoped their language would still be comprehensible after their death. In 1976 the Greek state adopted a law declaring *dimotiki* the official language of Greece at every level of communication. To Greeks educated after 1976, some writing from the nineteenth and early twentieth centuries seems as distant as the language of the Gospels.

But Greek is also a powerfully expressive tool. Its high degree of inflection means that grammatical endings rather than word order convey syntactical relations. Myriad word roots and prefixes easily join and recombine to form new compounds. Furthermore, Greek tends to absorb new words from every language with which it comes into contact and feeds people's pleasure in coining new words, so that Greek really has an infinite vocabulary. All this gives Greek users a multihued room for play.

Greek seems to require that its users write. The longevity of Greek as a written language seems to goad people to resurrect the dead letter and give it a new written form expressing a contemporary vision. The lexical wealth of Greek, its syntactical elasticity, and especially the value society puts in literature encourage everyone to write. Poets exist in every corner. They work day jobs as lawyers, shipowners, doctors, physicists, biologists, engineers, diplomats, dishwashers, civil servants, shopkeepers, and homemakers, then invest the end of their day in words, as if their country's future depended on their writing. Even the hardest of times have inspired Greeks to write. The surrealist painter and poet Nikos Engonopoulos, alluding to the Civil War of 1945–1949, offered a fractured set of lines to express his paradoxical need to put to words the harsh conditions that made it so impossible to write.[4] Yiorgos Chouliaras, a writer of the present day, refers to Greece's speculation in literary assets as "the industrial revolution" that Greece never experienced.[5]

Whatever the reasons for Greece's literary renaissance since 1821, the main point is that literature holds a huge place in the hearts and minds of Greeks. Greece continues to produce more than its share of great writers, and Greeks continue to communicate their grief, joys, frustrations, and beliefs not just by writing but also by reading aloud in very public settings. A legal defense, a televised program celebrating Greek music, an eminent person's funeral, even a political rally may become an occasion for a literary reading. For example, Dimitris Koufodinas, the operations chief of the November 17 terrorist group, recited a few lines from the work of poet Kostis Palamas in his own defense at his trial on August 25, 2003. He elicited spontaneous applause.[6] "We are living inside a poem" was the recent assessment of someone who witnessed a deputy of Parliament's emotional reading of poetry by Odysseus Elytis at the funeral of Dolly Goulandris, benefactor and founder of the Cycladic Art Museum.[7]

DIONYSIS SOLOMOS: NATIONAL POET

Until recently, poets were Greece's national bards. Their voices stood for the nation's. They aspired to make their poetry an expression of the national body.

Dionysios Solomos (1798–1857) is *the* national poet. The opening two stanzas of the "Hymn to Liberty," a poem of 158 stanzas, became the Greek national anthem, and his small body of mostly unfinished works has come to represent the aspirations of Greeks. The stanzas promise that Liberty personified is resurrected in exchange for rebels of the Greek War of Independence who sacrifice their "sacred bones" in battle.

While the resurrection of glorious ancestors from the bones of slain revolutionaries offered itself as a rich theme to Solomos, the poetic language for expressing this theme did not present itself automatically. In Solomos's time vernacular Greek was the language of oral poetry, composed, performed, and transmitted by illiterate subjects of the Ottoman Empire to express their fears, desires, and beliefs. Educated Greeks wrote in classicizing Greek, that is, in a learned form of Greek imitating an older, fifth-century B.C. form of ancient, classical Greek, or in other languages and moved in circles outside oral poetry. Greek vernacular poetry did not offer itself as a vehicle for writing. Solomos, the illegitimate son of Count Nikolaos Solomos and his Greek housekeeper from Venetian-controlled Zakynthos (the island found itself under Napoleonic rule the year Solomos was born), straddled the line between Greek literacy and orality. He sensed the expressive potential of vernacular Greek from the time he remembered his mother singing folk songs. But he was sent to Italy to study. He wrote Italian verse at the beginning and end of his poetic career. His Greek was broken even during his middle period, when he lived on the islands of Zakynthos and then Kerkyra (Corfu) and chose to write in Greek so as to chronicle Greece's War of Independence. When he felt the desire to express in the poetic language of the common people the self-realization of Greeks, he did not have the language adequate to the task he had given himself.

Solomos wanted to represent the cause of Greeks' hard-fought pursuit of freedom. The problem he faced was not just that he was not fluent in Greek. The instrument he needed to express his ideas did not yet exist. A large body of folk poetry had been composed and performed in vernacular Greek from the Byzantine through the Ottoman eras. There was *Diyenis Akritas*, an eleventh-century Byzantine epic about a border guard of mixed Greek and Arabic lineage, and *Erotokritos*, the very popular seventeenth-century Cretan verse-romance by Vitsentzos Kornaros. Shorter ballads presented human life as a heroic struggle with the elements, whether the subject was work, love, emigration, or death. "Night Journey," one of the first poems in modern Greek to reach an English readership,[8] narrates a haunting story of a brother who returns from the dead to fulfill his promise to his mother that he will bring his sister back from the foreign land where she is married. "The Bridge of Arta," another popular ballad, tells of human sacrifice of the master builder's wife, who is immured in a bridge's foundations to ensure engineering success. In addition there were Klephtic songs (songs of brigandage under Ottoman rule) that told stories of courage, contests, and death-defying endurance.[9] Though rich in its use of natural metaphors and supernatural figures, this body of poetry lacked the literary qualities that Solomos found in other modern national traditions, such as those of Germany or Italy.

After the success of the "Hymn to Liberty," Solomos wanted to give his poetry the kind of philosophical depth he found in Coleridge, Hölderlin, and Leopardi. He tried to adapt the language, meters, and figures he found in folk poems to express his German idealist notion of the human spirit's efforts to overcome physical limitations. He explored this theme in a series of poems about poisoned, dying, and dead women and men. To his own mind he failed miserably. He filled his Greek writings' marginalia with crude epithets expressing his feelings of inadequacy, then left his incomplete manuscripts to his successors to sort out. He found a dedicated editor in fellow writer Iakovos Polylas, whose "Prolegomena" and critical notes in his 1859 edition of Solomos's poetry imposed meaning on Solomos's fragmented oeuvre.

In Polylas's edition of Solomos's poetry, readers found a lasting, coherent body of literature. Though unfinished, poems such as "Lambros," "Kritikos," and "Porphyras" offered suggestions for literary solutions to language questions from which writers are still drawing lessons. Some critics even argue that Greek poetry since Solomos has been a footnote to his enigmatic, unfinished lines. Especially rich are certain phrases from his second draft of "Free Besieged"—a poem in three drafts in which Solomos tried desperately to capture the transcendent spirit of the dying Greeks besieged by the Ottomans at Messolonghi, where Lord Byron also met his death—such as "the eyes of my soul."[10] Solomos combined Greek words of philosophical depth such as *psyche* (soul) or *kosmos* (world) with the meters, rhyming patterns, and grace of oral poetry. The fifteen-syllable iambic rhyming couplets, the most common meter in Greek folk songs, gave Solomos's version of German idealism the rhythm and feel of folk poetry, while his incorporation of vernacular words with philosophical overtones transformed *dimotiki* into a language for learned poetry.

MODERN POETS, ANCIENT INHERITANCE

Solomos was one of the first learned writers of Greek to enter the fray of the language question on the side of the *dimotiki*. Many nineteenth- and twentieth-century poets followed suit, grounding their work in forms inspired by traditional oral poetry, interweaving ancient words of great cultural weight, while also attending carefully to the tone, rhythms, sounds, movements, and skeptical ideas that were reaching Greece from the West. Poets from Solomos's era to the present have tended to keep themselves well informed about artistic and philosophical developments in the great capital cities of Europe and America. Tensions and contradictions in their cultural inheritance between their twin roots of Eastern Christianity and pagan Classicism, on the one hand, and the influences of European and American writing, on the other hand, continue to give their poetry its electric charge.

Although deeply rooted in every aspect of its linguistic inheritance, Greek writing shuns obsequious appeals to tradition. Kostis Palamas (1859–1943) dominated the literary scene as a critic and poet from 1880 to 1930. His complete works fill sixteen volumes. More than any other poets of his era, including Yiorgos Drosinis (1859–1951), Ioannis Gryparis (1870–1942), and Apostolos Melahrinos (1880–1952), Palamas earned a reputation as a keeper of indigenous, vernacular traditions. Furthermore, his work synthesized elements from the entire span of the Greek past—classical, Byzantine, and Ottoman—with contemporary European intellectual developments. "A Hundred Voices," a poem in his collection called *Asalefti zoi* (The Inert Life), finds in the heroes, men, and gods of older literature something similar to clouds, angels, and dreams, which keep company with modern poets. Palamas did not subordinate the present to the past. For example, he put words of skepticism into the mouth of his nomadic, freethinking, postclassical, Nietzsche-inspired "gypsy" hero in his great epic poem, *O dodekalogos tou gyftou* (The Twelve Lays of the Gypsy, 1907). Addressing the "beautiful immortals" of antiquity he proclaimed: "Now there is another sun, another air, and you are only Apparitions."[11] The gypsy stands by to witness intellectuals leaving Constantinople during the last years of the Byzantine Empire with their own "beautiful immortals" in the form of classical texts. Anticipating that artists will try to recover these idols, too, he warns future poets not to "follow obsequiously" in their footsteps but to carve their own path.[12] Rather than lose himself in the worship of dead ancestors, Palamas's gypsy revels in the idea of turning ancient papyrus into kindling. This is Palamas at his most rebellious, as he tries to establish the poet as a new prophet of song.

Angelos Sikelianos (1884–1951) was another master of the folk and classical traditions. He understood that the dead speak to the living whether

Banners showing authors Andreas Embirikos and Angelos Sikelianos outside the Ethniko Kentro Vivliou (National Book Center) in Athens. Photo by author, October 2008.

through dead letters or dead bodies. It is the poet's job to keep the spirit of the word alive. Sikelianos also recognized that everyday occasions may reveal a sense of eternity, unity, and justice, especially when disaster looms on the horizon. In his many collections of poems and plays, Sikelianos did not distinguish between different mythological faces of death and its obverse, resurrection. His poetry crosses the divide between the classical and the Christian, the ancient and the modern. It moves freely between Mother Earth, Alcmene, and Theotokos (mother of God), Orpheus and Dionysus, Adonis and Christ. Yet it finds glimpses of revelation not in the myths or Christian texts themselves but in everyday occasions that bring myths to life and render them full of significance. Sikelianos's poem, "At the Monastery of St. Luke" finds occasion in the Greek Orthodox services of Good Friday and the Resurrection. The scene comes to life during the religious ritual when Vangelis, a young man the community counted as lost in war, walks into the church with a wooden leg. His mother falls to his feet and clasps the leg. The soldier's return turns the ritual of resurrection into a real resurrection of the flesh.[13]

On another occasion Sikelianos used a real funeral to inspire mass defiance. It was the early 1940s, and Greeks were facing repression and mass starvation under the Nazi occupation, which so greatly devastated Greek life in the countryside and cities and reduced Greece's population by as much as 10 percent. On February 28, 1943, Sikelianos delivered the eulogy at Palamas's funeral. Standing among the throngs in Athens, Sikelianos conjured up the spirit of Palamas and his literary ancestors as he declaimed: "On this coffin hangs all of Greece!" Then he called on the ghosts of "Orpheus, Herakleitos, Aeschylus, and Solomos" to receive the triumphal soul of Palamas. Offering a message of unity and continuity, his poem reached its climax in the final verse: "Resound in one body this land, from shore to shore. Sound the Paean! Terrible flags of Freedom, unfold the air to Freedom!" In defiance of the Nazi soldiers who stood guard, hundreds of thousands of mourners began singing Solomos's "Hymn to Freedom," the outlawed national anthem.[14]

Yannis Ritsos (1909–1990) gave a different nod to dead ancestors. A prolific writer (he published 117 books) and committed communist (he dedicated many poems to the KKE, the Greek Communist Party), Ritsos experimented with every idiom of modernism to capture the tone, feeling, and difficult sense of dramatic events from the 1930s to the 1970s. He found a national popular resonance in traditional folk poetry and classical myth. His early poem "Epitaphios" (1936) laments the death of a young man killed on May 10, 1936, in Thessaloniki in bloody street battles between striking tobacco workers and the Greek national guard. Ritsos was inspired by a newspaper image of the young man's mother reaching down to embrace her son's bloody body. The form and figurative language of Ritsos's fifteen-syllable rhymed iambic verse recalls Greek folk songs. Its title, "Epitaphios," alludes directly to a religious icon of the supine body of Christ and the ritual lament of the mourning Theotokos. "Epitaphios" also names the Good Friday evening service during which Greek Orthodox faithful chant lamentations and follow the icon in a long, slow ritual procession. The poem draws on the long-lived literary legacy of Greek without sacrificing the power of lament to inspire opposition. When Mikis

Theodorakis set the poem to music in 1960, the song was sung by millions of Greeks across generational and political lines, igniting a cultural revolution.[15] Ritsos's message of popular struggle against fascism and dictatorship flouted strict political censorship for decades and led to his exile at the end of the Civil War from 1948 to 1952 and again during the dictatorship from 1967 to 1971.

During that same period, Odysseus Elytis (1911–1996, winner of the Nobel Prize for Literature in 1979) wrote *Asma iroiko kai penthimo gia ton hameno anthipolohago tis Alvanias* (Heroic and Elegiac Song for the Lost Second Lieutenant of the Albanian Campaign, 1945), a powerful lament for an anonymous soldier who fell on the Albanian front, where Elytis also served as second lieutenant from 1940 to 1941. The poem draws on the conventions of oral poetry, especially the *moiroloi* (ritual lament), whose basic theme is the vivid trace of a living memory that contrasts starkly with the reality of the dead body. In Elytis's poem memory exaggerates the qualities of the life that was lost. A traditional lament might compare the dead person to a bird, a heavenly body, or a precious metal. Elytis compares his fine young man to the sun, and the passing of his life to a shadow cast over all of life. At his birth the mountains themselves kneel before him. The firmament participates in his every act.[16] The exaggerated picture of his participation in life brings more bitter mourning for his death. Cataclysmic forces participate in that event: mountains thunder; their snows melt and wash his body.[17] The poet too participates in communal grief. As he tries but fails to find reason in the young man's sudden death, he identifies a nameless, faceless enemy. To diminish the enemy, he catalogs the beauty and bitterness of Greek life. Elytis's lists are fresh and surprising, sometimes even jarring in their juxtapositions. Elytis identified with the surrealist movement and acknowledged the influences of European writers from France and Spain, including Federico García Lorca, whose "Llanto por Ignacio Sánchez Mejías" (1935) certainly touched Elytis's writing of this poem.

The poem does not end on a somber note. With the line, "In the distance ring bells of crystal," it anticipates the transition from mourning to celebration and perhaps also echoes Sikelianos's "thundering bells" pronounced a few years earlier on the occasion of Palamas's burial. Elytis anticipates that the soldier's death will become a transformative event that brings freedom for his people and rings: "Liberty."[18] This is a clear reference to Solomos's "Hymn to Liberty," where slain heroes become the occasion for "liberty restored."

Heroic and Elegiac Song is a precursor to Elytis's architecturally more elaborate, better-known epic, *The Axion Esti* ("It Is Worthy," the name of a Greek Orthodox icon and the hymn to the Virgin Mary it inspired). Published in

1959, *The Axion Esti* touches on the same cosmic themes. In both poems all of nature participates in a hero's epic story of birth, suffering, death, and an anticipated resurrection. The two poems also recall Greece's experiences during World War II. Moreover the poems fuse individual with collective experience and suggest that the death of the hero stands for the suffering of the entire nation, while the promise of resurrection touches the whole of Greece's natural and social world. With the organization of *The Axion Esti* in three parts— "The Genesis," "The Passion," and "The Gloria"—however, the later poem announces its much grander literary vision. Its prototypes are not confined to oral poetry but reach deep into the vast body of Hebraic-Christian Greek writing: the Septuagint, New Testament, Divine Liturgy of John Chrysostom, and Akathistos Hymn by Romanos the Melodist. The poem reaches back to ancient authors while recalling vernacular writers such Ioannis Makriyannis, hero of the Greek revolution.

Indeed *The Axion Esti* represents a kind of Mass. At its heart stands the figure of the celebrant-*poietes*, a Greek word signifying both the writer of poems and the maker of the universe. Elytis described the purpose of his writing thus: "'I am personifying Greece in my poems. . . . All the beautiful and bitter moments beneath the sky of Attica."[19] Indeed it seems that Elytis achieved his grand ambition to a degree. Despite its complexity, *The Axion Esti* became a kind of national hymn when composer Mikis Theodorakis set selections of it to music in 1964, and it continues to touch the national unconscious.[20]

If Elytis made the whole cosmos dance on the pinhead of his poetry, George Seferis (1900–1971), Elytis's contemporary and another recipient of the Nobel Prize for Literature (1963), moved in quite the opposite direction to grapple with the impossibility of containing anything in writing. Seferis believed that the intellect barely grasps the record of human activity. Language is but a pale reflection of reality. Outside language, in the peripheral vestiges of sight and touch, in lingering feelings, images, or dreams, Seferis sensed that there are much more lasting impressions of life from the past. These occasionally surface and touch present lives, whereas language can be as insubstantial as the screech of a bat. In Seferis's poetry readers of Greek writing come up against a new sense of the limits of human knowledge, as articulated in "The King of Asine," a poem that tries to recover the traces of a Bronze Age citadel represented by a gold death mask and two words in the Homeric corpus: *Asinen te*, "and Asine." Here Seferis's writing seems to envy hard, mute objects for the wordless traces they contain where words fall far too short: "a void everywhere with us."[21]

Seferis's poetry reaches into the hidden recesses of a life lived beyond the frequency of language. In his long poem *Mythistorema* (1935), a composition of twenty-four parts (like the twenty-four rhapsodies of Homer's epics), visual and literary fragments drawn mostly from Homer and the tragedians bear down with the force of a nightmarish absence on the crushed, ravaged, ill-directed souls of the present day, who occupy a barren landscape from which they can find no easy escape. The vision is dark and enigmatic. Some have read this frustrated Odyssey as an allegorical treatment of the Asia Minor catastrophe, an event that marked Seferis's life deeply, as his family was one of the 1.3 million Greek Orthodox Christians who lost their homes on the shores of Asia Minor. Certainly the rootlessness of a people forced to wander amid thousands of years of "ruined buildings which once, perhaps, were our homes" [22] is a recurring theme.

Thrush (1946) is a long, difficult poem, whose vision of dead castaways re-turning to advise the living was inspired by the shipwrecked *Thrush*, which had lodged itself off the coast of Poros during World War II. Viewing that shipwreck from his window, Seferis developed further the sense that modern writing needs to anchor itself in the ancients, even though it can never receive a clear signal from the past. Sophocles' *Oedipus at Colonus*, Plato's *Apology*, and Homer's *Iliad* appear in quoted fragments. More than any other text, the *Odyssey*, the prototype of stories of wandering, cuts into *Thrush*, though Seferis's poetic persona is no epic hero but a modern observer. Yet Seferis chose to enter what he called "that mysterious current which is Greece" as an Odysseus-like *outis*, an uninitiated nobody who is simply trying to make his way blindly out of the unilluminated cave of interwar Greece: "But the in-tellect thrown back upon itself sometimes needs freshness, like the dead who needed fresh blood before answering Ulysses."[23] So in *Thrush* Seferis found freshness in Odysseus's "Nekyia," the journey to the Underworld (*Odyssey*, book 11), where Odysseus feeds dead souls with living blood so that they will talk to him. As Seferis's narrator is contemplating the shipwreck, Odysseus's dead interlocutors emerge from "the dark side" of the sun. The narrator hears familiar voices but can't distinguish them. Then further interference. The poem cuts Homer's account short, as Socrates interrupts, thanking the Athe-nian law court for condemning him to drink poison, because he prefers death. "Who'll come out best only God knows."[24]

Thrush gave readers hard literary lessons.[25] Greeks today can neither move forward without the ancients nor anticipate what will come from their en-counter. They can neither control which voices from the past prevail nor fully comprehend what the ancestors are trying to tell them. Seferis's difficult mes-sage moves one step further. By replacing Teiresias, the blind seer who gave Odysseus a road map for his difficult journey home, with Socrates, the old man who asked hard questions without offering answers and chose death over life, the poem places the onus of interpretation on its readers. Published in 1946, when a harsh Civil War followed the devastating Nazi occupation, the poem's conversation with the dead offered no clear interpretive path out of the mined harbor of war and civil strife. It deferred to readers, requiring them to draw their own lines of connection and escape.

Readers who found *Thrush* difficult were more receptive to poems by Seferis with fewer philological demands. An earlier poem, "Arnisi" ("Denial") is among Seferis's most popular. People read into its words a more upbeat message, though Seferis was probably unsatisfied with the loss of ambivalence in the popular interpretation given to the poem when composer Mikis Theodorakis set it to music. The song bestowed on the poem a remarkable afterlife, beginning at Seferis's funeral, which took place on September 22, 1972, under the watchful eye of the dictatorship's police. Spontaneously and without any prompting, hundreds of thousands of mourners gathered in the streets of Athens to follow the coffin from the Church of Transfiguration on Kidathineon Street in the Plaka to Athens's First Cemetery. As they processed, mourners began singing "Denial" to the tune of Theodorakis's banned music.[26] Thus in a strange, unforeseen twist of fate, and hardly owing to the poem's words, Seferis's "Denial" became a kind of anthem of resistance signifying Greeks' refusal to accept any form of repression, and remains so to the present day.

ALTERNATIVE VISIONS

The formula of infusing Greek poetry with ghosts of the ancients while giving it the words, rhythms, and sounds of oral poetry that can be sung by the masses is not the only one found in Greek writing. Some poets have taken a different course, sidelining oral tradition while imitating the language and form and not just the stories of ancient precursors, or attaching themselves to foreign literary movements. Among those belonging in this category who deserve close attention but are not discussed in detail here but are Kostas Ouranis (1890–1953), Maria Polydouri (1902–1930), Nikos Engonopoulos (1907–1985), Nikos Kavvadias (1910–1975), Miltos Sachtouris (1919–2005), and Dinos Christianopoulos (b. 1931).

The most interesting contemporary of Solomos was Andreas Kalvos (1792–1869). Like Solomos, he was educated in Italy and wrote his first and last works in Italian. The Greek War of Independence inspired him to turn briefly to Greek. He published ten odes in 1824 in a collection entitled *Lyre* and another ten in 1926 under the title *Lyrika*. In his linguistic choices, poetic form, and content, his odes drew lines of direct connection with classical Greek. His language was archaizing, really an imitation of ancient Greek. His verse—consisting of five-line strophes of irregular rhyme schemes, with the last line consisting of five syllables stressed on the second-to-last syllable—recalled not just the sixth-century B.C. Greek poet Pindar's victory odes but also British imitations of Pindar in the eighteenth century. Kalvos's odes told of shepherds and nereids revisiting the same cool springs and forests as their ancestors, and they exhorted the people of Greece, burdened by "the yoke of slavery," to find virtue and courage equal to that of the ancients and adequate to achieving their goal of freedom. Kalvos's poetic creations were an interesting parenthesis in Greek writing.

Another writer whose rich, rhymed verses present a great challenge to translators is Kostas Karyotakis (1896–1928). Karyotakis acknowledged a poetic debt to Andreas Kalvos in "To Andreas Kalvos," a poem beautifully imitating Kalvos's verse as no other Greek poet has managed to do. Karyotakis found in Kalvos's voice "the divine spark." Yet for Karyotakis, Kalvos's idealism could not speak to his generation, because times had changed inexorably and "swept / away your ideals."[27]

Influenced by French symbolism, Karyotakis wrote dark, witty satiric and elegiac poems for unheroic times. Karyotakis's work takes its tone from the political divisions and military losses of the era of his greatest productivity, from 1922 until his suicide in 1928. It stands opposed to the lyricism of Palamas and Sikelianos, and although it anticipates the high modernism of symbolist George Seferis, who retained something of his tone, it exhibits a mood of utter hopelessness.

Karyotakis refused to embrace the role of the poet-visionary. He would not promise a message of eternal scope or lasting worth. Instead he wrote with vigilance about the hard realities of the contemporary moment, which inevitably turns sour: of love turned bitter, of the lover who submits to tenderness but "whom pain had turned to stone,"[28] of the civil servant who cannot find inspiration in his work, of the poets who "replace with sounds and syllables the feelings on our paper hearts."[29] Writing poetry was a kind of necessary exercise to be compared to playing a broken instrument that makes bad sounds: "We are just some battered guitars," he wrote. "When the wind blows over us, / it awakens verses and dissonant sounds / on strings that droop like watch chains."[30] Despite his protests to the contrary, and despite his very short life, Karyotakis left a corpus of worthy poems, some of great beauty and poignancy.

Kostas Varnalis (1884–1974) was another master of meter and form. What separated him from other poets of his era was his commitment to Marxism, which expressed itself in his deep sympathy for the oppressed and in the satire he directed at the existing social order. Varnalis scoured religious texts for examples he could turn on their heads to show the human potential for social renewal. Thus his poem "Magdalene" identifies as its hero not Jesus but the prostitute who, in despairing of "darkness...within" but also knowing the freedom a person learns to embrace from the condition of slavery, throws herself at Jesus' feet. She then offers to Christ a path to salvation from his destiny as a crucified godhead. Hers is not a miraculous resurrection granted by a distant deity but the gift of one human being relieving the other of human pain: a gift of empathy gained by living life in the margins of humanity: "I shall resurrect you!"[31]

The writer who has achieved the greatest international success in modern times is Constantine P. Cavafy (1863–1933). Like Solomos and Kalvos, he lived his entire life outside the Greek state. A native of Alexandria, Egypt, he was raised and educated in England and Constantinople before returning to Alexandria to live the remainder of his life. He spoke broken Greek with a foreign accent, wrote in English before he turned to Greek, and struggled to find satisfaction in his writing. Yet he developed "a shrewd sense of his own worth and seemed to know that the world would acknowledge his accomplishment if he played his cards right."[32] He found people to promote his work, most notably the British novelist E. M. Forster, who in 1923 introduced Cavafy to the English-speaking world with translations of three poems: "The God Abandons Antony," "Alexandrian Kings, and "In the Month of Athyr," and a verbal portrait of the poet that has become as famous as the poet himself: "a Greek gentleman in a straw hat, standing absolutely motionless at a slight angle to the universe."[33]

Cavafy's inspiration came from written rather than oral sources. He remained quite uninterested in the Greek nation's self-realization, which Solomos, Kalvos, Ritsos, and so many others sought to capture. Cavafy's is a poetry of unresolved scenes rather than plenitude or presence. It contemplates the passing image, lost reputation, burning memory, missing voices of persons who are long gone. It explores how these missing traces return "like music at night, distant, fading away."[34]

Cavafy's readings were in history and biography. He studied sources carefully to find the drama of the odd, transitional moment. Evidence of such drama also existed in the present day in his hometown of Alexandria, Egypt, a city that had risen to great power and declined more than once in its long history. All around him in Alexandria's antiquities but also in its coffee shops, hallways, places of passage, ephemeral glances, and exchanges was the raw material for poetry. Cavafy's memories of a youth full of nightly escapes from the claustrophobic environment of decency and order in Alexandria's wealthy neighborhoods into the mess, squalor, and excitement of shops and bars in Alexandria's poorer quarters of ill repute also entered his poetry, but not until Cavafy's youthful impressions had aged. Cavafy wanted time and memory to work their magic on human drama. In unpublished notes to himself, he recorded his mode of thinking. "To me, the immediate impression is never a starting point for work. The impression has got to age, has got to falsify itself with time, without my having to falsify it."[35]

Most readers of Cavafy's poetry know that Cavafy was a homosexual who kept his identity half hidden. He did not publish many of his poems in his lifetime. Partly this was to hide his homosexuality, the "hidden things" he referred to in one of his unpublished poems filed with the note: "to be kept but not published." Yet Cavafy can be seen plotting his future by alternately revealing and hiding himself. Cavafy seems to have foreseen the power of future readers to reevaluate his work, even as Cavafy had reshaped what he inherited from his precursors. Cavafy was a modern Plutarch, who read not just lives but historical moments past, present, and future in parallel. He understood that hindsight sees clearly history's unforeseen ironic turns, but the same eyes are blind to those same turns in the present. He set his art to dramatizing the emotions, desires, and reflections, however grand or mundane, that propel people to act unwisely, then to console themselves by reliving the past as they would have liked to play it out.

In large part, Cavafy's strategy of saving instead of publishing guaranteed surprise, a necessary element for sustained fame. Cavafy understood that a poet's death would transform his name. He wanted to ensure an affirming transformation. In his lifetime he circulated his work only partially, never as a whole. He sent hand-sewn printed copies of his poems to friends, acquaintances, and preferred readers. He handpicked his readers, and the list changed with each new mailing, depending on his previous reception. Thus Cavafy left his complete works to posterity to discover, bit by bit. Although his complete works have not yet seen the light of publication, Cavafy is the most translated Greek author in English or any other language. Surprisingly readable and eminently translatable, because not even a bad translation can destroy his voice, Cavafy's poetry presents a world of unsuspecting, disappointed, fearful, daydreaming, aging souls who have lost control of their lives. It challenges readers not to be caught off guard, like those "waiting for the barbarians" in Cavafy's most famous poem, but to use the poet's insights to anticipate, or at least interpret wisely, life's unexpected outcomes.

Nicolas Calas (1907–1988), one of several pseudonyms used by Nikos Kalamaris, was a revolutionary writer in many respects.[36] Identifying himself as a Marxist and surrealist, he embraced two mottos for change: "Marx said: Transform the world! Rimbaud said: Change life. These two commands are for us but one."[37] Calas resisted the strong presence of Kostis Palamas and embraced instead the classicizing romanticism of Andreas Kalvos and the learned aestheticism of C. P. Cavafy, whose writing was not well received in Greek circles in the interwar years when Calas made his literary appearance. In the early 1930s Calas wrote both an essay and a poem extolling the virtues of Cavafy's writing. In the poem "Cavafy," Calas drew the portrait of a Levantine figure whose "melody runs on the wind with Ionian currents and arrives at

Byzantium," but whose world is overwhelmed by the dark, raging "barbarous echoes" in the present.[38] What Calas found laudable in Cavafy's poetry was its understatement, irony, and skillful transformation of life's harsh realities into art.

Yet Calas's art was not imitative of Cavafy's, or of any other Greek writer's for that matter. Calas found himself in alignment with the Greek surrealists, especially Andreas Embeirikos, whose publication in 1935 of *Blast Furnace*, a collection of "automatic writing," provoked strong public reaction. Like Embeirikos, Calas was interested in how the unconscious shapes the world. In his poetic style, however, he was his own master. Calas's compressed line, his difficult sense, the torrent of unpunctuated phrases, and the flood of contemporary references reveal his awareness of contemporary European and American soundscapes: of jazz, on the one hand, and mechanized labor on the other. Calas pressed his readers to feel the forces of mass consumption that were transforming their world. His poem "Acropolis" (1933) sees the ancient monument as one of many "cylinders" of exchange in a hypermodern world, where coins changing hands, photographs processed and reproduced, products bought and sold, buildings razed and restored, are all implicated in the "processes of mechanization."[39]

Calas's intellectual independence led him to Paris after Prime Minister Ioannis Metaxas became dictator in 1936, suspending key articles of the constitution, banning political parties, and introducing broad censorship. With the outbreak of World War II he moved to New York, where he worked as an art critic. His writings in art journals brought attention to young artists and to the conditions that favored the creation of new art movements. Calas's contribution to Greek letters has taken many decades to assimilate.

New Language Questions after World War II

When one form of life passes before another takes root, political and social thought may remain static while innovation takes refuge in the dark corners of society. Out of the ashes of the Nazi occupation of Greece and the Civil War that followed, a generation of young women and men came of age. Their entrance into adult life took place under difficult circumstances, whether they joined the Greek resistance, fought on the losing side in the Civil War, suffered imprisonment or exile or were sentenced to death for their political views, or simply struggled to receive a good education and stand independently. With their hard experiences came not only a maturity of vision but also an acute sense that reality is not as it seems and won't reveal what it is really made of. Those who turned to poetry held no delusions about the power of poetry to reach a deeper layer of meaning. Poetry was without power. Poets found themselves simply condemned, in a sense, to write. So they used writing to question almost every dimension of life: ideological certainties, the power of words to offer inspiration, the notion that poetry can lead to praxis or even render an alternative vision. Their writing did have its effects, as it earned them the suspicion of ideologues from both ends of the political spectrum.

Writers who came of age after World War II were for decades overlooked by the critics and translators who were beginning to find an international platform for Greek writing. This was a time when a canon of modern Greek authors was being fashioned. Writers from the first half of the twentieth century took their place in the literary canon. Cavafy became an international phenomenon. English translations of the work of poet, novelist, and travel writer Nikos Kazantzakis became best sellers. George Seferis received the Nobel Prize for Literature in 1963, Odysseus Elytis the Nobel in 1979, and Yannis Ritsos the Lenin Prize for Poetry in 1977. Elytis's vision of a sun-filled Aegean took center stage in the image Greece presented to the world. In contrast many of the best poets of the second half of the twentieth century have been writing in relative obscurity. Yet their experiments have left an indelible mark on Greek writing. Important questions about the relationship of poetry and praxis, language and society lie at the heart of their work.

Manolis Anagnostakis (1925–2005) was not the first Greek poet of revolutionary politics. Solomos and Kalvos dedicated their poetry to the War of Independence. Varnalis imagined how a communist revolution could materialize. Ritsos took the side of losing leftists, yet remained optimistic of revolutionary change even after his years of political imprisonment. But Anagnostakis—who participated in a communist youth group during the Nazi occupation and as a partisan in the Civil War, and who after a commuted death sentence went from prison to prison from 1949 to 1952—wrote of the revolution's failure. Cool, self-mocking, almost chillingly without delusions, he wondered what is poetry's purpose after defeat. He pondered how to speak of suffering and death. He explored how to utter statements within the prescribed limits of a political order that prohibits free speech.

One way to answer these questions was to explore what it feels like to write under prohibition. This was one of Anagnostakis's strategies. In "Apologia of the Law Abiding," Anagnostakis tests the established order by pretending to comply with the laws of censorship and respect limits that do not allow poems to contain words such as *freedom* and *democracy*, or phrases like "down with tyranny" and "death to the traitor." He pretends to "write poems that do not turn against the established order."[40] Anagnostakis's language is terse. It hides emotion. Although he speaks in the first person, he subtracts the personality from the person. There is no hint of a past or future, only a present utterance stating whatever is required. This and other poems by Anagnostakis read like forced political confessions, where significance lies in all that has been silenced.

At the other end of the emotional spectrum is the angry, prophetic first-person voice of Michalis Katsaros (1920–1998), another major left-wing poet who lost faith in the direction of the communist revolution. Katsaros decried the loss of meaning that followed the doublespeak of official Soviet talk and wondered how a poet could work "in this cemetery of words? How shall we re-baptize the conflagrations: *Liberty, equality, Soviet, power?*"[41]

The most succinct articulation of the crisis of meaning in poetry appeared in a short poem by Titos Patrikios (b. 1928) titled "Verses 2," published in 1957. It contains a frank assessment of poetry's limits, claiming that verses embracing a revolution are untrue and boastful "because no verse today can overthrow the established order." These harsh lines became a kind of counterslogan for a disenchanted generation. Patrikios's corpus of sixty-five years, consisting of poetry, fiction, essays, reviews, and scholarly books, bears witness to both the range of his generation's experiences—from resistance to concentration camps, exile, military dictatorship, and social unrest, and to the vicissitudes of idealism. "Verses 2" exposed the hopeless idealism in the belief that poetry's "paper guns" might become weapons of any kind. It established a more modest, self-deprecating goal of using words "to cast a light on our counterfeit lives."[42]

A more analytical statement of the function of poetry in the face of defeat appeared in October 1962 in an influential journal of the arts that Patrikios helped found, *Epitheorisi Technis* (Arts Review, 1954–1967). A review essay by Vyron Leontaris (b. 1932) used the phrase "the poetry of defeat" to characterize the futility of social vision found in poetry by Leontaris's contemporaries, Patrikios, Thanasis Kostavaras (b. 1927), and others. The essay claims that this is the only honest stance writing can take in an era when humanity and civilization face defeat. Leontaris saw the failure of the political left in Greece after World War II as a sign that revolutions are always already defeated. Revolutions are ideals, and ideals are defined by their failure to materialize. Likewise poetry is an ideal that cannot materialize: it does not lead to action but instead is bound up with the expression of defeat. Leontaris has spent a lifetime writing poetry about poetry and trying to work out where exactly this leaves poets. "From the Ends" (1986), Leontaris's learned, lyrical poem, calls poets "the most ill-fated spirit."[43] Emptied of everything in which they once believed, purged of their desperate attachment to the past and hope for the future, they have no other subject but the story of their descent into the Hades of poetry, a place harboring leftover, discarded lines of poems.[44] This is their last stand. Although writing does not have the power to lead to action, it represents the effort of fallen human beings to retain their dignity in the face of defeat by recycling the words of others.

Zoe Karelli (1901–1988) posed a set of existential questions about language. She wanted to know if she could stretch the grammatical paradigm of "man" in the masculine gender to accommodate *i anthropos*, the feminine person, man in the feminine gender, or, as translated by Nanos Valaoritis, "She Male."[45] In part her question is theological. If God made man in his image, what likeness is there to woman? But *women* is also missing from the language of man, producing linguistic and social limitations that a woman must struggle painfully to overcome.[46] Karelli has been identified as a "modernist existentialist," who used the liberated, idiosyncratic verse of modernist poetry to explore "the emotional contradictions and situations of women in modern life."[47] Her modernism lies in her high degree of language consciousness. Her existential questions are bound up with questions about the limits language imposes on social relations and the human imagination. How much adjusting is required for woman to fit into the word *man*? Does the woman writer become alien to herself in the process?

Another intensely self-conscious poet is Kiki Dimoula (b. 1931), whose introduction of an intentionality of consciousness to the everyday creates an intense awareness of the larger questions of existence tucked away in the here and now. Dimoula's work is highly attentive to form. It almost seems to use the careful ordering of verse to reframe the chaos of everyday life. Its intensity lies in the disparity between her self-consciously phrased observations and the subject of her musings, scenes from a life on the verge of forgetfulness, atrophy, disintegration, decay. Her writing is a kind of literary mending. "The Adolescence of Forgetfulness," one of her great poems, gingerly puts back together what cannot finally be repaired while it offers insights on that temporary, and ultimately futile, process.[48]

Both Karelli and Dimoula can be said to belong to a long lineage of Greek poets who take seriously their role as creators. Poets are creators who make things with words. Their bottom line is that words are all they have to go on. Words are a poet's medium and to a large extent the vehicle of human interaction. Thus, to write poetry means to adjust the relationships between not just words but also the people who use words. Poetry can make people talk, feel, and see differently.

The degree of confidence in words varies. On the most pessimistic end of the spectrum we have seen the "poets of defeat," for whom words are always already sullied by doublespeak. Karelli and Dimoula are less pessimistic. Although Karelli struggles "to have my word" and Dimoula isn't sure that she actually "fixes" anything, neither condemns the act of writing poetry. For Katerina Anghelaki-Rooke (b. 1938), words are flexible, creative substitutes for what people cannot touch or know. A prolific poet and translator, Anghelaki-Rooke uses words to explore inner lives, to invent alternative worlds, to follow the traces of missing bodies, to wonder at all that is lost in translation, to speculate on the sides of myths that remain untold. "Says Penelope" imagines a patient, long-suffering wife whose ploy for putting off suitors is not weaving but "some writing I would start and erase." The writing contains double-edged words of crying and the physical grief those words deprive.[49]

On the more assertive end of those who see in poetry a creative promise is Nanos Valaoritis (b. 1921), perhaps the most important writer of the Greek diaspora since Cavafy. Valaoritis recognizes that language reinforces and is reinforced by conventions, yet believes that poetry still has the power to fashion things differently. Valaoritis has been involved in literary movements in England, France, the United States, and Greece. His work feeds on many sources of inspiration. It draws on both the surrealist promise that psychic automatism can pry open a marvelous dream world and the "upbeat" and "beatific" in the American Beat Generation. In much of his writing Valaoritis is a poet's poet, reflecting on the historical conditions of writing and trying out every possible position, as in his poems "The Poetic Art" and "The Poet & the Other Man: A Creation Myth."[50] Yet Valaoritis encourages creativity in his readers too. His poem "I Believe" offers a template for new creeds. The poem can be read as a kind of manifesto for a generation for which creative juxtapositions do not so much expose the underbelly of traditional myths as free the mind of dogmas that bind it.[51]

Most poets of the generations emerging after World War II can be located somewhere between Leontaris's position of resignation and Valaoritis's "upbeat" message. Agnosticism about the real power of language is also common. Eleni Vakalo (1921–2001), who was simultaneously one of the most important art critics in Greece in the late twentieth century and an award-winning poet, drew lessons from several media and conceptual movements and from the language people use to talk about the world everyday. She learned from the visual arts the process of abstraction and applied this to poetry to create distillations of language events in the world that could be used almost as charms, as in her poem, "A Charm for Women."[52] At the same time her work is attentive to the material production of words and the degree to which people's desires and lives are implicated in their circulation. Vakalo's playful collections of poems centered on heroine Lady Rodalina explore the idea that a human life may be a living out of possibilities already inscribed in language. If this is the case, writing implicates readers, who actively engage in the fashioning of a story but whose lives also reflect the story they are fashioning, and so on and on—in the hall of language mirrors.[53]

Greek poetry remains remarkably rich, varied, and vital. Besides those mentioned here, Manos Eleftheriou, Stefanos Rozanis, Markos Meskos, Dinos Siotis, Lefteris Poulios, Yannis Kontos, Yannis Varveris, Maria Laina, Pavlina Pampoudi, Maria Kyrtzaki, Jenny Mastoraki, Dionysis Kapsalis, Yannis Patilis, Haris Vlavianos, Stathis Gourgouris, Thanassis Hatzopoulos, and Athina Papadaki are just a few actively publishing today. Mention should also be made of Olga Broumas, who glides so effortlessly between Greek and English that she almost erases the line between the two languages. Lessons learned from post–World War II writers run deep. From the "poetry of defeat" there remains a sense that words have a limited power and little transparency. They do not open a window to the real or even surreal world. Instead words turn in on themselves as labyrinths or mirrors. Yet there is also belief in the value of language play, in the possibility, and even the requirement, that language will keep producing fresh, odd angles on a too-familiar view. To gain traction, to keep language alive and the vision of the universe fresh, poets today approach writing through layers of contemplation, which may be philosophical, as in the writing of Haris Vlavianos and Thanassis Hatzopoulos, or ironic. They reach across national borderlines, revisit generational divisions, explore gender lines, and generally stand at odd angles to common subjects. Michalis Ganas (b. 1944), for example, keeps a city dweller's nostalgic eye on life in dying villages while he also identifies the village ethos in the gestures and habits of city dwellers. Poets today move between linguistic registers, between rare and common words. According to Yiorgos Chouliaras, "It takes humble, everyday words to build simple and elegant linguistic designs."[54] They even explore mundane examples of creativity in order to learn better how to create. A recent poem by Sakis Serefas (b. 1960) plays on multiple meanings of the phrase "out of nothing" and suggests that if poetry is a materialization of the immaterial, it is second to his grandmother's art of living, which made something practically of nothing. The poet marvels at the miracle of his grandmother's creative "nothing" as he watches her embroidering silently in the dark. He wants to learn from her vital lessons: "'Hey,' I go, 'where did you learn how / to tame the darkness to make light eat from your hand?' / and she answers playfully, 'Out of nothing.'"[55]

Given the current level of sophistication, poets worry that their words no longer resonate with popular audiences, something that may reduce their body of work to a proper name in literary history with no living resonance. Dimitris Kalokyris (b. 1948) knows a great deal about book audiences. Besides writing many books of poetry, prose poems, and fiction, he has worked as publisher, translator, editor of the journals *Tram* and *Chartes*, author and editor of a series of children's books, book display designer, and book artist. In his poetry he combines traditions, stories, invented or real quotes from other writers, and even recipes with pseudo-commentaries. Kalokyris's recent poem "The Poet and the Muse" begins with a pompous recitation of an invented, highly lyrical poem about mythical heroes and bright archipelagoes, then breaks as the poet makes love to his muse. As she buttons her dress and adjusts her lipstick, the muse admonishes him for confusing an outdated approach to poetry with national foundations. She then implicates the poet in a self-referential game and urges him to stop. Times are changing, and neither she nor his readers are listening:

> Drop the wheel, take up the oar,
> your verses don't move me any more. . . .
>
> Look, your readers hang out in arenas apathetic,
> and tomorrow they will certainly find you pathetic.
> While you drench yourself in ink, something is amiss:
> You dream of seducing me with hard, glass kisses,
> but you will only win me over in theory
> and from here to eternity be just a name, "Kalokyris."[56]

"The Poet and the Muse" summarizes beautifully both the playful self-awareness of poetry in Greece today and its loss of audience share to other forms of writing.

THE RISE OF FICTION

Fiction is the most popular form of writing in Greece today. This has not always been the case. From the emergence of the Greek state through the years of repression and dictatorship after World War II, prose took a secondary role to poetry. Prose writers were never Greece's bards. Instead the writers of memoirs, satire, realist, and naturalist fiction in the nineteenth and early twentieth century and of modernist and postmodern fiction of the past sixty years have been offering evidence of a difficult, fractured community consciousness.

Some of Greece's revolutionary heroes wrote memoirs in order to record the stories of their involvement in the Greek War of Independence, justify their actions, and castigate their opponents. Ioannis Makriyannis (1797–1864) reportedly learned to read and write in order to compose his memoirs. His simple, direct style has found a place in the Greek canon, inspiring other works. *Loukis Laras*, a popular patriotic novel by Dimitris Vikelas (1835–1908), was serialized in a literary journal in 1879 and translated almost immediately into English and several other languages. It is a fictional memoir of a rich old Greek merchant of London, who reflects on his adventures as a refugee of war following the massacre of civilians on the island of Chios at the beginning of the War of Independence. In the twentieth century, testimonial narratives were used to represent new experiences of trauma in the Greek national psyche: World War I,[57] the Asia Minor catastrophe,[58] the occupation,[59] Civil War, and the 1960s.[60]

While social and political upheavals have offered primary material for fiction writing, many authors found richer fodder in the problems plaguing Greece since it gained independence: brigandage, corruption, bureaucratic waste, struggling agricultural communities, the social inferiority of women, and in the twentieth century, class divisions and the unplanned growth of Athens. For many decades the topographies of Greek fiction tended to be centripetal, focusing their attention on Greece or neighboring areas where Greeks lived, with just a few narratives set abroad and very few involving characters that were not Greek.

Thanos Vlekas (1855) is a biting satire exposing the inequalities in Greek society. Published anonymously in 1855 by Pavlos Kalligas (1814–1896), a politician, professor of law at the University of Athens, judge, and historian, the satire finds the symbol of inequality in two brothers, the one virtuous, brave, immune to corruption but unable to improve his condition, the other ruthless in his pursuit of wealth and socially successful through his illegal manipulation of Greece's political machinery. Emmanuel Roidis (1836–1904) is best known for his novel *Pope Joan* (1866), an elaborate work of fiction based on a historical rumor that a woman managed to hide her sexual identity and sit on the papal throne from 855 to 858; but he also wrote caustic essays satirizing daily life in Greece's cities, where, he believed, the rising middle class simply did not know how to behave. In a handful of stories written between 1882 and 1895, Georgios Vizyenos (1849–1896), a native of a village in Thrace, explored village life outside the Greek state in the Ottoman Europe, a battleground for competing nationalities. The perspective he offered was that of a grown son who, returning from his university studies in Western Europe, is comfortable neither in his newly acquired skin nor in his former Greek Ottoman incarnation. An outsider at home, he views with skepticism the supernatural, superstitious interpretations people give to puzzles lying at the heart of each story's drama. Yet he cannot offer an educated answer of his own to these puzzles, because the social phenomena are too layered and complex to grasp, no matter what approach is taken to understand them. Vizyenos's stories cut through his era's rigidly drawn lines of ethnicity, gender, religion, and even rationality and sanity.[61]

While some prose works written at the turn of the twentieth century tried to uncover survivals of the ancient past, the continuities of Greek history, and the unity of Greek society, others achieved a dramatic depth by exposing discord, dysfunctionality, and conflict in Greek village life. *The Beggar* (1896), a novella by Andreas Karkavitsas (1865–1922), shows villagers in Thessaly so illiterate and destitute that they fall victim to a ring of counterfeit beggars who play on their superstitions and vulnerabilities. *The Murderess* (1903) by Alexandros Papadiamantis (1851–1911) depicts a village woman's descent into madness. The woman is pressed by poverty, worn out by life, and downtrodden by the inequality that she and other women must endure because their fate depends on their families' ability to provide a dowry. She takes it upon herself to kill a series of young girls born to families that cannot afford them in order to save them from her own fate. The woman's madness is especially poignant because her thinking is as logical as her actions are monstrous. *The Life and Death of the "Hangman"* (1920) by Konstantinos Theotokis (1872–1923) depicts an old man so obsessed with money and profit that he alienates his neighbors, who in turn use his greed as bait to steal his possessions and make the end of his life a living hell. In Theotokis's anatomy of social drama, the confusion of profit with value and of financial deals with human intimacy lies at the heart of abusive conflicts. Theotokis's fiction also explores what happens when individuals seek to impose their will over social destiny. Theotokis introduced social philosophy to prose writing.

Several decades later, Nikos Kazantzakis (1883–1957) turned Theotokis's critique of the individual on its head.[62] In Kazantzakis's novels, all of them translated into English and popular with international audiences in the 1960s and 1970s, strong individuals rise to overcome society's constraining forces. Kazantzakis's work dramatizes philosophical issues. It is driven by the question of how human beings can express their desire to be free—individually, socially, politically, spiritually—in the face of a brutal social order and universe without meaning. Zorba is the antirational, spontaneous hero of Kazantzakis's most popular novel, *Zorba the Greek* (1949). He represents a "primitive man" who experiences life's "basic problems"—work, friendship, food, drink, sex—as "urgent necessities.[63] "Boss," the story's erudite narrator with an ascetic nature and socialist ideals, hires Zorba to manage a mine he has inherited in Crete. The two travel and live together in Crete. Having none of Zorba's vitality, "Boss" tries to learn from the uneducated, older man how to overcome his evasion of life. But when he exposes himself to society, he finds it cruel and immoral. In the end he decides to leave Crete, part with Zorba, and return to his home abroad. He promises to apply Zorba's lesson of throwing himself completely into the "here and now" not to live like Zorba but to devote himself heart and soul to his original love, book learning.

Kazantzakis's novels, written near the end of his life in the 1940s and 1950s, treated the theme of the individual's tense relationship with the social order without attending to the contemporary political landscape of Greece.

Kazantzakis's point of reference, the era of his youth, when Greeks were embroiled in nationalist battles with the Ottomans, deflected attention from the political and social contests brewing at home. These would spill into the streets and countryside from 1944 to 1974 and force fiction writers of the next generation to face the drama of individuals in Greece who found themselves at odds with the political and social order at home.

Traumatic events of the occupation and Civil War, conflicts between the political left and right, conflicts within the political left, political prison and exile, intragenerational battles of the 1960s and 1970s, and uneven development after the return to democracy in 1974 have absorbed Greek authors during the sixty years since World War II.[64] Yiannis Beratis (1904–1968) was one of the first to give an account of divisions in the Greek Resistance to the Nazi occupation in his *Itinerary of '43* (1946). Others who treated the Civil War and its aftermath in the 1950s were Costas Taktsis, Alexandros Kotzias, Rodis Roufos, Nikos Kasdaglis, and Renos Apostolides.[65] Melpo Axioti (1905–1973), a high modernist whose difficult experimental fiction published just before the war challenged readers, returned to experimental writing in the 1960s after producing popular works of socialist realism in the late 1940s and 1950s. In 1965 she published *My Home*, a memoir organized as a set of related short stories. The stories register the author's frustrated efforts to recollect her island home of Mykonos while she is living in political exile in East Berlin. Meanwhile she knows that her home is changing with the invasion of tourism. Scenes from childhood filled with beggars, a blind archaeologist piecing together the nation's history, and donkeys making their way between villages offer local color and nostalgia. But the book also explores the island's difficult economic conditions, which have made it perennially dependent on others, as it dramatizes the author's impossible task of grasping the island's current state of dependency without seeing the place for herself. The storytelling shifts between formal Greek and local dialects, between description and quotations from documents and archival letters, as it moves back and forth between the place of exile and the homeland. Aris Alexandrou's (1922–1978) *The Mission Box* (1975) is another masterpiece of the era. Alexandrou wrote poetry and prose in his short life but broke new ground with this novel. The language with which he recounts the Greek Civil War seems simple and direct, like a testimony, but the accounting involves a complex mystery that implicates the narrator in ways he cannot grasp. The book is multilayered and enters a rich dialogue with other European literature about the failure of revolution. Menes Koumandareas, Yiorgos Ioannou, Thanassis Valtinos, Christoforos Milionis, Marios Hakkas, Vassilis Vassilikos, Maro Douka, Yorgis Yatromanolakis, Dimitris Nollas, and others worked through many of these same topics and themes while they also took fiction in new directions. They introduced the variables of the everyday, where people live out private dreams, anxieties, passions, and perversions that matter more to them, finally, than the political ideals they may work briefly to promote.

Achilles' Fiancée (1987), a novel by Alki Zei (b. 1925), a writer best known for her children's books, exemplifies this last trend. The book explores the disillusionment of the Greek left through alternating chronological and ge-ographic angles. The narrative moves back and forth between the heroine's interior processing of events in the 1940s and 1950s that send her and thou-sands of Greek communists into political exile in Tashkent, Uzbekistan, at that time a part of the Soviet Union, and a third-person account of relations between some of those same former communists now in self-imposed exile in Paris in the late 1960s, as they contemplate taking a stand against the Greek military dictatorship. The book is about a lost generation, lost opportunities, and lost Greek histories that have taken place elsewhere; but it is also about the frustrated efforts of the heroine, a women known by her nom de guerre Eleni and her other name, Daphne, to make a life for herself. Although its historical reference point is the Civil War and its aftermath, *Achilles' Fiancée* is most representative of trends in Greek writing in the last decades of the twentieth century.

CONTEMPORARY PROSE: CENTRIFUGAL TOPOGRAPHIES AND FORGOTTEN HISTORIES

Modernism and postmodernism give to Greek writing its current orien-tation, techniques, topics, and tropes. Telemachus Alavera, Dimitris Hadzis, Tatiana Gritsi-Milliex, Yiorgos Heimonas, Margarita Karapanou, Takis Koufopoulos, Mimika Kranaki, Yiorgos Maniatis, Kostoula Mitropoulou, Mona Mitropoulou, Yiannis Panou, Nikos Politis, and Alexandra Schina introduced techniques of high modernist prose in the years after World War II. Niki Anastasea, Maria Efstathiadi, Dimitris Dimitriadis, Nikos Houliaras, Alexandros Isaris, Alexandra Keligiorgi, and Yiorgos Xenarios emphasize the intertextual horizons of writing as they expose the conditions of literary production. Evgenios Aravitsis, Apostolos Doxiadis, Michel Fais, Rhea Galanaki, Eleni Giannakaki, Christos Homenides, Hristos Hristopoulos, Dimitris Kalokyris, Achilleas Kyriakidis, Klairi Mitsotaki, Thomas Skassis, Ersi Sotiropoulou, Phaidon Tamvakaki, Takis Theodoropoulos, Petros Tatsopoulos, Nasos Vayenas, Kostas Voulgaris, and Zyranna Zatelli put to use postmodernism's techniques to produce a pastiche of genres and codes. Their writing mixes genres, blurs the lines between fiction and nonfiction texts by embedding the one in the other, and gives new life and form to historical fiction and fictional biography. Besides foregrounding the conventions of fiction writing, their writing also revisits forgotten or repressed histories that have been left unfinished or untold. Their stories concentrate on people on the move. They tell stories of emigration, the contact of Greeks with others, the impossible quest for origins. They bring to the surface traces of Greece's invisible others—non-Greeks living within Greek society and Greeks living out their dramas abroad—who challenge the appearance of national homogeneity. The body of prose work published in the past two decades has forced even the most conservative coterie of critics in Greece to explore questions of Greek identity, otherness, gender, textuality, hybridity, and historicity.

Rhea Galanaki's *Life of Ismael Ferik Pasha* (1989) was one of the first novels to revitalize historical fiction. It tells the story of a young Cretan boy who is kidnapped and taken to Egypt in his youth and raised as a Muslim. He rises to the position of minister of war in the Ottoman Empire and leads the Egyptian army to suppress the Cretan uprising against the Ottomans. In Crete the novel shifts to Ismael Ferik's first-person musings as he comes face-to-face with his Christian brother and struggles with some rather unyielding questions of history, national myths, and individual identity. Galanaki has written several works of fictionalized biography, revisiting the forgotten lives of individuals such as writer and critic Andreas Rigopoulos in *I Shall Sign as Loui*, and in *Eleni or Nobody*, Eleni Altamura, who may be Greece's first woman painter, and most recently stirring up controversy by fictionalizing an account told by a living woman about her kidnapping in Crete. Michel Fais's *Autobiography of a Book* follows the efforts of a local historian to piece together the complex history of Komotini, a town with a strong Muslim, Christian, Asia Minor refugee, and Jewish presence, as he sifts through personal testimonies and nonfictional documents referring to the same sets of events but telling the story in conflicting ways.

A current focus on human movement and ethnic interaction and mixing has brought stories of emigration and immigration into the spotlight. Most people living in Greece have close relatives who emigrated from Greece in the past century. While mass emigration from Greece was a phenomenon of the early and mid-twentieth century, it did not become a recurring theme in fiction writing until quite recently. Two postwar novels stand as early landmarks. *The Life of Andrea Kordopatis, Book 1: America* (1964) by Thanassis Valtinos (b. 1932) appeared ahead of literary trends but two generations after the first wave of labor emigration to the United States (1890–1920s) to which it refers. Here Valtinos introduces a chronicle style of writing based on oral testimony, with the fictional Kordopatis, a dirt-poor laborer born in the Peloponnese in the 1880s, narrating his story in a reworked version of the nonfictional Kordopatis's testimony. The narrator's voice is flat and unreflective. It obscures his inner world while giving weight to each episode equally, as if unfolding a

life with no causes or consequences, highs or lows. There is no search for explanations, no exploration of drama; only a series of episodes. Why travel under the worst possible conditions to the United States? Why wander out west,
then forcibly return to Greece after being discovered by American authorities?
Valtinos's emigration story offers no answers—only a deadpan narration. This
is not an epic story of an emigrant named Kordopatis but the unheroic record
of every "Kordopatis" whom embarrassing circumstances forced to leave family and home.

Dimitris Hadzis's *The Double Book* (1974) was another trailblazer, a book
about a Greek Gastarbeiter in Germany. Hadzis offered a second, contrapun-
tal voice to the emigrant Kostas's flat testimony. While Kostas, the poor Greek
who went to Germany to find work, is trying to tell his story simply, an unnamed narrator in this "double" book, an "author" in search of a good story,
presses him for explanations, raising questions of history, causality, and identity. What was Kostas's story prior to emigration? What moved him to emi-
grate? How does he feel among strangers? Where is his homeland? What is his
identity? How does he understand the "Romeic"? Kostas demurs. He has no
homeland, no positive identity, no past he wants to remember, just the drive
to live and understand the present. He doubts the author can get anything
of out him. Through the fits and starts in the dialogue between author and
subject, the book develops the picture of a life adding up to both more than
is expected and less than is hoped for.

Recent prose works probe Greek emigrations from different angles. These
include Thanassis Valtinos's *Data from the Decade of the 1960s* (1989), Dimitra
Sideri's *Homelands* (1992), Mimika Kranaki's *Philhellenes* (1992), Theodores
Kalifatidis's *The Last Rose* (1996) and *In the Light of the North* (2000), Sophia
Dangle-Panagiotidou's *Two Homelands* (1997), and Christos Kolyvas's *Em-
igrants to Another World* (1996). There are also books about Greek repatri-
ation, among them Sotiris Dimitriou's *May Your Name Be Blessed* (1993),
Alexis Stamatis's *Bar Flaubert* (2000), Ioanna Karystiani's *Men's Suit in the Dirt*
(2000), and Vassilis Alexakis's *Paris-Athens* (1989), *Mother Tongue* (1995), and
Foreign Words (2006). Two kinds of stories have taken form, roughly following
Valtinos's and Hadzis's prototypes. The one chronicles episodes of migration,
focusing on the passage to the foreign land, work, the state, acts of remem-
bering the homeland, and occasionally, the fate of foreign-born children. It
contains a kernel of intense human drama, but the narrative does not develop
the drama any more than a formal document explores people's lives. Modeled
on oral testimony, like Valtinos's *Kordopatis*, this type of story does not create
an emotional center to draw a reader in; yet it converges on a migrant life
narrative so familiar one feels one has lived it oneself. The other type adds a
layer of reflection. Just as the second narrator in Hadzis's *Double Book* presses

Kostas for insights, books such as Mimika Kranaki's *Philhellenes* and Alexis Stamatis's *American Fugue* break the verisimilitude of the story to underscore key points in the drama of belonging nowhere. The protagonists in these narratives are likely to be literate and highly reflective. While they may be political exiles crossing borders under stress, still the obstacles they face are different from those of labor immigrants who struggle for work, shelter, legal standing, and respect. Their drama consists in their trying to fit into containers carved out by forces of history, geography, and politics beyond their making. They neither fit comfortably into the confines of the homeland nor find an easy place in the host country.

Gazmed Kapllani's, *Border Syndrome* is another "double book." Kapllani is an Albanian immigrant who arrived in Greece in the early 1990s when he was in his twenties. He worked as a laborer, then enrolled in Panteion University in Athens, and there completed a Ph.D. in sociology. Although he learned Greek as an adult, Kapllani writes and speaks fluently, and he works as a journalist for the Greek newspaper *Ta Nea*. The subject he treats in this book is the story of a group of young Albanian men's difficult, illegal entry into Greece in the early 1990s, a time when Greece made known its desire to receive immigrants but treated them as if they were unwanted after they arrived. Kapllani gives this reason for the narrative: "You cannot understand an immigrant unless you hear his story."[66] The immigrant's story has two voices. One voice gives a third-person account of the group's border crossing and internment in a detention center whose purpose is to manage illegal immigration. Interspersed in this account is the second voice of thoughtful, first-person reflections. Like journal entries, these process the internal steps the immigrant takes to wrest himself from a delinquent motherland, which has for decades proved its incompetence in caring for its young, and to adjust to a wary step-fatherland. He describes the initial fantasy of living outside a state where there is no occasion for conspicuous consumption, whether of goods or sex—the obsession of several young men. He remembers crossing the border's invisible line, which is marked only by the presence of border guards. He describes his response to Greek television news clips about crimes allegedly executed by Albanians. He recalls how it feels to adopt new gestures, mouth Greek words, enter a foreign skin, and finally recognize that his own child feels more comfortable in the foreign language than in the immigrant's mother tongue and skin.

It is too soon to know if Gazmend Kapllani's book will inaugurate a new trend in Greek writing or stand as a literary exception. Yet the publication of this book serves as a reminder that several of Greece's literary giants—Solomos, Kalvos, and Cavafy—wrote Greek as foreigners, even though they saw themselves as Greeks. Moreover it begins to pry the Greek language apart from its automatic association with a certain national group and history. This does not mean that Greek is losing any of its expressive power or richness as a long-lived literary language. Today's Greek writing is adding to the rich history of Greek by creating a vehicle for more than one group of people to explore dimensions of their identity, community, and geography.

NOTES

1. Linear B is an early script consisting of syllabic signs and logograms used to record Mycenaean Greek, the oldest recorded Greek dialect. See Geoffrey Horrocks, *Greek: A History of the Language and Its Speakers* (London: Longman, 1997), 305.

2. Odysseus Elytis, "Nobel Lecture," December 9, 1979 (accessed January 8, 2008), http://nobelprize.org/nobel_prizes/literature/laureates/1979/elytis-lecture-e.html.

3. Brian D. Joseph, "Modern Greek," Ohio State University Department of Linguistics (accessed October 16, 2008), http://www.ling.ohio-state.edu/~bjoseph/articles/gmodern.htm, cites 10 million speakers in Greece, 500,000 in Cyprus, more than 1 million in Australia, and the remainder elsewhere in the Greek diaspora.

4. Nikos Engonopoulos, "Poetry 1948," trans. David Connolly, N. Engonopoulos (accessed August 31, 2008), http://www.engonopoulos.gr/_homeEN/poem10.html.

5. Yiorgos Chouliaras, "Regarding the Investment of the Shipowner Mr. Andreas Embeirikos in a Blast Furnace (March 1935)," in *Bread of Words* 6, trans. David Mason and Yiorgos Chouliaras, unpublished ms.

6. "N17 a Political, Revolutionary Organization, Koufodinas Tells Court," Hellenic Resources Network, July 25, 2003, http://www.hri.org/news/greek/ana/2003/03-07-25.ana.html#17.

7. E-mail message to the author, February 19, 2008.

8. David Ricks, *Modern Greek Writing* (London: Peter Owen, 2003), 27, mentions the poem's popularity with English readers. It appeared in an almost-instant English translation (1825) in Claude Fauriel, *Chants populaires de la Grèce moderne* and "struck a chord with English readers in the Romantic period."

9. See Michael Herzfeld, *Ours Once More, the Making of Modern Greece* (New York: Pella, 1986), 36.

10. Author's translation from Greek.

11. Kostis Palamas, *The Twelve Lays of the Gipsy*, trans. George Thomson (London: Lawrence and Wishart, 1969), 77.

12. Palamas, *Twelve Lays*, 76.

13. See Angelos Sikelianos, "At the Monastery of Saint Luke," trans. Thanasis Maskaleris, in *Modern Greek Poetry: An Anthology*, ed. Nanos Valaoritis and Thanasis Maskaleris, (Jersey City, NJ: Talisman House, 2003), 41.

14. Mark Mazower, *Inside Hitler's Greece* (New Haven, CT: Yale University Press, 1995), 117–118, narrates this event.

15. Gail Holst-Warhaft, *Dangerous Lament: Women's Laments and Greek Literature*. (London: Routledge, 1992), 179–184.

16. Odysseus Elytis, *Heroic and Elegiac Song*, trans. Edmund Keeley and Philip Sherrard, in *A Century of Greek Poetry 1900–2000: Bilingual Edition*, ed. Peter Bien et al. (River Vale, NJ: Cosmos, 2004), 373.

17. Elytis, *Heroic and Elegiac Song*, 374.

18. Elytis, *Asma Iroiko kai Penthimo gia ton Hamenon Anthypolohago tis Alvanias* (Athens: Ikaros, 1979), part 14, my translation.

19. Mel Gussow, "Odysseus Elytis, 84, Poet and Nobel Laureate Who Celebrated Greek Myths and Landscape," *New York Times*, March 19, 1996.

20. Vangelis Calotychos, *Modern Greece: A Cultural Poetics* (Oxford, UK: Berg, 2003), 221.

21. George Seferis, "The King of Asine," in *George Seferis Collected Poems*, trans. Edmund Keeley and Philip Sherrard (Princeton, NJ: Princeton University Press, 1981), 267.

22. Seferis, *Mythistorema* XXII, trans. Nanos Valaoritis and Bernard Spencer, in *Modern Greek Poetry*, 100.

23. Seferis, "Some Notes on Modern Greek Tradition," *Nobel Lecture*, December 11, 1963 (accessed September 1, 2008), http://nobelprize.org/nobel_prizes/literature/laureates/1963/seferis-lecture.html.

24. George Seferis, "Thrush," in *George Seferis Collected Poems*, 333–335.

25. Roderick Beaton, *George Seferis: Waiting for the Angel* (New Haven, CT: Yale University Press, 2003), 271, relates the poem to Seferis's personal "Descent into Hades" during the first years after World War II.

26. Beaton, *George Seferis*, 404–405, translates the poem and gives an account of the funeral and demonstration.

27. "To Andreas Kalvos," in Kostas Karyotakis, *Battered Guitars: Poems and Prose*, trans. William W. Reader and Keith Taylor (Birmingham, UK: Modern Greek Translations, 2006), 121.

28. Kostas Karyotakis, "Love," in *Battered Guitars*, 14.

29. Karyotakis, "We Set Out All Together," in *Battered Guitars*, 125.

30. Karyotakis, "We Are Just Some Battered Guitars," in *Battered Guitars*, 103.

31. Kostas Varnalis, "Magdelene," trans. Kimon Friar, in *Modern Greek Poetry*, 64.

32. C. P. Cavafy, Artemis Leontis, Lauren E. Talalay, and Keith Taylor *"What These Ithakas Mean": Readings in Cavafy* (Athens: ELIA, 2002), 18–19.

33. Edward Morgan Forster, *Pharos and Pharillon* (London: Hogarth Press, 1961), 193. Peter Jeffreys, *Eastern Questions: Hellenism and Orientalism in the Writings of E. M. Forster and C. P. Cavafy* (Greensboro, NC: ELT Press, 2005), explores Forster's and Cavafy's relationship.

34. C. P. Cavafy, "Voices," trans. Edmund Keeley and Philip Sherrard, in *C. P. Cavafy Collected Poems* (Princeton, NJ: Princeton University Press, 1992), 22.

35. See Artemis Leontis, "Who Is C. P. Cavafy?" Modern Greek, University of Michigan (accessed September 1, 2008), http://www.lsa.umich.edu/modgreek/about/whoiscavafy.

36. Effie Rentzou, "Nicolas Calas: A Life in the Avant-Garde," February 15, 2004, Greekworks.com (accessed September 1, 2008), http://www.greekworks.com/content/index.php/weblog/extended/nicolas_calas_a_life_in_the_avant_garde/.

37. Nicolas Calas, "Surrealist Pocket Dictionary," in *New Directions in Prose and Poetry*, ed. James Laughlin (Norfolk, CT: New Directions, 1940), 403.

38. Nicolas Calas, "Cavafy," trans. Avi Sharon, in *Modern Greek Writing*, ed. David Ricks (London: Peter Owen, 2003), 260.

39. Nicolas Calas, "Acropolis," trans. David Ricks, in Liana Giannakopoulou, "Perceptions of the Parthenon in Modern Greek Poetry," *Journal of Modern Greek Studies* 20, no. 2 (October 2002): 260–261.

40. Manolis Anagnostakis, "Apologia of the Law Abiding," trans. David Posner, in *Modern Greek Poetry*, 376.

41. Michalis Katsaros, "In the Dead Forest," trans. Thanasis Maskaleris, in *Modern Greek Poetry*, 356.

42. Titos Patrikios, "Verses 2," in Kimon Friar, *Contemporary Greek Poetry* (Athens: Greek Ministry of Culture, 1985), 262–263.

43. Vyron Leontaris, "From the Ends," trans. Amarinth Sitas and Nanos Valaoritis, in *Modern Greek Poetry*, 388.

44. Leontaris, "From the Ends," 384.

45. Zoe Karelli, "She Male," trans. Nanos Valaoritis, in *Modern Greek Poetry*, 255.

46. Karelli, "She Male," 256.

47. Valaoritis and Maskaleris, eds., *Modern Greek Poetry*, 254.

48. Kiki Dimoula, "The Adolescence of Forgetfulness," trans. Don Schofield and Harita Mona, in *A Century of Greek Poetry*, 569, 571.

49. Katerina Anghelaki-Rooke, "Says Penelope," trans. Christina Lazaridi, in *A Century of Greek Poetry*, 621.

50. See Friar, *Contemporary Greek Poetry*, 119–121.

51. Nanos Valaoritis, "I Believe," in Friar, *Contemporary Greek Poetry*, 118.

52. Eleni Vakalo, "A Charm for Women," trans. Paul Merchant, in *A Century of Greek Poetry*, 431 (from her collection *Genealogy*).

53. Vakalo, "Oh, Eloise, Oh Chateaubriand," from *The Mad Words of Lady Rodalina*, trans. Nanos Valaoritis, in *A Century of Greek Poetry*, 312–313.

54. "Poet Yiorgos Chouliaras: 'Poetry is an Inquiry into the Universe,'" *Kathimerini*, May 12, 2005 (accessed September 1, 2008), http://www.ekathimerini.com/4dcgi/news/content.asp?aid=56228.

55. Sakis Serefas, "*Ap' to tipota* (Out of Nothing)" (Athens: Kedros, 1994), 17, translated by the author.

56. Dimitris Kalokyris, "The Poet and the Muse," *Entefktirio* 79 (December 2007), translated by the author.

57. On World War I, see Stratis Myrivilis, *Life in the Tomb*, trans. Peter Bien (Hanover, NH: University Press of New England, 1987).

58. On the Asia Minor catastrophe, see Stratis Doukas, *A Prisoner of War's Story*, trans. Petro Alexiou (Birmingham, UK: Modern Greek Translations, 1999); Stratis Myrivilis, *The Mermaid Madonna*, trans. Rick Abbott (Athens: Efstathiades Group, 1981); George Theotokas, *Leonis: A Novel*, trans. Donald E. Martin (Minneapolis: Nostos, 1985); Elias Venezis's "Mycene" and Ellie Alexiou's "Fountain of Ali Baba," both in *Greece: A Traveler's Literary Companion*, ed. Artemis Leontis (San Francisco:

Whereabouts, 1997); Dido Sotiriou, *Farewell Anatolia*, trans. Fred A. Reed (Athens: Kedros, 1991). Venezis's *Number 31328: The Book of Slavery*, about his life in a concentration camp after the Asia Minor catastrophe in 1922, has not been translated into English.

59. On World War II, see George Psychoundakis and Patrick Leigh Fermor, *The Cretan Runner: His Story of the German Occupation* (London: Penguin, 1999), and Iakovos Kambanellis, *Mauthausen*, trans. Gail Holst (Athens: Kedros, 1995).

60. On the 1960s, see Thanassis Valtinos, *Data from the Decade of the 1960s*, trans. Jane Assimakopoulos and Stavros Deligiorgis (Evanston, IL: Northwestern University Press, 2000).

61. See Margaret Alexiou, *After Antiquity: Greek Language, Myth, and Metaphor* (Ithaca, NY: Cornell University Press, 2002), 275–286.

62. Dimitris Tziovas, *The Other Self: Selfhood and Society in Modern Greek Fiction* (Lanham, MD: Lexington Books, 2003), 13–54, compares Theotokis's and Kazantzakis's work.

63. Nikos Kazantzakis, *Zorba the Greek*, trans. Carl Wildman (New York: Simon and Schuster, 1996), 151.

64. See Roderick Beaton, *Introduction to Modern Greek Literature* (Oxford: Oxford University Press, 1994), 229–245.

65. English translations exist of Alexandos Kotsias, *Jaguar*, trans. H. E. Criton (Athens: Kedros, 1991); Costas Taktsis, *The Third Wedding*, trans. Leslie Finer (Harmondsworth, UK: Penguin, 1969) and trans. John Chiolis (Athens: Ermis, 1985); and Stratis Tsirkas, *Drifting Cities*, trans. Kay Cicellis (Athens: Kedros, 1995).

66. Gazmend Kapllani, *Border Syndrome* [*Mikro Imerologio Synoron*, in Greek] (Athens: Livanis, 2006), 14. Author's translation.

6

Music and Dance

GREEK MUSIC AND dance cast their spell on the world in 1960 when *Never on Sunday* became an international hit and composer Manos Hadjidakis won an Oscar for the title song. There was the opening scene in the Greek tavern, with the *bouzouki* orchestra playing and Yiorgos (Titos Vandis), one of the customers, dropping his head, snapping his fingers, raising his arms like wings for a *zeibekiko* solo. The world applauded along with Homer Thrace (Jules Dassin), the film's American tourist, as Yiorgos slowly turned, dipped, brushed his shin with his palm, leaped in the air, then came down to his knees—arms pulsing at his sides—and lifted a bottle of ouzo from the dance floor with his mouth, bottoms up. People wanted to join in the fun when Homer started breaking plates in the film's *hasapiko* finale. And they wanted to learn "Zorba's dance" exactly as Zorba (Anthony Quinn) taught it to his introverted boss (Alan Bates) in *Zorba the Greek* (1963) with Mikis Theodorakis's irresistible *bouzouki* arrangement.[1]

Although these scenes are now almost fifty years old, their image of Greece has not really aged. The world still associates Greece with the *bouzouki*, its most distinguishable sound, and with dancers, whether male or female, who in a flash of Dionysian ecstasy will cast off all restraint.[2] It's hard to imagine a Greek party, wedding, or festival that does not live up to this image. Indeed, the *bouzouki* fills many corners of the Greek social world, and an evening with friends often reaches its climax when beloved songs from the repertoire of *laika*, popular urban songs with Eastern roots like the ones Hadjidakis and Theodorakis adapted for the big screen, inspire one *zeibekiko* after another.

This style of music seems to be the cultural form without which Greeks would be least themselves.

Yet the *bouzouki* is not the only instrument in Greece's vibrant music scene, and *laika*, though remarkably long lived and still a dynamic presence, is only one of many musical styles. Byzantine music in Greek Orthodox churches is presently attracting an unprecedented numbers of young men and women who wish to learn to chant in the tradition. *Dimotika* (folk songs) and *paradosiaka* (traditional music) are enjoyed in many venues and inspire new songs. Western and Eastern crosscurrents—classical, jazz, rock, Latin, rap, French and Italian song traditions, pop, Turkish, Slavic, Jewish, Persian, Roma, and Indian influences—can be traced in everything from instrumentation to melodies. And Greek traditional dances of enormous regional variety continue to be danced in many settings. There are also interesting gender and class lines running through the traditional music world, some of which have been disturbed by city life, though other barriers seem harder to overcome. (There are many female singers and some great lyricists but very few composers, for example.)

Perhaps the best way to appreciate the variety of scenes and sounds is to attend to the places where music is played, shared, and enjoyed, and to linger where the strongest influences are most evident.

BYZANTINE CHANTING

Greek Orthodox Churches are an important first stop. Here *psaltes* (chanters) cultivate not just the Byzantine, unaccompanied, monophonic vocal style but also its paths to composition, all of which reach back to centuries-old practices. Church canon law prohibits the use of instruments, as the church fathers felt that the human voice is the only instrument pure enough to praise God. This means that Byzantine music is unaccompanied. It is also modal, meaning that its scales are more complex than major and minor Western scales, with elaborate intervals that differ from those of the Western octave and give the music its Eastern sound. These scales may owe something to ancient Greek musical theory, but there was also heavy borrowing from the Jewish temple. The Eastern sound of the chanting as it is practiced today owes its defining traits to influences and important composers from Palestine and Syria. After 1453 there was a give-and-take between Ottomans and Greeks, as Ottomans borrowed heavily from the sumptuous Byzantines and employed Greek chanters to write music. Indeed, the mixture of Roman, Jewish, Hellenic, Slavic, and Ottoman influences can be considered the defining post-Byzantine synthesis in music and other Greek arts.

More important, the dominant aesthetic factor in shaping the music is the rich hymnographic poetic tradition—a factor seen also in the unique fusion of high poetry and popular twentieth-century Greek song. The melodic line of a given hymn is defined by its mode and by a traditional formula, or melody type. This melody type is claimed to preserve the transmission of the hymn from the earliest time of its composition when the music founds its inspiration in the poetry. There are legends relating those melodies to angels, for example, the story of a boy lifted up to heaven to hear the angels singing, "Agios, Agios" ("Holy, Holy") and repeating it once he returned to the earth so that communities of faithful could sing it with every Divine Liturgy. This is not to say that compositions remain anonymous. While Romanos the Melodist (early sixth century A.D.) is one of the great composers of longer works, Kassia (ninth century A.D.), stands out as the woman who composed numerous hymns, including Kassiani, chanted on the Tuesday vespers services of the Holy Week before Easter.

Chanters are trained both to sing in unison the melody types of thousands of hymns and to elaborate on melodies through ornamentation and melisma, a run of notes on a single syllable. A choir of chanters stands in front of the icon screen on the side and responds to the priest's petitions. In longer hymns, the *Protopsaltis* (lead chanter) chants the melody with improvised ornamentation, while the choir anchors the melody and keeps it from losing its tone by holding the *ison* (bass drone). Byzantine harmonization is not polyphonic. The bass line does not provide a counterpoint to the melody or running harmonies. Instead it holds the tonic note of the scale. The *ison* gives the music its solemnity and gravity. To anyone accustomed to Western choral music, the singing style is elaborate and unmistakably Eastern, some would say "austere and haunting" or even "otherworldly."[3] Whether the voices are all male, as in the traditional Byzantine choir, or male and female, as is increasingly the case, the music aspires to convey the transcendent sublimity of pure chant.

The singing style of Byzantine chant continues to work its way into Greek popular music. Precursor Simon Karas (1903–1999) played a big role in raising the profile of Byzantine music among urban elites, counteracting pre–World War II tastes that favored Western styles of music. Today many male singers of secular music either have been chanters or have learned at the side of chanters. Indeed, the claim is made that among those singing popular Greek music, the majority have a connection to Byzantine music. Makis Christodoulopoulos, better known to his fans as "Makis," sings exactly in the style of Byzantine chant. Petros Gaitanos, who attracts a different audience, records both secular songs and Byzantine hymns. Even female stars such as Haris Alexiou and Alkisti Protopsalti follow the style.

DIMOTIKA AND PARADOSIAKA

A second foundation of Greek music can be found in the improbable number of places of entertainment—from taverns to high-end clubs to large open-air theaters—that offer their stage to musicians who play *dimotika* (folk music) and *paradosiaka* (traditional music) from different regions of Greece. Music from Crete is especially popular. Musicians such as composer Yiannis Markopoulos and the late, legendary singer Nikos Xylouris brought the island's traditions to the national stage in the 1970s by singing rebel songs known as *rizitika* and the epic love poem *Erotokritos*. Behind their success were artists such as Thanasis Skordalos and Kostas Moundakis, who helped popularize the *lyra* (three-stringed lyre that is bowed). Now others are extending that fame. With his long hair, beard, and eccentric, frenzied playing style, singer and lyra player Psarantonis (Xylouris's brother) has a kind of rock-star image in the world music circuit. Another singer and master of strings is Loudovikos of Anogeia, who finds inspiration for his original compositions in the rich musical traditions of Anogeia, a place high on Mt. Psiloritis famous for its music, stock breeding, and fierce independence. Several musicians are taking a broad approach to Cretan *paradosiaka*. Chainides, a group formed in 1990, blends original compositions with themes and songs not just from Crete's musical traditions but also from Turkey, Afghanistan, and Bulgaria. Ross Daly, an Irish musician who speaks Greek with a Cretan accent and plays the *lyra* and several other Cretan and Near Eastern instruments (*laouto, outi, tambur, saz, kemence,* and *ranbab*) with great flair, has helped extend the reach of Greek *paradosiaka* by bringing them into contact with world music. His Labyrinth Musical Workshop, held since 1982 in the village of Houdetsi, Crete, near Iraklion, has "the goal of initiating young people, primarily, into a creative approach to traditional musical idioms from various parts of the world."[4] These musicians and their passionate audiences are giving new relevance to *paradosiaka* not as an idiom of the *parelthon* (past) but of *kathimerinotita* (the everyday)—a Greek "jazz," as they like to call it.[5]

Greek traditional music consists of a broad category of songs and dances identified as *dimotika* or *paradosiaka*. These two terms refer to the same body of material, but *dimotika* are folk songs performed by people who have always shared this music, whereas *paradosiaka* is a newer term and coincides with the rediscovery of folk music by urban elites since the 1960s. *Paradosiaka* tend to be associated with urban musicians who play traditional instruments with historical accuracy. There is a renaissance of this kind of playing, spawned in part by *mousika gymnasia* (state-sponsored musical high schools) introduced in the 1980s to teach young people Byzantine and traditional music.[6] The traditions consist of *tragoudia* (songs) and *horoi* (dances). But they represent music that has evolved over such a wide area, where Greeks lived alongside Vlachs, Albanians, Slavs, Turks, Jews, Armenians, Arabs, Roma, and others, that, on the surface at least there seems to be little coherence. For one thing, instruments differ from region to region. On the Greek mainland what dominates is the *klarino*, an Albert-system clarinet in C imported in the nineteenth century, or the more traditional *zournas*, *karamoutsa*, and *pipiza*, double-reed instruments with a piercing sound. The *tsabouna* or *gaida* (bagpipe) supplies the drone. Lead instruments in other areas are the *lyra*, a three-string lyre whose shape and playing technique differ from region to region; the violin played like a Near Eastern fiddle; the mandolin; or the *tabouras* or traditional *bouzouki*, an older, smaller, less resonant version of the modern *bouzouki*. The *laouto* (lute), *outi* (oud), *santouri* (hammered dulcimer), and sometimes the guitar offer the accompaniment, and the *daouli* (bass drum) punctuates the beat. In northern Greece, ensembles of *halkina* (brass bands) offer another sound.

There is even greater variety in the dances. People claim that more than five hundred Greek dances are known and many more lost. Regional traditions are identified with the Peloponnese, Central Greece, Thessaly, Epirus, Macedonia, Thrace, Ionian Islands, Aegean Islands, Crete, Cyprus, Asia Minor, Constantinople, and the Black Sea, but there are many locally specific dances. Just a few of the countless regional dances are the *tsakonikos* from the Peloponnese; *karagouna* from Thessaly; *koftos* from *Epirus*; *gaida*, *baidoushka*, *leventikos*, and *mikri Eleni* from Macedonia; *zonaradikos* and *podaraki* from Thrace; *ballos*, *syrtos*, *kerkyraiikos*, from the Ionian islands; *ballos*, *sousta* from the Aegean Islands; *pentozalis*, *kastrinos*, *syrtos*, and *sousta* from Crete; various "spoon dances" from central Anatolia, and the *tik*, *kotsari*, and *serra* from Pontos, the area around the Black Sea where Greek communities once thrived.

What joins these traditions is the folkloric and media attention they have received for more than fifty years. *Paradosiaka* comprise a unified tradition in Greece today because they have been studied, performed, and enjoyed as such across all of Greece and in the Greek diaspora. Forces of mass migration that took Greeks out of their villages and brought them together in cities have contributed to the creation of a Panhellenic body of dances. The *kalamatianos*, a semicircular dance in 7/8 derived from Kalamata; the *tsamikos*, a leaping male dance in 3/4 from the mainland; the fast *hasapiko* or "butchers' dance" in 2/4 from Constantinople; the Cretan *syrtos* and *pentozalis* are traditional dances with regional origins that form a Panhellenic repertoire.

Yet there are traditional musical principles connecting locally distinct practices. Performers of *dimotika* follow musical paths similar to those of Byzantine music. The music is modal and, for the most part, monophonic. An accompaniment may keep the rhythm or supply the drone. A song has a *skopos* (melody) consisting not of fixed notes assigned to words but of a set of musical themes that arrange themselves in relation to the words. Performers do not reproduce prior performances exactly. Instead they retain the integrity of the *skopos* and the lyrics while adding exclamations (*aman! more! ela! aide!*), repetitions of syllables, and *melisma* (long vocal runs on a single syllable) to give the song rhythmic variety, and glisandos and ornaments to enrich the melody. Musicians bring to the performance their own repertoire of *stolidia* (ornamentation), which is part of their style of performing. In traditional communities men and sometimes women both sing, but until recently rural women played only small percussive instruments such as the *defi* (tambourine) and *koutalia* (spoons). Besides these unifying principles, there is the reality that musicians perform music, and musicians travel. Wherever musicians go, they introduce their instruments and playing styles. For a very long time now professional Roma musicians, for example, have been playing across the broad region of the Balkans and eastern Mediterranean, appearing in groups with the *zournas*, *gaida*, and *daouli*, excelling on the clarinet or violin, mixing their repertoire of ornamentation into the regional sounds.

In dance Greeks have a preference for the semicircular formation, which performs the social function of bringing people together, face-to-face, in a celebratory spirit, while offering individuals a chance to lead the group. Circles travel counterclockwise and are open at one end. The person on the left end is the lead dancer, who keeps the beat, maintains the steps, introduces variations, and improvises with a set of figures, including jumps and turns, depending on the dance. Circle dances consist of two kinds: the *syrtos* (shuffling) type danced with hands joined by handkerchiefs, bodies erect, and feet executing elaborate footwork close to the ground; and the more acrobatic *pidiktos* (leaping) dance type with higher kicks, jumps, and more impressive turns. Tradition assigns the shuffling dances to women, with men joining in. Leaping dances are exclusively a male domain. There are also the *antikrista* (paired dances) such as the *ballos* and *karsilamas*.

All of this may sound a bit technical, but the reality is that Greeks understand the rules of traditional music and dance rather intuitively and know many dance steps, for they are exposed to them early in their lives at home and in school. People who identify themselves as Greeks outside Greece are especially keen to preserve dances that their immigrant ancestors brought with them to foreign lands. When formally performing dances, they follow strict gender divisions, but informally women and men mix things up. Still leaping dances such as the *tsamikos* will bring a male dancer to the lead, who uses the opportunity to show off his strength and acrobatic skill.

National and local societies exist, whether formally or informally created, to keep *paradosiaka* alive. Folklorist Domna Samiou pioneered in this with her Kalitechnikos Syllogos Dimotikis Mousikis (Artistic Society of Folk Music), founded in 1981. The Archive of Hellenic Music, another group, does important work collecting, digitizing, reconstructing, and recording older Greek music, and collaborating with dancers. Local societies focus on local traditions or music from *hamenes patrides* (lost homelands) from which members are descended.[7] For example, the Lyceum of Greek Women, a nonprofit organization founded in 1910, has fifty-one branches inside Greece and sixteen outside the country, each devoted to traditions of a particular area. A branch operating in Rafina recently appeared on national public television. Although Rafina lies on the east coast of Attica, the group focuses on traditions of Asia Minor, the lost homeland of many Rafina residents. It performs dances such as the *karsilimas*, *hasapiko*, *syrtos*, *ballos*, and traditional *zeibekiko*. When national television host Bilio Tsoukala of the daily afternoon program *Ehei Gousto* (It's Fun) featured "Dances of Eastern Hellenism," she invited Rafina's Lyceum of Greek Women to perform with musicians from the Archive of Hellenic Music, featuring the great violinist Kyriakos Gouventas. The show became an occasion for pronouncements about the grace, charm, and importance of *paradosiaka*.

The Dora Stratou Greek Dances Theatre in Athens, founded in 1953 as a "living museum of Greek dance"[8] is continuing its ethnographic research and commitment to the authenticity of performances under the direction of Alkis Raptis.[9] It also houses more than two thousand handmade costumes collected from villages and towns decades ago. The theater is best known for its tourist-oriented summer performances in its open-air performance space on Philopappos Hill. But the theater sets aside *Vradies tis Pemptis* (Thursday evenings) from September to May for those truly dedicated to *paradosiaka*.[10] These are free gatherings in the theater's main building on Scholeiou Street in the Plaka. Someone lectures on traditions of particular region, with live examples by a local dance group. A *glenti* (party) follows with food, spirits, live music, and an open dance floor. When the weather is good, the *glenti* spills into the theater's courtyard, and one corner of the Plaka in Athens fills with the sounds of traditional instruments: the piercing *zournas*, beating *daouli*, and joyous cries of dancers and onlookers. Whatever the tradition, the party lasts until the food and drink are gone and the musicians are ready to return home.

HYBRIDS OF GREEK AND WESTERN MUSIC, FROM JAZZ TO HIP-HOP

Outside the traditional music scene, *paradosiaka* combine with other musical sounds to produce new hybrids. Places such as the Half Note Jazz Club and Avlaia in Athens and Xylourgeio in Thessaloniki feature offbeat artists whose work combines non-Greek and Greek, modern and traditional, sounds.

Thursday-evening *glenti* (party) with musicians and dancers at Dora Stratou Dances Theatre, Plaka. Photo courtesy of Stephen Snyder, May 2008.

One night, internationally acclaimed vocal artist and composer Savina Yannatou might be performing. Formally trained in early music and Baroque, she has worked with groups such as Primavera en Salonica and other ensembles to sing, voice, speak, and play Mediterranean and Mediterranean-inspired songs, including Sephardic music, works by Hadjidakis, poems by Borges. She crosses over freely from traditional to jazz to avant-garde improvisation. On another night, the powerful vocalist and pianist Diamanda Gallas, a Greek American with family roots in Mani, may make a dramatic appearance, using her near-four-octave operatic range to reinterpret everything from Johnny Cash songs to a Maniat woman's ritual *moiroloi* (lament). Trio Balkano also performs there. Grounded in jazz but working through Balkan musical traditions in its Roma-inspired playing, the group performs songs like "Tik Florinas" and "The Handkerchief Dance." Estudiantina, a group from Volos, plays music in the tradition of the trained musical orchestras of Constantinople and Smyrna, which, at the turn of the twentieth century, bridged musical sounds, styles, and repertoires of the Greek, Turkish, and Arabic East and European West. Florina Brass Band is another group. Formed in the 1960s by the late Tassos Valkanis and revived by saxophone player Floros Floridis in the 1980s, its frenetic playing follows the style of Balkan brass bands of the Ottoman era. Its greatest hit was "Paradehtika kai zoi kai thanato" ("I Have Accepted Both Life and Death," 1991), the product of an inspired collaboration between singer Alkisti Protopsalti, lyricist Lina Nikolakopoulou, and double-born Bosnian Croat–Serb composer Goran Bregovich, who translated into a Greek idiom his Balkan-influenced Gypsy songs from Emir Kusturica's movie, *Time of the Gypsies*. All over Greece people still dance to the Florina Brass Band's complex rhythms in "Petrol Station," "I Got Pardoned," and "I Wish Joy Was a Plot of Land" from that album. At these same clubs Dionysis Savvopoulos's original songwriting and hybrid combination of *paradosiaka*, *laika* (Greek popular music), American folk music, and rock-and-roll continues to find new audiences among the children and grandchildren of those who first embraced the long-haired hippy when he was strumming his guitar on street corners in Thessaloniki in the 1960s.

Western crosscurrents are heard in everything from Greek classical music and jazz to rock, techno, rave, rap, and pop-inspired songs. These influences sometimes enrich and at other times impoverish music, depending on the composers, the venue, and the spirit of the times. In the 1960s, Nikos Mastorakis's radio show of American and European rock-and-roll, *Leoforeio i melodia* (A Bus Named Melody), inspired Greek rock bands Forminx and Socrates Drank the Conium, with its keyboardist Vangelis Papathanasiou (known to the world today as "Vangelis"). Recent rock and alternative artists Pavlos Sidiropoulos, Vasilis Papakonstantinou, Trypes, Diafana Krina, Xylina Spathia, Pyx Lax, Onar, Ble, Anastasia Moutsatsou, Iro, Zak Alexandrou, and Foivos Delivorias have continued filling airwaves, clubs, and stadia with memorable songs and thoughtful lyrics. Electronic music, acid, house, and techno music also have a strong presence. Kbhta (Konstantinos Vita),

"1st Athens Hip Hop Festival … 4th October Technopolis" posters, Kerameikos metro stop, Athens. Photo by author, October 2008.

formerly of Stereo Nova, received international attention for his musical contribution to the Athens 2004 Olympics Opening Ceremony. Hip-hop groups Imiskoumbria, Goin' Through, and Active Member have also influenced the Greek musical mainstream. *Laika* singer Yiorgos Mazonakis scored a blockbuster rap hit in 2004 with "Gucci forema" (Gucci Dress). Meanwhile alienated subgroups create their own hip-hop scene in more hidden spaces. In the town of Volos, for example, Albanian immigrant teenagers have been rapping in fluent Greek to express the complexity of their standing between immigrant parents and Greek society.

Since the beginning of the twenty-first century, however, pop has been dominant. There is little variety in the musical videos on Greek television or the music blasting in trendy clubs. Rather than create new hybrids out of the old, the assimilative energy here works in the manner of a remix, reducing musical variation to a club beat. In the past few years the Greek music industry, too, has turned its attention to creating pop hits for a Euro-pop audience, especially in its entries for the Eurovision contest. Elena Paparizou's "My Number One," the winning song of 2005, topped charts in Greece, Cyprus, and Sweden, and entered top ten charts in several countries. Besides its success that year, Greece entered the semifinals in 2004 and a top-ten

position with songs performed by Sakis Rouvas ("Shake It," 2004), Anna
Vissi ("Everything," 2006, her second entry, after "Autostop" in 1980), the
British Cypriot and Lebanese pop singer Sarbel Michael ("Yassou Maria,"
2007), and the Greek American Kalomira ("Secret Combination," 2008).[11]
The songs are notable for what they do not exhibit: the Greek language,
Greek musical influences, originality, and apart from "My Number One,"
any lasting power. Where there is more creative energy is in the work of
certain DJs, who display their vast knowledge of music and intuition for
creating unexpected juxtapositions. Some of the best-known DJs in Athens
in 2008 were G Pal, Amy X, and Mahi Lamar, who play alternative and
electronic music; Tsilihristos, who plays Greek and other mainstream; Miss
Lefki, with fusion; and Grigoris Psarianos, a lover of African American and
Latin sounds who works a day job as a deputy to Parliament representing the
left-wing political coalition Synaspismos. Here and there, an old song from
the *rebetika* repertoire may be thrown into the very rich mix.

REBETIKA

Rebetika hold a special place in the story of Greek popular song. They are the
lynchpin of contemporary Greek music, the sine qua non of its development.
They made the *bouzouki* the lead instrument of Greek songs and brought
dances such as the *zeibekiko*, *hasapiko*, and *tsifteteli* to the center of the dance
floor. Without *rebetika* there would be no *laika*. Greek music would have
different scales, different harmonies, different sounds.

Rebetiki Istoria, a *magazi* (establishment) in the Athenian neighborhood
of Exarcheia, is the perfect place to hear *rebetika*.[12] It has been around for
more than thirty years, yet remains humble and true to its original mission of
making authentic *rebetika* accessible to audiences in a spirit true to their legacy.
The place barely advertises its existence, and it's easy to miss the inconspicuous
sign above its door. Even after crossing the threshold and passing through a
narrow hallway into the main room, a customer isn't convinced this is the
right place. A small stage decorated with strings of Chinese lantern–style lights
stands on a slightly raised platform against one wall. Benches stand along the
walls with about twenty-five tables surrounded by wooden chairs scattered
through the *magazi*. There's a small space in front of the stage for dancing.
On the wall are photographs of all the great legends of *rebetika*. One is signed
tellingly, "To Pavlo, with love, Sotiria Bellou."

Rebetika refer to songs of the urban underclass composed from the 1920s
through the 1940s. At first the songs had different names (*mourmourika*,
yiouroukika, *karipika*, *mangika*, *mortika*). They only became broadly labeled
rebetika after 1935, when the recording industry began using the term to
identify a certain musical sound, and more systematically in the 1950s and

Musicians at Rebetiki Istoria in Exarcheia, Athens. Photo by author, May 2008.

1960s among people who collected their recordings. There is little agreement on the etymological roots of the name, only competing claims that it comes from the Greek *remvazo*, "to wander or dream"; the Turkish *rebet*, a person who does not submit to authority; the Serbian *rebenok*, "rebel"; or some unidentified root. *Rebetika* were once accompanied by the three-stringed *bouzouki* and *baglamas* as lead instruments, with the guitar providing chordal accompaniment.[13] Today the four-stringed *bouzouki* is ubiquitous, though Rebetiki Istoria uses the more historically authentic three-stringed *bouzouki*. Sometimes the violin, bass, accordion, or even the banjo joins in. The lyrics are plainspoken in the manner of *dimotika* but narrate urban experiences using the jargon of the subgroup that produced them.

  Rebetika are the product of a wonderful alchemy of musical elements.[14] In the nineteenth and early twentieth centuries, men living in the margins of Athenian society in the neighborhoods of Psyri and later Piraeus composed songs about their lives: about prison, hashish smoking, street fights, illness, passions of all kinds, love interests, and generally the values and lifestyle of the *koutsavakis*, later known as the *mangas*, street toughs. Their instruments were the *bouzouki*, *tzouras*, and *baglamas*, pear-shaped, long-necked *trichorda* (with three paired strings) instruments of different sizes, also known by the name *tabouras*. This was an exclusively male-centered world, with women as the occasional subjects but never the singers or performers of songs. A key feature of the playing style was the open lower string providing a bass drone. The lyrics were distinctive. In coded language, they described a scene without an excess of sentiment, in sharp, clearly articulated, clipped words. The music was modal, and the tuning of the instruments depended on the *dromos*, as musicians call the "path" or mode of composition in which the song was sung. The best known of these tunings was the *karadouzeni*, which is also the title of an early recording by *bouzouki* player, composer, and singer Markos Vamvakaris.

At about the same time in Smyrna, musicians formally trained on instruments such as the violin or mandolin and proficient in both Italian-influenced, polyphonic styles and the free-form, monophonic, Persian- and Turkish-influenced *amanes* (plural *amanedes*, improvisations on the Turkish/Arabic word *aman*, meaning "mercy") found a way to combine Western polyphonic and Eastern monophonic forms. Yiankos Alexiou, or "Yiovanikas," a man from Lesvos who is rumored to have studied the violin with *tsiganoi* (Roma) in Romania and who played to raving audiences in Smyrna, is credited with that great innovation. He concentrated his efforts on taming an Eastern mode with intervals no smaller than halftones so he could harmonize it with broken minor chords. Thus he produced the *Smyrneiko minore* or *minore tis avgis* (minor scale of Smyrna or the East), combining natural and harmonic elements. With this innovation he produced the musical foundation for Greek popular music in the twentieth century: a scale capable of harmonizing Eastern sounds, or conversely, of giving Western music an Eastern feel.

The Asia Minor catastrophe created the conditions for a new fusion of sounds. Of the 1.3 million refugees forced from their homes by the Greek defeat in the Greco-Turkish war and burning of Smyrna's Christian quarters in September 1922 and the Treaty of Lausanne in 1923, more than 100,000 reached Piraeus, already a crowded, unhygienic port city of 130,000. The hopelessly tight living conditions of Piraeus brought Smyrna and Piraeus musicians into close proximity. A sense of solidarity developed between them. Piraeus musicians invited the refugees to visit their *tekedes* (hashish dens) as customers and performers, though for nearly a decade the two groups performed their own styles of music separately. *Bouzouki* players such as Vamvakaris, with his Piraeus Tetrada (quartet) consisting of himself and Anestis Delias on the *bouzouki*, Yiorgos Batis on the *baglamas*, and singer Stratos Payioumtzis, continued playing their songs in the margins of Greek society, for the *bouzouki* was déclassé. Meanwhile the Smyrna Company of Piraeus, a group of trained male and female musicians from the cosmopolitan cities of Smyrna and Constantinople, rose quickly to dominate not just tavern life but also recordings. The company's musical repertoire included *amanedes* in the Eastern style, something Athenians associated with the *café aman*, an establishment imported in the late nineteenth century. The great singer Rosa Eskenazi gave her high-pitched voice to many of these performances, though she also performed every other genre of Greek music. Instruments were many, from the *outi*, *santouri*, *klarino*, and *doubeleki* (drum) to the violin, guitar, mandolin, accordion, and tambourine.

Then in 1932 the first recording of a *bouzouki* reached the shores of Greece from the United States. Jack Gregory, the American name of Yiannis Halikias, recorded "Minore tou teke," a hash-den tune in a minor key, the first example of a *bouzouki* playing not in the *karadouzeni*-style with a bass drone but with broken chords accompanying a tune inspired by Yiovanikas's "Minore tis avgis." It is not surprising that this innovation came from the United States. The first recordings of Greek music were made there in the early 1900s, nearly two decades before the recording industry reached Greece. These precursors of *rebetika* reflect the multiplicity of sounds and fluidity of the state of Greek music not just in the United States but wherever Greeks lived. Musicians performing on these recordings are of various ethnic backgrounds representing the Balkan and Ottoman mix of the day. The same musicians sing *amanedes* in Turkish and Greek. They play Greek, Sephardic, Roma, and Armenian songs. They also show innovation in relation to the musical environment found in the United States. Among the masters is Yiorgos Katsaros, a composer of hundreds of songs, who continued to his dying day at 107 years singing in a style peculiar to singers from Eastern Europe to Afghanistan in the late nineteenth century, with a loose, protruding jaw moving rapidly back and forth to produce a vibrato sound.

When Jack Gregory's "Minore tou teke" became a hit in Greece, Odeon Records invited Vamvakaris to record himself playing and singing with his harsh, untrained voice. In 1933 "O Dervisis" (The Dervish) and "O Harmanis," two hashish songs, were the first Vamvakaris recordings to hit the streets, played by itinerant carriers of record players known as *fonografitzides*. At about that time Smyrna musicians invited *bouzouki* musicians to join forces. From this point on, Piraeus and Smyrna, male and female, trained and untrained, musicians performed together.

These musicians introduced Athens's upper classes to songs of illicit pleasures and the hard life. *Rebetika* featured *bouzouki* solos, direct and unsentimental lyrics, bent notes, and musical melodies and harmonies based on the *Smyrneiko minore* and other modes and scales. Passions ran deep in the lyrics but were controlled on the surface. The rhythms of the songs would eventually typify Greek music: the slow *hasapiko* in 4/4 and fast *hasapiko* or *hasaposerviki* in 2/4, the slow solo *zeibeiko* in 9/4 and the faster, paired *karsilamas* in 9/8, the smooth *syrtos* line dance in 7/8, and the sinuous *tsifteteli* in 4/4 with stress on the first and fourth beat.

When the government of Ioannis Metaxas imposed strict censorship on music in 1936, illegalizing songs with "unethical material" and performance styles and instruments that sounded Eastern, the whole operation went underground. It moved its base to the edges of cities, where it sang newly whitewashed words to old tunes and attracted even bigger crowds in the late 1930s and early 1940s, until the arrival of the Nazis in Athens in 1941. The dark period of the occupation cut back on entertainment but still inspired some powerful songs, including "Saltadoros" (Jumper) by Michalis Yenitsaris, about a man who steals fuel from the back of Nazi trucks, and Vassilis Tsitsanis's "Synnefiasmeni Kyriaki" (Overcast Sunday), which might be dubbed Greece's alternative national anthem, about a cloudy, rainy Sunday and a heart darkened by a bloody massacre by the Nazi occupying forces. There's also a rumor that the composer was mourning the loss of his favorite soccer team.

Tsitsanis was one of the most prolific Greek composers of all time. He enjoyed wide popularity from the time he began recording in 1937 until his death in 1984. He collaborated with Sotiria Bellou, perhaps the greatest singer of *rebetika*. With her uncompromising, androgynous manner, perfect phrasing, and subtle, agile ornamentation, Bellou gave *rebetika* a distinctive voice. When she and Tsitsanis had a falling out, Tsitsanis turned to Marika Ninou, a flirtatious personality who tried to keep Tsitsanis exclusively in her orbit. But Tsitsanis calmly road waves of high drama, including Ninou's self-destructive behavior. Of all the old *rebetes*, Tsitsanis was one of the few who survived seismic changes after the 1940s, when *rebetika* gave way to *laika*.

Musicians at Rebetiki Istoria are careful not to mix *rebetika* with *laika*. On this particular evening they begin with a cluster of "songs of consumption." The first is by Yiorgos Katsaros:

Mother I'm consumptive

Mom I have TB
guard my other brother, Mom
so he won't be ...[15]

The song epitomizes a vital characteristic of *rebetika*: its economy of expression. There is nothing sentimental or saccharine in the lyrics. This is a key element of *rebetika*, more important even (according to *rebetika* specialist Markos Dragoumis) than the instrumentation or style of musical performance.[16] And it is the reason why the songs have aged so well.

Although the group plays some obscure songs at the beginning and end of the evening, between midnight and 2 A.M. better-known *rebetika* satisfy customers, who love to sing along. There's Vamvakaris's "Frankosyriani," about a love interest who is a "Frank," Catholic woman on the island of Syros; Tsitsanis's "Synnefiasmeni Kyriaki"; Yannis Papaioannou and Kostas Manesis's "Pente Ellines ston Adi" (Five Greeks in Hades), a song about five young men whom the lyricist saw die in the Greek-Italian War of 1940–1941 and whom he honored by imagining them in hell, singing and dancing and "driving all the devils mad"; Apostolos Kaldaras's "Nychtose horis fengari" (Nightfall with a New Moon), written and immediately censored in 1947 for its lyrics describing a young political prisoner incarcerated in Thessaloniki during the Greek Civil War; and Yiorgos Mitsakis's "Valentina," a prophetic song written in 1950 about a tomboy with short hair and boyish grace:

> When you go to the *bouzoukia*
>
> and dance the *hasapiko*,
> All of Athens goes wild
> and all the men love you
> . . . soon you will be wearing pants![17]

The song makes explicit an undercurrent of the *rebetika* world as it was evolving after the war. Independent women existed at the edges of that world, offering excitement but also challenging some crucial social barriers.

Pavlos has the voice of legends. At times he almost sounds like Antonis Dalgas, an Asia Minor singer with a remarkable vocal range. But Pavlos doesn't bring attention to himself. He does whatever he can to shun publicity and won't even allow himself to be recorded. He simply sings the songs— thousands of songs over the course of a year, perhaps the biggest repertoire in all Athens. *Rebetika*, not he, are the heroes of his establishment. Following his artistic direction, the *magazi* takes a purist approach to *rebetika*. Musicians perform an immense but finite corpus of older music. Pavlos draws a stylistic line between *rebetika* from everything that followed, and he sticks to the former. The musicians' playing style is supposed to be historically accurate. Pavlos winces when the main *bouzouki* player draws out a solo, gliding between notes and adding excessive ornamentation. He draws back disapprovingly when a customer dances a *zeibekiko* too quickly, and when a second dancer, a woman, adds hip and shoulder movement to the dance as if it were a *tsifteteli*. Pavlos is a purist. For him the *zeibekiko* is a men's dance of Doric severity. The history of Greek music is at stake every night of the year. As night yields to morning, the lyrics of his songs grow especially dark, touching on women who destroy their men and on the generous *mangas* who ends up destitute on the street. Pavlos's face remains impassive, as it has been all evening. His articulation is crystal clear. His voice doesn't break. His singing draws on deeply felt but carefully controlled emotions. Rebetiki Istoria lives and breathes the legacy of *rebetika*.

LAIKA

Bouzoukia, the name people lovingly give to establishments where people hear *laika*, are just a few miles from Rebetiki Istoria, though worlds apart. For nearly fifty years, they have lined segments of the road from Athens to Eleusis, still called by its ancient name Iera Odos (Sacred Way), and Leoforos Poseidonos (Poseidon Avenue) along the Attic Peninsula's southern coast. "Pame sta *bouzoukia*" (Let's Go to the *Bouzoukia*) signifies not just going to hear a certain instrument but embracing a lifestyle.[18] The attitude toward this avenue of consumption is summarized by the phrase "Kai o minas ehei ennia" (literally, "it's the ninth of the month," meaning there's money to be spent).[19] *Bouzoukia* mean a very late night and money conspicuously spent on prior reservations, stiletto heals, suit jacket and tight jeans, a generous tip for a table as close as possible to the stage, expensive trays of carnations tossed on the dance floor or at the feet of the beloved singer, and exorbitantly priced bottles of whiskey—lots of whiskey. The scene inspires people to sing, dance, and lean back *meraklomenoi* (high) in their chairs to feel the lyrics deep in their hearts. *Bouzoukia* are about listening to the heart, reacting spontaneously, and throwing money on the dance floor for a *parangelia* (paid request) for a dear friend, who may be too tipsy to stand but can turn, jump, dip, snap her fingers, stare back at her love interest, and still keep a cigarette between her lips while dancing the *zeibekiko*. The night lasts into the early morning hours and sometimes requires a visit to another establishment for *patsa* (tripe soup), a known hangover cure, or, crepes, a more recent taste.

A straight line connects *rebetika* to *laika*. But the two genres of music do not sound the same. Whereas *rebetika* are rough around the edges but understated, *laika*, music that became popular with rural migrants during the decades after World War II and eventually all segments of the population, exaggerate everything. A number of factors contributed to these radical changes.

The *bouzouki's* physical transformation had a huge effect. The sound emanating from taverns and bars in Greece's urban centers changed dramatically when the *bouzouki* acquired a fourth string, an innovation attributed to the virtuoso *bouzouki* player Manolis Chiotis. At about the same time the *bouzouki* grew in size and acquired amplification. The effect of these changes was to make it a loud, solo instrument dominating all others. In the hands of Chiotis and Yiorgos Zambetas, two exceedingly charming performers, the instrument eventually entered posh entertainment haunts of the rich and famous. It became a fetish of all classes, high and low.

Stelios Kazantzidis's arrival on the scene was also groundbreaking. A singer with a deep, dark voice, a huge vocal range, and a peculiar style, Kazantzidis did not just sing melodies. He slid between notes, working his way around them even after reaching his destination. His augmented vowels stretched words out. He filled his songs with exclamations of pain ("Ach!") all bringing to the surface the bitterness and longing that Greece's working classes needed to share, while *rebetika* had kept these hidden beneath the surface.

A third innovation followed the popularity in Greece of sentimental Indian films, more than one hundred of them, presenting family drama, beginning with *Aan* (renamed *Mangala, the Rose of India*).[20] The films inspired Greek songs with Indian musical themes, beats, and melodies, some of them borrowed wholesale. "Madhubala" ("Aajao tarapt hai arma..." from *Awaara*) with lyrics by Eftychia Papayiannopoulou, Greece's prolific female lyricist of the era, was an especially big hit, as was "Kardia mou kaimeni" ("Dunia me ham aaye" from *Mother India*) by composer Babis Bakalis.

Laika are the songs that emerged from these changes. *Laika* use the song type and instruments of *rebetika* but with dusky female voices and plaintive male voices filled with sentimentality. Their lyrics speak of love lost and dignity defied, as exemplified by the following two verses of "To Agriolouloudo" (The Wildflower), a song made popular by Kazantzidis and recorded more recently by Haris Alexiou:

Do not feel sorry for me, throw me out tonight

cut my life like a wildflower.

...
I started off naked,
I go on alone,
grief is my home,
the journey is my song.
Throw me out and don't feel sorry,
don't care about what becomes of me,
the wildflower endures
whether it rains or snows.[21]

Laika's lyrics of pain, humiliation, and endurance are embellished by an exaggerated style of ornamentation. As performed by singers such as Kazantzidis and Grigoris Bithikotsis—two luminaries of *laika* from the 1950s through the 1970s, the latter a favorite of the urban working class, the former much loved by rural migrants—*laika* personified the losses, cares, and desires of Greek people as they tried to recover from World War II. Other popular singers of *laika* from the early years are Poly Panou, Keti Grei, Mairi Linta, Yiota Lydia, Marinella, Manolis Angelopoulos, Stratos Dionysiou, and Dimitris Mitropanos. The *zeibekiko* became the favored rhythm and dance no longer of the underclass but of a large number of Greeks, a superstructure onto which each person could hang his or her individual complaint—and momentary overcoming—of society's injustices. As the conditions in Greece improved, the dance has changed, too, becoming more elaborate, with faster turns, higher jumps, deeper dips, and more impressive effects in its present-day incarnations.

Among the singers performing *laika* at the *bouzoukia* in the early twenty-first century, whether along the Sacred Way or the road running from Athens to Sounion, or in upscale clubs in towns where people have money to spare or spare more than they have are Paschalis Terzis, Peggy Zina, Notis Sfakianakis, Yiannis Ploutarhos, Antonis Remos, Despina Vandi, Vasilis Karras, Nino, Apostolia Zoi, Yiorgos Margaritis, Angela Dimitriou, Antypas, Yiorgos Mazonakis, and Mihalis Hatzigiannis. These are the current stars of *laika*. They sing new songs but also older repertoire by the major composers of *laika*, Babis Bakalis, Hristos Nikolopoulos, Alekos and Irini Hrisovergi, Akis Panou, Zambetas, and many others.

The déclassé version of *bouzoukia* is a certain kind of dive known by the charming name *skyladiko*, meaning "haunt of dogs" and sometimes translated "woof-woof." (The singers are endearingly called *skylades*, or "big dogs.") *Skyladika* are shabby, disreputable bars located near the Ethniki Odos (Greek National Road). Some of the best known are Embati north of Athens, Mon Repos on the road heading to Marathon, and a variety of places near Larissa and Thessaloniki, two cities famous for their *skyladika* and the *skylades* they promote. Here amplified *bouzoukia* supported by electronic instruments blast out songs from midnight to morning, sometimes as late as 10 A.M. Under the umbrella of this amplified sound, the places offer remarkably decadent, artfully clumsy songs about *kapsoura*, burning love, desire, and pain: "You're burning me, you're burning me, whenever I see you you're burning me, because I love you, because I hurt for you. You're killing me you're killing me, come back, you're killing me" (each line repeated many times).[22] *Skyladika* attract a special mix. Farmers, students (if there is a university nearby), and marginal types, including pimps and prostitutes, frequent establishments in the countryside, while laborers mix with intellectuals and even actors and stars in *skyladika* near cities. Some *skyladika* stars are Angela Dimitriou before she became a pop star, Makis Christodoulopoulos, "Doukissa," Litsa Diamanti, Pitsa Papadopoulou, and Bougas, who is nicknamed "O Planitarhis" (ruler of the planet).

ENTECHNO TRAGOUDI, "ART SONG"

Rebetika and *laika* also have their upscale side. In 1957, when 78 rpm recordings were withdrawn from Greek markets, suddenly songs that had been

Billboard in Monastiraki announcing 2007 as the year of the soprano Maria Callas. Photo by author, May 2008.

cut during the first half of the century became collectable, with *rebetika* acquiring extra value because some records were especially rare due to long periods of censorship. Collectors are known to have increased the rarity of their collections by buying and destroying extant copies. This phenomenon gradually led to *rebetika*'s rediscovery, canonization, and emergence as a field for ethnomusicological study. At about this time, classically trained composers Manos Hadjidakis, Mikis Theodorakis, and Stavros Xarhakos identified *rebetika* as an art form worthy of imitation. Hadjidakis was one of the first trained musicians to embrace *rebetika* with a lecture he delivered in 1949 praising the musical genre, just as Greek audiences were following with pride the meteoric rise of two Greek classical music stars: prima donna operatic soprano Maria Callas, "La Divina" (the Divine), and conductor Dimitris Mitropoulos.

Hadjidakis, Theodorakis, and Xarhakos found that they could satisfy people's middle- and highbrow tastes by giving *laika* a classical twist. In his *Exi laikes zografies* (six popular sketches after *rebetika* songs), Hadjidakis, an accomplished pianist, imitated the sounds of the *bouzouki* and *baglamas* on the piano. He gave his transcriptions and original *laika*-inspired songs to classically trained singers from Nana Mouschouri and Fleury Dantonakis in the

1960s to Elly Paspala in the 1980s. He continued to write classical compositions with a Greek twist for theater as well as orchestra, even as he became Greece's most famous composer of film music. Xarhakos orchestrated both *rebetika* and *laika* and wrote art songs with lyrics by Lefteris Papadopoulos in the style of *laika*. Theodorakis's compositions moved in the opposite direction, setting poetry to *bouzoukia*. In 1960 Theodorakis composed music for Yannis Ritsos's "Epitaphios" in two versions, one sung by Nana Mouschouri with a string quartet accompaniment and another featuring popular singer Grigoris Bithikotsis accompanied by *bouzouki* player Manolis Chiotis. The second version became a popular hit.

With the formula Theodorakis unexpectedly discovered for delivering poetry with a *bouzouki* accompaniment, something important happened to Greek music. The reception of artfully written *laika* was so positive across such a wide social spectrum that *entechno* effectively eclipsed Greek classical music—for a Greek national school of classical music had been a growing force in the first half of the twentieth century, with composer Manolis Kalomiris as its leading representative and Manos Hadjidakis one of its students.[23] In the decades after World War II, Greeks lost their appetite for Greek classical music, especially experimental, atonal compositions, with the exception of Nikos Skalkottas's "36 Greek Dances" (1931–1936, rearranged in 1949). Composer Iannis Xenakis, a major international figure of contemporary music, never even entered their radar screen. Greek classical music's loss of audience share happened despite its systematic promotion by Hadjidakis, Theodorakis, and Xarhakos.[24] Even cultivated urban elites found a more satisfying musical language in artfully crafted *laika*, whether these took the form of a large song cycle with a complex musical structure such as Hadjidakis's *Amorgos* and Theodorakis's musical rendition of Elytis's *The Axion Esti*, or a song such as Theodorakis's "Strose to stroma sou gia dio" (Make Your Bed for Two).

The international success of Hadjidakis and Theodorakis's popular songs enhanced Greece's profile in the world by producing a recognizable sound attached to an image of Greece. That sound reverberated in Greece for decades. From the mid-1960s to the turn of the twenty-first century, it inspired numerous talented composers to produce tens of thousands of songs. Just a few of the best-known composers of the past forty years are Nikos Antypas, Eleni Karaindrou, Loukianos Kelaidonis, Stamatis Kraounakis, Mariza Koch, Linos Kokotos, Stavros Kouyioumtzis, Christos Leontis, Manos Loizos, Sokratis Malamas, Yannis Markopoulos, Notis Mavroudis, Dimos Moutsis, Thanos Mikroutsikos, Hristos Nikolopoulos, Vassilis Papakonstantinou, Nikos Papazoglou, Orfeas Peridis, Mimis Plessas, Dionysis Savvopoulos, Pantelis Thalassinos, Marios Tokas, and Nikos Xydakis. Each has been working with a singular palette combining traditional and popular Greek with other Western and Eastern sounds. Lyricists of exceptional talent, including Manos Eleftheriou, Lina Nikolakopoulou, Lefteris Papadopoulos, and Manolis Rasoulis, have been adding their voices to those of poets C. P. Cavafy, Odysseus Elytis, Nikos Gatsos, Kostas Karyotakis, Nikos Kavadias, Tasos Leivaditis, Yannis Ritsos, and George Seferis, whose work is regularly set to music. Arletta, Haris Alexiou, Eleftheria Arvanitaki, Yiorgos Dalaras, Dimitra Galani, Glykeria, Kaiti Homata, Melina Kana, Haris and Panos Katsimichas, Manolis Mitsias, Viki Moscholiou, Alkisti Protopsalti, Dionysis Savvopoulos, Tania Tsanaklidou, and Nena Venetsanou are well-known singers of *entechno* and *laika*. Some had their beginnings in *Neo Kyma* (new wave), a movement that combined Greek rhythms with folk-rock styles in the 1960s. They stirred small but passionate audiences in venues known by the French word *boîte* (box). Adding to the attraction of the intimate setting were politically charged messages during the dictatorship (1967–1974), when people found in their songs references to common women and men struggling to rise from the blow of injustice.

Some of those same singers are now legends of Greek music who fill large, prestigious concert halls. A large-scale spectacle is likely to feature a megastar such as Yiorgos Dalaras in a carefully produced show. In the past years concerts would have highlighted new songs, but now they review old hits. Dalaras has released more than sixty-five albums of his own and multiple collaborations in the forty-two years since the mid-1960s, when he began performing as a sixteen-year old. His distinctive voice is that of a lyric baritone, with ringing highs and rich lows, though his style draws on Byzantine chant. His concerts inspire enthusiastic crowds. In the 1980s a record 160,000 people attended a concert held in the Athens Olympic Stadium. Albums such as *O Yiorgos Dalaras Tragouda Apostolo Kaldara* (Yiorgos Dalaras Sings Apostolos Kaldaras) and *Mikra Asia* (Asia Minor) have reached platinum status in the Greek market, and his live recording of a concert at the Orfea in Alexandroupolis in 1983, titled *Ta tragoudia mou* (My Songs), is the best-selling album in Greek history.[25]

The winter and spring of 2008 found Dalaras performing "San tragoudi magemeno" (Like a Bewitched Song), a staged historical review of *rebetika*, in Greece's large music halls. These venues are distinctly different from the makeshift *tekedes* where the urban underclass shared hashish and played banned music, but for Dalaras what has always really mattered is the quality of the songs and their performance.[26] Director Sotiris Hatzakis staged the show; Panayiotis Kounadis researched it;[27] Anna Dalara, the singer's manager and wife, supervised it; lyricist Lefteris Papadopoulos wrote the introduction to the program notes; and poet Yiorgos Skabardonis wrote the dramatic text. With the support of a thirteen-member orchestra, Dalaras sang songs representing stations in the story of Greek music in the twentieth century: songs of Smyrna and Constantinople composed before 1922; songs by the same musicians after their forced exodus from Asia Minor to Greece or the United States, including the classic Smyrna-style works of Toundas, Peristeris, Skarvelis, and Papazoglou; songs by the Quartet of Vamvakaris, Payioumtzis, Batis, and Delias; classic *rebetika* composed when the two groups merged, and so on. The program moved deep into the second half of the twentieth century, where Dalaras revisited his favorite *laika* and *entechna*. The stage distance between performer and audience diminished each time Dalaras started a familiar song and audiences joined in, as if singer and audience were part of a small group of friends. Then dramatic acts between song sets reasserted the theatrical distance. These turned on an imagined dream in which Dalaras saw his father, *rebetika* musician Loukas Daralas (Dalaras switched the two middle consonants of his father's name to create his stage name) with a circle of friends telling stories of struggle and success.

The program reached a moment of truth when Dalaras recalled an early memory of his first hearing of Markos Vamvakaris's "Frankosyriani." The narrative became personal but also yielded a social-political message, as often happens at a Dalaras concert. "I was a small child yet I sensed that the song touched me. I stood up, barefoot, and danced an improvised *hasapiko*," Dalaras recalled.[28] He moved from his own youthful response to the song to the observation that younger generations who frequent clubs today "with their depressing *laiko*-pop songs, end up dancing to the *rebetika* which are necessary play at the high point of the night."[29] Here he was drawing a clear contrast between the old and the new, "*laiko*-pop," in their effect on the hearts and minds of young people. He was making the point that *rebetika* and *laika* still claim the heart and soul of Greeks—even of the young people who enjoy *laiko*-pop.

This quote reveals the anxiety people feel about the direction music is taking in Greece today. At the same time it expresses faith in the power of *rebetika* to touch new generations of Greek revelers. Many people share Dalaras's conviction that *rebetika*, *laika*, and the form of entertainment they spawned—late-night *bouzoukia*, group singing, and dancing with friends—continue to exist not just as icons but "deep in the consciousness and inspirational field" of all Greeks.[30]

MUSIC IN THE TWENTY-FIRST CENTURY

The musical and dance forms inherited from the nineteenth century and developed during the twentieth do reach the hearts and minds of ever-new consumers seeking to find pleasure in song, but they have ceased to sell new songs. The repertoire of songs Greeks love to sing is growing backward and inward but not forward. The Internet, with sites such as www.stixoi.info and www.kithara.vu collecting lyrics and others with data, narratives, histories, pictures, and video and audio recordings, has become a schoolroom teaching people old Greek songs.

Television is also contributing to the expanding repertoire. Every day Greek national television reviews some aspect of Greek music and dance or some artist's career. *Stin ygeia mas* (To Our Health!), a weekly Saturday-night program devoted to reviewing music as Greeks are accustomed to sharing it—with food, drink, conversation, song, laughter, and dance—has been especially successful. Beginning in the fall of 2004, new shows have been taped almost weekly from September through June. On the set, host Spyros Papadopoulos, who also works as an actor and game-show host, is seen dining with his honored guests, consisting of a composer, singer, lyricist, performer, specialist, or fellow actors, accompanied by a long table of friends. The group shares music as musicians play for as long as the evening lasts—anywhere from two to four hours. Between sets Papadopoulos chats with guests about the topic of the day. He has dedicated programs to nearly every genre of Greek music, every decade of its production, every circumstance and region of its creation, and hundreds of music makers. He conveys to the audience his intense pleasure in receiving guests and his astonishing command of the lyrics of thousands of songs. Furthermore he communicates a deep desire to keep Greek music alive. Part of his mission is to introduce audiences to new performers or remind them of the qualities of the older one.

There is a feeling in the air, which is supported by the music accountants' spreadsheets, that the music business has lost its old rhythm. It is not that the taste for music has disappeared. A visitor to Greece will be astonished to observe people of all ages and generations singing the verses and the refrains of hundreds of songs, sharing them in groups together. As in so many other places in the world, however, the recording industry has lost its ability to feed a hungry audience with something it wishes to buy. The process of discovering new artists and moving them from the margins to the center through a sequence of venues—from local bars to places of entertainment along the national highway, to clubs along the Sacred Way or Poseidon Avenue, to recording studios on Mesogeion Street and large concert halls, to the marketplace, and finally to people's listening devices—has broken down at two key points. A small coterie of powerful agents with an eye to large profits monopolize contracts with the big clubs and record companies, and so promote only a small number of artists for brief periods of stardom. On the production end this means too much attention to a few attractive singers and little effort to cultivate a larger group of composers, lyricists, musicians, and singers over the long period that it takes a body of good work to mature. At the same time CD sales have been languishing due to high CD prices, piracy on several fronts, and people's lack of enthusiasm for what finally reaches the *agora* (marketplace). It may also be that the old formula for *laika* is no longer productive, while *laiko*-pop, no matter how deafeningly loud, makes no dent in the Greek subconscious. Something new may be in the making, but people aren't really sure what's next.

For now, the mix of ephemeral pop and long-lived favorites serves even if it doesn't completely satisfy Greeks' appetite for music and dance, as countless scenes from everyday life suggest. New songs fill the airwaves, but old songs continue to find new life in present-day performances. On a breezy morning in late spring, the deck of a ferryboat from Piraeus to Aegina unexpectedly becomes a dance floor for *gymnasio* (junior high school) students on an end-of-the-year excursion. Teachers chaperoning the group have set the students loose, so nearly a hundred 15-year-olds are wandering through the boat, talking and laughing and moving their hips to a subliminal club beat. Suddenly "Dyo portes ehei i zoi" (Life Has Two Doors), an old song written and performed by Kazantzidis with words by Eftychia Papayiannopoulou, begins to play on an amplified iPod. The lyrics describe a man reflecting on his past and future destination at the end of his life, when everything seems so fleeting:

Where I'm going

there's no room for tears or pain;
cares and hurts stay here in life
and I walk away alone.

It's all just a *psema* (lie),
a single breath in and out.
One day a hand cuts our life short
like a flower at dawn.[31]

The song is a *zeibekiko*. It used to be danced as if a man's manly dignity depended on it. The solo *zeibekiko* was fraught with tensions. It was a performance of self. While the dance was an intensely personal improvisation directed by the dancer's body and emotions, the dancer could not escape the consciousness of doubleness that is part of performance. Even as the dancer pretended he was dancing for himself, he was also making a statement to the world about himself, his independence, his manliness, as if to say, "I dance the *zeibeikiko*, therefore I am."[32] This was not a statement he could make alone. It needed an audience. The *zeibekiko* dancer walked a tightrope between introspection and exhibitionism; self-expression and audience expectations; living

Students dancing *zeibekiko* on ferryboat between Piraeus and Aegina. Photo by author, May 2008.

in the moment, recalling every *zeibekiko* danced before, and caring about the opinion of friends. It was the balance of tensions that gave the dance its force.

The opening scene of the film *Never on Sunday* showed what could happen if the delicate balance was tested. When Homer applauded Yiorgos as if he were an entertainer, Yiorgos punched him in the eye. Why? Ilya, Melina Mercouri's character, explained: "In Greece when a man dances it is for himself. It makes him feel better in his—how do you say in English, *psyche?*" In *Parangelia!* (Request!), a film directed by Pavlos Tassios (1980), a man's traumatized psyche was especially edgy. The film revisited a historical incident involving a man named Nikos Koemtzis in a nightclub fight during the dictatorship. While nursing several wounds from assaults on his personal dignity (unemployment, a girlfriend's infidelity, harassment by the security police for his father's communist beliefs), Koemtzis paid musicians to play a song for his younger brother to dance. But his political enemies provocatively took over the dance floor, so he pulled a knife and slashed and killed three of them and wounded another half dozen.

On the ship's deck in May 2008, several very lively 15-year-olds mark a spot. Three begin dancing the *zeibekiko* together in a huddle, jumping and clicking their fingers. One breaks away while the others drop to their knees. They're clapping the beat for his solo, belting the words with the chorus of other ninth graders. The soloist is doing acrobatics. He's having fun. He's showing off. Others join in the dance, incorporating their devil-may-care youthful attitude into their moves, happy to accept the applause of fellow students and tourists on the boat. The dancers have taken on the challenge of performing a song about life's bitter *psema* as an affirmation of their confident, youthful European Greek existence. This may not be the *zeibekiko* of the dancers' working-class grandfathers, yet the *bouzouki*, the singing, the sunshine, the wind, the spontaneous party with countless songs of every imaginable kind waiting to be heard on the iPod dock are casting their spell.

NOTES

1. Theodorakis's "Zorba's Dance" was an arrangement of "Armenohorianos Syrtos" by Yiorgis Koutsourelis, a Cretan composer and performer. The dance is a *syrtaki*, a version of the slow *hasapiko*.

2. Gail Holst-Warhaft, "Rebetika: The Double-Descended Songs of Greece," in *The Passion of Music and Dance*, ed. William Washabaugh (Oxford: Berg, 1998), 112 calls this the "Zorba factor."

3. Allan Kozinn, "Byzantine Chant, Rich Challenge to Its Gregorian Counterpart," *New York Times*, April 20, 2004.

4. "Labyrinth Musical Workshop" (accessed June 3, 2008), http://labyrinthmusic.gr/laby/index.php?option=com_frontpage&Itemid=1&lang=en.

5. Haris Pontida, "Yiorti ton Kreton sto Theatro Vrahon: Kritiki paradosi me jazz diathesi kai kefi" (Cretan Celebration at the Theatro Vrahon: Cretan Tradition with a Jazz Mood and *Kefi*," *Ta Nea*, July 8, 2008 (accessed October 17, 2008), http://ta-nea.dolnet.gr/default.asp?pid=2&ct=4&artid=74599.

6. Zoe Dionyssiou, "The Effects of Schooling on the Teaching of Greek Traditional Music," *Music Education Research* 2, no. 2 (September 2000): 141–163.

7. *Hamenes patrides* refer to places in Turkey where Greeks lived until the first decades of the twentieth century, when ethnic cleansing destroyed their communities.

8. "Dora Stratou Greek Dances Theatre" (accessed June 15, 2008), http://www.grdance.org/.

9. Dora Stratou published her research in *The Greek Dances: Our Living Link with Antiquity* (Athens: [s.p.], 1966) and *Greek Traditional Dances* (Athens: Greek Educational Books Organisation, 1979). Alkis Raftis continues her work with *The World of Greek Dance* (Athens: Finedawn Publishers, 1987). The author benefited from a long conversation with him in May 10, 2007.

10. The author took part in *Vradies tis Pemptis* on May 10, 2007 and May 8, 2008.

11. "Eurovision Song Contest" (accessed June 13, 2008), http://www.eurovision.tv/page/history.

12. The description of Rebetiki Istoria draws on the author's visit on May 6, 2008, an evening when Pavlos Vasileiou spoke about his *magazi* and the music he loves to play before launching into a marathon of more than five hours' playing. Yona Stamatis describes entering the same *magazi* in "Rebetika, At Last," her Monday, September 10, 2007 entry at http://yonainthefield.blogspot.com.

13. Risto Pekka Pennanen, "The Development of Chordal Harmony in Greek Rebetika and Laika Music, 1930s to 1960s," *British Forum for Ethnomusicology* (1997) discusses the chordal harmonization in *rebetika*, which is neither Eastern nor Western but something unique to the form.

14. This account of *rebetika* draws on many sources, including Kostas Ferris, *I istoria tou rebetikou tragoudiou* (The History of *Rebetiko* Song), 2006 DVD.

15. Author's translation from Greek.

16. Kostas Ferris, *I istoria tou rebetikou tragoudiou*, part 3.

17. Author's translation from Greek.

18. Title of a song by singer-songwriter Nikos Gounaris (1954).

19. The phrase is the title of a song by Yiorgos Tzavellas (1953) and refers to a time when civil servants were paid on the ninth of each month.

20. Helen Abadzi, "When India Conquered Greece: Hindi Films of the 50s in Greece," March 17, 2003 (accessed June 14, 2007), http://helen-abadzi.sulekha.com/blog/post/2003/03/when-india-conquered-greece-hindi-films-of-the-50s.htm.

21. Author's translation from Greek.

22. Author's translation from Greek.

23. Hadjidakis studied music theory with Menelaos Pallantios, an important presence in the Greek National School, from 1940 to 1943.

24. Hadjidakis's greater investment was in promoting classical music, whereas his soundtracks and popular songs paid his bills. Hadjidakis thought so little of his popular music that he even renounced the ever-popular "Paidia to Peiraia" (Never on Sunday)!

25. Vasilis Loukas, *I hrisi platina* (Gold Platinum) (Athens: Livani, 2007), 216.

26. This description draws on Natali Hatziantoniou, "To rebetiko mageve kai tous estemenous" (*Rebetiko* Bewitched Even Those with Crowns), *Eleftherotypia*, February 5, 2008 (accessed October 17, 2008), http://www.enet.gr/online/online_hprint?q=%F1%E5%EC%F0%DD%F4%E9%EA%E1&a=&id=70442632.

27. Iota Sykka, "Rebetika Is Alive and Well," *Kathimerini*, February 12, 2008 (accessed June 1, 2008), http://www.ekathimerini.com/4dcgi/_w_articles_civ_1_12/02/2008_9324.

28. Hatziantoniou, "To rebetiko mageve kai tous estemenous."

29. Hatziantoniou, "To rebetiko."

30. Sykka, "Rebetika Is Alive and Well."

31. Author's translation from Greek.

32. Although women now dance the *zeibeikiko*, their *zeibekiko* seems to be about women's access to a man's world.

7

Media, Theater, and Cinema

NEWSPAPERS ARE ONE of the first things Greeks see whenever they leave their homes. They hang in streams from kiosks and shop windows. They cling to clothespins, like laundry being aired. Greeks want to see how current events, issues, and trends are presented, so that they can judge for themselves whether the laundry is dirty. The country's experience of foreign rulers, civil unrest, and military dictatorships has seeped deep into its collective being. It has made Greeks alert to the threat of not just autocratic governments but also the media itself and its manipulation of public opinion. It has earned them the freedom to peruse the front page of every paper on display and even flip to the underside without the requirement to buy.

The very public display of newspapers indicates the kind of attention Greece gives to public culture. Much can be learned from the newspapers themselves. Their numbers are bewildering.[1] In a country of some 11 million residents there are twenty-five national dailies, most of them published in Athens, with three in Thessaloniki, and many appearing on the Internet. There are six daily financial papers and nine daily sports papers. The regional dailies are countless. *Proto Thema*, a weekly tabloid published Sundays since 2005, is the top-selling newspaper, often surpassing two hundred thousand copies sold per issue. And there are several free papers, including the daily *Metrorama* and several weeklies with information about happenings in Athens (*Lifo, Athens Voice, FAQ, Athens Plus*) and Thessaloniki (*Simera*). Many newspapers include special inserts such as magazines, toys, CDs, DVDs, and even pornography to promote themselves. Newspapers represent a very broad political spectrum,

Periptero (kiosk) selling newspapers and periodicals in downtown Athens. Photo by author, October 2008.

from communist (*Rizospastis*), left (*Avgi*), and socialist or center left (*Eleftherotypia, Ethnos, Ta Nea, I Niki, O Logos, To Vima, Avriani*) to center right (*Kathimerini*), right (*Adesmeftos Typos, Apogevmatini, Eleftheros Typos, Estia, I Hora*), and right nationalist (*Eleftheri Ora*). They give free range to politicians, artists, intellectuals, and common citizens to elaborate their viewpoints on a wide variety of topics. Another interesting feature is their daily coverage of culture. Most daily newspapers devote a section to the *technes* (arts) or *politismos* (civilization), with reviews, analysis, and listings. Television and radio channels also regularly present concerts, exhibits, plays, films, and documentaries from their archives as well as discussions with creators and critics. Clearly there's a market for culture, and newspapers make it their business to keep it in public view.

Greeks are alert to both the dangers and powerful returns of public forms of culture. In a sense, all culture is public, as it involves behaviors learned through socialization. Yet some forms—theater, exhibits, parades, festivals, and all kinds of displays—are more public than others because they are staged for a large audience. Others—cinema, print and Internet publications, radio and television broadcasting—reach out to a mass audience to shape its opinions and tastes. These cultural forms create a nexus where audiences, artists, opinion makers, and those who benefit from shaping public opinion meet, with a variety of results. In Greece, a country whose roots are tied to the origins of tragedy and whose latest century of existence is filled with so much drama, public culture is especially potent. Revivals of ancient Greek theater nourish a sense of national pride but also bring attention to the hubris that leads individuals to transgress social boundaries, or the underlying absurdity of their actions. Cinema, radio, and television offer mind-numbing staples together with some hard-earned, reflexive, and ground-shaking interventions. A closer look at key moments in the history of these forms indicates just how vital public culture is in Greece.

RADIO

Greek radio came into being under conditions of dictatorship. For the following fifty years the only legal broadcast enterprise was a monopoly of the Greek state. Dictator Ioannis Metaxas established the first radio service in 1936. When Nazi occupying forces seized control of Greece in April 1941, they placed radio's management in the hands of collaborators. The Greek State again took over after the retreat of the German army on October 20, 1944. It controlled broadcasting through periods of emergency government, parliamentary monarchy, and military dictatorship. With the restitution of democracy and abolition of the monarchy in 1974 came the guarantee of freedom of expression and the press (article 14 of the constitution of 1975); yet article 15, section 2, of the same constitution placed radio and television under direct state supervision. Deregulation came finally under pressure from market forces, especially actions taken by the pressure group Channel 15, formed in 1985 by communication specialist Roussos Koundouros with support from thirty-three well-known personalities (including composer Manos Hadjidakis, author Costas Taktsis, and architect and computer scientist Nicholas Negroponte) who recognized the potential of free radio.[2] The mayors of three cities, Athens, Piraeus, and Thessaloniki, also "decided to promote media pluralism and set up municipal radio stations."[3] By the time of deregulation, Greek national radio had three stations operating from Athens and several from other cities in Greece (Thessaloniki, Volos, Patras, Chania, Corfu, and Iraklion).[4]

Yet even during its fifty years of state monopoly, the radio landscape in Greece was rich. Some of the more dramatic moments show just how aware people were, even from the first moments in its history, that radio technology can reach audiences. On April 27, 1941, as German tanks were entering Athens and rushing to take over the radio station, the announcer managed to utter these words before shutting down his program: "Brothers and sisters, heads high! In a little bit this station will not be Greek. Stop listening to it. The *agonas* (struggle) continues."[5] Although the Nazis used technology as efficiently as they could to shut out all voices of resistance, they were not able to fully control the message that reached the occupied country. When in 1943 they confiscated radios to reprogram them so that they could only receive certain channels, certain technicians found ways to make the reprogramming reversible. Then in August 1944 the announcer Dinos Tsaloglou at the Athens station managed to broadcast cheers for the Greek resistance movement's successes on the Nazi occupying forces' station without the occupiers hearing it.[6] The Nazis were most successful in silencing stray voices during their retreat, when they destroyed the transmitter at the station and many antennas, leaving Greece without a radio station to announce its liberation.

Pirate radio stations cropped up in the 1960s as a way to broadcast alternative voices to the state radio that was the only legal provider and, during the years of the military junta from 1967 to 1974, a force limiting political discourse through strict censorship. Pirate stations tended to come and go, offering nonconfrontational musical programming, sometimes with a very specific subject: songs by the Animals or the music of Stelios Kazantzidis. Derti FM 98.6, a very popular private station, continues to this day with its motto from that era, "Mono laika!" (which means "only *laika*," or Greek popular music for the masses). "Their illegality was their charm,"[7] as they offered a kind of intimacy and love for their subject that was missing in the conservative radio of the state. Most of these stations tended to be weak and short lived, leaving few traces of their experiments with broadcasting. When Greek students occupied the Polytechnic in November 1973, however, their success in setting up a pirate radio station for broadcasting their appeal to the people of Greece to revolt against the dictatorship changed the political dynamic in the country. This "was the first serious challenge to the fascist colonels since they had seized control in 1967."[8] It was especially effective because it captured on live radio the confrontation of the night of November 16–17, when the dictatorship sent in troops with military tanks to break down the Polytechnic's gates and suppress the uprising.

Although state radio led the way in the long periods of political censorship during dictatorships, occupation, and civil unrest, its cultural programming managed to introduce polyphony. One of Greek radio's most important experiments was the serialized performance of adapted translations from the great repertoire of world theater. The programming reached its apogee from 1946 to 1956, years of the Civil War and hard-line anticommunist governments, with its creative adaptations that included experimental theater by authors such as Jean-Paul Sartre, Samuel Beckett, and Eugène Ionesco. One critic has suggested that theatrical programs on Greek national radio became the "*protoporia* [avant-garde] of Greek theater" during this era.[9] Some of Greece's great theater directors (Karolos Koun), actors (Katina Paxinou, Alexis Minotis, Anna Kyriakou, Marika Kotopouli, Despo Diamantidou, Melina Mercouri, Dimitris Horn, and Dimitris Papamihail), educators (Antigone

Metaxa), composers (Manos Hadjidakis), authors (Iakovos Kambanellis and Nikos Gatsos), translators, and musicians took part in the project. The list of names is remarkable. These were some of Greece's greatest artists working at the time. And in some cases their artistic, social, and political ideas differed from the views promoted by the ruling political regime. Thus while politics was working to shrink people's ideological horizons, national radio's dramatic performances were giving voice to alternative worlds. This kind of programming contributed to Greeks' sense that culture could provide an alternative site for political expression.

Manos Hadjidakis's *Trito Programma* (Third Program, or ERA 3, Greek national radio's classical station) opened another free, experimental space where polyphony ruled. From 1975 to 1982, the buoyant years immediately following the fall of the military dictatorship and restitution of democracy, Hadjidakis took over as director of ERA 3. Hadjidakis changed the direction of the station's programming without diminishing the weight given to classical music. He brought together youthful new talent in a highly creative atmosphere. *Edo Lillipoupoli* (Lillipoupoli Here), a children's musical program with words by Marianina Kriezi set to music by Lena Platonos, Nikos Kypourgos, and Dimitris Maragopoulos, entertained a generation of Greek children in ways comparable to American public television's *Sesame Street*. As time went on, Hadjidakis broadened the circle of his collaborators to include artists, philosophers, and researchers who had never participated in the mass media. Into the mix he threw his own charismatic leadership and restless searching. He cast new light on classical music by juxtaposing it with jazz, *rebetika*, tango, Italian film scores, and so on, leading his very broad audience into a rich exploration of sounds.

Today the radio dial in Greece gives a different meaning to polyphony. The airwaves are overcrowded. Around 1,200 stations operate on land, according to one source, most of them privately owned with a local character and without an official license.[10] The state-owned presence remains important, though it is declining in audience figures and advertising revenue. State-owned radio includes five national stations (NET, Second, Kosmos, ERA3, and ERA SPORT), one station with international coverage (ERA5 "The Voice of Greece") and another international network (ERA), a station for immigrants living in Greece (Filia), nineteen regional stations with local coverage, and two shortwave programs in Macedonia with international coverage. Private stations now dominate the radio sector. According to Radiourgies Blogspot, the ten most popular radio stations in the last two months of 2007 were SKAI 100.4, SuperSport FM 94.6, Lampsi 92.3, Derti FM 98.6, Rhythmos 94.9, Kiss FM 92.8, ERA Sport 101.8, Sfera 102.2, Melodia 99.2, and Red 96.3.[11] Ant1, broadcast on 97.5 FM and 97.2 in Athens, is a popular station.

Today's political battles over radio include questions about how the state issues licenses, where "collusive relationships between politicians and owners of radio stations" exist, and whether privatization freed radio from repressive state controls or created new monopolies.[12]

TELEVISION

Television's emergence under the military dictatorship in Greece (1967–1974) is the subject of a popular film of 1984 and a television series (2006–2008), both called *Loufa kai parallagi* (Loafing in the Army).[13] A group of soldiers is assigned to the cinematic unit of YENED (Armed Forces Information Service), the television station created by the Greek Army to "provide 'national, moral, and social education' to the armed forces and the public."[14] Their job is to produce propaganda films and newsreels but also to entertain. They find themselves in a challenging position because, while their talent and prior experience in the film business recommend them for their positions, their morals, politics, and tastes do not exactly match the dictatorship's ideology. Yet they end up doing pretty much what they please. The comedy comes from the incongruity of their approach to show business with the officers' weighty sense of their mission, and of the absurd situations the soldiers actually found themselves in (many episodes are faithful to history) with the tragic national adventures of the period.

In many ways *Loufa kai parallagi* represents the absurd situation of Greek television during those formative early years. Television, like radio, was a state monopoly from its first broadcast in Athens on February 23, 1966, under parliamentary monarchy through seven years of military dictatorship and another fifteen of parliamentary democracy until its deregulation in 1989. The dictatorship of April 21, 1967, with its "revolution to save the nation," named as enemies of the state communism, atheism, and rock-and-roll music "composed by drug-addicted hippies."[15] Yet television under the dictatorship embraced American and British popular culture. The colonels wished to be loved, people loved pop culture, and so, to boost its lagging popularity, the dictatorship broadcast—alongside its own parades and reenactments of ancient battles—programs on pop culture, including rock-and-roll and its idols. It operated two television channels in black and white for about eight hours every evening beginning at about 5:30 P.M. One was EIRT (today's ET1), run by the Hellenic Radio and Television Foundation, and the other YENED, the propaganda medium of the Greek army.[16] Although the two channels were state monopolies, they found ways to compete for the country's limited television audience. Thus when YENED discovered Nikos Mastorakis, a successful television personality, EIRT hired him too for its programs.

Mastorakis is the perfect symbol of television's contradictions under the dictatorship. He became a television pioneer in Greece as an importer of pop celebrity rather than a mouthpiece for the dictatorship's reactionary motto, "Ellas Ellinon Hristianon" (Greece of Christian Greeks). His most influential program introduced Greeks to rock-and-roll: its lifestyles, its stars. His *Afti einai i zoi sou* (This Is Your Life, after the American program) and *Bingo* were so popular they cut into movie and theater sales on weekend nights. Yet Mastorakis, the ultimate media entrepreneur, found himself without work in Greece after the restitution of democracy because people thought he had collaborated too closely with the dictatorship, especially in a series of army-supervised interviews he conducted with students incarcerated after the military's November 17, 1973, raid on the Polytechnic. He left the country to make B movies in the United States, then returned after 1989 to lead the way in the privatization of Greek television. In contrast to Mastorakis, Freddy Germanos, another personality of YENED during the dictatorship, survived the transition to democracy. His *Alatopipero* (Salt and Pepper) featured interviews with world celebrities such as John Lennon and Yoko Ono and, after the fall of the dictatorship, with Melina Mercouri, Mikis Theodorakis, and other returning political exiles. In 1982 Germanos opened his show *Proti selida* (First Page) to Manolis Glezos, deputy of PASOK (Panelliniko Sosialistiko Kinima, Panhellenic Socialist Movement), to narrate for the first time on television the story of how during the first weeks of Nazi occupation he and Apostolos Santas climbed up to the Acropolis by night and tore down the Nazi war flag. The show created an enormous sensation and was repeated many times.[17]

Greek national television introduced many of the staples of scripted entertainment in the first decade after the return to democracy, the period when Greek households acquired a television set and television replaced cinema as the popular medium of entertainment. Adaptations of novels became common, and new ones continue to be produced and broadcast to the present day. Greek television has produced good serialized versions of wonderful works by Alexandros Papadiamantis, Maria Ioardanidou, Kosmas Politis, Konstantinos Theotokis, Nikos Kazantzakis, Margarita Lymberaki, and many others. Dramatic works also found their way to the television screen, though over time serialized novels proved more popular. Seven plays by Grigoris Xenopoulos appeared on television between 1977 and 1988. And the channels encouraged in-house production of news programs, situation comedies, social drama, and adventure shows. The American hits *Charlie's Angels, Fame, The Muppet Show, Dynasty, Dallas, Love Ship,* and the British *Benny Hill* were as popular in Greece as they were in their home countries. Gradually unscripted television began to appear: *Ta tetragona ton asteron* (Stars' Squares, after *Hollywood Squares*), vigilante television, talk shows—some of them highbrow with ethnomusicologists, linguists, and specialists in theater, politics, history, and every other academic field, and others as lowbrow as television can go—historical accounts narrated by firsthand witnesses, reportage on everyday life. And Greek cinema, the old black-and-white films from the 1950s and 1960s at least, began replaying on television.

The 1980s brought a different revolution to the structure of broadcasting. When PASOK, the Panhellenic Socialist Movement elected in October 1981, created the first socialist government in Greek history, it sought to make its mark on television. The new government canceled many shows in the pipeline, putting in their place its own programming, including the first Greek show with a leftist political perspective, *Ta Lavreotika* (Events in Lavrion), a serial about labor strikes in the mines of Lavrion.[18] Then in 1982 PASOK took YENED away from the military and placed it under Hellenic Radio and Television, creating ET2 (today's NET), a station dedicated to news, information, and commentary, alongside ET1, which focused on entertainment. To increase regional exposure, PASOK government introduced a third channel based in Thessaloniki with a regional focus on northern Greece but national coverage (today's ET3) in 1987.

Deregulation of television took place in 1989 under a coalition government between the center-right New Democracy Party and the Communist Party, with pressure applied by some of the same market and municipal political forces that transformed Greek radio. In addition to these forces, there were strong feelings from PASOK's political opponents that PASOK had used television for political ends. Prior to deregulation, TV100, owned by the city of Thessaloniki, began broadcasting as the first nonstate television station, followed by TV Plus in Athens. Then law 1866/96 gave license to two private channels, Mega and Nea Tileorasi. Mega began broadcasting on November 20, 1989, and continues to the present day with many of the best-scripted programs on Greek television, whereas Nea Tileorasi disappeared before it ever aired, replaced by ANT1 on December 31, 1989. Alpha (previously Skai) and Star soon followed. With the proliferation of private channels has come a proliferation of *sapounoperes* (soap operas), sitcoms, foreign programs and films, and thousands of unscripted variety shows, reality shows, game shows, talks shows, music shows, and so on, many of them based on foreign models but responding to local tastes and trends.[19] As might be expected, popular shows, such as ANT1's soap opera *I Lampsi* (The Shining, Greece's longest running soap opera, from 1991 to 2005 for 3,457 episodes, with an audience share reaching 45 percent), or its reality show *Fame Story* (2002–2007), the equivalent of *American Idol*, drastically cut national television's audience and market share. Responding to the loss of viewership, ERT has shifted its priorities to include competitive mass-audience programming, without completely eliminating cultural programming or investigative news, and introduced ERT world satellite and three digital channels: CINE+, SPOR+, and PRISMA+. In addition to ERT, Hellenic Parliament operates its own public, national channel, featuring Parliament in plenary and committee sessions and, when Parliament's business is concluded, concerts, plays, films, and high-quality documentaries on history and the arts.

Deregularization has produced more than its share of trash television but also a few gems. *Sto para pente* (In the Nick of Time, 2005–2007) was a detective comedy that became the most popular hit ever, generating online communities. *Loufa kai parallagi* (2006–2008, mentioned earlier) found absurdity in the history of Greek television itself. *S'agapo m'agapas* (I Love You, You Love Me, 2000–2001 on Mega), an adaptation by Dimitra Papadopoulou of the French *Un gars, une fille* (1999), cast the daily routine of couples in a hilarious light. Yet even veterans of television such as Papadopoulou observe, "Times are hard for television, what else can I say? Television is for heroes, not for ordinary people. There is a lack of humor, we have people who mimic the humorists, people who are not by nature humorists" but rather people who value humor "in the market . . . as . . . a tradable commodity."[20] In terms of television policies, authorities are debating questions of "the amount of broadcast time allocated to advertising, program quotas, protecting minors, and the private ownership of multiple forms of the media by one person or organization."[21]

One very popular television personality deserves special comment. Lakis Lazopoulos has been director of programming for Alpha television since 2003. He is a stand-up comedian, writer of his own material, and comic talent who has played straight and comic roles in film, *epitheorisi* (variety entertainment), and revivals of ancient Greek drama in his own modern Greek translations. His translation of Aristophanes' *Lysistrata* reached the stage in a very memorable production of 1986 directed by Andreas Voutsinas, with music by Stamatis Kraounakis, lyrics by Lina Nikolakopoulou, and Lazopoulos in the title female role. He gave his voice to Hercules in the Greek version of the Disney film. Currently he plays the commentator on *Al Tsandiri News*, a two-hour weekly satirical program comparable to Jon Stewart's *Daily Show* or the news portion of Jay Leno's *Tonight Show*, but with humor and verbal pyrotechnics peculiar to Greece. The show has been running on Alpha television since November 2004, with "the highest ratings and perhaps the highest revenues from advertising on Greek television today."[22] But Lazopoulos's television masterpiece is certainly *Deka mikroi Mitsoi* (Ten Little People Named Mitsos, 1992–1997 Mega), a caustic social satire conducted entirely through Lazopoulos's impersonation of about fifteen fictional personalities of his own making. Lazopoulos completely disappears into each of the characters, male and female, "bumbling sailors and rich old dames,"[23] and convincingly gives voice, gestures, nervous ticks—a complete physical and verbal presence—to their worldview. Lazopoulos quit the show at its peak of popularity so it would remain strong in people's memory.

Lazopoulos may be the most brilliant comic talent of his generation, and he is certainly Greece's most successful at present, but he is not unique in his artistic range or the versatile career he has carved out. Other talented personalities have also moved between media. Indeed, the door between television, film, *epitheorisi*, and performances of all kinds, including revivals of ancient drama, has been a revolving one. Many artists sharpen their tools in one form and carry hard-earned lessons to another of the many venues Greece offers for performances.

FESTIVALS AND OTHER VENUES

The performing arts scene in Greece is rich, with prominent international festivals filling the summer and fall months, which then give way to national and private companies performing in winter theaters. The wealth of events really stands out in a country of 11 million people.

The International Thessaloniki Film Festival, a member of the International Film Federation of Film Producers Association, began as a festival of Greek films but took a new direction in 1992, transforming itself into the most important film event in the Balkans. The nine-day festival takes place in the fall. An international competition yields the first and second features. The festival also includes a Balkan survey, the independence days noncompetitive showcase of independent films, a noncompetitive Greek section with an overview of the year's production, and the Ministry of Culture's presentation of the State Film Awards. Exhibitions, discussions, concerts, and tributes to leading film directors make the festival especially rich. The festival sponsors a separate documentary festival in March and the Video Dance Festival in May.

Thessaloniki's Dimitria Festival of dance, drama, cinema, art, and music runs from September through November. It has been running since the 1960s, when it modernized a local *panigyri* dedicated to St. Dimitrios. It mixes traditional folk presentations, classics, and cutting-edge, contemporary works. Thessaloniki is also known for its Greek Song Festival, held during the period of the Dimitria.

The ten-day Kalamata International Dance Festival, founded in 1995, has become a leading showcase of dance in the Mediterranean, featuring international artists, commissioned works by Greek choreographers, new companies, and experimental work. The festival brings together professionals, students, and audience members through events, which educate and promote creativity and awareness in dance.

The Renaissance Festival in Rethymnon, founded in 1987, is a three-week event held in July, followed by the six-day Rethymnon Summer Arts Festival from late July to mid-August. The former supports exchanges in the Mediterranean, Balkans, and Europe through musical concerts, theater, storytelling, film, and exhibits. The latter gives more weight to theater.

The month long Ionian Concerts Festival in Corfu is the culmination of a summer academy organized by the Ionian University's department of music in collaboration with music schools worldwide. Seminars and lectures focus on classical music and music education. Concerts feature the orchestras, ensembles, and choirs of Corfu and groups from outside Greece. A music festival concentrating on contemporary music of Greece and the Balkans is the Nestorio River Party, a four-day festival held at the end of July on the Aliakmon River in northern Greece.

Together with these are international festivals in Halkidiki (Sani Jazz Festival), Ikaria, Kavala, Patras, Rhodes, Samothraki, Sitia, and Syros (Ermoupolis Classical Music Festival), and most substantial of all, the Hellenic Festival, held since 1955 in Athens and Epidaurus from June through August. These are the festival settings for performances in Greece. Overall, the scene is bountiful. The Hellenic Festival is a case in point. In its first years the world-famous conductor Dimitris Mitropoulos and the soprano Maria Callas were its stars. Now it draws on talent from the entire world. In the summer of 2008, it presented ninety-five events in eighty-four days at nine separate venues. A large concentration—thirty-three theater performances, seven operas, one musical drama, one event celebrating songs from Greek theater—took place on the theatrical stage, while the exhibit Heroes and Gods of Ancient Drama was also dedicated to the stage.

The winter season adds to the opportunities for concerts, film, and theater, with theater occupying an important place. About two hundred plays are performed from October through April. Most are in Athens, with more than one hundred theaters, though the state supports, in addition to the National Theatre in Athens, the State Theatre of Northern Greece in Thessaloniki and fifteen regional theaters, and Thessaloniki has many semiprivate or private theater companies.[24] State organizations benefit from the stability of public funding. Privately run companies survive with state subsidies or grants from foundations or, if they are well established, income from performances, donations, and their drama schools. Or they simply struggle to carve out makeshift spaces, rehearsing without pay and publicizing on the Web and by word of mouth.

Only by putting together a composite picture of the festivals and winter performances is it possible to grasp the range of events people have to choose from. The point can be sharpened a bit through careful observation of just the theater scene. Much of the world's drama reaches the Greek stage, some in its original language and more in Greek translation. Greek writers have been producing their own works, too, which are conversant with European and American drama. Yet Greece really specializes in performing classical Greek drama. Even in this narrow category, the variety is dizzying. There are revivals of the ancient plays, experimental adaptations, and new works on ancient themes played by Greek and non-Greek companies. For example, the 2008 Hellenic Festival presented revivals of Aristophanes' *Birds*, *Frogs*, and *Plutus*, Aeschylus's *Agamemnon*, Sophocles' *Ajax*, *Oedipus Rex*, and *Oedipus at Colonus*, and Euripides' *Orestes*, *Phoenician Women*, and *Andromache* (in French and Arabic), as well as works inspired by classical myths, including Glück's *Orfeo and Eurydice* performed by the Ballet de l'Opéra national de Paris with Pina Bausch; Heiner Müller's *Philoctet*; the mime troop Theater of Silence's *Seeking Oedipus*, Thomas Moschopoulos's staged reading of *The Bacchae* featuring the band Artifacts; and Lee Breuer and Bob Telson's *The Gospel at Colonus*, a coupling of ancient Greek theatrical rituals with their African equivalents. Dimitris Papaioannou, the visual artist and director whose direction of the Athens 2004 Olympics Opening Ceremony "is widely considered a high-water mark of large scale spectacle,"[25] presented his dance-theater piece, *Medea 2*, a wordless, water-bound retelling of the ancient story that made an "international splash."[26] And Stamatis Kraounakis organized a review of Greek stage music, including pieces from four Aristophanic revivals.

Performances at the Hellenic Festival have the added dimension of ancient venues and well-tested audiences. Two ancient amphitheaters offer their stages to modern productions: the Herodeion, a second-century music hall built by Herod Atticus on the south slope of the Acropolis, and the ancient theater of Epidaurus, built in the fourth century B.C. as the sanctuary of Asclepius and famed for its acoustics. Both theaters were excavated in the nineteenth century and restored with marble seating in the 1950s. The Herodeion holds five thousand spectators and the Epidaurus fourteen thousand. Each new performance, standing on the ground of previous productions, must contend with the afterlife of those older performances. The theaters themselves, with their evocative, ruined presence, enter into dialogue with the plays. The audience is another interactive element, as many spectators are well versed in both the texts and the history of their modern performances. There's even a rumor that the villagers of Ligourio near Epidaurus, who have been feeding theater companies and attending free rehearsals for years, are some of the strictest critics around. In short, there may be no more intriguing place in the world than Greece to see adaptations of ancient drama.

THEATER

With its collection of films from old productions, the ERT (Greek Radio and Television) audiovisual archive, established in 1990 to safeguard the audiovisual legacy of the Greek media, supplements photographs, playbills, costumes, memorabilia, scripts, and newspaper articles in theater archives at the National Theatre, Theatre of Epidaurus, Museum and Study Centre of the Greek Theatre at the Cultural Center in Athens, and other university programs and research institutes. Early film footage in the ERT archive bears out the depth of Greece's modern engagement with ancient drama. One interesting document is the filming of *dromena* (performances) on classical sites at Delphi, Olympia, Eleusis, Sounion, the Herodeion, and the Acropolis. Of these, the staging of ancient tragedies at Delphi in 1927 and 1930 represent landmarks in Greek theater.

Eva Palmer Sikelianos, a New Yorker married to poet Angelos Sikelianos, directed Aeschylus's *Prometheus Bound* and *Suppliants* in the ancient amphitheater at Delphi as part of two privately funded festivals. In many ways the performances set the course for revivals of ancient drama in Greece. Some aspects of Palmer-Sikelianos's direction (masks, hand-woven costumes, angular choreography inspired by modern dance) did not catch on. But Palmer-Sikelianos showed that contemporary aesthetics could give new life to classical texts, and that ancient tragedy, with a strong chorus responding to transgressions of justice, could move a modern audience. She tried to obliterate the gap between the dead letter and living spectators by using spoken Greek and drawing on folk music and dance to animate a large, well-rehearsed, disciplined chorus. Adding to the play's dynamism was the natural setting of Delphi. The sharp peaks of Mt. Parnassus, the sun following its course across the sky, and the eagles soaring over Prometheus's head contributed to the feeling of old drama coming back to life. Open-air performances and modern, vernacular translations became standard principles of Greek revivals in the decades that followed. In due time, directors also deployed folk and popular traditions to make the plays' messages accessible to contemporary audiences.

Palmer-Sikelianos's revival of Aeschylus's plays was revolutionary in many respects but not entirely out of line with other developments. The history of Greek theater is an interrupted one, as both Byzantine and Ottoman rulers issued prohibitions against theater in the centuries between antiquity and modernity. People's theatrical aspirations grew with their exposure to the West in the 1800s. Always the specter of ancient drama stood somewhere close at hand. A tantalizing moment in theater writing involves Elizabet Moutzan-Martinengou (1801–1832), an aristocratic woman from the Ionian island of Zakynthos who received an education despite her father's strong opposition and who "wrote no fewer than [twenty-two] plays,"[27] including comedies and tragedies following neoclassical and romantic prototypes. The moment is evocative because none of Martinengou's creative work survives while her extant autobiography describes her literary activities.[28] It also brings attention to two phenomena: women's involvement in Greek theater from its early stages and the centrality of the Ionian Islands in that same story. Dimitrios Gouzelis's *Hasis* (1795), a satirical comedy written in the tradition of popular theater, with stories and jokes exchanged between a performer and audience during Apokries (Carnival), has been called the "first really Modern Greek play."[29] There are other important moments and localities, including an earlier renaissance of theater in Crete in the seventeenth century, which spread to the Aegean and Ionian islands,[30] and the rise of Greek theater in cosmopolitan centers—Patras, Ermoupolis, Odessa, Constantinople, Smyrna, and Alexandria—in the nineteenth century. Many of the works staged in the early nineteenth century belonged to the "baroque and neoclassical repertoire. Foreign adaptations of ancient myths...were more popular than the original tragedies that had inspired them."[31] As the century wore on, neoclassical works had to compete with comic satires, *epitheorisi* (variety entertainment), and Karagiozis shadow puppet theater.

A word about Karagiozis and *epitheorisi* is in order, as they are significant in themselves and eventually mix with other theater, including classical revivals. Karagiozis shadow theater, performed behind a white, translucent screen with flat figures of animal skin or cardboard and moving parts, was popular from the years of Greece's liberation to the first decades of the twentieth century. The trickster protagonist, derived from the more raunchy, Ottoman Karagioz (literally, "black eye"), dispensed with his precursor's obscenities and replaced his phallic appendage with a "very long arm ready to dispatch blows to any character weaker than himself."[32] He became the big-nosed, hunchbacked Karagiozis, a poor Greek of infinite ingenuity in an Ottoman world. The scenery depicts Karagiozis's position at the bottom of the social heap. His poor, neglected cottage is to the left, while the sultan's palace stands to the right. Karagiozis stories are variations on the theme of the poor, hungry Karagiozis, with his wife and three impish sons, outmaneuvering his socioeconomic superiors by clever posturing. There are heroic stories, too, in which Karagiozis assists a historical figure, for example, Alexander the Great or one of the heroes of the Greek revolution. Traveling *Karagiozopaiktes* (Karagiozis players) were the key to Karagiozis's success. They moved him and the theater's other stock characters with sticks and gave each character a distinctive voice. They lived by roaming "all over Greece, adding figures and stories and technical innovations as they went along."[33] As they performed, they kept their ears tuned to the audience, listening to people's comments, responding with rapid quips, and adapting the story to the prevailing spirit. Over time they added an array of characters representing the mixture of dialects, classes, and mentalities that coexisted in Greece. Karagiozis reached a peak of popularity in the 1920s, then began to wane as cinema and other forms of popular culture took its place. Today Karagiozis is part of a small arsenal of cultural forms representing the nation. Karagiozis made his appearance in the Athens 2004 Olympics both on a float in the opening ceremony and as a happening, with the *Karagiozopaiktis* Kostas Makris performing his "Karagiozis Olympic Winner." Greeks embrace Karagiozis nostalgically. He is a key figure in the social imaginary that views Greeks as history's surviving underdogs. Evgenios Spatharis, a *Karagiozopaiktis* who helped keep the genre alive from 1942 through the turn of the twenty-first century, recently stated in a television interview, "Karagiozis represents the Greek people... their hunger, thirst, ill-treatment, rushing about pursued and in pursuit."[34] Spatharis popularized two lines identified with a Greek national character, "*Tha fame, the pioume, kai nistikoi tha koimithoume*"("We'll eat, we'll drink, and we'll fall asleep hungry") and "*E re glentia*" ("Ah, the parties!"), uttered with Karagiozis's inimitable enthusiasm.

Epitheorisi was "undoubtedly the most popular theatrical genre in Greece between roughly 1894 and the early 1930s"[35] and again from 1947 to 1967.[36] The first *epitheorisi* on record is *Ligo ap' ola* (A Little of Everything), written by Mikios Lambrou and Iosef Kaisaris and staged by Dimitris Kotopoulos the summer of 1894. Inspired by satirical comedies, comic idylls, and foreign variety shows, *epitheorisi* consists of a series of comic sketches performed by a set of actors in different combinations. The actors play stock characters, but there is a development in their relationships, which gives the show its episodic structure. Each sketch culminates in a song and dance, with witty Greek lyrics sung to Western-style tunes and orchestrations, complete with bright lights, live music, sparkles, spectacle, and glamour. In its first incarnation, *epitheorisi* celebrated "the city, contemporary fashions, modernization, Westernization, and social (and sexual) 'liberation.'"[37] It contained "messages of freedom from rules and conventions, both social and artistic"[38] but within limits. While *epitheorisi* introduced one of the first feminist songs in Greece, "*Ego eimai i nea gynaika*" ("I'm the New Woman," sung by Marika Kotopouli in "Panathinaia 1908"), it also satirized a short-lived women's suffrage movement at the turn of the century.[39] Under conditions of free expression, "the satirical dimension of the genre... allowed it to develop a distinct national identity, as the sketches and the content of the songs often referred to recent and local events and situations."[40] During periods of censorship, *epitheorisi* became a theater of escape. After World War II *epitheorisi* shared its stars with radio, television, and the big screen: actors Vasilis Avlonitis, Georgia Vassiliadou, Mimis Fotopoulos, Dinos Iliopoulos, Dimitris Horn, Alekos Alexandrakis, and many others began their careers in *epitheorisi*. *Epitheorisi* "was and still is a form that reflects the perpetual flow of things (indeed, numbers can be withdrawn or added to accommodate current events), uses mixed media, offers possibilities for experimentation, and has an acute sense of stage rhythm."[41] Today's *epitheorisi* struggles to attract audiences, who have easier access to rapidly changing spectacles on television, yet *epitheorisi* continues to feed other forms of theater.[42]

Athens emerged as a center of theater at the turn of the twentieth century. It featured dramatic idylls, comic satire, *epitheorisi*, and domestic drama, which linked "the techniques and spirit...found in Ibsen, Strindberg, Chekhov, Maeterlinck, [and] Hauptmann" to "modern Greek realities."[43] Ibsen was especially influential with popular playwrights from Grigoris Xenopoulos (1867–1951), the most prolific writer in the first half of the century, to Iakovos Kambanellis (b. 1922), the "patriarch of modern Greek drama."[44]

In the early years of Athenian theater, people did not take to classical tragedies, performed in ancient Greek or *katharevousa* ("purified," archaizing modern Greek). The revivals pleased elite circles but "failed to excite nonacademic, general audiences."[45] A set of tragedies produced for the 1896 Olympic Games were the exception because they had a captive audience. Of all the ancient tragedies, adaptations of Euripides' *Medea* proved popular.[46] The comic poet Aristophanes was even better received. Two very different adaptations reached the stage in 1868, one a prose adaptation in *dimotiki* (vernacular, spoken Greek) of the *Plutus*, and the other a conservative academic performance of the *Clouds* in a scholarly *katharevousa*. There was also a "landmark performance of Aristophanes' *The Clouds*" for Greeks in Alexandria in 1901.[47] Generally, however, the philological effort to recover the fifth-century moment through the pedantic revivals did not engage modern spectators.

A precursor of Palmer-Sikelianos's idea that performances of ancient drama should reach out to modern audiences was Konstantinos Hristomanos (1867–1911), founder of the short-lived *Nea Skini* (New Stage, 1901–1905). He spoke at the ancient Theater of Dionysus in Athens on February 27, 1901, urging artists not to cultivate drama in Greece as a direct imitation of the classical: "I am not talking about retracing our steps backwards in the centuries, and I am not asking you to build Parthenons because we are Greek. The Greek poet does not need to shape words or ideas in the rhythms of Pindar or Sappho, rhythms gone with the waves."[48] Rather than treat classical texts as monuments of the past, *Nea Skini* tried to breathe in new life. It performed Euripides' *Alcestis* in a *dimotiki* in 1901. The Royal Theatre in Athens, inaugurated in 1901 with a purpose of reviving ancient Greek drama and producing serious theater in Greece, followed suit, performing Aeschylus's *Oresteia* in *dimotiki* in 1903. The performance wreaked havoc. University students marched to defend the purity of Aeschylus's Greek and killed an innocent bystander in an event Greek history books refer to as the *Oresteiaka* (*Oresteia* events). At that time the ministry of Dimitris Rallis took steps to forbid "any further performances of the offending trilogy."[49] The Royal Theatre closed its doors in 1908 for lack of funds.

When reestablished on May 3, 1930, the National Theatre, successor of the Royal Theatre, "considered it of paramount importance to revive the tradition of staging ancient plays."[50] The theater's first production was Aeschylus's *Agamemnon* (1932), performed in a *dimotiki* under the direction of Fotos Politis, a veteran visionary of the theater who focused on training actors to convey the sense of the words and used lighting to reveal tragic meaning. From this point on, the National Theatre began working, often under stressful conditions of dictatorship, foreign occupation, war, and censorship[51]—to bring carefully researched, philologically sound productions of classical and modern drama to the Greek stage. It inaugurated the use of the ancient, open-air theater at Epidaurus under the Metaxas dictatorships. Throughout its history the National Theatre has continued performing ancient and modern classics. A few of its actors—Katina Paxinou, Alexis Minotis, Melina Mercouri—have achieved international fame.

The productions and companies mentioned here are just a few key events. A more complete survey would include information about the theater scene in Thessaloniki and other cities. It would touch on children's theater and discuss private companies, especially the Art Theatre of Karolos Koun (1942–present), founded under conditions of occupation, creating a small theater-in-the-round (220–230 spectators) on the ground floor of the Orpheus Cinema, influencing theater to the present day. It would linger on playwrights, including Pavlos Nirvanas, Xenopoulos, Spyros Melas, Pantelis Horn, and Konstantinos Hristomanos at the turn of the century; Nikos Kazantzakis, Angelos Sikelianos, and Angelos Terzakis in the interwar years; Iakovos Kambanellis, Yiorgos Skourtis, Kostas Mourselas, Vasilis Ziogas, Pavlos Matesis, Loula Anagnostaki, Dimitris Kehaidis, Yiorgos Dialegmenos, and Marios Pontikas in the decades after the World War II; and Dimitris Dimitriadis, Andreas Staikos, and others in the present day. And it would look at stage designs by prominent artists, from Nikos Hadjikyriakos-Ghikas, Yiannis Moralis, Yiannis Tsarouchis, Spyros Vassiliou, and Nikos Georgiadis to Dionysis Fotopoulos, a stage designer of international fame in the present day.

Karolos Koun Art Theatre poster for Benaki Museum exhibit displayed in shop window. Photo by author, October 2008.

In addition to foundational moments, there have been some lodestones: productions in the tumultuous postwar years with a magnetism of their own. Here are just three indicating the complex role theater has played in public life.

Under the most extraordinary circumstances political prisoners of the Greek civil war exiled on islands in the Aegean staged Greek tragedies—Sophocles' *Philoctetes* and *Antigone* and Aeschylus's *Prometheus Bound* and *Persians*.[52] Interned as communists, the prisoners were accused of trying to undermine Greek civilization. As part of their political reeducation, they were forced to labor building amphitheaters and models of the Parthenon in their barren places of exile. They were made to perform classical drama for the same purpose. Yet through the plays prisoners generated "performative and protest statements that, despite the constraints of censorship and constant surveillance, went well beyond the scripts, their staging and performance."[53] For example, their staging of *Philoctetes*, the play about a wounded soldier of the Trojan War left to suffer alone in exile on the island of Lemnos, managed to "pass political and personal comments" about the inmates' torture, mutilation, and malnourishment on the prisoner island of Makronisos.[54]

On August 29, 1959, the Herodeion offered its stage to a vanguard production of Aristophanes' *Birds* performed by a theater company other than the National Theatre: the Art Theatre of Karolos Koun. Koun's team of collaborators was the best in town: Vasilis Rotas (translation), Yiannis Tsarouchis (scenery and costumes), Manos Hadjidakis (music), and Ralou Manou (choreography, later reworked by Zouzou Nikoloudi). They produced a revolutionary performance, with a large chorus dressed in costumes inspired by African ritual singing and dancing to Hadjidakis's irrepressible folk- and pop-inspired songs as protagonists equal to the actors in the play. They also tested the limits of classical revivals as they pointed the sharp, satirical knife at the present day. The ancient priest conducting sacrifices in the play, dressed and chanting like a Greek Orthodox priest, bordered on sacrilege. And there were references to the contemporary practice of grabbing public lands for development. These gibes were not lost on the audience. The performance brought frenzied applause from the upper tiers but also a "ban on further performances" by the conservative government of Constantine Karamanlis.

In the summer of 1973, the sixth year of the military dictatorship, *To megalo mas Tsirko* (Our Grand Circus), a play by Kambanellis with film and theater stars Jenny Karezi and Kostas Kazakos and music by Stavros Xarhakos, offered a "mirror image" to the dictatorship's self-promoting "military parades, victory festival, and historical reenactments."[55] Like the dictatorship's spectacles, *To megalo mas Tsirko* presented a version of modern Greek history but with a different message. The play faced an impossible challenge: to retell history in a suggestive way that encouraged audiences to oppose the dictatorship and to pass the dictatorship's strict censorship. It achieved these ends by performing a kind of circus, using every available device: "All the recognizable codes were there: characters and designs from the popular shadow theater, *Karagiozis*...songs from the period of German occupation, a narrator instructing a street urchin, and an exquisite Cretan singer, Nikos Xylouris, whose singing and general demeanor kindled ancient memories of heroes, epics, and bards."[56] The traditional elements and historical scenes convinced the censors that this was a proud historical pageant. But the history featured moments of conflict between people and autocratic rulers. Furthermore the performance pushed pageantry in a different direction: it "reclaimed theater...as a place for self-display and self-fashioning,"[57] while it also suggested that the dictatorship was a misplaced circus that ought to be toppled. The regime did not respond favorably to the production. Karezi and Kazakos spent several nights in jail for their part in the performance.

The 2008 season of the Hellenic Festival gave more than a nod of recognition to magnetic moments in Greek theater, with strong audience response. The Karolos Koun Art Theatre brought down the house with its revival of the 1959 *Birds* production at the Herodeion. And spectators at the Herodeion were visibly moved by the end of Stamatis Kraounakis's review of twentieth-century theater music, "On Stage: Burning Down the House," as Kraounakis introduced one blockbuster show tune after another, with his own musical-theater company Speira Speira offering choral accompaniment. Songs from Koun's *Birds* and Kambanellis's *To megalo mas Tsirko* came second and third among fifty-three selections. Their position at the beginning of the performance signaled their importance. Otherwise the program moved mostly chronologically through songs from *epitheorisi* (including Marika Kotopouli's feminist "Panathinaia 1908"); operettas; two versions of Aristophanes' *Lysistrata* (National Theater's with music by Hadjidakis and Lazopoulos's with music by Kraounakis) and one of the *Acharneans* with music by Dionysis Savvopoulos; productions of plays by Federico García Lorca, Tenessee Williams, Kambanellis's *Neighborhood of Angels* with music by Mikis Theodorakis, and Nikos Kazantzakis's *Kapetan Mihalis* with music by Hadjidakis. When Kraounakis brought out veterans of *epitheorisi* Sperantza Vrana and Anna Kalouta to sing songs from the 1940s and 1950s, there wasn't a dry eye left in the house. "Tears and apotheosis...I can't take it any more," one critic wrote. What stood out in the scene was its consistent effect: people of all generations were present, taking old songs as cues for recovering a sentiment of warm community belonging. Music from a century of theater reached through time and touched a crowd of five thousand as if they had experienced the original performances together.

Down the way in an industrial part of town, Piraios 260, a theater created in a 1970s office furniture factory, opened the 2008 Hellenic Festival with a performance in stark contrast to Kraounakis's celebration of the Greek stage: Dimitris Dimitriadis's short novel *Pethaino san hora* (I'm Dying as a Country), reworked for theater and directed by Michael Marmarinos, and performed by the Theseum Ensemble with a chorus of two hundred volunteers. The work turns on the premise that a foreign occupation has crushed a country's culture and thrown it into a progressively worsening state of sterility, anarchy, and self-destruction. The historical references to Greece's history from 1936 through 1974 are obvious; yet the story, written after the fall of the dictatorship, offers no sense of recovery. As the chorus—comprising people of all national groups, ages, backgrounds—moves silently through the theater, with individual faces projected on a large screen, but no collective voice, five actors approach a microphone and give speeches exuding symptoms of their existential exhaustion in a dense language of despair. At one point members of the chorus attempt to enter into dialogue with an actor, but the dialogue is unproductive: a speaker of Korean responds in her own language to Greek words she takes as Korean; another set of Greek speakers hear her words as the beginning of different Greek jokes. In the end, Beba Blanche, a singer of *laika* (popular, working-class songs) from the 1960s, recites a seven-minute diatribe: "I despise this country.... It has eaten my guts.... I don't want to be a country.... I'm dying as a country."[58] The play's unrelentingly critical stance brought accusations of anti-Hellenism. Yet the question it raised, whether people today can thrive within a national framework, resonated with its audience. It became an occasion for audience members collectively to work through their frustrations with the course of events in Greece since the fall of the dictatorship. While this unexpected hit of 2007 and 2008 stood as a sign that serious theater was alive and well in Greece today, it expressed a general uncertainty about the state of the nation.

CINEMA

Cinema has several of its own moments of reflection. Filmmaking has not been big business in Greece since the 1970s, when "television combined with censorship to put an end to" Greece's powerful studio system of the 1950s and 1960s.[59] Meanwhile the Greek Film Center became a key source for funding, replacing studios that relied on success in the box office, and directors turned their ambitions to making films of artistic merit. One film more than any other, *Thiasos* (Traveling Players, 1975) by Theo Angelopoulos (b. 1935), created hopes that cinema in Greece could become exceptional by being contemplative, experimental, and deeply political.

The screening of *Thiasos* in 1975, the year after the fall of the dictatorship, was probably the most electric moment ever in Greek cinema. Made under difficult conditions of strict censorship during the dictatorship and with a very low budget, the nearly four-hour film sold more admissions (six hundred thousand) than any other film before it, despite Angelopoulos's inimitably slow pace.[60] It did so by breaching a forbidden topic: the events leading to and including the Civil War of 1945 to 1949. The film suggested what historians had detailed before but no one had dared to declare before a mass audience: "that many Greeks who were not necessarily communist worked with the Partisans to help liberate Greece from the Germans and then continued to side with the communists because they were even more disenchanted by right wing monarchists who catered more often to foreign interests than to the needs of the people."[61] The film broke ground in its meditative approach, too, not just through slow long shots, which deliberately resisted the trend toward faster editing, but also in nonsequential, multilayered storytelling, which regularly broke cinematic conventions so as not to allow spectators to identify with characters. It won Best Film Award at the Thessaloniki Film Festival and awards in Japan, Britain, Italy, and the Cannes and Berlin film festivals in 1975. It has been recognized with the FIPRESCI (the International Federation of Film Critics) prize as one of the top films in the history of cinema. After *Thiasos*, Angelopoulos won many more awards. *To vlemma tou Odyssea* (Ulysses' Gaze, 1995), about an expatriate Greek filmmaker's (Harvey Keitel) journeying through the war-torn Balkans in search for undeveloped reels of film by the Manaki brothers, symbols of a lost shared history, won the Grand Jury Prize at the Cannes Film Festival and the Critics Award of the European Film Academy. *Mia aioniotita kai mia mera* (Eternity and a Day 1998), with Bruno Ganz playing the terminally ill writer Alexander, who spends his last day with a young illegal immigrant from Albania, won the won the Palme d'Or, the top prize at Cannes. Throughout his artistic journey, Angelopoulos has been crossing Greece's geographical, historical, visual, mythological, and ideological boundaries, looking for other repressed or neglected worlds.

Thiasos follows a traveling theater company from 1939 to 1952 as the company plays under the difficult conditions of the Metaxas dictatorship (1936–1941), German occupation (1941–1944), Dekemvriana (December 1944), and Civil War (1945–1949). The company's repertoire consists of a single play, the pastoral drama *Golfo, the Shepherdess* (1899). It should be noted that *Golfo* was not just a very popular rural drama but also the subject of the first Greek feature film in 1914, a 1932 remake that was the first talking picture,[62] and another 1955 remake. The play tells of Golfo's and Tassos's love, which is frustrated when Tassos accepts a dowry for marriage with a wealthy girl and drives

Golfo mad. But the troop never finishes the play. Each time it brings *Golfo* to the stage, offstage drama interrupts the story.

Some of the drama comes from the actors, whose lives imitate the *Oresteia*. The players' unnamed members are Agamemnon (the troop leader), Clytemnestra (his unfaithful wife), Aegisthus (the actor with whom she is having an affair), Orestes, Elektra, and Chrysothemis (children of the troop leader and his wife), and Pylades (a friend and accomplice of Orestes). After Agamemnon joins the resistance against the German occupation, Aegisthus, a Nazi informer, betrays him and so brings about his execution. Orestes executes his revenge on stage, shooting his mother and her lover while reciting the play's lines: "You've gone too far, *tselinga* [wealthy sheep owner]; you've cut me to the quick." The audience gives a resounding ovation as the curtain falls. Orestes then disappears into the mountains to rejoin ELAS, the military arm of the resistance to the occupation, now in armed revolution against the Greek state, but is captured and executed as a communist. Pylades takes Orestes' place when Elektra reestablishes the troop in 1952, but only after he has endured imprisonment and torture on the barren Aegean prison isle of Makronisos and signed a statement denouncing his beliefs. The film's last scene shows the traveling players arriving in the town of Aigion, as they did in 1939 before the dramatic events tore them apart. It refers back to the film's first scene, in which the traveling players reached the same spot in their 1952 configuration.

A second source of offstage drama is history. From different corners of Greece, the film offers glimpses of political posters, banners, uniforms, battles, and executions. It captures snippets of conversations, songs, slogans, and personal testimonies of repression. Political rallies, scenes of occupation, acts of resistance, and hangings keep interrupting the company's tours and shows. Through all these interruptions, the film presents the turbulence of the era.

Thiasos thus operates on three levels: the theatrical, historical, and personal, which overlaps with the myth of the *Oresteia*.[63] It produces meaning through the confluence and diversion of these three levels. The scene of Orestes' revenge brings the three levels of reality together in a stunning way, as a murder happens on stage, with the actor playing an actor's part, uttering verses from *Golfo*, and the public mistaking his action for an act in the play. Here theater becomes the stage for history and life. In another scene, a shot fired from offstage into the crowd of spectators kills a British soldier in the audience as the players perform on the beach for the Allies. Here history intrudes on the theater, a reminder that theater's suspension of disbelief does not keep realities from intruding.

As with Kambanellis's *To megalo mas tsirko*, Angelopoulos's *Thiasos*, another vast epic of Greek history, succeeded in passing the dictatorship's censorship through its layering of tradition and myth to camouflage political intentions. In some ways the *Oresteia* myth was an alibi to receive the censorship committee's permission to make the film. Yet the family's imperfect embodiment of the *Oresteia* became another elucidator of meaning—and one that could speak to a broader public familiar with Greek myths. Clytemnestra betrays and brings about the murder of Agamemnon, a refugee Asia Minor who has committed none of mythical Agamemnon's crimes. Orestes executes his anticipated revenge but does not meet the *Oresteia*'s happy end. Whereas the mythical Orestes found justice in the Athenian court, the player Orestes, like the player Agamemnon, is executed by history's winners. At his funeral Electra bids him farewell with a verse from *Golfo*, and the actors applaud his performance in life. The film's denouement comes not by deus ex machina but through Pylades' release after his forced denouncement of his beliefs. History is harsher than myth, the film suggests, and one survives it only by acting.

Angelopoulos's *Thiasos* shares with other monumental Greek works a complex vision that operates on multiple levels. In cinema, it can be seen to divide the history of Greek cinema in two parts. Before *Thiasos* the biggest players in Greek cinema were the studios—Anzervos Films, Kalagiannis-Kalatzopoulos, Spentzos Films, Damaskinos Michailidis, and Finos Films. These dominated Greek cinema from 1949 to 1977, producing popular cinema for entertainment of the masses. The studio era drew on talent from theater to create new stars and countless wildly successful films. They played in indoor neighborhood cinemas in winter and open-air *therina* (summer) cinemas through the warmer months: open spaces surrounded by aromatic vines, where people sit in folding chairs facing a giant screen or the blank side of a building, talking and eating *pasatempo* (sunflower or pumpkin seeds). With no competition for cheap, nightly entertainment, "the Greek film industry reached a production peak when it released 177 Greek films in 1966 and sold a total of 137 million tickets in 1968."[64]

Comedies with a musical dimension were one type of film, with simple plots giving room to famous singers to take to the stage. Actors trained in *epitheorisi* and improvisational theater played stock characters and devised rapid-fire dialogue with smart jokes and clever *attakes* (from Italian *attacca*, a quick, one-line response). *Laterna, ftohia kai filotimo* (Barrel Organ, Poverty, and Honor), a 1955 film by Alekos Sakelarios with Jenny Karezi, Vasilis Avlonitis, Mimis Fotopoulos, and Alekos Alexandrakis, is a perfect example. It features a wealthy runaway (Karezi) and two poor, wandering organ grinders (Avlonitis and Fotopoulos) who find her in their path and take her under their wing. When they read her father's newspaper announcement of a reward for her return, they consider turning her in but decide instead to reunite her with her lost love (Alexandrakis). In their adventures they cross paths with a group

Man grinds *laterna* (barrel piano) decorated with poster from *Laterna, ftohia, kai filotimo*, a 1955 film starring Jenny Karezi and Vasilis Avlonitis and featuring "Garyfallo st'afti" (Carnation on the Ear), a song by Manos Hadjidakis. Photo by author, February 2006.

of *tsiganes* (Roma), who sing Hadjidakis's hit song "Garyfallo st'afti" (Carnation on the Ear), and a violinist on his way to a *panigyri*. Other comic actors who regularly appeared as stock types in films were Kostas Hadjichristos (the newly arrived villager in the capital city), Lambros Konstandaras (upright, successful citizen), Thanasis Vengos (migrant laborer on the run), Georgia Vassiliadou (unattractive flirt), and Dinos Iliopoulos (master of every role). Aliki Vougiouklaki, the most popular film star in Greece ever, played the eternally youthful, flirtatious, but fundamentally good girl in forty-two films and plays between 1954 and her death in 1996. She played in musical comedies and melodrama. Her performance in *Mantalena* in 1960 won her an award for best actress at the Greek Film Festival in Thessaloniki and a nomination at the Cannes Festival.

There were dramatic works of note, some challenging the conventions of their times. *Stella* (1955), based on a bold theatrical work by Iakovos Kambanellis, featured the restless heroine Stella (Melina Mercouri), a singer in a bar who despises marriage and wishes to choose her lovers freely. Director

Michael Cacoyannis (b. 1922) collaborated with Manos Hadjidakis and actors Mercouri, Giorgos Foundas (Miltos), Alekos Alexandrakis (Alekos), and singer Sophia Vembo (Maria) to re-create the *laika* bar scene in the then-impoverished area of Monastiraki. *O drakos* (1956), directed by Nikos Koundouros (b. 1926), entered an even more marginal Athenian neighborhood of pimps and thugs. It featured an insignificant bank accountant mistakenly pursued by the police as a criminal who takes refuge in a bar. There his resemblance to the criminal gives him the status to lead a planned theft of antiquities until the mistake is discovered. Greece's darker underside comes through in these and other films. The same world inspired *Kokkina Fanaria* (Red Lights, 1965), a film that earned Karezi an Oscar nomination. It also occupied *Evdokia* (1971), a landmark film about the doomed marriage of a prostitute and sergeant. Under the hard lens of director Alexis Damianos, *Evdokia* makes the existentially bared protagonists seem like extension of the rocky, dry, unforgiving landscape. But it was two English-language films—Jules Dassin's *Never on Sunday* (1960) with Mercouri, Dassin, Foundas, Titos Vandis, and Despo Diamantidou and music by Hadjidakis, and Cacoyiannis's *Zorba the Greek* (1964) with Anthony Quinn, Alan Bates, Lila Kedrova, and Irene Papas and music by Mikis Theodorakis—that gave the subject of Greece's underside international exposure. Paradoxically, it was film's depiction of Greek life in brothels and other hidden places that begat the ubiquitous stereotype of the earthy, lusty, life-embracing Greek. A third category of films from this period is classical revivals by Cacoyannis and Dassin, including *Electra* (1962), *Phaedra* (1962), *The Trojan Women* (1971), *Iphigenia* (1977), and *A Dream of Passion* (1978).

One commercial film from the studio era moved in a completely new direction, probably because it was not a Greek studio product but made in France. Costa-Gavras's (b. 1933) *Z*, winner of an Oscar for Best Foreign Film in 1969, stunned audiences with its deliberate unraveling of events surrounding the 1963 assassination of Grigoris Lambrakis (Yves Montand), a doctor and leftist member of Parliament from Thessaloniki. The film follows the investigative work of prosecutor Christos Sartzetakis (Jean-Louis Trintignant) as he uncovers the vast conspiracy leading to Lambrakis's death and the cover-up, involving the chief of police, military, and government officials. Banned by the dictatorship, *Z* resonated with audiences abroad that were trying to learn how democracy in Greece had been undermined. Gavras has devoted his career to making films with a political agenda, just as Angelopoulos has, though Gavras makes commercial films. *Z* helped define Costa-Gavras's approach to political-commercial cinema and gave him themes for future works: the abuse of power, dangerously centralized authority, paramilitary groups, spies, investigations, and sabotage.

After the release of Angelopoulos's *Thiasos*, film took an excessively artistic turn. Angelopoulos continued to make astonishing, difficult cinema, and many directors tried to imitate his formal style, with unfortunate results. Cinema in Greece became almost self-absorbed, running on borrowed ideas and poor scripts. "Directional idiosyncrasies . . . often tried to pass as style and individual vision."[65] Film directors ignored public tastes, and the public lost interest in them. An unintended consequence was that the 1980s and early 1990s brought about a reassessment of the old studio films, which were replaying endlessly on television. To a generation of Greeks coming of age in the twenty-first century, black-and-white comedies and melodramas are landmarks of their youth just as they were to their parents or grandparents.

Since the mid-1990s, Greek filmmakers have begun capturing a wider audience by registering the changing face of Greece in a way that speaks to a larger audience. Some directors of note are Nikos Nikolaidis (1939–2007), Pantelis Voulgaris (b. 1940), Nikos Panayiotopoulos (b. 1941), Tonia Marketaki (1942–1994), Nikos Perakis (b. 1944), Sotiris Goritsas (b. 1955), Constantine Giannaris (b. 1959), Olga Malea (b. 1960), and Renos Haralambidis (b. 1970). Their films have set the agenda for the present century, bringing to the foreground a very different picture of Greece.

Disruptions in the social order since the opening of borders with Greece's northern neighbors is one recurring theme. Angelopoulos brought attention to illegal immigrants arriving from Albania with *To meteoro vima tou pelargou* (The Suspended Step of the Stork, 1991). The film includes scenes from Greece's border with Albania. It reaches a climax with a wedding uniting a bride and groom, who stand on opposite sides of the river that divides the two countries. Goritsas' *Ap'to hioni* (From the Snow, 1993) was the first to focus on the social effects of illegal immigration. The film drew on Goritsas's acquaintance with two young men from Albania and a short narrative he read in a newspaper, published by the fiction writer Sotiris Dimitriou. It indicated the high level of expectations immigrants were carrying with them as they endangered their lives to cross the border and Greeks' complete lack of preparation to deal with the impact of their arrival. Giannaris's *Ap' tin akri tis polis* (From the Edge of the City, 1998) features teenage children of ethnic Greek immigrants from the Black Sea, with their mixed language of Russian and Greek, in their fast pursuit of a life of petty crime and prostitution in the marginal western suburbs of Athens. Lucia Rikaki's documentary film *O allos* (The Other, 2006) captures unrehearsed moments in the lives of a teacher and the six students attending a small school in Patsidero, a small village in northern Crete, where all but one student are Albanians. With a sensitive ear and eye attuned to the delicate matters of immigration through her own experiences as a child of a immigrants, Rikaki brings to the screen villagers' notions of how to handle their coexistence with others different from them, and the children's much freer sense of what binds them with one another.

A second theme is the loosening of social values and its effects on individuals and society. This theme was present in films from the studio era, but today's social satire and drama bring the subject to the screen without restrictions of censorship or audience expectations for a happy or cathartic ending. The characters pursue their desire for sex (Perakis, *Thiliki etaireia*, Company of Women, 1999; Thanasis Papathanasiou and Michalis Reppas, *Safe Sex*, 1999; Malea, *Diakritiki goiteia ton arsenikon*, The Mating Game, 1999; George Panoussopoulos, *Mia mera ti nichta*, Athens Blues, 2001), fame (Haralambidis, *No Budget Story*, 1997, and Panayiotopoulos, *Afti i nichta menei*, Edge of Night, 1998), drugs (Panayiotopoulos, *Delivery*, 2004), and money (Goritsas, *Balkanisateur*, 1997, and *Brazilero*, 2001) with no end but individual satisfaction, and little satisfaction in the end. Or the same theme may be viewed from the eyes of a person who sees the game of pursuit in a different light (George Panoussopoulos, *Mia mera ti nychta*, Athens Blues, 2001, and Katerina Evangelakou, *Tha to metanioseis*, Think It Over, 2002).

A third theme is Greek history's untold stories of emigration, moments with little play in the big history books that nevertheless occupy a crux in the social imagination. Angelopoulos wove stories of emigrants returning to Greece into several films. He brought to the foreground the absence of reconciliation: the returnee and the world to which he returns are out of sync. His most recent work *Trilogy* (which is in progress, as only the first and second films, *The Weeping Meadow*, 2003, and *The Dust of Time*, 2008, have been released, while *Return* is slated as upcoming[66]), follows Greeks away from Greece through historical events they experience elsewhere: in the Soviet Union, Austro-Hungarian borders, Italy, and New York. Greek emigration has been occupying other directors too in popular and critically successful films of the past decade. Voulgaris's *Nyfes* (Brides, 2004) follows seven hundred so-called mail-order brides in 1922 as they travel on a ship, steerage class, from the eastern Mediterranean and Black Sea to the United States, to marry men whom they have never met. The camera of Norman (Damian Lewis), a disillusioned American photographer, brings attention to their faces, gestures, desires, and grief as they leave behind their families and voyage into the unknown. Tassos Boulmetis's hero Fanis in *Politiki Kouzina* (Touch of Spice, 2003) is another Greek emigrant, though the home he leaves behind is in Turkey and the strange one where he arrives is Athens. Through smells and flavors and the art of cooking, he keeps alive memories from the world left behind in the 1960s, when his family's deportation from Kostantinoupoli (Istanbul) separated him from his grandfather and so much else that was a part of him. Maria Iliou's *The*

Journey: The American Dream (2007) recovers uncataloged footage and pho-tographs of Greek immigrants in the United States, pictures without words, whose specific context is lost. Commentators discuss aspects of Greeks' stay in the United States without filling in the gaps. Pictures of emigration suggest that dreams of the abandoned homeland enter the emigrant's imagination just as the emigrant enters the new home. They take the form of a boat called *Nea Hellas*, or a man reading a newspaper in Greek. Although they mirror an image of the world left behind, their precise content is impossible to pin down.

Greeks pride themselves in the very public display of the day's news and in the passion they feel when perusing it. It's a sign that they care about the public good no matter how anxious they may be about the direction public life is taking. A cartoon by Kostas Mitropoulos indicates one level of anxiety. Mitropoulos is just one of many cartoon artists of international reputation living and working in Greece. Greek newspapers and magazines support car-toonists by including political cartoons in every publication. In Mitropoulos's cartoon, a very Greek-looking *periptero* (the awning and roof are blue and white, and a Greek key decorates the cornice) is covered with newspapers and magazines hanging by clothespins—more than fifty of them in French, English, and German, none in Greek. Inside a shopkeeper with a proud, han-dlebar moustache dons a *fustanella* (the national costume of Greece) and tas-seled red fez.[67] Cartoons, like films, visualize a social group's deepest anxi-eties. Films attach social fears to imaginary people's stories, while cartoons create a sudden burst of self-recognition. Here Mitropoulos nips at Greek pride that dwells on nonessentials while missing the obvious. The Greek press isn't what it used to be. Multinationals threaten its autonomy. Private compa-nies compete to make a profit. Greeks themselves aren't reading newspapers cover to cover, or coming together as a public body to discuss their contents as they used to.[68] They appear on the verge of losing control over their public sphere.

Yet a glimpse at how people in Greece produce and share culture shows a strong awareness of what's at stake in keeping public debate alive. The best way to understand Greek culture is to see how its plays out in the public domain. It's not just the most public cultural products—newspapers, me-dia, theater, cinema—but every element of culture that becomes a piece of the civic fabric. The message may sometimes be as dire as Dimitris Dimitri-adis's apocalyptic *I'm Dying as a Country*. Yet the audience remains alert, on edge, ready to argue otherwise, knowing well that the day when people in Greece stop debating their future will signal the end of their history as they know it.

NOTES

1. There are 1,788 national, local, and regional newspapers, 252 of them dailies, according to Cathie Burton and Alun Drake, *Hitting the Headlines in Europe: A Country-by-Country Guide to Effective Media Relations* (London: Kogan Page Publishers, 2004), 128. Stylianos Papathanassopoulos, "Greece," in *The Media in Europe*, ed. Mary Kelley et al. (London: Sage, 2004), 97, calls the "excess of supply over demand ... a kind of tradition in Greece."

2. Yiannis Tzannetakos, "Eleftheri Radiofonia" (Free Radio) in Peggy Kounenaki, ed., "Meres Radiofonou" (Days of Radio) *Epta Imeres-Kathimerini*, December 31, 1995, 26.

3. Cathy Burton and Alun Drake, *Hitting the Headlines in Europe, A Country-by-Country Guide to Effective Media Relations* (London: Kogan Page, 2004), 128.

4. "Radio," ERT Online,(accessed July 28, 2008), http://tvradio.ert.gr/radioen/radiohistory.asp.

5. Ionas A. Moschanas, "To radiofono stin Katohi" (Radio under Occupation), in "Meres Radiofounou" (Days of Radio), ed. Peggy Kounedaki, *Epta Imeres-Kathimerini*, December 31, 1995, 12.

6. Moschonas, "To radiofono," 13.

7. Makis Milatos, "Oi erasitechnes ton FM" (Amateurs of FM), in "Meres Radiofounou," ed. Peggy Kounedaki, *Epta Imeres-Kathimerini*, December 31, 1995, 22.

8. John Downing, with Tamara Villarreal Ford et al., *Radical Media: Rebellious Communication and Social Movements* (Thousand Oaks, CA: Sage Publications, 2000), 184.

9. Yiorgos Hatzidakis, "Theatro apo ton 'aera'" (Theater from the Air), in "Meres Radiofounou," ed. Peggy Kounenaki, *Epta Imeres-Kathimerini*, December 31, 1995, 18.

10. Papathanassopoulos, "Greece," 97. According to Andrew Yoder, *Pirate Radio Stations: Tuning in to Underground Broadcasts in the Air and Online* (New York: McGraw-Hill, 2002), 197, unlicensed private radio in Greece is allowed to broadcast as long as it remains noncommercial.

11. "Radiofonikes akroamatikotites apo Oktovrio 2007 eos Ianouario 2008" (Radio Ratings from October 2007 to January 2008) (accessed August 24, 2008), http://radiourgies.blogspot.com/2008/01/2007-2008.html.

12. Isaac A. Blankson and Patrick D. Murphy, *Negotiating Democracy: Media Transformations in Emerging Democracies* (Albany: State University of New York Press, 2007), 248.

13. A second film, *Loufa kai parallagi, seirines sto Aigaio* (2005), has a different subject. Nikos Perakis directed both films and several episodes of the television series.

14. Thimios Zaharopoulos and Manny Paraschos, *Mass Media in Greece: Power, Politics, and Privatization* (New York: Praeger, 1993), 44.

15. Linda Martin and Kerry Segrave, *Anti-rock: The Opposition to Rock 'n' Roll* (New York: Da Capo Press, 1993), 156.

16. According to Lena Papadimitriou and Christodoulos Papadimas, "100 stigmes stin istoria tis ellinikis tileorasis" (100 Moments in the History of Greek Television), *To Vima*, November 21, 1999 (accessed August 24, 2008), http://tovima.dolnet. gr/print_article.php?e=B&f=12764&m=C14&aa=1, YENED broadcast its first show on February 27, 1966, under the name *TED*, and so preceded the military junta by fourteen months; but the channel grew in the hands of the dictatorship.

17. Papadimitriou and Papadimas, "100 stigmes."

18. Papadimitriou and Papadimas, "100 stigmes."

19. Angeliki Koukoutsaki, "Greek Television Drama: Production Policies and Genre Diversification." *Media, Culture and Society* 25, no. 6 (2003): 715–735.

20. "Dimitra Papadopoulou: Television Is for Heroes," *Kathimerini*, February 3, 2006 (accessed August 24, 2008), http://www.ekathimerini.com/4dcgi/ _w_articles_ell_2_03/02/2006_65966.

21. "Greece Press, Media, TV, Radio, Newspapers," August 13, 2008, http://www. pressreference.com/Fa-Gu/Greece.html.

22. P. Mandravelis, "Slapdash Comedy and Greek Myths," *Kathimerini*, April 18, 2008 (accessed August 24, 2008), http://www.ekathimerini.com/4dcgi/ _w_articles_columns_2_18/04/2008_95676.

23. Andrew Horton, *Screenwriting for a Global Market: Selling Your Scripts from Hollywood to Hong Kong* (Berkeley: University of California Press, 2004), 27.

24. Bacopoulou-Halls, "Theatre System in Greece," in *Theatre Worlds in Motion*, ed. H. Van Maanen, S. E. Wilmer, and H. Van Maanen (Amsterdam: Rodopi, 1998), 261.

25. "Interview with Dimitris Papaioannou, Director of Medea II" (accessed August 9, 2008), http://www.cityweekend.com.cn/beijing/articles/blogs-beijing/ film_stage_blog/interview-with-dimitris-papaioannou-director-of-medea-ii-by-omega-dance-company/.

26. "Master of Olympic Pageantry Prepares One Final Blowout," *New York Times*, August 29, 2004 (accessed August 31, 2008), http://www.nytimes.com/2004/08/29/ sports/olympics/29closing.html?ex=1220328000&en=8b502146f463b3eb&ei= 5070.

27. Anna Tabaki, "The Long Century of the Enlightenment and the Revival of Greek Theater," *Journal of Modern Greek Studies: Modern Greek Theater* 25, no. 2 (2007): 294.

28. Elisavet Moutzan-Martinengou, *My Story*, trans. Helen Dendrinou Kolias (Athens: University of Georgia Press, 1989).

29. Bacopoulou-Halls, "Theatre System in Greece," 265.

30. See Walter Puchner, "Early Modern Greek Drama," *Journal of Modern Greek Studies* 25, no. 2 (2007): 243–266.

31. Gonda Van Steen, *Venom in Verse: Aristophanes in Modern Greece* (Princeton, NJ: Princeton University Press, 2000), 45.

32. Bacopoulou-Halls, "Theatre System in Greece," 267.

33. Bacopoulou-Halls, "Theatre System in Greece," 268.

34. *Al Tzandiri News*, Mega Channel, March 13, 2007.

35. Bacopoulou-Hall, "Theatre System in Greece," 269

36. Kostas Georgousopoulos, "Hronia akmis 1947–1967" (Peak Years, 1947–1967), in "Epitheorisi," *Epta Imeres-Kathimerini*, April 4, 1998, 15–18.

37. Lydia Papadimitriou, "More than a Pale Imitation: Narrative, Music and Dance in Two Greek Film Musicals of the 1960s," in *Musicals*, by Bill Marshall and Robynn Jeananne Stilwell (Bristol, UK: Intellect, 1999), 118.

38. Bacopoulou-Halls, "Theatre System in Greece," 269.

39. Kyriaki Petrakou, "I emfanisi tou feminismou sto neoelliniko theatro" (The Appearance of Feminism in Modern Greek Theater), European Modern Greek Studies Society Third Congress (accessed August 6, 2008), http://www.eens-congress.eu/?main_page=1&main_lang=de& eensCongress_cmd=showPaper&eensCongress_id=230.

40. Papadimitriou, "More Than a Pale Imitation," 118.

41. Aliki Bacopoulou-Halls, "Greece," in *The World Encyclopedia of Contemporary Theatre*, ed. Don Rubin, Peter Nagy, and Philippe Rouyer (London: Routledge, 1994), 405.

42. Myrto Lomverdou, "Akmi kai parakmi tis epitheorisis" (Peak and Decline of *Epitheorisi*), *To Vima*, "Nees Epoches," July 6, 1997 (accessed August 18, 2008), http://tovima.dolnet.gr/print_article.php?e=B&f=12436&m=B10&aa=1.

43. Martin Banham, *The Cambridge Guide to Theatre* (Cambridge: Cambridge University Press, 1995), 448.

44. Bacopoulou-Halls, "Greece," 404.

45. Van Steen, *Venom in Verse*, 49.

46. Van Steen, *Venom in Verse*, 50.

47. Chrysothemis Stamatopoulou-Vasilakou, "Greek Theatre in Southeastern Europe," *Journal of Modern Greek Studies* 25, no. 2 (October 2007): 275.

48. Quoted in Bacopoulou-Halls, "Theatre System in Greece," 274.

49. William Miller, *Greek Life in Town and Country* (London: George Newnes, 1905), 8.

50. Bacopoulou-Halls, "Greece," 409.

51. Kostas Myrsiades, *Cultural Representation in Historical Resistance* (Lewisburg, PA: Bucknell University Press, 1999), 59–69, describes the conditions of theater in Greece's urban centers under Nazi occupation.

52. A comparison might be made to theater in German concentration camps in World War II. See Rebecca Rovit and Alvin Goldfarb, eds., *Theatrical Performance during the Holocaust: Texts, Documents, Memoirs* (Baltimore: Johns Hopkins University Press, 1999).

53. Gonda Van Steen, "Forgotten Theater, Theater of the Forgotten: Classical Tragedy on Modern Greek Prison Islands," *Journal of Modern Greek Studies* 23, no. 2 (October 2005): 335.

54. Van Steen, "Forgotten Theater," 357.

55. Gonda Van Steen, "Joining Our Grand Circus," *Journal of Modern Greek Studies* 25, no. 2 (October 2007): 301.

56. Bacopoulou-Halls, "Greece," 404.

57. Gonda Van Steen, "Joining Our Grand Circus," 303.

58. Dimitris Dimitriadis, *Pethaino san hora* (I'm Dying as a Country) (Athens: Agra, 1985), 48–53.

59. Dan Georgakas, "Greek Cinema for Beginners: A Thumbnail History," *Film Criticism* 27, no. 2 (2002): 4.

60. Georgakas, "Greek Cinema for Beginners," 3.

61. Andrew Horton, "O Thiasos" (accessed August 8, 2008), http://www. filmreference.com/Films-Str-Th/O-Thiasos.html.

62. Georgakas, "Greek Cinema for Beginners," 5.

63. Christina Grammatikopoulou, "A Junction of Myth, History, Cinema: Aeschylus's *Oresteia* in Theo Angelopoulos's Film *Thiasos* (The Traveling Players, 1975)," Interactive: Platform for Contemporary Art and Thought (accessed August 8, 2008), http://www.interartive.org/christina_grammatikopoulou_en.htm.

64. Stratos E. Constantinidis, "Greek Film and the National Interest," *Journal of Modern Greek Studies* 18, no. 1 (May 2000), 6.

65. Georgakas, "Greek Cinema for Beginners," 6.

66. *The Dust of Time* premiered at the Thessaloniki Film Festival on November 22, 2008. See 49th International Film Festival (accessed December 31, 2008), http://tiff.filmfestival.gr/default.aspx?lang=en-US&loc=4&page=721&Section ID=68&MovieID=1209.

67. The cartoon appeared on the back of an issue of *Kathimerini*'s Sunday magazine, *Epta Imeres*, dedicated to "Oi ellines geloiografoi" (Greek cartoonists) (February 19, 1995).

68. See Gregory Jusdanis, *Belated Modernity and Aesthetic Culture* (Minneapolis: University of Minnesota Press, 1991), 129–135.

8

Architecture and Art

GREECE IS A country of celebrated traditions in architecture and art. Most significant for Greek culture today, buildings from all eras, including the archaic, classical, and Byzantine, are still standing. The Acropolis, a limestone plateau rising abruptly to about two hundred feet at the center of Athens and topped with world-famous classical buildings from the fifth century B.C.—the Propylaia, Erectheion, Temple of Nike, and, an inspiration worldwide, the Parthenon (447–432)—is visible to Athenians every day as they turn street corners or look up from their morning coffee.

There is something distinct about the way Greeks assimilate older traditions that are still in plain view. The process is no simple matter. It is wrought with tensions and challenges. The plastic and visual arts are cultural forms with an extended synchronicity. Their material existence does not suffer instant decay, like music and dance, for example, but extends beyond the temporal duration of their creation. So they tend to accumulate over time, unless they are demolished or left to disintegrate. In Greece the extended synchronicity of buildings in particular operates on a grand scale. Remnants from five thousand years of architectural history are a piece of the landscape, their protection a vital article of the Greek constitution.[1] Newer buildings must not only select their sources of inspiration from all these extant remnants; they must compete for a place in the sun.

The Acropolis looms especially large on the horizon. Its echoes can be overwhelming as designers plan new creations to meet current needs. Yet the results of trying to create a dialogue with ancient monuments are never entirely predictable. A present-day controversy surrounding the New Acropolis Museum, the most important monumental building Greece has undertaken in decades, is a case in point. This controversy offers a point of entry into the dramatic story of the architecture and art in Greece in the modern period.

THE NEW ACROPOLIS MUSEUM AND THE CONTESTED ACROPOLIS VIEW

The controversy erupted on July 3, 2007, when the Ministry of Culture's panel of overseers voted to override historical listings in order to expropriate and tear down two buildings on Dionysiou Areopagitou Street, a pedestrian walkway that lines the southern edge of the archaeological site of the Acropolis. The buildings are No. 17, an art-deco apartment block by architect Vassilis Kouremenos listed as a historical monument by the Ministry of Culture, and No. 19, a neoclassical villa belonging to composer Vangelis Papathanasiou and listed as protected by the Ministry of Public Works. They stand along a row of distinguished houses boasting what may be the best view in all of Europe. The Acropolis is less than eight hundred feet away. Although the facades of these buildings are lovely, the Ministry of Culture claims that their unsightly backs disrupt the "visual link to the Acropolis" from the New Acropolis Museum, which stands behind these buildings.[2]

The view of the Acropolis is the most salient feature of the New Acropolis Museum, the reason why this new public building stands where it does. It is a purpose-defined building, designed by Bernard Tschumi with Michael Photiadis to provide the best possible conditions to exhibit the decorative marble sculptures from the Parthenon. These sculptures have been divided between two countries for nearly two hundred years. An old Acropolis Museum, built on the Acropolis in 1863, became the holding ground for some of the sculptures. But the British Museum in London possesses the lion's share, the so-called Elgin marbles, purchased in 1816 from Lord Elgin, who forcibly removed the sculptures from the Parthenon between 1803 and 1811. In an ongoing controversy over the sculptures' rightful place—perhaps the most famous international disagreement about art relating to Greece—the British Museum continues to argue that its Duveen Galleries provide the best environment for the sculptures' display. The New Acropolis Museum has the benefit of location. Taking advantage of its outstanding view of the Acropolis from the top floor is a glass-encased gallery oriented and proportioned in perfect alignment with the Parthenon. Natural lighting, a protective controlled environment, and the clear view of the Parthenon make this the perfect space to exhibit the Parthenon's surviving sculptures, Greek authorities argue. The Ministry of Culture's wager is that the British Museum will eventually return its share. For as long as the British Museum remains intransigent, the New Acropolis Museum will apply subtle pressure by displaying visually distinct stand-ins where the missing marbles are meant to be, a sign that the marbles in Greece are patiently awaiting reunification with their compatriots.

The New Acropolis Museum is attentive to the view of antiquity in other directions, too. Beneath the museum is another most extraordinary sight: a 2,500-square-meter (26,909 square feet) archaeological excavation representing four thousand years of continuous inhabitation in this neighborhood of Athens from 3000 B.C. to A.D. 1200. The archaeological site includes a thriving mix of houses, workshops, bathhouses, and even several villas dating from late antiquity. The excavation's innovation was that it maintained samples from all the successive building phases it uncovered even as it worked to unearth older layers. The New Acropolis Museum protects the excavation by hovering over it on concrete piers. Glass tiles on its ground floor give visitors a clear view of what lies below.

Yet for all the museum's attention to creating the ultimate visual dialogue with its surroundings, the New Acropolis Museum has alienated many Athenian residents in this neighborhood of Makriyanni, as it is called—named after the revolutionary hero and memoir writer Ioannis Makriyannis, who bought property here after Greece gained independence. In the late 1990s, excavation of the site required the demolition of ten houses and apartment blocks. Then at the beginning of this century the Ministry of Culture brought down several more buildings to give "breathing space" to the museum.[3] And in July 2007 it announced the planned expropriation of Nos. 17 and 19 Dionysiou Areopagitou. The ministry appealed to cultural legacy to argue that the buildings marked for demolition hindered the desired unity between the museum and the ancient monuments. Responding to that appeal, residents of the neighborhood, citizens from around the country and abroad, and architects worldwide countered with a unified chorus of protests. They complained that the ministry has taken a high-handed approach to life in the neighborhood, sacrificing historical buildings to create an optimal museum view. Marina Kouremenou-Flenga, granddaughter of the architect of No. 17, who lives in one of the apartment flats, set the tone and agenda with her statement, "We simply claim that both can coexist."[4] More than twenty-two thousand people signed petitions asking the ministry to overturn its decision. Moreover, 172 experts responded to a call for proposals to enhance the buildings' backs with screens and landscaping. Those protesting the ministry's decision expressed their desire to keep the old with the new and not to sacrifice the modern for the ancient. The immediate effect of this grassroots campaign was to stay the buildings' execution until after the New Acropolis Museum opens its doors in 2009.

The neighborhood of Markriyanni is not unusual in the uneasy coexistence of classical antiquities, "neoclassical" homes built in a classicizing style during the nineteenth and early twentieth centuries, architect-designed apartment blocks in varying styles, and developer-generated apartment buildings from the years of Athens's massive expansion after World War II. It simply represents an exaggerated case of the difficult balancing act that architects and artists must manage between Greece's emerging needs and historical legacies. With the Acropolis in clear view from every rooftop in the neighborhood and millennia of history underfoot, Makriyanni, together with a few other neighborhoods in Athens—Plaka, Psiri, Kerameikos, and Metaxourgeio (and just a few towns in Greece, such as Nafplion, Aegina, Chania, and Ermoupolis)—have a relatively large aggregation of neoclassical houses compared to the rest of Athens, where 80 percent of the pre–World War II housing was demolished between 1952 and 1975.

Before exploring further the meaning of the contest over the fate of Nos. 17 and 19 Dionysiou Areopagitou, it is worth taking visual cues from Makriyanni to grasp the general course of the history of the plastic and visual arts from the foundation of the modern state to the present day.

Neoclassicism in Architecture, Sculpture, and Painting

Outside the line of vision connecting the New Acropolis Museum with the Acropolis, Makriyanni creates its own effective unity with classical Greek antiquity through the large number of surviving neoclassical buildings. Stylistic features of the Athenian school of neoclassicism are symmetry, simplicity of mass, precision in the proportions, clarity of details, and the warm tones of the building materials.[5] The buildings make direct reference to the Acropolis through these formal elements and their decorations. Columns in the Doric, Ionic, or Corinthian styles, the three classical Greek orders from simplest to most ornate, flank their entrances. Pilasters, flattened columns attached to the face of a building, may frame a central window on an upper floor. Windows and doors are decorated above with pediments, nonstructural triangular elements that echo the triangular pediments under the pitched roof. Roofs are clay tiled and decorated along their edges with *akrokerama* (*akroteria*, terracotta roof ornaments). Niches on the facades of buildings are filled with earthenware urns or sculptures of classical deities.

Some Greeks refer to neoclassical homes as examples of *paradosiaki architektoniki* (traditional architecture) even though the style is technically a foreign import developed through Western Europeans' encounter with Greek and Roman temple forms in the eighteenth and early nineteenth centuries. Greeks' reappropriation of this once homegrown style speaks to the complexity of artistic borrowings, especially under the conditions of Greece's emergence as a modern state. It should be remembered that the independent Greek state took shape under the rule of a foreign king, the Bavarian Otto. He was selected by leaders of the Great Powers, France, Britain, and Russia, who felt that Greeks could not govern themselves. King Otto was responsible for neoclassicism's importation. Together with the style, he also imported architects from Germany and Denmark and two German-trained Greek architects, Stamatios Kleanthis (1802–1862) and Lysandros Kaftantzoglou (1812–1885), to design monumental buildings for the capital city. Money to fund the buildings came from wealthy Greeks who lived abroad.

The oldest postrevolutionary building in Makriyanni is the Military Hospital, built by the Bavarian engineer Wilhelm von Weiler between1834 and 1836. It stands on the same block as the New Acropolis Museum. People refer to it as neoclassical though technically its round-arched windows identify it with Rundbogenstil, another style of the era.[6] Yet the building is in harmony with true neoclassical homes in the neighborhood built on a much smaller scale.

Athens' more monumental neoclassical buildings lie beyond Makriyanni to the north of the Acropolis. The Old University of Athens, once the home of Kleanthis, is in the Plaka. The National Observatory (1843–1846) is on the Hill of the Nymphs to the west. More imposing is the Athenian "neoclassical trilogy" on Panepistimiou (University Street). These three buildings consists of the National Library (1887–1902), with its six Doric columns imitating the facade of the Hephaestion in the Ancient Agora and a double Renaissance staircase; the University of Athens (1839–1864), an Ionic building with columns replicating those on the Propylaiea and a long, painted portico; and the Academy (1859–1885), another Ionic building with pediment sculptures depicting the birth of Athena and statues of Athena and Apollo on very high freestanding pedestals. Down the street from the trilogy are a number of impressive buildings in different styles. The Eye Clinic (1847–1869) is neo-Byzantine. The luxurious, Renaissance-style Iliou Melathron (1878–1880), mansion of the archaeologist Heinrich Schliemann Mansion, is decorated up and down with Ionic columns. Old Parliament (1858–1871) is a graceful neoclassical building with an Ionic porch, while the present-day Parliament on Syntagma Square, built as the Royal Palace (1836–1843), has an austere Doric facade. Next to Parliament are the National Gardens, with Zappeion Exhibition Hall (1874–1888) to the south and the Presidential Mansion, once the New Palace (1891–1897) built for King George I, and the Maximos Mansion (1924) to the east. Heading in the opposite direction on Panepistimiou Street to the north one reaches the Athens Polytechneio (National Technical University, 1862–1957) and the National Archaeological Museum (1866–1891).

Scattered throughout the city center are the Arsakeion School for Girls (1900–1925) on Stadiou Street, businesses and hotels around Syntagma and Omonia squares and along Ermou Street, and many architect-designed mansions and hospitals of all sizes along Vasilissas Sofias Avenue. All of these are neoclassical buildings. At the time when they were built, they created the impression that Athens was a wealthy, powerful city. Yet quite the opposite was true. In 1898 Athens had no paved roads and no electric generator. The per capita income was $72 per year, compared to $94 in Romania and $419 in the United Kingdom.[7]

The rulers and many of the subjects of the new Greek state preferred neoclassicism in Athens's planning for two reasons. First, neoclassicism highlighted Greece's connections with its classical past and expressed its modern European aspirations. Second, neoclassicism serves to erase the Eastern face of Greece as it had evolved under Ottoman rule, which represented years of repressive rule to the Greeks and a foreign, Eastern despotism to Western Europeans. Indeed, neoclassicism erased the traces of architecture from the years before Greek independence so successfully that local architecture from Ottoman times has been effectively lost, at least in Athens. Only one building from prerevolutionary years is still standing in Athens: the eighteenth-century Benizelos House at 96 Adrianou Street in the Plaka, which is currently undergoing restoration after years of neglect.

Architecture in the Greek state's first years of existence managed to develop into a kind of native language, despite the importation of styles. Neoclassical buildings in Athens quite literally incorporated earlier building sources. Leo von Klenze, Otto's family's court architect, was particularly effective in reshaping a classical, Hellenic Greece from the ruins of prior occupations. He linked the revival of Greece with the restoration of the Acropolis's classical monuments at the expense of all other layers of the site's history, "the remains of barbarity," as Klenze called them. His proposal became in reality a foundation for the new state. Following his plan, archaeologists excavated the Acropolis to its bedrock and then threw over the south side of the plateau "any material which could neither be reincorporated into the ruins nor made into a picturesque display on the Acropolis."[8] They sold off the detritus of their excavations as building material for the new city. Thus this material was built into the foundations of many of Athens's neoclassical buildings.

Greece's neoclassicism also benefited from a firsthand view of the Acropolis and other archaeological sites. Architects were close enough to ancient buildings to copy their motifs directly. They developed a sense of locality through their use of stone drawn from ancient quarries: Pentelic marble for decorative features on the tops of buildings and Piraeus limestone in the lower parts of

Acropolis from Philopappos Hill with Herodeion. Debris from the archaeological excavation of the Acropolis has been thrown over the south slope, © 1865. Courtesy of the Library of Congress.

the building. Planners oriented streets and squares so that people could view ancient monuments on their evening *volta* (stroll). They regulated building heights to keep the Acropolis visible from the city's high points.[9] Architecture and planning thus offered strong visual evidence of Greece's classical lineage, a condition Europeans had established for lending their support to Greece.

Nineteenth-century Greek sculpture also developed along neoclassical lines with strong German influences.[10] Some of the best examples are in Athens's First Cemetery about half a mile southeast of Makriyanni. The cemetery has been operating since 1837 as a quiet, dreamlike mirror to an ever-expanding, changing modern city. Paths are devoid of cars and lined with well-watered pine and olive trees. White marble neoclassical monuments take the form of ancient temples, carved funerary steles, urns, and freestanding sculptures. Older graves stand alongside newer monuments. Near the cemetery's entrance is the grave of Melina Mercouri, the actress turned politician who as minister of culture in Greece advocated for the return of the Elgin marbles. A tall funerary stele topped with a decorative palmette marks her grave with respectful classicizing minimalism.

I koimomeni (The Sleeping Girl, 1877) sculpture by Giannoulis Chalepas in Athens First Cemetery. Photo by author, May 2007.

The most famous sculpture in the cemetery is *I koimomeni* (The Sleeping Girl) (1877), a reclining figure in a state of eternal sleep carved in white marble. The artist, Giannoulis Chalepas (1851–1938), came from a long lineage of stone carvers from Tinos, an island famous for its marble workers. His work was academic in its conception and neoclassical in its achievement of the "noble simplicity and quiet grandeur" attributed to the Greeks,[11] but its exceptional technique and close attention to form and expression owed a great deal to traditional marble cutting.

Chalepas's work stands as a reminder that sculpture in Greece did not arise out of a void. Generations of artisans were working in Greece prior to the foundation of the modern state, creating two- and three-dimensional art primarily for decorative and religious purposes. Traditional products were sculpted crosses, icon screens for churches, and decorative door frames and skylights for wealthy patrons. Stone and wood carvings adorned aristocratic homes, shepherd's sticks, and the figureheads for ships' prows. The names of most artists do not survive with their work, but their long-lived tradition of craftsmanship prepared their descendents well for the work of decorating the new state capital. After Athens became the capital, its construction needs brought artisans to the city to carve architectural decorations. The great stone-carving artisans from Tinos, people like Chalepas, were especially welcome. One finds their work on nearly every neoclassical building. In a few cases the artists' vernacular language comes through, as in a small house at 45 Agion Asomaton (c. 1880) in Psiri, with its "twin Caryatids, which, tradition claims, commemorate the early deaths of two beautiful girls of the neighborhood."[12]

While artisans carried out the work of decorating the city and occasionally became well-known artists, they were not given the lead in determining the direction art would take. When King Otto's court established the School of Fine Arts in Athens in 1837, it appointed the German sculptor Christian Siegel (1808–1883) as its first professor of sculpture. Siegel brought with him a classicizing spirit and ties to the Royal Academy of Fine Arts in Munich. With this appointment, the court was passing over significant local talent—people such as the Iakovos brothers (d. c. 1903) and Frangiskos Malakates (d. 1914) from Tinos and the Italian-trained Pavlos Prosalentis (1784–1837), founder of an art school on his native island of Kerkyra. It was thus signaling the direction it wanted Greek art to take. The leaders of the new state envisioned Greece as a heroic, classical partner of Europe, with all signs of its Ottoman past erased. The generation of Greek sculptors to which Chalepas belonged, even when they came from Tinos, studied in Athens or Munich, and there learned techniques for sculpting the human form that drew on careful observation of classical sculptures in Greece and Rome. Leonidas Drosis (1843–1884), for example, another artist from Tinos and Chalepas's teacher at the School of Fine Arts in Athens, studied in Munich in preparation for his work of decorating buildings in Athens, which included the sculptures of the Academy of Athens.

Painting also shared in creating a vision of Greece as a Western European player. As with sculpture, painting repressed local traditions and embraced the academic style of nineteenth-century Northern European painting. The repressed traditions were Greek Orthodox iconographic art, with its "two-dimensional ascending perspective," and decorative painting.[13] Of course, naive artists continued to work in their traditions into the twentieth century, and some even achieved national prominence. Panayiotis Zographos, a mural painter working in northern Greece, was commissioned by General Ioannis Makriyannis to paint twenty-five scenes from the Greek War of Independence. But for the most part "the Greek artists who dominated the nineteenth century . . . all studied in Munich,"[14] where they learned to paint as Europeans. They include Theodoros Vryzakis (1814–1878), who painted images of the Greek revolution "in a formal Neoclassical style reminiscent of Jacques-Louis David";[15] Nikiphoros Lytras (1832–1904), painter of "Antigone before

the Dead Polyneices" (1865); Nikolaos Gyzis (1842–1901); and Georgios
Iakovidis (1853–1932), first director of Greece's National Gallery. Their style
of painting is called academic, a technical term used by art historians to identify nineteenth-century art as learned in the academies and universities of
Europe, which drew its subjects from history, mythology, and landscapes.
While academicism used shading, color, and light to create an illusion of depth
on a two-dimensional surface, it tended to sacrifice realism for idealism—an
idealization of its subjects subordinating them to an idea or theme.

Greek artists put academicism to work to depict scenes from the Greek
revolution and from village life. They sought a synthesis of neoclassicism and
romantic nationalism, both movements with tangible links to Europe: to the
inheritance of revolutionary France and the folkloric interests of German
nationalists. In *Apokries* (Carnival), *Kryfo Scholeio* (Secret School, both by
Gyzis), *O Galatas* (The Milkman), *To filima* (The Kiss), or *Psariano moiroloi*
(Lament in Psara, all painted by Lytras), they highlighted the role the anonymous *laos* (folk or people) played in preserving national identity from classical antiquity to the present. It is one of the paradoxes of Greek culture
that its academic painters of the nineteenth century repressed local visual
styles cultivated in Greece's villages even as they depicted scenes from village
life.

The neoclassical aesthetic in architecture, sculpture, and painting was remarkably long lived in Greece. It lingered on during the first two decades of
the twentieth century, long after its visual message of an enduring, timeless
harmony, reason, and beauty had begun to clash with the spirit of the times—
for the nineteenth century closed with Greece's declaration of bankruptcy on
European loans (1893) and the great defeat in Greece's war with the Ottoman
Empire (1897), while the twentieth century opened with the Goudi military
coup (1909) against the royal family's intervention in Greece's military affairs
and brought the liberal Eleftherios Venizelos into power. While the popular
desire for a progressive turn found its voice briefly in politics, new approaches
to architecture and art came in fits and starts.

ECLECTICISM IN ARCHITECTURE: FROM THESSALONIKI TO ATHENS

In architecture, the spirit of experimentation found fuel first in eclecticism,
a concept that became important in Europe in the second half of the nineteenth century. Eclecticism borrows and combines various styles from different sources to create something new. Because European eclecticism did not
rule out classicism but instead allowed the mixing of classicism with elements
from many other periods, it held the potential to open new paths for architects
and artists working Greece without their having to abandon the old.

Porch of the Villa Atlantis in Kifisia designed by Ernst Ziller in an eclectic style with classical, Renaissance, and romantic elements. Photo by author, July 2007.

Traces of the boldest experiments in architecture from the turn of the century lie some distance from Makriyanni. They took shape not in Athens's center but further afield, for example, in Kipseli, then lying at the outskirts of Athens, the wealthy Athenian suburb of Kifisia, and especially in Thessaloniki, an important, multiethnic city that remained under Ottoman rule until 1912. The fact that Thessaloniki was not annexed by Greece until the early part of the twentieth century meant that it developed a modern architectural heritage independent from the influences of neoclassicism. Furthermore, its cosmopolitan residents worked with an international pool of architects, who constructed buildings representing the most contemporary currents.

Some architectural gems from the late Ottoman period are still standing. Casa-Bianca is an art nouveau mansion of 1912 designed by Italian architect Pierro Arrigoni for Dino Fernandez, a prominent member of the very substantial Jewish community that was the majority in Thessaloniki at the time. The Villa Mordoch, built in 1905 by the Greek architect Xenophon Paionidis, is an eclectic work with a different architectural style—neoclassical, Renaissance, baroque, and art nouveau styles—on each of its four sides, "accentuating the pluralism of the structure."[16] The customs building of

1910 by architect Eli Modiano combines the "excessive decoration . . . of late eclecticism"[17] with reinforced concrete, a new building technique, used here for the first time in Thessaloniki.[18] Most remarkable of all is the Yeni Tzami (New Mosque), designed by the Italian architect Vitaliano Poseli in 1902 for Jews who had converted to Islam. Although a mosque, the building retains "much of the form and decorative symbolism of a synagogue"[19]

These and a few other one-of-a-kind buildings survived the disastrous fire of 1917 that destroyed the Jewish city center and left 73,448 people homeless.[20] But even with the implementation of French architect Ernest Hébrard's plan for a new, Greek city following "modern Western principles . . . based on a grid system with spectacular diagonal broad avenues,"[21] Thessaloniki did not submit to design rules that would have linked it to the classical Greek past. It retained visible vestiges of its Hellenistic, Roman, Byzantine, and Ottoman past in its city walls, old buildings, and marketplaces. It kept intact the Ano Polis (Upper Town), the city's onetime Muslim neighborhood, with its narrow streets and small, inward-looking homes. Moreover, in the city's new monumental buildings, streets, and squares, architects took cues from the city's past and combined these with the form of modern European buildings. Surrounding the magnificent Aristotelous Square, for example, is a set of long, concave buildings that accentuate the plaza's U-shape with arched, colonnaded porticos on the ground floor and patterns of repeated or mixed arched and rectangular windows decorating the upper parts. The immediate effect of these buildings was one of elegant, Eastern European grandeur, while in the long run Thessaloniki contributed to the countrywide sense that Greek architects could explore their past more fully while imagining their future a bit more freely.

A related message reached Athens through a different emissary, also from the north: the architect Aristotelis Zachos (1872–1939) from Kastoria, a town in the region of western Macedonia famous for its traditional stone and stucco *arhondika* (aristocratic homes) with their decorative wood carvings. In 1911 Zachos published an article titled "Laiki architektoniki" (Vernacular Architecture) proposing that architects should look to Greece's traditional buildings for inspiration for their modern creations.[22] Soon architect Dimitris Pikionis (1887–1968), supported by the Greek Folk Art Association, would lead a group to begin documenting vernacular architecture in Greece, starting in western Macedonia. The group's work would be cut short by World War II but eventually yield books on Zachos's native Kastoria (1948) and nearby Kozani and Siatista. The group also "succeeded in getting many mansions listed for preservation."[23]

The turn to vernacular traditions in architecture and art was an idea waiting to happen, given the number of artists and artisans working in Greece's cities with roots in traditional crafts. In fact, such an experiment was already taking place in marginal neighborhoods in Athens where people were building illegally. Such is the neighborhood known today as Anafiotika (1847–1863), which is nestled above the Plaka and around the corner from Makriyanni on the northeast slope of the Acropolis. Here stone, plaster, and wood artisans and builders from the Aegean island of Anafi and other islands, who had found work as builders in Athens but no place to rest their own heads, perched a small village of Cycladic-style, whitewashed, stucco homes.

Even though there were models in place to explore, Zachos was borrowing his idea not from Greece's artisans but from a group of European and American modernists who argued that the artistry and craftsmanship of vernacular traditions were not only a good source of inspiration but also an antidote to the soulless, machine-made production that was overtaking the world. Zachos put his ideas to work in designing the house of folklorist Angeliki Hatzimichali (1924–1927), today the Municipal Museum of Folk Culture in Athens's Plaka. He mixed modern and traditional elements: clean lines and a flat, undecorated surface with rectangular and arched windows in irregular positions; rounded bay windows; an arched, colonnaded veranda; and elaborate woodcut decorations in the home's interior, designed by Hatzimichali herself.

The decade of the 1920s, when Zachos and Hatzimichali were reintroducing folk traditions to urban Greek architecture, was the period when the area of Makriyanni along Dionysiou Areopagitou Street was attracting wealthy residents and new, luxury building projects. No. 17 Dionysiou Areopagitou (1932), the apartment block whose planned demolition in 2007 has caused such a stir, is a prime example. Architect Vassilis Kouremenos was trained in the Academy of Fine Arts in Paris. His architectural language was art deco, a style that was gaining popularity in Greece's new middle-class neighborhoods. For about a decade, art deco's streamlined reinterpretation of traditional designs perfectly expressed the spirit of the times. Since No. 17 has been catapulted to fame by controversy, with multitudes stopping by admire its grace, symmetry, and artistic detail, it is worth a closer look, whether or not it survives the controversy. The building's pink marble face is pure art deco, as is its delicately crafted ironwork entrance. Two stylized bas-reliefs of Greek peasant women—one carrying a jug of water and the other a basket of fruit on her head—flank the entrance. Here are "echoes of folklore... reminiscent of the trend of folk tradition which took shape after 1920."[24] Folklore and Byzantine iconography also inform the style of two colorful mosaics on the building's top floor. But the subject is classical. Odysseus in his sailing vessel dominates one frame, while Oedipus outsmarts the sphinx in the other. Subtle hints of classicism run through the building. The sculptures are carved in white marble. They each stand as a piece of a modified, fluted Doric column, with ornaments of a Doric frieze overhead. A balustrade of fluted columns decorates a balcony too narrow to sit on. The building is carrying on a restrained conversation with the neighboring Parthenon. As the architect reportedly said, "You have no idea how sacred this place is, underneath the Acropolis. You can't sit out on a balcony eating your biscuits here."[25]

MODERNISM IN ARCHITECTURE

1917 marked the opening of the first school of architecture in Greece in the Polytechneio (National Polytechnic) in Athens.[26] From here, the first Greek-taught alumni emerged as practitioners of modernism. They found direction not from their instructors but in their collective experience of the gap between architectural practice in Greece and the historical moment in the wider world.[27] They also drew inspiration from ideas introduced by Le Corbusier—simplified form, reduced ornamentation, mass-produced materials—which had special resonance in Greece because of Le Corbusier's strange passion for Greek architecture as one of the foundations of modernism.[28] Additionally, Dimitris Pikionis, a modernist with strong traditionalist leanings, contributed greatly to their thinking after he began lecturing at the school in 1925.

Pikionis was trained in the Polytechneio's School of Engineering in the first decade of the century but became a frequent visitor to its School of the Fine Arts, where he was a friend of artists Giorgio de Chirico (1888–1978) and Konstantinos Parthenis (1878–1967). He was also drawn to art critic Perikles Yiannopoulos (1869–1910), who was working toward defining a native aesthetic for contemporary Greek art emphasizing the "Attic light." Pikionis moved on to study art in Munich and Paris before he settled on architecture as his "object of aesthetic contemplation," as he put it.[29] He was well acquainted with modernism in Europe and, when he returned to Greece, encouraged his students to break free of their country's intellectual introversion and draw lessons from modernism in the visual arts. Throughout his career he collaborated with artists and writers of his day. But Pikionis's main contribution to Greek architecture was his insistence on "the harmony of the architecture with its given site—the concept of genius loci."[30] Following a revelation that came to him as he returned to Greece, when his "eyes were struck by the cold, dazzling whiteness of a piece of marble lying in the mud,"[31] his stylistic focus turned to the qualities of the Greek landscape and the vernacular architecture. In the Aegean Islands, he found hard angles and round curves, whiteness and shade, hot and cold, creating sharp antitheses, a characteristic he found to be true to the Greek landscape. It should be noted that Pikionis's interest in Aegean architecture runs parallel to Le Corbusier's fascination with "the play of masses brought together under light."[32]

Pikionis's theories relating building to local history and the natural environment have survived him in the idea that architecture should draw on native resources without depleting them or destroying social quality. Pikionis put this theory to work in the landscaping of the Acropolis and Philopappos Hill (1951–1957), which thousands of people enjoy everyday.[33] Among its gems, the church of St. Dimitrios Loubardiaris, Pikionis's imaginative reconstruction of a fifteenth-century church on Philopappos Hill, is a popular destination for weddings, baptisms, and evening walks. His free-form geometric walkways are sui generis. Working on-site with a hands-on approach approximating the methods of vernacular architects, he integrated new and old materials—concrete blocks, potsherds, and fragments of ancient sculptures—to create an organized space that feels like an extension of the natural environment. According to one critic, "The immense care and attention to detail exercised by Pikionis and his team have resulted in one of the most perfect man-made landscapes of the period."[34]

Greece's first generation of architects, trained in the School of Architecture, joined forces with others returning from their studies abroad to create designs suitable for new conditions that were evolving in Greece. Several social projects gave architects occasion to develop a systematic design program. The largest was an extensive school building project (1928–1932) involving more than a thousand buildings, supported by Greece's liberal Prime Minister Eleftherios Venizelos and his minister of education, George Papandreou. The project's minimal funding challenged architects to create functional designs on a tight budget, for which modernism's mass-produced materials, subordination of form to function, and absence of ornamentation was perfectly suited. Another social project was housing for refugees from the population exchange that followed the Asia Minor catastrophe (1922). Many of these buildings have suffered demolition or neglect. A few are extant but under threat. The eight-building housing complex on Alexandras Avenue (1933–1935) by Kimon Laskaris and Dimitris Kyriakos was set for demolition prior to the Athens 2004 Olympics. But government officials gave in to public pressure when people rallied against the buildings' demolition and instead covered their neglected facades with a giant tarpaulin.[35] The building awaits decision about its restoration and reuse. Other buildings of the era are some of the first city apartment blocks in Athens, all built by progressive architects for wealthy landowners with high standards of taste. It should be noted that private citizens funded the buildings according to their tastes, as the state did not take any housing action before or after the war. Modernist apartment blocks and private homes from the era are among the most carefully designed buildings in Athens. Their architects lavished as much attention on the use of basic forms to produce the effects of symmetry, equilibrium, and regularity as the previous generation had given to architectural ornamentation.

Then, as suddenly as it appeared, the modernist experiment ceased for nearly fifteen years when Metaxas's conservative dictatorship, followed by the occupation and the Civil War, forcefully put an end to progressive architecture. With each new wave of repression more architects disappeared. Some were killed, others went out of practice, and the majority left the country.[36] One who remained was Constantine A. Doxiadis (1913–1975). Before going on to acquire world fame as a town planner in the 1960s, Doxiadis headed the Office of Research on Spatial and Urban Planning under the Nazi occupation, taking advantage of his position to send architects into the field to document the country's destruction, which amounted to four hundred thousand buildings in ruins and a quarter of a million people left homeless.[37] After the war he took charge of coordinating the country's reconstruction. But ideological upheavals combined with the self-interest of powerful individuals to make it impossible to implement a policy or plan.

Modernism returned with a vengeance in the 1950s, though not as a building program carried out by experienced architects trained in its analytical methods. Conservative architects from the prewar period embraced it as an inexpensive building style that fulfilled people's desire to move forward. Additionally they recognized it as a lucrative way to satisfy the country's desperate need for mass housing, a result of massive destruction of the countryside and certain cities during World War II and the mass migration of villagers to cities in the decades after the war.

Ambitious, cash-poor developers also jumped at the opportunity to turn profits. They used an enterprising system for funding apartment buildings. It became known as *antiparohi*, meaning "exchange." Developers would eye a neighborhood of old houses in the city. They would let it be known that they were interested in building and try to convince owners of neighboring houses to give them their land in exchange for a two- or three-bedroom flat in the planned apartment building. They would sell the remaining apartments to people who did not own any land and rent the first floor to shopkeepers or technicians. The developers would usually plan the buildings themselves, with little help from architects, who usually just sign their names on this kind of project. They would then demolish the city's pre–World War II housing (in Athens they destroyed 80 percent of it during the city's development from 1952 to 1975) and replaced it with unpainted concrete eyesores known as *polykatoikies* (apartment flats). Because they excelled in getting around the city's minimal codes, they introduced all kinds of irregularities in the shape, height, and placement of buildings. And they hugely increased the cities' congestion, for they made no effort to widen streets, plan for parking, or carve out public spaces. The only green space that remained was that of old church squares or abandoned houses that did not match the developers' plans. Out of this system of exchange, Greece's cities (Iraklion, Argos, and Larissa are representative, but Athens is the prime example) grew taller, uglier, and overcrowded. Yet the system had its benefits. It retained the scale and mixed use of older neighborhoods and—with butcher shops, dry cleaners, pharmacies, beauty shops, seamstresses, workshops, *kafeneia* (coffeeshops), restaurants, and bars on ground floors—gave people everything they needed to survive and even prosper.

The building boom of the 1960s and 1970s saturated the landscape with a multitude of visual stimulants that did not relate to one another. In the resulting pastiche, a few projects by a talented group of younger architects stand out. As head of the Design Department of the National Tourist Organization from 1958 to 1967, Aris Konstantinidis (1913–1993) oversaw the building of the Xenia hotel chain, archaeological museums, and beach pavilions throughout Greece. Many were bold statements of modernism yet sensitive to their environment. One of his own great achievements is the Archaeological Museum of Ioannina. The Hilton Hotel (1958–1962), built in Athens by P. Vasiliadis (1912–1977), E. Vourekas, and S. Staikos with a mural by artist Yiannis Moralis, is an outstanding example of the international style, though it met with wide disapproval as an "injur[y to] its site, which happens to be Athens, whose Acropolis it rivals in size."[38] Takis Zenetos was one of the most uncompromising innovators in the use of new materials and forms, as exhibited in his design of the Fix Brewery (now undergoing renovation to become the New Museum of Contemporary Art) and the open-air theater on the hill of Lykavittos. These and other modern works served the purpose of visually aligning Greece with Europe.[39]

A belated form of modernism continues to dominate architecture to the present day. Greece has outstanding architects who are aware of current trends and in dialogue with colleagues worldwide. T. Bobotis's high-tech Würth Hellas building (1989–1991) is very successful in its imaginative postmodern design. The late Kyriakos Krokos's Museum of Byzantine Culture in Thessaloniki (1989–1993) raises questions of collective memory without nostalgia, as it reactivates in a visibly modern building older Byzantine architectural forms: the textured juxtaposition of brick- and stonework, the rhythm of shadows from a line of recessed windows. The group of Mario Botta with Irena Sakellaridou, Morpho Papanikolaou, and Maria Pollani built the National Bank of Greece's new administrative headquarters (1998–2001) on Aiolou Street after winning first prize in an open competition. The new building stands opposite the eclectic Melas Building (1887, E. Ziller architect) and adjacent to Athens's Plateia Kotzia, a square with a small archaeological site in one corner and neoclassical buildings all around. The National Bank's ultramodern design, which includes a glass pyramid with a view of the ancient city walls below ground, creates a visual dialogue with surrounding buildings as it adds to the pleasures of loitering in the square.

Yet for every outstanding achievement there are many deficient designs. It is noteworthy that the Athens 2004 Olympics did not produce an architectural heritage—apart from some of Santiago Calatrava's designs and the Attiko Metro, Athens's new underground public-transport system, a by-product of the games—chiefly due to procedures that were not followed.[40] A pattern of irregularities is something architects complain of: competitions disregarded, architects marginalized or ignored, plans abandoned in favor of unrelated objectives.[41] "The architectural capacity of the country was not utilized," is architects' frequent complaint.[42] The Megaro Mousikis (Athens's music hall) is one building that singled out as an example of underachievement. Originally planned in 1975, it was completed in 1991 following a long, changing list of architects, contractors, and experts.[43] Its resulting exterior design stands too contentedly alongside Walter Gropius's American embassy (1961), as if both came from the same period.

From the general public one hears another chorus of complaints: that contemporary designs don't sit well in their neighborhoods; that modernism destroyed something better than it created. People who had abandoned drafty old neoclassical homes in the 1960s complain today about all those demolitions. Thus a residual dissatisfaction characterizes the feelings of both experts and nonexperts when they think about Greece's buildings, though they disagree on the diagnosis. Architects of large-scale buildings think that they have not been allowed to carry through their work. The public complains that arrogant architects have gone too far. These divergent viewpoints on modernism are the context for present-day tensions as they play out over the slated demolition of the art-deco and neoclassical houses blocking the view of the ultramodern New Acropolis Museum.

TWENTIETH-CENTURY ART

A few blocks from the New Acropolis Museum at 5 Webster Street is the Atelier of Spyros Vassiliou, which functions today as a "space for viewing the Greek environment, natural and constructed, as seen through the eyes of an artist who loved and was deeply involved in the world around him."[44] The studio's terrace stands opposite the Parthenon's west facade. From this house, the artist Spyros Vassiliou (1903–1985) chronicled changes in the Athenian cityscape after World War II. He even hired the modernist architect Patroclos Karandinos to raise the roof of his wife's neoclassical home in order to improve his view as Athens's buildings grew taller. Hundreds of Vassiliou's paintings (his total output was more than five thousand) render everyday objects against a flat background, as if they were Byzantine saints living in eternity. Some of these objects (kerosene lamps, gramophones, a dish of homemade preserves with a silver spoon) represent a disappearing way of life. But many of Vassiliou's paintings interpose objects between the viewer and the cityscape. Several paintings render an Acropolis view blocked by the frame of the author's window, a lamp, a ruined house or rising construction. Sometimes Vassiliou turned his view downward to the street level to find activity on the ground, for example, a neoclassical house announcing its availability for demolition, *didetai me antiparohi* (offered for exchange), and giving a phone number. The body of Vassiliou's works thus offers a steady viewpoint from which to follow Athens's postwar transformation, as rooftops kept rising to compete for a better view.

Vassiliou's work also says a great deal about the evolution of Greek art in the twentieth century. Even though his painting style is realistic, his subject matter and viewpoint stand at a great distance from academic paintings that idealized the Greek revolution and countryside in the nineteenth century. It presupposes the artistic revolution of the first half of the twentieth century.

The move from academism through abstraction to a new examination of representation followed a quicker path with more routes and byways in the visual arts than it did in architecture. Paintings, drawings, printmaking, and photography are cheaper, lower-risk, more portable media than buildings, so it's easier to experiment with them. Sculpture is also a piece of this story but to a lesser degree. Many of the greatest crafters of stone continued to take on traditional projects for the public sector rather than creative work of their own. As with architecture, sculpture is costly and requires patronage, so its evolution depends on what people will pay for. Michalis Tombros (1889–1974) was an exception. He worked alongside painters to find the roots of three-dimensional abstraction, and he found them in archaic art and fourth-century B.C. terra-cotta figurines. Yiorgos Zongolopoulos (1903–2004) was more groundbreaking at every step. In the 1930s he collaborated with architects on the public school project. He then sculpted abstract human figures from 1934 to 1958, but as he moved to work with metal he abandoned the human figure and collaborated with architects to set his constructions in motion. A kinetic piece with moving umbrellas was an entry in the Venice Biennale Centenary (1995) and is now installed on Thessaloniki's *paralia* (waterfront). Another related piece, *Aithrio* (Ether) consisting of umbrellas, ladders, nails, tubes, springs, and rods, moves within a dome-shaped ceiling of the Syntagma metro stop.

In painting, Konstantinos Parthenis is considered the first to have broken with the academic teachings of the Munich school. His landscapes in the first decade of the 1900s used the techniques of impressionism and postimpressionism, on the one hand, and imagery from Byzantine art, on the other, to create a sense of atmosphere. They also tested the limits of the illusion of space by introducing multiple perspective points and cubist disfigurement. The psychologically penetrating portraits and landscapes of Nikolaos Lytras (1883–1927) used the gestural brushstrokes and thick painted surfaces of expressionist painting. Others who explored the nature of their painterly medium while distorting the human figure to an even greater degree were Georgios Hatzopoulos (1859–1935), Konstantinos Maleas (1879–1928), and Georgios Bouzianis (1885–1959).

Of special note in the story of representational art in this period are a woman engraver and two women photographers. As in every other field of Greek culture except for the arts of the everyday, women's names are absent from the history of the fine arts and architecture before World War II. This is not to say that women were not producing art. Eleni Altamura, for example, is considered Greece's first woman painter, but she disguised herself as a man so that she could paint.[45] Most women's creative energy was directed elsewhere. Women were expected to work in textiles. Women of all classes embroidered, and women in villages spun wool and wove cloth with intricate designs they picked up from one another, altered, and developed. This was an area where women excelled. Significantly, Vaso Katraki (1914–1988), a student of Parthenis and printmaker Ioanis Kefalinos, who designed posters to encourage soldiers fighting on the Albanian front in 1940 and resistance fighters of EAM and who held individual exhibits and won awards for her prints after World War II, was the daughter of an internationally recognized weaver of woolen and cotton *kilimia* (kilims or carpet tapestries). Undoubtedly, most women were discouraged from entering formal training in the arts, as Altamura's case and the near-complete absence of women artists with a national profile prior to World War II suggest.

The first two woman artists of note are both photographers. Elli Souyioultzoglou-Seraidari (1899–1998), who signed her work "Nelly's,"[46] was born to a cosmopolitan family in Constantinople. She studied in Germany before moving to Athens to open a studio. She made her living taking portraits and scenes from the Greek countryside, including its artistic happenings such as the Delphic festivals in 1927 and 1930. Her pictures for the Ministry of Tourism in the mid-1930s "contributed to creating the earliest visual symbols of Greece's philosophy regarding tourism."[47] But Nelly is best known for two subjects: the human nude and Greece's ancient temples, including some of the Acropolis, where she managed to defamiliarize the site through lighting and odd angles. She brought these two richly overladen visual icons together in 1929 in a set of photographs of seminude dancers on the Acropolis. In one set Mona Paova is standing modestly before the Parthenon's fluted columns, while in another Nicolska is soaring between them. Neither dancer is wearing anything but transparent cloth. While the images give a rather classic interpretation of the "human body in absolute harmony with the grace and symmetry of the ancient monuments,"[48] the fact that the bodies are female and nude and seen against the Parthenon, a symbol of feminine virginity, under the natural light continues to provoke scandal to this day.[49]

Voula Papaioannou (1898–1989) studied at the Polytechneio and became the exhibit photographer for the National Archaeological Museum.[50] She took up documentary photography during World War II, using her camera as a weapon to expose the effects of famine under the Nazi occupation. She worked as a photographer for the United Nations Relief and Rehabilitation Administration (UNRA) in 1945 and from that time continued to photograph the harsh realities of life in the sun-drenched countryside. Her hard, realist eye shaped the tourist image of Greece after the war.

Artists who came of age in the 1930s and consolidated their presence in the 1950s and 1960s were especially effective in combining the tendencies toward a more analytical approach to making art with attachments to Greek tradition. They succeeded in bringing European trends closer to Greek ideas in ways that previous generations had not anticipated. A key formal element was their analysis of color as it related to the source of light, a tendency toward abstraction, which, paradoxically, reproduced the appearance of things under the intense summer sun in Greece. Thematically their work refers to a much broader historical spectrum than academic painting. Gone are the depictions of heroic or folkloric scenes. Classical motifs enter their work, but their juxtaposition with modern figures creates a surreal effect, as in the work of Nikos Engonopoulos (1907–1985). Artists also leaned heavily on other eras of the Greek past ignored by their predecessors: the prehistoric and archaic (Yiannis Moralis, b. 1916), Hellenistic and Roman (Yiannis Tsarouchis, 1910–1989), Byzantine (Spyros Papaloukas, 1892–1957), and folk (Giorgos Sikeliotis, 1917–1984). Notably missing is the Ottoman era, which people to this day view as a repressive digression in their history. Besides incorporating elements from the broad sweep of Greek history they also tried to distil the elementary forms and colors of the countryside and energy of the city.

Despite the trend toward abstraction, representational images continued to have a powerful presence. Gavriil Pentzikis (1908–1993), a painter and writer of Thessaloniki, made Byzantine icons his prototype. Without imitating their subjects, he worked to re-create their color, texture, and flatness to a degree that made the object almost disappear in the paintings' rich surface. Photis Kontoglou (1895–1965) also embraced the techniques of Byzantine frescoes, but without transgressing painting's iconographic purpose. As a religious painter he revitalized Greek Orthodox art by recovering its pre-Western style. When treating other subjects he replaced verisimilitude with Byzantine techniques such as ascending perspective, stylized bodies, and landscapes. He added expressive distortions and solid backgrounds to produce the feeling of a lack of depth. Paintings such as his *Laocoön* (1938) reveal his debt to El Greco, the famous seventeenth-century painter from Crete known for his paintings in Spain, who painted his version of the Laocoön scene in 1610–1614. Kontoglou and other artists revised Greeks' aesthetic sensibilities, giving people a new view of their history and style. His work, together with the critical writings by poets and critics of his day, opened the way for a new appreciation of Greece's vernacular painters, including Theophilos Hatzimichail (c. 1870–1934), an itinerant artist from Lesvos who painted for a plate of food. Just before his death, Theophilos's name began circulating as a kind of legend when Tériade (Stratis Eleftheriades), a Greek art critic and patron living in Paris, publicized his work. The authors Stratis Myrivilis, George Seferis, and Odysseas Elytis all wrote about Theophilos after his death. Today at least two museums—one in his native Lesvos and another in a mansion he painted outside Volos—are devoted solely to his work. He overshadows many experimental artists of his day, a sign that Greeks found greater comfort in the emotive break with realism offered by vernacular artists than in the analytical approach of those who moved Greek art in the direction of abstraction. Theophilos is considered a national artist, while artists who pushed the visual arts to the limits of abstraction—for example, Theophrastos Triantafyllidis (1881–1955), Gerasimos Steris (1898–1987), Giorgos Vakalo (1902–1991), Angelos Spachis (1903–1963), Alekos Kontopoulos (1904–1975)—remain little known. Greeks' attachment to images just would not give way to iconoclasm.

A few artists were especially successful in producing a modernist "myth of Hellenicity," that is to say, images that looked both modern and Greek.[51] Their work remains popular today. Nikos Hadjikyriakos Ghikas (1906–1994), a collaborator with Pikionis on the journal *To trito mati* (The Third Eye, 1936–1937), found inspiration in cubist approaches to form and light, but he produced landscapes and still-life compositions whose distortions seem to be refractions of the Greek light. Like Pikionis's architecture, Ghikas's paintings fit into the Greek landscape. The work of Yiannis Moralis (b. 1916) also became iconic. Moralis followed a path of figurative painting reduced to geometric abstraction. Over time he rid his painting of tonal variation and details. He began to make pictures and sculptures consisting entirely of solid geometric shapes. These shapes, with rounded curves and colors of beige, terra-cotta, blue, and black, reproduce the feeling of carved stone masses under the Greek sun. Moralis's paintings connect their viewers with something Doric or, going further back, the Greek Stone Age. In Greece it is extremely visible. For example, his untitled metal installation on the marble walls of the Panepis-timiou stop of the Attiko metro is seen by thousands of people each day. He became hugely influential as a professor in Athens's School of the Fine Arts. Alecos Fassianos (b. 1935), one of Moralis's most successful students, found his visual language when he moved from abstract painting back to figurative painting to create stylized, flat, solid-colored silhouettes of people engaged in everyday activities. His *Myth of My Neighborhood* in Athens' Metaxourgeio metro stop shows folk-inspired, almost cartoonlike figures engaged in the ev-eryday activities of buying and selling things.

Fassianos's success came after he took up residence in Paris. His departure from Greece together with others who would become world-famous artists changed the course of Greek art. The list of Greece's important expatriate artists is long, and should include children of immigrants such as Theodore Stamos (1922–1997) and William Baziotes (1912–1963), two of the New York school "irascibles" who helped American art break out of its provin-cialism. Among those born in Greece who left the country, Chryssa, Jannis Kounellis, and Loukas Samaras are the most famous. Chryssa (Vardea Mavromihali, b. 1933) found a luminous iconography in the blinking signs on Times Square and began making sculptures from colored neon tubes. She moved on to use other hard, heavy materials. Her genius lies in the way she gives them a graceful calligraphic motion. Lucas Samaras (b. 1936) has been called the most versatile artist of the twentieth century.[52] His work places the artist's body and face at its center and gives new meaning to the word *self-image*. In an especially influential series of works, Samaras photographed himself in the 1970s with a Polaroid camera. Having discovered that he could chemically manipulate the Polaroid prints, he used the discovery to introduce a range of distortions he called *Photo-Transformations*. The effect was a series of self-portrait photographs of beauty and terror. Here the fine line between seduction and threat collapses. Samaras's personal imagery, narrative photog-raphy, and concentration on the human body, enhanced with spikes, pins, and other signs of torture, has been especially influential at the turn of the twenty-first century. Jannis Kounellis (b. 1936) studied in Rome, where he continues to breath new life into galleries by filling them with instillations of found ob-jects and detritus, indicators of the world of commerce and transportation. One of many works of note is a 1994 installation consisting of thirty years of his work, which he deposited on a boat called *Ionian* and sent to his native port of Piraeus.

The effect of this diaspora of Greek artists on art in Greece was galvaniz-ing. These artists and others—Yannis Gaitis (1923–1984), Takis (b. 1925), Nikos Kessanlis (1930–2004), Kostas Tsoklis (b. 1930), Dimitris Mytaras (b. 1934), Chryssa Romanou (1931–2006), Achilles Droungas (b. 1940), Opy

Zouni (b. 1941), Costas Varotsos (b. 1955), and Yannis Bouteas (b. 1941) are just a few—transformed art. They opened doors to galleries outside Greece, encouraging women and men to choose art as a career. They also liberated art from the imperatives of an obvious visual or thematic link to Hellenicity. Exposure to centuries of making and philosophizing about art in Greece became a conceptual starting point rather than a stylistic or thematic handicap. Their work has moved beyond classically inspired, geometric abstraction to an exploration of the conceptual, technological, and institutional grounds for making art.

The permanent exhibition of highly conceptual works of art in high-traffic locations such as the waterfront of Thessaloniki, busy street corners in Athens, and the stops of the Attiko Metro is a testament to artists' success in broadening public sensibilities.[53] *O dromeas* (The Runner, by Costas Varotsos) on Vasilissas Sofias Avenue in Athens depicts a human figure in motion, but the figure is made of layers upon layers of glass, which slice through the boundaries between created and uncreated space and leave the figure both visible and amorphous, still and moving through space. *Dexileos* (by Dimitris Mytaras) at the Dafni metro stop, a three-meter by eleven-meter (9.8-foot by 36.1-foot) bas-relief, deconstructs the elements of a fourth-century funerary stele from the ancient Kerameikos cemetery. The subject is Dexileos, who died in a battle in Corinth in 394. B.C. The relief topples and dissects the gravestone's inscription, letter by letter.

Mott Street (by Chryssa), a dark aluminum and retoned neon sculpture at the Evangelismos metro stop is named for a street in New York's Chinatown, but it might just as well have been called *Kerameikou Street* after the heart of Athens's new Chinatown.[54] Like many of Chryssa's works, it gives homage to the language of contemporary cities: the "gleaming surfaces of skyscrapers, the blaring intensity of shop signs," and the babel of languages—in this case flashing Chinese letters as they might be seen by one ignorant of Chinese from a speeding car.[55] The message of this glowing, gnarled piece of metal is ambivalent. One struggles to decide whether *Mott Street* celebrates today's cities or finds their angled, kinetic energy menacing. *Mott Street* perfectly expresses the ambivalence of life in Greece's cities, and, as urban living has become a reality for the plurality of Greeks in the past fifty years, for life in Greece today. People appreciate the almost limitless opportunities for self-expression city life gives them. They love the city's energy, its constant motion, the veil of anonymity behind which they sometimes hide. They thrive on contacts with people they don't know, even people from other countries whose languages they can't understand. But the explosive growth of cities has come at great expense to quality of life. People have paid dearly for their narrow apartment view.

THE URBAN LANDSCAPE TODAY

Some of Greece's best designers are aware that they cannot repair the damages of modernization by adding more hard-edged buildings to their cities' endless horizons of concrete. So they are finding new approaches to keep up with the demands of the times, exploring possibilities, such as building downward as well as upward. Perhaps no engineering or building project has improved life for so many people to such positive communal effect as the Attiko Metro in Athens, the underground transport system inaugurated in January 2000 with work continuing into the future. Construction of the Thessaloniki metro, begun in June 2006, will have a similarly positive effect on life in that city.

A key approach designers are putting into effect is adaptive reuse: improving and upgrading through adjustments. It's an old approach with deep roots in Greece. The Parthenon exists today as a ruined classical Greek temple, having survived 2,500 years of invasions, war, and occupations precisely because it found reuse as a Christian church, a Muslim mosque, and today as a UNESCO World Heritage monument. Throughout Greece, *spolia*, building

The New Acropolis Museum (*right*) in Makriyanni, Athens, opposite the Weiler Building of the Center for Acropolis Studies, built as a military hospital (1834–1836). The glass floor reveals the archaeological site below. Photo by author, May 2008.

material from old monuments, appear in later constructions. As already noted, nineteenth-century Athens built its foundations on *spolia* discarded from the Acropolis excavations. In the mid–twentieth century Dimitris Pikionis integrated *spolia* in his harmonious paths on the Acropolis and Philopappos hills. At the end of the same century planners extended Pikionis's work to create an archaeological park in the center of Athens by closing major streets to automobile traffic around the Acropolis—Dionysiou Areopagitou, Agiou Pavlou, Ermou—and turning them into carefully landscaped pedestrian walkways. While the "clarification of the ancient topography" on and around the Acropolis has certainly "enriched the experience of visitors,"[56] as the Ministry wished, more important, it has enhanced the quality of everyday life.

Strategies of adaptive reuse carry the message that Greeks can appreciate their past while enhancing—rather than sacrificing—their quality of life. Coexistence is no easy matter, as the early–twenty-first-century controversy surrounding the New Acropolis Museum and plans to demolish Nos. 17 and 19 Dionysiou Areopagitou make evident. The interests of heritage management, archaeology, planning, development, people in need of housing, tourism—which contributes 18 percent to the country's gross domestic product—and individuals wishing to enjoy an evening stroll just don't coincide. Yet the message from people protesting the planned demolition is equally clear. *Spolia* can become building material. Ruins can become parks. The backsides of buildings that are eyesores can become a garden. Present-day living requires adaptation. It requires the determination to coexist.

The view of the Acropolis is just one of the pleasures of a *volta* (stroll) in Makriyanni. The walk down Dionysiou Areopagitou may become congested, what with street vendors, musicians, and motorcycles illegally taking their stands, and stray soccer balls threatening passersby. Yet for a split second, just as the ball is in hand and ready to fly back in the face of that careless teen, it also becomes obvious that Athens is not just a sea of concrete surrounding ancient monuments. Greece is not just a country of islands and glorious beaches, on the one hand, and environmental problems, on the other. It's a place of vitality and—dare one say it?—beauty: the kind that comes into view where people feel the precarious weight of their variable ancestors, and are determined to coexist with both ancient ghosts and modern neighbors.

NOTES

1. See "The Constitution of Greece," article 24, no. 1, *Hellenic Resources Network* (accessed September 2, 2008), http://www.hri.org/docs/syntagma/artcl25.html.

2. Cordelia Madden, "Museum Viewpoint Dooms Houses," *Athens News*, July 13, 2007 (accessed September 3, 2008), http://www.athensnews.gr/athweb/nathens.prnt_article?e=C&f=13243&t=01&m=A04&aa=1.

3. Mary Adamopoulou, "Katedafiseis ktirion yper tou neou mouseiou" (Demolitions of Buildings for the New Museum), *Ta Nea*, March 28, 2008 (accessed July 14, 2008), http://www.tanea.gr/default.asp?pid=2&ct=4&artid=62374.

4. "Facelift Could Save Landmarks," *Kathimerini English Edition*, June 2, 2008 (accessed September 4, 2008), http://www.ekathimerini.com/4dcgi/_w_articles_politics_2_02/06/2008_97299.

5. Georgios A Panetos, "The Formation of Athenian Neoclassicism," in *Athens: From the Classical Period to the Present Day (5th century B.C. to A.D. 2000)*, ed. M. Korres and Charalambos Bouras (Athens: Kotinos; New Castle, DE: Oak Knoll Press, 2003), 398–435.

6. "Stratiotiko Nosokomeio Makriyanni" (Makriyanni Military Hospital) *Archaeology of the City of Athens* (accessed July 14, 2008), http://www.eie.gr/archaeologia/gr/arxeio_more.aspx?id=163.

7. Andreas Yakoumakatos, *Istoria tis ellinikis architektonikis 20os aionas* (History of Greek Architecture, the Twentieth Century) (Athens: Nefeli, 2004), 17.

8. Mary Beard, *The Parthenon* (London: Profile Books, 2002), 100.

9. Eleana Yalouri, *The Acropolis: Global Fame, Local Claim, Materializing Culture* (Oxford: Berg, 2001), 55.

10. The National Gallery of Greece Web site (accessed July 14, 2008), http://www.nationalgallery.gr/, gives the history of each art form and examples of artists' work from the gallery's collections.

11. The phrase comes from Johann Joachim Winkelmann (1717–1768), whose influential guide to ancient art, *Geschichte der Kunst des Altertums* (Dresden, 1764), idealized the contribution of the Greeks and deeply influenced European neoclassicism.

12. Nikos Vatopoulos, *Facing Athens* (Athens: Potamos, 2003), 33, gives many examples of the popular caryatid type on old Athenian houses.

13. Andreas Ioannou, *Greek Painting: The 19th Century* (Athens: Melissa, 1999), 42. See also Robert Shannon Peckham, *National Histories, Natural States: Nationalism and the Politics of Place in Greece* (London: I. B. Tauris, 2001), 26.

14. Peckham, *National Histories*, 26–27.

15. Peckham, *National Histories*, 27.

16. "Municipal Gallery of Thessaloniki" (accessed July 15, 2008), http://www.thessalonikicity.gr/English/Art_Gallery/municipal_art_gallery.htm.

17. Manos Bires and Maro Kardamitse-Adame, *Neoclassical Architecture in Greece* (Los Angeles: J. Paul Getty Museum, 2004), 284.

18. Savas Condaratos and Manos Bires, *Twentieth Century Architecture—Greece* (Munich: Prestel, 1999), 121.

19. Nikos Papastergiadis, "Glimpses of Cosmopolitanism in the Hospitality of Art," *European Journal of Social Theory* 10, no. 1 (2007): 139–152.

20. Robert D. Kaplan, *Balkan Ghosts: A Journey through History* (New York: Macmillan, 2005), 236.

21. Karin Skousbøll, *Greek Architecture Now* (Athens: Studio Art Bookshop, 2006), 174.

22. Yakoumakatos, *Istoria tis ellinikis architektonikis*, 31–32.

23. Vatopoulos, "Vernacular Architecture in Greece," *Kathimerini English Edition*, July 7, 2005 (accessed September 3, 2008), http://www.ekathimerini.com/4dcgi/_w_articles_civ_2_07/07/2005_58353.

24. Vatopoulos, *Facing Athens*, 141.

25. Cordelia Madden, "Museum Viewpoint Dooms House," *Athens News*, July 13, 2007, A4.

26. Dimitris Rigopoulos, "A New Approach to Greek Buildings of Interwar Period," *Kathimerini English Edition*, November 3, 2005 (accessed September 3, 2008), http://www.ekathimerini.com/4dcgi/_w_articles_civ_2_03/11/2005_62611.

27. Yakoumakatos, *Istoria tis ellinikis architektonikis*, 39.

28. Yakoumakatos, *Istoria tis ellinikis architektonikis*, 45–46, tells how Le Corbusier selected Athens as the site of the fourth Congrès International d'Architecture Moderne (CIAM) in 1933.

29. Dimitris Pikionis, "Autobiographical Notes," from "Dimitris Pikionis, Architect 1887–1968 'A Sentimental Topography,'" *Myrobiblios* (accessed September 3, 2008), http://www.eikastikon.gr/arxitektoniki/pikionis/texts.html in Greek, and http://www.myriobiblos.gr/afieromata/pikionis/en_txt_cv_self.html.

30. Skousbøll, *Greek Architecture Now*, 40.

31. Pikionis, "Autobiographical Notes."

32. Le Corbusier, *Toward a New Architecture* (1927), trans. Frederick Etchelles (New York: Dover, 1986), 20.

33. Eleni Bastéa, "Dimitris Pikionis and Sedad Eldem: Parallel Reflections on Vernacular and National Architecture," in *The Usable Past. Greek Metahistories*, ed. K. S. Brown and Yannis Hamilakis (Lanham, MD: Lexington Books, 2002), 159.

34. Michael Lancaster, *The New European Landscape* (St. Louis: Butterworth Architecture, 1994), 120.

35. "The Endangered Refugee Housing Complex...," *Kathimerini English Edition*, September 1, 2004 (accessed September 3, 2008), http://www.ekathimerini.com/4dcgi/_w_articles_politics_2_01/09/2004_46799.

36. Yakoumakatos, *Istoria tis ellinikis architektonikis*, 59–63, describes the conditions for architects.

37. Skousbøll, *Greek Architecture Now*, 47, quotes these figures. Doxiadis's team produced maps and books documenting Greece's destruction.

38. Vincent Scully, "The Athens Hilton: A Study in Vandalism," *Architectural Forum* (July 1963): 102, quoted in Yalouri, *The Acropolis*, 154.

39. Yakoumakatos, *Istoria tis ellinikis architektonikis*, 99.

40. "Five Greek Architects Speak Out," *Kathimerini English Edition*, March 13, 2004 (accessed September 3, 2008), http://www.ekathimerini.com/4dcgi/_w_articles_ell_2_13/03/2004_40645.

41. Yakoumakatos, *Istoria tis ellinikis architektonikis*, 153–165, discusses short circuits in the processes Greece follows in building public buildings.

42. "Five Greek Architects Speak Out."

43. Eleni Fessa-Emmanouil, "I proti fasi tis ktiriakis istorias" (The First Phase of the Building History), *Kathimerini* (issue of *Epta Imeres* devoted to the Megaro Mousikis),

November 2, 2003, http://www.kathimerini.gr/4dcgi/_w_articles_kathglobal_2_02/11/2003_1281108.

44. Drossoula Vassiliou Elliott, "Message from the Founders of the Museum," *Atelier Spyros Vassiliou* (accessed September 3, 2008), http://www.spyrosvassiliou.org/atelier/index_en.html.

45. For a fictionalized account of the life of Altamura, see the historical novel by Rhea Galanaki, *Eleni, or Nobody*, trans. David Connolly (Evanston, IL: Northwestern University Press, 2002).

46. The Benaki Museum holds Nelly's photographic archive and gives a description of her work and samples of her work on its Web site at http://www.benaki.gr/index.asp?id=1020102&lang=en.

47. http://www.benaki.gr/index.asp?id=1020102&lang=en.

48. Introduction to the exhibit, "Nelly: From Athens to New York: The Work of Elli Seraidari" at the International Center of Photography (December 5, 1997–February 22, 1998) (accessed July 18, 2008), http://museum.icp.org/museum/exhibitions/nelly/.

49. Eleana Yalouri describes present-day reactions to the photographs in *The Acropolis: Global Fame, Local Claim* (Oxford: Berg, 2001), 159–162.

50. The Benaki Museum holds Voula Papaioannou's photographic archive and gives a description and samples of her work on its Web site at http://www.benaki.gr/index.asp?id=1020103&lang=en.

51. The phrase is from Eleni Vakalo, *I fysiognomia tis metapolemikis technis stin Ellada* (The Physiognomy of Postwar Art in Greece), vol. 3, *The Myth of Hellenicity* (Athens: Kedros, 1983).

52. *Charlie Rose*, "A Discussion about the PaceWildenstein Gallery," with Arne Glimcher, Lucas Samaras, Chuck Close, Kiki Smith, December 28, 2000 (accessed September 3, 2008), http://www.charlierose.com/shows/2000/12/28/2/a-discussion-about-the-pacewildenstein-gallery.

53. "Art Program" (accessed September 3, 2008), http://www.ametro.gr/page/default.asp?la=1&id=41.

54. Johanna Kakassis, "Athens: Take One Forlorn Ancient District, Add Chic and Stir," *New York Times*, January 21, 2007 (accessed September 4, 2008), http://travel.nytimes.com/2007/01/21/travel/21next.html.

55. David Ebony, "Chryssa at Castelli, *Art in America* 84 (October 1996): 117–118.

56. Hellenic Ministry of Culture, "Unification of the Archaeological Sites of Athens" (accessed July 21, 2008), http://www.yppo.gr/4/e40.jsp?obj_id=90.

Glossary

Asia Minor catastrophe   Greek *mikrasiatiki katastrofi*, or simply *katastrofi*, refers to events following the Greek defeat in the Greco-Turkish war of 1922, when the Christian population living in Asia Minor, the west coast of what is now Turkey, was ravaged and Smyrna's Christian quarters burned. Greek civilian casualties in Asia Minor are estimated at 100,000 dead, 160,000 deported to an almost-certain death, and 190,000 missing. With the Treaty of Lausanne in 1923, 1.3 million Greek Orthodox refugees arrived in Greece.

bouzouki   A plucked string instrument in the lute family with a pear-shaped body and long neck, related to the ancient Greek *pandouris*, Turkish *saz*, and traditional *tabouras*. Historically the bouzouki was *trichordo* (with three pairs of strings). It became *tetrachordo* (with four pairs of strings) in the 1950s and aligned its tuning with the guitar. The plural, *bouzoukia*, refers to nightclubs with loud bouzouki music, popular singers, and crowds dancing and throwing carnations (formerly plates).

Byzantine   Word used to name the eastern Roman Empire (A.D. 330–1453) centered in Constantinople (formerly *Byzantium*, renamed by Emperor Constantine), which flourished as Rome went into decline. It merged Christianity and Greek culture, using Greek as the language of religion, culture, commerce, and administration. The Byzantine Empire ruled over Greek territory through most of this period.

Civil War   Greek *emfylios*. The textbook dates are 1945 to 1949, but the war had roots in rivalries between resistance movements fighting the Axis occupation: communist-led EAM-ELAS (Ethniko Apeleftherotiko Metopo, Greek

Resistance Movement–Ellinikos Laikos Apeleftherotikos Stratos, Greek People's Liberation Army) and anticommunist EDES (Ethnikos Dimokratikos Ellinikos Syndesmos, National Republican Greek League). Disagreements centered on who would rule Greece after World War II. Fighting broke out from December 1944 to February 1945 in the Battle of Athens, then in the countryside from 1946 to 1949 between the Communist Democratic Army of Greece (DAG) and the Greek army with U.S. reinforcements. The war ended in communist defeat.

demotic   From Greek *demos* (people), the adjective means "folk" or "vernacular" in several contexts, depending on the inflection. Demotic Greek (*dimotiki*) refers to vernacular Greek as the language evolved through the centuries from ancient Greek. In the nineteenth and twentieth centuries it found itself in a contest with *katharevousa*, an archaizing form that purged Greek of foreign words and modified its grammar to approximate ancient Greek. *Dimotiki* became official, standard Greek in 1976. Demotic music (*dimotika*) is folk music.

dictatorship   Greek *diktatoria*, also known as the junta. The repressive regime of 1967–1974 led by colonels who organized a coup on April 21, 1967, on the pretext that scheduled May elections would have opened the door to communists. The dictatorship imploded after its failed efforts to overthrow Cyprus's President Makarios resulted in Turkey's invasion and occupation of 37 percent of Cyprus.

Evzones   Greek *eu* + *zone* (well belted). Members of the elite unit who guard the Tomb of the Unknown Soldier before Greek Parliament. Their full dress uniform, worn on national holidays and Sundays, includes the *fustanella*, a white skirt with four hundred pleats, each representing a year in the Ottoman occupation.

filotimo   Literally "love of honor," this highly desirable social value does not have an exact equivalent in English, though *integrity* is a close approximation. It bears the sense that a person has internalized the inclination to do the right thing. *Filotimo* is not a self-attribute but a quality that others recognize in a person. It requires standing tall under various circumstances, carrying through with one's duties in a decent, noble, principled, generous way, and rising above the call of duty to do right at the right moment. It involves a display of personal dignity, sacrifice, and respect for others and oneself. *Filotimo* carries the weight of national honor and is part of a Greek national unconscious. The opposite is *afilotimia* (lack of *filotimo*), a strong insult implying almost a dispossession of Greekness.

filoxenia   Greek *filos* + *xenos*, love of stranger, the word means hospitality and signifies a generous approach to treating strangers with food, spirits, and feelings of warmth and family togetherness. Greeks see this as a nationally defining attribute.

frappé   A cold, frothy coffee drink made from Nescafé instant coffee, with optional milk and sugar, and drunk slowly with a straw. Invented in Thessaloniki in 1957, it has become a kind of national drink in Greece.

frontistirio   Private tuition centers for grade and high school students. The majority of Greek students attend *frontistirio* in grade school to learn at least one foreign language (English is first, followed by German, French, Italian, and Spanish). High school *frontistirio* is a cramming school for all subjects that prepares students for *Panelladikes exetaseis*, required college entrance exams. Greek parents spend a large proportion of their salaries on *frontistiria* (plural) for their children.

hasapiko   "Butcher's dance" in 4/4 (slow *hasapiko*) and 2/4 (fast *hasapiko* or *hasaposerviko*). The *syrtaki* is a relatively new, choreographed version of the *hasapiko*. The best-known *syrtaki* is "Zorba's Dance" by Mikis Theodorakis.

icon   Greek *eikon* (image), a religious picture of a sacred person and scene used in Greek Orthodox practices. Icons refer generally to all such two-dimensional images, whether freestanding or murals, and more narrowly to painted images on wood. Icons are venerated but not worshiped, as Greek Orthodoxy holds to the commandment against the worship of idols. *Iconostasis* is the icon-decorated altar screen that divides the altar from the nave of a Greek Orthodox Church. Iconoclasm was an eighth-century movement that condemned the use of icons in the church. The movement failed, and icons are a key element of Greek Orthodox religious practices.

komboloi   Worry beads: a string of an odd number of traditionally amber beads (turquoise, obsidian, resin, glass, metal, and plastic are also used) with a fixed bead and tasseled end, manipulated in the hands, usually of men, to release tension. *Komboloi* (from Greek *kombos*, or "knot") is etymologically related to *komboskini* (knotted prayer rope) but bears no religious significance.

koumbaria   From Italian *compare*, the institution whereby an individual (masculine *koumbaros*, feminine *koumbara*) sponsors a couple in marriage or a child in baptism, thus creating a tie as strong as kinship. *Koumbaria* is used to affirm friendships but also to create patron–client ties of political significance.

laika   From Greek *laikos* (popular), *laika* (singular *laiko*), popular music developed in the 1950s and 1960s, when the bouzouki became a mainstream instrument. *Rebetika*, music from Indian films, the singing styles of Turkish and Arabic singers, and Byzantine chanting were strong influences.

laiki   From Greek *laikos*, the name for farmers' market.

March 25   Greece's national and religious holiday commemorating both the beginning of the Greek War of Independence in 1821 and the feast day of the Annunciation.

mati   Greek word for *eye* also used to name blue-eyed charms that guard against the *kako mati* (evil eye). Greek culture considers eyes to be powerful outward emitters of psychic energy. *Kako mati* is the conscious or unconscious gaze of *fthonos* (envy, jealous admiration, or jealousy) that causes harm. The Greek Orthodox Church as well as popular belief recognizes the *kako mati*, which it calls *vaskania* (from Latin *fascinare*, to cast a spell). Prayers and popular practices are used to dispel its ill effects.

Megali Idea   The "Great Idea" put forth by Ioannis Kolettis in 1844 challenging Greece to expand its borders to encompass historically Greek territories with large Greek populations. This idea sparked Greece's territorial expansion from 1844 to 1922 and ended with the *mikrasiatiki katastrofi*.

metanastes   Greek word for immigrants, emigrants, and internal migrants. From 1893 to 1974 more than 1.5 million Greeks emigrated worldwide, especially to the United States, Canada, Australia, Germany, and South Africa. Since 1989 Greece has received more than 1 million immigrants from Eastern Europe, Asia, and Africa. Throughout the century, people were also moving from the countryside to cities. Greece continues to lose its educated population to universities and jobs abroad.

metapolitefsi   Greek *meta + politevma* (change of political system) names the period after the dictatorship's fall in July 1974 when Greece made its transition to democracy. An interim government under Constantine Karamanlis prepared the country for legislative elections (November 1974), followed by a referendum to abolish the monarchy (December 1974), and the promulgation of a new constitution defining Greece as the Hellenic Parliamentary Republic.

name day   Greek *onomastiki yiorti*, the saint or feast day associated with a person's given name. For many people name days are more self-defining than birthdays. People celebrating name days fill their homes with sweets to treat anticipated visitors.

occupation   Greek *katohi* (*kata + eho*, hold against), refers to the joint German, Italian, and Bulgarian Axis occupation of Greece from April 1941 to October 1944.

Orthodox   Greek *orthodoxia* (*ortho + doxa*, true belief), the Christian faith with which more than 97 percent of Greek citizens identify on some level. The Greek Orthodox Church is part of the Eastern Orthodox Church, the second-largest single Christian communion in the world, which believes it is the authentic, original church established by the apostles of Jesus Christ, and as such, preserves the teachings and traditions of early Christianity.

Ottoman   The Turkish empire with its capital in Constantinople. It ruled over much of Greece from 1453 to 1832. Greeks refer to Ottoman rule as *Turkokratia* (Turkish occupation) and remember it as a period of oppression.

Panayia   Greek *pan + ayia* (all holy), the popular name for the Virgin Mary. Other names are Theotokos (birth giver of God) and Despoina (lady)—never Maria or Parthena (virgin). *Panayia* yields two common Greek names, the feminine Panayiota and masculine Panayiotis.

Panelladikes   Greek *pan + ellada* (all Greece), Panhellenic entrance university exams compulsory for high school graduates who wish to attend a public university or technical institution. Students take six exams, whose subjects depend on their orientation (humanities, science, or technology) and an additional one to two exams for entrance to certain schools. Subjects are ancient Greek, biology, business organization and administration, chemistry and biochemistry, economics, electronics, history, Latin, mathematics and statistics, modern Greek, Greek literature, physics, and programming.

panigyri Greek *pan* + *gyro* (all around), this "gathering of everyone from all around" takes place when a village or neighborhood church celebrates its saint or feast day. It begins the day before the event and continues through the feast day. The celebration consists of religious services and the two-day party (*glenti*) of food, music, and dancing in the church *plateia* (square). Itinerant vendors line the square and surrounding streets with their goods.

paradosi Greek *para* + *dido* (give over), the name for "tradition," something Greeks believe links them to ancestral customs. The adjective *paradosiakos* (traditional) yields words like *paradosiaka*, referring to traditional houses, music, and so on.

parea Group of friends.

periptero Kiosk, usually a four-sided, enclosed booth with a broad awning extending beyond its four external walls and protecting the merchandise that faces outward to the sidewalk or street where the kiosk stands. *Periptera* (plural) vend newspapers, magazines, cigarettes, snacks, drinks, maps, and other merchandise. They are ubiquitous in Greece.

rebetika A type of popular music that developed in Greece after Asia Minor refugees arrived in the 1920s, when refugee musicians combined their talents with musicians of the poor neighborhoods of Athens, Piraeus, and other port cities who sang songs about drug abuse, prison, and violence. *Rebetika* popularized the bouzouki as the lead instrument in Greek music. There are thousands of *rebetika* songs, many still in circulation and enjoyed by people of all ages.

rousfeti Reciprocal dispensation of favors, especially between civilians and politicians, who exchange votes for favors. *Rousfeti* is widespread, though also publicly criticized, and connects people in patron–client relations.

Syntagma Greek word for constitution (*syn* + *tasso*, to arrange or appoint together), which has also attached itself to the large square where a military coup and popular uprising on September 3, 1943 (in front of what was then the palace and today is the *vouli*, parliament building) forced King Otto to produce a constitution.

vouli Greek word for council, names both Parliament and the parliament building facing Syntagma Square.

xenitia From Greek *xenos* (stranger, foreigner), *xenitia* is the experience of living as a stranger in a foreign land. The word has been in usage for centuries and suggests estrangement, alienation, and nostalgia for the distant homeland.

zeibekiko Solo improvisational dance in 9/4 traditionally by a man, though women now also perform it.

Selected Bibliography

CHAPTER 1: THE LAND, PEOPLE, AND HISTORY

About Greece. Athens: Ministry of Press and Mass Media, Secretariat General of Information, 2007.

Athanassoglou-Kallmyer, Nina M. *French Images from the Greek War of Independence (1821–1830): Art and Politics under the Restoration.* New Haven, CT: Yale University Press, 1989.

Brewer, David. *The Greek War of Independence: The Struggle for Freedom from Ottoman Oppression and the Birth of the Modern Greek Nation.* Woodstock, NY: Overlook Press, 2001.

Brown, Keith, and Yannis Hamilakis, eds. *The Usable Past: Greek Metahistories.* Lanham, MD: Lexington Books, 2002.

Campbell, John, and Philip Sherrard. *Modern Greece.* New York: Praeger, 1968.

Carabott, Philip, and Thanasis D. Sfikas, eds. *The Greek Civil War: Essays on a Conflict of Exceptionalism and Silences.* Aldershot, UK: Ashgate, 2004.

Clark, Bruce. *Twice a Stranger: Greece, Turkey and the Minorities They Expelled.* London: Granta, 2005.

Clogg, Richard. *A Concise History of Greece.* Cambridge: Cambridge University Press, 2002.

Clogg, Richard. *The Movement for Greek Independence, 1770–1821: A Collection of Documents.* New York: Barnes & Noble, 1976.

Close, David H. *Greece since 1945.* London: Pearson Education, 2002.

Close, David H., ed. *The Greek Civil War, 1943–1950: Studies of Polarization.* London: Routledge, 1993.

Constantinidis, Stratos E. *Greece in Modern Times: An Annotated Bibliography of Works Published in English in Twenty-Two Academic Disciplines during the Twentieth Century.* Lanham, MD: Scarecrow Press, 2000.

Dakin, Douglas. *The Greek Struggle for Independence, 1821–1833.* Berkeley: University of California Press, 1973.

Damaskos, Dimitris, and Dimitris Plantzos. *A Singular Antiquity: Archaeology and Hellenic Identity in Twentieth-Century Greece.* Athens: Mouseio Benaki 3rd Supplement, 2008.

Dobkin, Marjorie Housepian. *Smyrna 1922: The Destruction of a City.* New York: Newmark Press, 1998.

Eugenides, Jeffrey. *Middlesex.* New York: Picador/Farrar, Straus & Giroux, 2003.

Faubion, James D. *Modern Greek Lessons: A Primer in Historical Constructivism.* Princeton, NJ: Princeton University Press, 1993.

Fermor, Patrick Leigh. *Mani: Travels in the Southern Peloponnese.* [1955]. New York: New York Review of Books, 2006.

Fermor, Patrick Leigh. *Roumeli: Travels in Northern Greece.* New York: Harper and Row, 1966.

Fleming, K. E. *Greece: A Jewish History.* Princeton, NJ: Princeton University Press, 2008.

Fleming, K. E. *The Muslim Bonaparte: Diplomacy and Orientalism in Ali Pasha's Greece.* Princeton, NJ: Princeton University Press, 1999.

Gage, Nicholas. *Portrait of Greece.* New York: New York Times Book, 1971.

Gallant, Thomas W. *Modern Greece.* Brief Histories. London: Arnold, 2001.

Gerolymatos, André. *Red Acropolis, Black Terror: The Greek Civil War and the Origins of Soviet-American Rivalry, 1943–1949.* New York: Basic Books, 2004.

Gerolymatos, André. *The Balkan Wars: Conquest, Revolution, and Retribution from the Ottoman Era to the Twentieth Century and Beyond.* New York: Basic Books, 2002.

Gourgouris, Stathis. *Dream Nation: Enlightenment, Colonization, and the Institution of Modern Greece.* Stanford, CA: Stanford University Press, 1996.

Halkias, Alexandra. *The Empty Cradle of Democracy: Sex, Abortion, and Nationalism in Modern Greece.* Durham, NC: Duke University Press, 2004.

Harlaftis, Gelina. *A History of Greek-Owned Shipping: The Making of an International Tramp Fleet, 1830 to the Present Day.* London: Routledge, 1996.

Herzfeld, Michael. *Anthropology Through the Looking-Glass: Critical Ethnography in the Margins of Europe.* Cambridge: Cambridge University Press, 1987.

Herzfeld, Michael. *Portrait of a Greek Imagination: An Ethnographic Biography of Andreas Nenedakis.* Chicago: University of Chicago Press, 1998.

Hionidou, Violetta. *Famine and Death in Occupied Greece, 1941–1944.* Cambridge Studies in Population, Economy and Society in Past Time. Cambridge: Cambridge University Press, 2006.

Hoe, Susanna. *Crete: Women, History, Books and Places.* Of Islands and Women, livret no. 2. Oxford, UK: Women's History Press, 2005.

Holden, David. *Greece without Columns: The Making of the Modern Greeks.* Philadelphia: Lippincott, 1972.

Holland, R. F., and Diana Weston Markides. *Britain and the Hellenes: Struggles for Mastery in the Eastern Mediterranean 1850–1960.* New York: Oxford University Press, 2006.

Iatrides, John O., and Linda Wrigley, eds. *Greece at the Crossroads: The Civil War and Its Legacy.* University Park: Pennsylvania State University Press, 1995.

Kaloudis, George Stergiou. *Modern Greek Democracy: The End of a Long Journey?* Lanham, MD: University Press of America, 2000.

Kalyvas, Stathis N. *The Logic of Violence in Civil War.* New York: Cambridge University Press, 2006.

Karakasidou, Anastasia. *Fields of Wheat, Hills of Blood. Passages to Nationhood in Greek Macedonia, 1870–1990.* Chicago: University of Chicago Press, 1997.

Kessel, Dmitri. *Hellada tou '44.* Athens: Amos, 1997.

Kitromilides, Paschalis, ed. *Eleftherios Venizelos: The Trials of Statesmanship.* Edinburgh: Edinburgh University Press, 2006.

Koliopoulos, John S., and Thanos M. Veremis. *Greece, the Modern Sequel.* London: Hurst, 2002.

Kontogiorgi, Elisabeth. *Population Exchange in Greek Macedonia: The Rural Settlement of Refugees 1922–1930.* Oxford, UK: Clarendon, 2006.

Koundoura, Maria. *The Greek Idea: The Formation of National and Transnational Identities.* New York: I. B. Tauris, 2007.

Kourvetaris, George A., and Betty A. Dobratz. *A Profile of Modern Greece: In Search of Identity.* Oxford, UK: Clarendon, 1987.

Lavdas, Kostas A. *The Europeanization of Greece: Interest Politics and the Crises of Integration.* New York: St. Martin's, 1997.

Lewkowicz, Bea. *The Jewish Community of Salonika: History, Memory, Identity.* London: Vallentine Mitchell, 2006.

Matsas, Michael. *The Illusion of Safety: The Story of the Greek Jews during World War II.* New York: Pella, 1997.

Mazower, Mark. *Inside Hitler's Greece: The Experience of Occupation, 1941–44.* New Haven, CT: Yale University Press, 1995.

Mazower, Mark. *Salonica, City of Ghosts: Christians, Muslims, and Jews, 1430–1950.* New York: Alfred A. Knopf, 2005.

Mazower, Mark, ed. *After the War Was Over: Reconstructing the Family, Nation, and State in Greece, 1943–1960.* Princeton, NJ: Princeton University Press, 2000.

Michaels, Anne. *Fugitive Pieces.* New York: Vintage, 1998.

Milton, Giles. *Paradise Lost: Smyrna 1922: The Destruction of a Christian City in the Islamic World.* New York: Basic Books, 2008.

Panourgia, Neni. *Dangerous Citizens: The Greek Left and the Terror of the State.* Bronx, NY: Fordham University Press, 2008.

Paxson, Heather. *Making Modern Mothers: Ethics and Family Planning in Urban Greece*. Berkeley: University of California Press, 2004.

Peckham, Robert Shannan. *National Histories, Natural States: Nationalism and the Politics of Place in Greece*. London: I. B. Tauris, 2001.

Petrakis, Marina. *The Metaxas Myth: Dictatorship and Propaganda in Greece*. London: Tauris Academic Studies, 2006.

Pettifer, James. *The Greeks: The Land and People since the War*. London: Viking, 1993.

Pirounakis, Nicholas G. *The Greek Economy: Past, Present and Future*. New York: St. Martin's Press, 1997.

Psychoundakis, George, and Patrick Leigh Fermor. *The Cretan Runner: His Story of the German Occupation*. 1955. Reprint, London: Penguin, 1999.

Sevillias, Errikos. *Athens, Auschwitz*. Athens: Lycabettus Press, 1983.

Sfikas, Thanasis D. *The British Labour Government and the Greek Civil War 1945–1949: The Imperialism of "Non-Intervention."* Keele, Staffordshire: Ryburn Publishing, 1994.

Smith, Michael Llewellyn. *Ionian Vision; Greece in Asia Minor, 1919–1922*. New York: St. Martin's Press, 1973.

Talalay, Lauren E. *Deities, Dolls, and Devices: Neolithic Figurines from Franchthi Cave, Greece*. Bloomington: Indiana University Press, 1993.

Triandafyllidou, Anna, and Ruby Gropas. *European Immigration: A Sourcebook*. Aldershot, UK: Ashgate, 2007.

Vakalopoulos, Apostolos E. *The Greek Nation, 1453–1669: The Cultural and Economic Background of Modern Greek Society*. New Brunswick, NJ: Rutgers University Press, 1975.

Valakos, Stratis, et al. *The Amphibians and Reptiles of Greece*. Frankfurt: Chimaira, 2008.

Van Dyck, Karen, and John Chapple. *Greece: Insight Guides*. Hong Kong: APA Publications, 1995.

Veremis, Thanos M. *The Military in Greek Politics: From Independence to Democracy*. Black Rose Books, 1997.

Veremis, Thanos M., and Mark Dragoumis. *Historical Dictionary of Greece*. Metuchen, NJ: Scarecrow, 1995.

Veremis, Thanos M., and Mark Dragoumis. *Greece*. World Bibliographical Series 17. Santa Barbara, CA: Clio Press, 1998.

Vlachos, Helen. *House Arrest*. London: Deutsch, 1970.

Voglis, Polymeris. *Becoming a Subject: Political Prisoners in the Greek Civil War*. Oxford, U.K. Berghahn Books, 2002.

Vryonis, Spyros. *The Mechanism of Catastrophe: The Turkish Pogrom of September 6–7, 1955, and the Destruction of the Greek Community in Istanbul*. New York: Greekworks.com, 2005.

Woodhouse, C. M. *The Rise and Fall of the Greek Colonels*. New York: Franklin Watts, 1985.

Zacharia, Katerina. *Hellenisms: Culture, Identity, and Ethnicity from Antiquity to Modernity.* Aldershot, UK: Ashgate Variorum, 2008.

WEB SITES

"The Constitution of Greece" at the Hellenic Resources Network Document Archive, http://www.hri.org/docs/syntagma/.
"Generation €700," http://g700.blogspot.com/.
Greekworks.com, http://www.greekworks.com/content/index.php.
Hellenic Ministry of Foreign Affairs, http://www.mfa.gr/en.
Kathimerini English Edition online, www.ekathimerini.com.
"Odysseus" at the Hellenic Ministry of Culture, http://odysseus.culture.gr.
Ta Nea online, www.tanea.gr.

CHAPTER 2: RELIGION

Alexiou, Margaret. *The Ritual Lament in Greek Tradition.* Cambridge: Cambridge University Press, 1974.
Cavarnos, Constantine. *Modern Greek Thought.* Belmont, MA: Institute for Byzantine and Modern Greek Studies, 1986.
Danforth, Loring M. *The Death Rituals of Rural Greece.* Photography by Alexander Tsiaras. Princeton, NJ: Princeton University Press, 1982.
Danforth, Loring M. *Firewalking and Religious Healing: The Anastenaria of Greece and the American Firewalking Movement.* Princeton, NJ: Princeton University Press, 1989.
Dubisch, Jill. *In a Different Place: Pilgrimage, Gender, and Politics at a Greek Island Shrine.* Princeton, NJ: Princeton University Press, 1995.
Florenskii, Pavel Aleksandrovich, et al. *Iconostasis.* Trans. Olga Andrejev and Donald Sheehan. Crestwood, NY: St. Vladimir's Seminary Press, 1996.
Gonomos, Dimitri. *Byzantine Hymnography and Byzantine Chant.* Brookline, MA: Hellenic College Press, 1984.
Hart, Laurie Kain. *Time, Religion, and the Social Experience in Rural Greece.* Lanham, Md.: Rowman & Littlefield, 1992.
John of Damascus. *On the Divine Images: Three Apologies against Those Who Attack the Divine Images.* Crestwood, NY: St. Vladimir's Seminary Press, 1980.
Markides, Kyriacos C. *The Magus of Strovolos: The Extraordinary World of a Spiritual Healer.* London: Arkana, 1985.
Markides, Kyriacos C. *The Mountain of Silence: A Search for Orthodox Spirituality.* New York: Doubleday, 2001.
Merrill, Christopher. *Things of the Hidden God: Journey to the Holy Mountain.* New York: Random House, 2005.
Norwich, John Julius. *A Short History of Byzantium.* New York: Vintage Books, 1999.

Ouspensky, Léonide, and Vladimir Lossky. *The Meaning of Icons*. Crestwood, NY: St. Vladimir's Seminary Press, 1982.

Panourgia, E. Neni K. *Fragments of Death, Fables of Identity: An Athenian Anthropography*. Madison: University of Wisconsin Press, 1995.

Papanikolaou, Aristotle and Elizabeth Prodromou, eds. *Thinking through Faith. New Perspectives from Orthodox Christian Scholars*. Crestwood, NY: St. Vladimir's Press, 2008.

Patrinacos, Rev. Nicon D. *A Dictionary of Greek Orthodoxy*. Minneapolis: Light and Life Publishing, 1984.

Ricks, David, and Paul Magdalino. *Byzantium and the Modern Greek Identity*. Aldershot, UK: Ashgate, 1998.

Samaras, Nicholas. *Hands of the Saddlemaker*. New Haven, CT: Yale University Press, 1992.

Samaras, Nicholas. *Survivors of a Missing Earth*. Salzburg, Austria: University of Salzburg Press, 1997.

Sherrard, Philip. *Athos, the Mountain of Silence*. Oxford: Oxford University Press, 1960.

Sherrard, Philip. *Church, Papacy, and Schism: A Theological Enquiry*. London: S.P.C.K., 1978.

Sherrard, Philip. *The Greek East and Latin West: A Study in the Christian Tradition:* London: Oxford University Press, 1959.

Sherrard, Philip. *The Sacred in Life an Art*. Ipswich: Golgonooza, 1990.

Sherrard, Philip, G. E. H. Palmer, and Kallistos Ware, trans. *The Philokalia: The Complete Text, Compiled by St. Nikodimos of the Holy Mountain and St. Makarios of Corinth*. 4 vols. London: Faber and Faber: 1979–1995.

Stavropoulos, Archimandrite Christoforos. *Partakers of Divine Nature*. Trans. Rev. Dr. Stanley Harakas. Minneapolis: Light and Life Publishing, 1976.

Stewart, Charles. *Demons and the Devil: Moral Imagination in Modern Greek Culture*. Princeton, NJ: Princeton University Press, 1991.

Studites, Theodore. *On the Holy of Icons*. Trans. Catharine P. Roth. Crestwood, NY: St. Vladimir's Seminary Press, 1981.

Theokritoff, Elizabeth. *The Cambridge Companion to Orthodox Christian Theology*. Ed. Mary B. Cunningham. Cambridge, UK: Cambridge University Press, forthcoming.

Tolidis, Tryfon. *An Almost Pure, Empty Walking*. New York: Penguin, 2006.

Tyneh, Carl S. *Orthodox Christianity: Overview and Bibliography*. Hauppauge, NY: Nova Publishers, 2002.

Ware, Timothy. *The Orthodox Church*. London: Penguin Books, 1963.

Yannaras, Christos. *Elements of Faith: An Introduction to Orthodox Theology*. Edinburgh: T&T Clark, 1991.

WEB SITES

Greek Orthodox Archdiocese of America, http://www.goarch.org/.

Mt. Athos, http://www.inathos.gr/.

CHAPTER 3: SOCIETY

Campbell, John K. *Honour, Family, and Patronage: A Study of Institutions and Moral Values in a Greek Mountain Community.* Oxford: Clarendon Press, 1964.

Cowan, Jane. *Dance and the Body Politic in Northern Greece.* Princeton, NJ: Princeton University Press, 1990.

Doumanis, Mariella. *Mothering in Greece: From Collectivism to Individualism.* London: Academic Press, 1983.

Dubisch, Jill, ed. *Gender and Power in Rural Greece.* Princeton, NJ: Princeton University Press, 1986.

Dubisch, Jill. "'Foreign Chickens' and Other Outsiders: Gender and Community in Greece." *American Ethnologist* 20, no. 2 (1993): 272–287.

Du Boulay, Juliet. *Portrait of a Greek Mountain Village.* Oxford: Clarendon Press, 1974.

Friedl, Ernestine. *Vasilika: A Village in Modern Greece.* New York: Rinehart and Winston, 1962.

Georgas, J. "Changing Family Values in Greece: From Collectivism to Individualism." *Journal of Cross-Cultural Psychology* 20 (1989): 80–91.

Halkias, Alexandra. *The Empty Cradle of Democracy: Sex, Abortion and Nationalism in Modern Greece.* Durham, NC: Duke University Press, 2004.

Herzfeld, Michael. *The Poetics of Manhood: Contest and Identity in a Cretan Mountain Village.* Princeton, NJ: Princeton University Press, 1985.

Herzfeld, Michael. "The Significance of the Insignificant: Blasphemy as Ideology." *Man,* n.s., 19, no. 4 (December 1984): 653–664.

Hirschon, Renee. *Heirs of the Greek Catastrophe: The Social Life of Asia Minor Refugees in Piraeus.* Oxford: Clarendon Press, 1988.

Holst-Warhaft, Gail. *Dangerous Voices: Women's Laments in Greek Literature.* New York: Routledge, 1992.

Just, Roger. *A Greek Island Cosmos: Kinship and Community on Meganisi.* Oxford: J. Currey, 2000.

Kalfopoulou, Adrianne. *Broken Greek: A Language to Belong.* Austin, TX: Plain View Press, 2006.

Kanelli, Sheelagh. *Earth and Water: A Marriage into Greece.* New York: Coward-McCann, 1965.

Karafili, Dora. *Things of the Household* (in Greek). Athens: Maistros, 2003.

Kirtsoglou, Elizabeth. *For the Love of Women: Gender, Identity and Same-Sex Relations in a Greek Provicial Town.* New York: Routledge, 2004.

Lardinois, André, and Laura McClure, eds. *Making Silence Speak: Women's Voices in Greek Literature and Society.* Princeton, NJ: Princeton University Press, 2001.

Loizos, Peter, and Evthymios Papataxiarchis, eds. *Contested Identities: Gender and Kinship in Modern Greece.* Princeton, NJ: Princeton University Press, 1991.

Mazower, Mark, ed. *Networks of Power in Modern Greece: Essays in Honour of John Campbell.* New York: Columbia University Press, 2008.

McNeill, William H. *The Metamorphosis of Greece since World War II.* Chicago: University of Chicago, 1978.

Moutsatsos, Chrisy. *Transnational Beauty Culture and Local Bodies: An Ethnographic Account of Consumption and Identity in Urban Greece.* Ph.D. diss., University of California, Irvine, 2001.

Panourgia, E. Neni K. *Fragments of Death, Fables of Identity: An Athenian Anthropography.* Madison: University of Wisconsin Press, 1995.

Papadiamantis, Alexandros. *The Murderess.* Trans. Peter Levi. London: Writers and Readers Publishing, 1983.

Papandreou, Nick. *A Crowded Heart.* New York: Picador, 1999.

Pettifer, James. *The Greeks: The Land and People since the War.* London: Penguin, 1993.

Pollis, Adamantia. "Political Implications of the Modern Greek Concept of Self." *British Journal of Sociology* 16, no. 1 (March 1965): 29–47.

Sant Cassia, Paul, ed. *The Making of the Modern Greek Family: Marriage and Exchange in Nineteenth-Century Athens.* New York: Cambridge University Press, 1992.

Sarrinikolaou, George: *Facing Athens: Encounters with the Modern City.* New York: North Point Press, 2004.

Storace, Patricia. *Dinner with Persephone.* New York: Pantheon Books, 1996.

Sutton, Susan Buck. *Contingent Countryside: Settlement, Economy, and Land Use in the Southern Argolid.* Stanford, CA: Stanford University Press, 2000.

Triandis, Harry C. "Education of Greek Americans for a Pluralistic Society." In *Education and Greek Americans: Process and Prospects*, ed. Spyros D. Orfanos, Harry J. Psomiades, and John Spiridakis, 19–34. New York: Pella, 1987.

Valtinos, Thanassis. *Data from the Decade of the Sixties.* Trans. Jane Assimakopoulos. Evanston, IL: Northwestern University Press, 2000.

Veikou, Christina. *Kako Mati: I koinoniki kataskevi tis optikis epikoinonias* [Evil Eye: The Social Construction of Optical Communication]. Athens: Ellinika Grammata, 2004.

Zinovieff, Sorka. *Eurydice Street: A Place in Athens.* London: Granta Books, 2005.

CHAPTER 4: LEISURE, HOLIDAYS, AND THE GREEK TABLE

Bozi, Soula. *Mikrasiatiki kouzina* [Asia Minor Cooking]. Athens: Ellinika Grammata, 2005.

Hart, Laurie Kain. *Time, Religion, and Social Experience in Rural Greece.* Lanham, MD: Rowman and Littlefield, 1992.

Herzfeld, Michael. *Ours Once More: Folklore, Ideology, and the Making of Modern Greece.* New York: Pella, 1986.

Herzfeld, Michael. *A Place in History: Social and Monumental Time in a Cretan Town.* Princeton, NJ: Princeton University Press, 1991.

Kochilas, Diane. *The Food and Wine of Greece: More than 300 Classic and Modern Dishes from the Mainland and Islands of Greece.* New York: Macmillan, 1993.

Kochilas, Diane. *Glorious Foods of Greece: Traditional Recipes from the Islands, Cities, and Villages.* New York: Harper Collins, 2001.

Kochilas, Diane. *The Greek Vegetarian: More than 100 Recipes Inspired by the Traditional Dishes and Flavors of Greece.* New York: St. Martin's Griffin, 1999.

Kochilas, Diane. *Mediterranean Grilling: More Than 100 Recipes from across the Mediterranean.* New York: Macmillan, 2007.

Litsas, Photis K. Litsas. *Our Roots: Holidays and Customs.* New York: Greek Orthodox Archdiocese of North and South America, 1982.

Malaby, Thomas M. *Gambling Life: Dealing in Contingency in a Greek City.* Urbana: University of Illinois Press, 2003.

Rodd, Rennel. *The Customs and Lore of Greece.* 1892. Reprint, Chicago: Argonaut 1918.

Rouvelas, Marilyn. *Guide to Greek Traditions and Customs in America.* Brookline, MA: Holy Cross Bookstore, 2004.

Seremataki, C. Nadia. *The Last Word: Women, Death, and Divination in Inner Mani.* Chicago: University of Chicago Press, 1991.

Stewart, Charles. *Demons and the Devil.* Princeton, NJ: Princeton University Press, 1991.

Sutton, David. *Memories Cast in Stone: The Relevance of the Past in Everyday Life.* Oxford, UK: Berg, 1998.

WEB SITES

Greek-Recipe.com, http://www.greek-recipe.com/.

The Official Greek Gate to Agrotourism, http://en.agrotravel.gr/.

"Greece Traditions: Information about the Customs and Traditions of Greece," Greek Island Specialists, http://www.greeka.com/greece-traditions.htm.

Greek Music Information, http://www.musicportal.gr/traditional_music_concerts?lang=el.

Hellenic Republic-Ministry of Tourism, Greek National Tourism Organization, http://www.gnto.gr/.

Komboloi Museum, http://www.komboloi.gr/.

"Greece," Travel Medicine, http://www.travmed.com/maps/country.epl?c=Greece.

CHAPTER 5: LANGUAGE AND LITERATURE

Alexakis, Vassilis. *Foreign Words.* Trans. Alyson Waters. Iowa City: Autumn Hill Books, 2006.

Alexandrou, Aris. *The Mission Box.* Trans. David Ricks. Athens: Kedros, 1997.

Alexiou, Margaret. *After Antiquity: Greek Language, Myth, and Metaphor.* Ithaca, NY: Cornell University Press, 2002.

Alexiou, Margaret. *The Ritual Lament in Greek Tradition.* Cambridge: Cambridge University Press 1974.

Anagnostakis, Manolis. *The Target: Selected Poems.* Trans. with intro by Kimon Friar. New York: Pella, 1980.

Anghelaki-Rooke, Katerina. *Beings and Things on Their Own: Poems by Katerina Anghelaki-Rooke*, Trans. Katerina Anghelaki-Rooke and Jackie Willcox. Brockport, NY: Boa Editions, 1986.

Anghelaki-Rooke, Katerina. *The Body Is the Victory and the Defeat of Dreams*. Trans. Philip Ramp. San Francisco: Wire Press, 1975.

Anghelaki-Rooke, Katerina. *Notes on Modern Greek Poetry*, http://genesis.ee.auth.gr/dimakis/Gramma/8/02-Anghelaki.htm.

Anghelake-Rooke, Katerina. *The Scattered Papers of Penelope: New and Selected Poems*. Ed. Karen Van Dyck, trans Jane Assimakopoulos. London: Anvil Press Poetry, 2008.

Barnstone, Aliki, and Willis Barnstone. *A Book of Women Poets from Antiquity to Now*. New York: Schocken Books, 1980.

Beaton, Roderick. *Folk Poetry of Modern Greece*. Cambridge: Cambridge University Press, 2004.

Beaton, Roderick. *George Seferis: Waiting for the Angel: A Biography*. New Haven, CT: Yale University Press, 2003.

Beaton, Roderick. *An Introduction to Modern Greek Literature*. Oxford: Oxford University Press, 1994.

Bien, Peter, et al., eds. *A Century of Greek Poetry 1900–2000: Bilingual Edition*. River Vale, NJ: Cosmos, 2004.

Browning, Robert. *Medieval and Modern Greek*. Cambridge: Cambridge University Press, 1983.

Calotychos, Vangelis. *Modern Greece: A Cultural Poetics*. Oxford, UK: Berg, 2003.

Cavafy, C. P. *Collected Poems*. Trans. Edmund Keeley and Philip Sherard. Princeton, NJ: Princeton University Press, 1992.

Cavafy, C. P., Artemis Leontis, Lauren E. Talalay, and Keith Taylor, eds. *"What These Ithakas Mean": Readings in Cavafy*. Athens: ELIA, 2002.

Connolly, David, ed. and trans. *Angelic and Black: Contemporary Greek Short Stories*. River Vale, NJ: Cosmos, 2006.

Crist, Robert. *Grind the Big Tooth: A Collection of Contemporary Greek Poetry*. Pittsburgh, PA: Sterling House, 1998.

Dimaras, C. T. *History of Modern Greek Literature*. Trans. M. P. Gianos. Albany: State University of New York Press, 1976.

Dimitriou, Sotiris. *May Your Name Be Blessed*. Trans. Leo Marshall. Birmingham, UK: Modern Greek Translations, 2002.

Dimoula, Kiki. *Lethe's Adolescence*. Trans. David Connolly. Minneapolis: Nostos, 1996.

Douka, Maro. *Come Forth, King*. Trans. David Conolly. Athens: Kedros, 2003.

Douka, Maro. *Fool's Gold*. Trans. Roderick Beaton. Athens: Kedros, 1991.

Douka-Kabitoglou, Ekaterini. "Fantasies of the Feminine in Contemporary Greek Women Poets," http://genesis.ee.auth.gr/dimakis/Gramma/8/05-Kabitoglou.htm#n01.

Doukas, Stratis. *A Prisoner of War's Story*. Trans. Petro Alexiou. Birmingham: Modern Greek Translations, 1999.

Doulis, Thomas. *Disaster and Fiction: Modern Greek Fiction and the Asia Minor Disaster of 1922*. Berkeley: University of California Press, 1977.

Doulis, Thomas. *Out of the Ashes: The Emergence of Greek Fiction in the Nineteenth Century*. Philadelphia: Xlibris, 2003.

Elytis, Odysseus. *Asma iroiko kai penthimo gia ton hamenon anthypolohago tis Alvanias*. Athens: Ikaros, 1979.

Elytis, Odysseus. *The Axion Esti*. Trans. Edmund Keeley and G. Savidis. Pittsburgh, PA: University of Pittsburgh Press, 1974.

Forster, Edward Morgan. *Pharos and Pharillon*. London: Hogarth Press, 1961.

Friar, Kimon. *Contemporary Greek Poetry*. Athens: Greek Ministry of Culture, 1985.

Friar, Kimon. *Modern Greek Poetry*. Athens: Efstathiadis Group, 1982.

Galanaki, Rhea. *Eleni, or Nobody*. Trans. David Conolly. Evanston, IL: Northwestern University Press, 2003.

Galanaki, Rhea. *I Shall Sign as Loui*. Trans. Helen D. Kolias. Evanston, IL: Northwestern University Press, 2000.

Galanaki, Rhea. *The Life of Ismael Ferik Pasha: Spina Nel Cuore*. Trans. Kay Cicellis. London: Peter Owen Publishers, 1996.

Gianos, Mary P. *Introduction to Modern Greek Literature; An Anthology of Fiction, Drama, and Poetry*. New York: Twayne Publishers, 1969.

Güthenke, Constanze. *Placing Modern Greece: The Dynamics of Romantic Hellenism, 1770–1840: Classical Presences*. Oxford: Oxford University Press, 2008.

Hakkas, Marios. *Heroes' Shrine for Sale*. Trans. Amy Mims. Athens: Kedros, 1997.

Hatzopoulos, Thanassis. *Quasi present=As if Present=Presque Present*. Trans. David Connolly, Michel Volkovitch, and Paola Maria Minucci. Chalkida, Greece: Diametros, 1997.

Holst-Warhaft, Gail. *Dangerous Voices: Women's Laments and Greek Literature*. London: Routledge, 1992.

Horrocks, Geoffrey C. *Greek: A History of the Language and Its Speakers*. London: Longman, 1997.

Jeffreys, Peter. *Eastern Questions: Hellenism and Orientalism in the Writings of E. M. Forster and C. P. Cavafy*. Greensboro, NC: ELT Press, 2005.

Jeffreys, Peter. *The Forster-Cavafy Letters: Friends at a Slight Angle*. Cairo: American University in Cairo Press, forthcoming.

Jeffreys, Peter. *C. P. Cavafy: Selected Prose Writings*. Birmingham, UK: Centre for Byzantine, Ottoman, and Modern Greek Studies, University of Birmingham, and University of Michigan Press, forthcoming.

Joseph, Brian D. "Modern Greek," Ohio State University Department of Linguistics, http://www.ling.ohio-state.edu/~bjoseph/articles/gmodern.htm (accessed October 16, 2008).

Joseph, Brian D., and Irene Philippaki-Warburton. *Modern Greek*. Croom Helm Descriptive Grammars Series. London: Croom Helm, 1987.

Jusdanis, Gregory. *Belated Modernity and Aesthetic Culture: Inventing National Literature*. Theory and History of Literature, vol. 81. Minneapolis: University of Minnesota Press, 1991.

Jusdanis, Gregory. *The Poetics of Cavafy: Textuality, Eroticism, History*. Princeton, NJ: Princeton University Press, 1987.

Kalligas, Pavlos. *Thanos Vlekas*. Trans. with introduction by Thomas Doulis. Evanston, IL: Northwestern University Press, 2001.

Kalvos, Andreas. *Odes*. Trans. George Dandoulakis. Nottingham, UK: Shoestring, 1998.

Kambanellis, Iakovos. *Mauthausen*. Trans. Gail Holst. Athens: Kedros, 1995.

Kapllani, Gazmend. *Mikro imerologio synoron* [Border Syndrome]. Athens: Livanis Publications, 2006.

Karkavitsas, Andreas. *The Beggar: A Novel*. Trans. William F. Wyatt Jr. New Rochelle, NY: Caratzas Brothers, 1982.

Karyotakis, Kostas. *Battered Guitars: Poems and Prose*. Trans. William W. Reader and Keith Taylor. Birmingham, UK: Modern Greek Translations, 2006.

Kazantzakis, Nikos. *Zorba the Greek*, 50th ed. Trans. Carl Wildman. New York: Simon and Schuster 1996.

Keeley, Edmund. *Inventing Paradise: The Greek Journey, 1937–47*. New York: Farrar, Straus, & Giroux, 1999.

Klironomos, Martha. "Ancient *Anamnesi*, National *Mneme* in the Poetry of Giorgos Seferis." *Greek Worlds, Ancient and Modern*. Special issue of *Journal of Modern Greek Studies* 20, no. 2 (October 2002): 215–239.

Klironomis, Martha. "George Seferis." *Dictionary of Literary Biography*, vol. 322, ed. Matthew J. Bruccoli and Richard Layman, 146–156. Detroit: Gale Research, 2007.

Kolokotronis, Theodore. *Memoirs of the Greek War of Independence, 1921–1933*. Trans. G. Tertzetis. Chicago: Argonauts, 1969.

Kostis, Nicholas, ed. *Beyond the Broken Statues: Modern Greek Short Stories*. River Vale, NJ: Cosmos Press, 2006.

Kotzias, Alexandros. *Jaguar*. Trans. H. E. Criton. Athens: Kedros, 1991.

Koumandareas, Menes. *Their Smell Makes Me Want to Cry*. Trans. Patricia Felisa Barbeito and Vangelis Calotychos. Birmingham, UK: Modern Greek Translations, 2004.

Lambropoulos, Vassilis. *Literature as National Institution*. Princeton, NJ: Princeton University Press, 1988.

Layoun, Mary, ed. *Modernism in Greece? Essays on the Critical and Literary Margins of a Movement*. New York: Pella, 1990.

Leontis, Artemis. *Topographies of Hellenism: Mapping the Homeland*. Ithaca, NY: Cornell University Press, 1995.

Leontis, Artemis. *Greece: A Travelers' Literary Companion*. San Francisco: Whereabouts, 1997.

Lexicon of Neohellenic Literature: People, Works, Movements, Terms (in Greek). Athens: Pataki, 2007.

Mackridge, Peter. "Greece." In *The Oxford Guide to Contemporary Writing*, ed. John Sturrock, 184–193. Oxford: Oxford University Press, 1996.

Makriyannis, I. *Memoirs of General Makriyannis, 1797–1864*. Ed. and trans. H. A. Lidderdale. London: Oxford University Press, 1966.

Merchant, Paul, ed. *Modern Poetry in Translation*, series 3, no. 7, *Greece*. New York: Grossman Publishers, 1968.

Miller, Henry. *The Colossus of Maroussi*. New York: New Directions, 1958.

Merry, Bruce. *Encyclopedia of Modern Greek Literature*. Westport, CT: Greenwood Press, 2004.

Moutzan-Martinengou, Elisavet. *My Story*. Trans. Helen Dendrinou Kolias. Athens, GA: University of Georgia Press, 1989.

Myrivilis, Stratis. *Life in the Tomb*. Trans. Peter Bien. Hanover, NH: University Press of New England, 1987.

Myrivilis, Stratis. *The Mermaid Madonna*. Trans. Rick Abbott. Athens: Efstathiadis Group, 1981.

Nagy, Gregory, Anna Stavrakopoulou, and Jennifer Reilly. *Modern Greek Literature: Critical Essays*. New York: Routledge, 2003.

Palamas, Kostis. *The Twelve Lays of the Gypsy*. Trans. George Thomson. London: Lawrence and Wishart, 1969.

Papadiamantis, Alexandros. *The Murderess*. Trans. Peter Levi. London: Writers and Readers, 1983.

Patrikios, Titos. *The Lion's Gate: Poems of Titos Patrikios*. Trans. Christopher Bakken and Roula Konsolaki. Kirksville, MO: Truman State University, 2006.

Philippides, Dia Mary L. *Census of Modern Greek Literature: Check-List of English-Language Sources Useful in the Study of Modern Greek Literature (1824–1987)*. New Haven, CT: Modern Greek Studies Association, 1990.

Polites, Linos. *A History of Modern Greek Literature*. Oxford: Oxford University Press, 1973.

Rentzou, Effie. "Nicos Calas: A Life in the Avant-Garde," February 15, 2004, http://www.greekworks.com/content/index.php/weblog/extended/nicolas_calas_a_life_in_the_avant_garde/.

Ricks, David. *Modern Greek Writing: An Anthology in English Translation*. London: Peter Owen, 2003.

Seferis, George, Edmund Keeley, and Philip Sherrard. *George Seferis, Collected Poems*. Princeton, NJ: Princeton University Press, 1981.

Siotis, Dinos. *Foreign Territory*. Santa Rosa, CA: Philos Press, 2001.

Siotis, Dinos. *Ten Women Poets of Greece*. San Francisco: Wire Press, 1982.

Siotis, Dinos, and John Chioles, eds. *Twenty Contemporary Greek Poets*. San Francisco: Wire Press, 1979.

Solomos, Dionysios. *The Free Besieged and Other Poems*. Trans. Peter Thompson, Roderick Beaton, Peter Cocaclides, Michael Green, and David Ricks. Ed. Peter Mackridge. Nottingham, UK: Shoestring Press, 2000.

Sotiriou, Dido. *Farewell Anatolia*. Trans. Fred A. Reed. Athens: Kedros, 1991.

Stamatis, Alexis. *American Fugue: A Novel*. Trans. Diane Thiel and Constantine Hadjilambrinos. Wilkes-Barre, PA: Etruscan Press, 2008.

Taktsis, Costas. *The Third Wedding*. Trans. Leslie Finer. Harmondsworth: Penguin, 1969.

Taktsis, Costas. *The Third Wedding Wreath*. Trans. John Chioles. Athens: Ermis, 1985.

Theodoropoulos, Takis. *The Power of the Dark God. A novel.* Trans. David Connolly. River Vale, NJ: Cosmos Publishing, 2007.

Theotokas, George. *Leonis: A Novel.* Trans. Donald E. Martin. Minneapolis: Nostos, 1985.

Trypanis, C. A. *Greek Poetry: From Homer to Seferis.* London: Faber and Faber, 1981.

Tsirkas, Stratis. *Drifting Cities.* Trans. Kay Cicellis. Athens: Kedros, 1995.

Tziovas, Dimitris. *The Other Self: Selfhood and Society in Modern Greek Fiction.* Lanham, MD: Lexington Books, 2003.

Vakalo, Eleni. *Genealogia=Genealogy.* Trans. Paul Merchant. Exeter: Rougemont Press, 1977.

Valaoritis, Nanos, and Thanasis Maskaleris. *Modern Greek Poetry: An Anthology.* Jersey City, NJ: Talisman House, 2003.

Valtinos, Thanassis. *Data from the Decade of the Sixties: A Novel.* Trans. Jame Assimakopoulos and Stavros Deligiorgis. Evanston, IL: Northwestern University Press, 2000.

Van Dyck, Karen. *Kassandra and the Censors: Greek Poetry since 1967.* Reading Women Writing. Ithaca, NY: Cornell University Press, 1998.

Van Dyck, Karen. *The Rehearsal of Misunderstanding: Three Collections by Contemporary Greek Woman Poets.* Hanover, NH: Wesleyan University Press, 1998.

Vassilikos, Vassilis. *The Few Things I Know about Glafkos Thrassakis.* Trans. Karen Emmerich. New York: Seven Stories Press, 2002.

Vassilikos, Vassilis. *Z.* Trans. Marilyn Calmann. New York: Farrar, Straus, & Giroux, 1968.

Vikelas, Dimitris. *Loukis Laras: Reminiscences of a Chiote Merchant during the War of Independence.* Trans. John Gennadius. London: Macmillan, 1881.

Vizyenos, Georgios. *My Mother's Sin and Other Stories.* Trans. William F. Wyatt. Hanover, NH: University Press of New England, 1988.

Vlavianos, Haris. *Adieu.* Trans. David Connolly. Birmingham, UK: Centre for Byzantine, Ottoman, and Modern Greek Studies, 1998.

Yatromanolakis, Yorgis. *History of a Vendetta.* Trans. Helen Cavanagh. New York: Hippocrene, 1992.

Zei, Alki. *Achilles' Fiancée.* Trans. Gail Holst. Athens: Kedros, 1991.

WEB SITES

"Contemporary Authors," Greece 2001 Frankfurt Book Fair, http://www.greece2001.gr/13.html.

Greece: Poetry International Web, http://greece.poetryinternationalweb.org/.

"Window to Greek Culture," University of Michigan Modern Greek, http://www.lsa.umich.edu/modgreek/wtgc.

Engonopoulos, Nikos, http://www.engonopoulos.gr/_homeEN/poem10.html.

"Nikos Kazantzakis," Historical Museum of Crete, http://www.historical-museum.gr/kazantzakis/en/index.html.

CHAPTER 6: MUSIC AND DANCE

Alexiou, Margaret, *The Ritual Lament in Greek Tradition: Interdisciplinary Approaches.* Revised by Dimitrios Yatromanolakis and Panagiotis Roilos. Lanham, MD: Rowman and Littlefield, 2002.

Auerbach, Susan. "From Singing to Lamenting: Women's Musical Role in a Greek Village." In *Women and Music in Cross-Cultural Perspective*, ed. Ellen Koskoff. 25–44. Urbana: University of Illinois Press, 1989.

Cavarnos, Constantine. *Byzantine Chant: A Sequel to the Monograph Byzantine Sacred Music, Containing a Concise Discussion of the Origin of Byzantine Chant, Its Modes, Tempo, Notation, Prologoi, Prosomoia, Style, and Other Features.* Belmont, MA: Institute for Byzantine and Modern Greek Studies, 1998.

Cavarnos, Constantine. *Byzantine Sacred Music: The Traditional Music of the Orthodox Church. Its Structure, Purpose, and Execution.* Belmont, MA: Institute for Byzantine and Modern Greek Studies Church Music, 1985.

Cowan, Jane. *Dance and the Body Politic.* Princeton, NJ: Princeton University Press, 1990.

Emery, Ed. "Rebetika: A Brief History" (accessed June 2, 2008), http://www.geocities.com/HydraGathering/emery1.html. Reprinted from Elias Petropoulos, *Rebetika: Songs of the Greek Underworld.* London: Saqi Books, 2000.

Gauntlett, Stathis. *Rebetika: Carmina Graeciae Recentioris.* Athens: D. Harvey and Co., 1985.

Harley, James. *Xenakis: His Life in Music.* New York: Routledge, 2004

Holst, Gail. *Road to Rembetika: Music from a Greek Sub-Culture, Songs of Love, Sorrow and Hashish.* Athens: Anglo-Hellenic, 1977.

Holst, Gail. *Theodorakis: Myth and Politics in Modern Greek Music.* Amsterdam: Hakkert, 1980.

Holst-Warhaft, Gail. *Dangerous Voices: Women's Laments and Greek Literature.* London: Routledge, 1992.

Holst-Warhaft, Gail. "The Female Dervish and Other Shady Ladies of the Rebetika." In *Music and Gender: Perspectives from the Mediterranean*, ed. Tullia Magrini, 169–194. Chicago: University of Chicago Press, 2003.

Holst-Warhaft, Gail. "Rebetika: The Double-Descended Songs of Greece." In *The Passion of Music and Dance*, ed. William Washabaugh, 111–127. Oxford, UK: Berg, 1998.

Levy, Kenneth, and Christian Troelsgård. "Byzantine Chant." Grove Music Online, Oxford Music Online (accessed June 14, 2008), http://www.oxfordmusiconline.com.proxy.lib.umich.edu/subscriber/article/grove/music/04494.

Mathiesen, Thomas J., et al. "Greece." Grove Music Online, Oxford Music Online (accessed June 14, 2008), http://www.oxfordmusiconline.com.proxy.lib.umich.edu/subscriber/article/grove/music/11694pg4.

Pappas, Nicholas G. "Concepts of Greekness: The Recorded Music of Anatolian Greeks after 1922." *Journal of Modern Greek Studies* 17, no. 2 (October 1999): 353–373.

Pennanen, Risto Pikko. "The Development of Chordal Harmony in Greek Rebetika and Laika Music, 1930s to 1960s." *British Journal of Ethnomusicology* 6 (1997): 65–116.

Pennanen, Risto Pikko. "Greece." *Continuum Encyclopaedia of Popular Music of the World VII: Europe*, 114–118. London: Continuum International, 2005.

Pennanen, Risto Pikko. "Greek Music Policy under the Dictatorship of General Ioannis Metaxas (1936–1941)." In *Grapta Poikila I. Papers and Monographs of the Finnish Institute at Athens 8*, ed. Leena Pietilä-Castrén and Marjaana Vesterinen, 103–130. Helsinki: Foundation of the Finnish Institute at Athens, 2003.

Pennanen, Risto Pikko. *Westernisation and Modernisation in Greek Popular Music*. Ph.D. diss., Acta Universitatis Tamperensis 692, University of Tampere (Finland) Press, 1999.

Petropoulos, Elias. *Songs of the Greek Underworld: The Rebetika Tradition*. Ed. and trans. Ed Emery. Illustrated by A. Kavanakis. London: Saqi, 2000.

Raftis, Alkis. "The Legacy of Dora Stratou." *Dance Studies* 16 (1992): 35–55.

Raftis, Alkis. *The World of Greek Dance*. Athens: Finedawn Publishers, 1987.

Schwartz, Martin. "Notes." *Greek-Oriental Rebetica Songs and Dances in the Asia Minor Style, 1911–1937*. CD. El Cerrito, CA: Arhoolie, 1991.

Shand, Angela. "The Tsifte-telli Sermon: Identity, Theology, and Gender, in Rebetika." In *Music and Gender: Perspectives from the Mediterranean*, ed. Tullia Magrini, 127–132. Chicago: University of Chicago Press, 2003.

Stratou, Dora. *The Greek Dances: Our Living Link with Antiquity*. Athens: n.p., 1966.

Stratou, Dora. *Greek Traditional Dances*. Athens: Greek Educational Books Organisation, 1979.

Torp, Lisbet. *Salonikiós:* "The Best Violin in the Balkans." Copenhagen: Museum Tusculanum Press, 1993.

Tsounis, Demeter. "*Kefi* and *Meraki* in Rebetika Music of Adelaide: Cultural Constructions of Passion and Expression and Their Link with the Homeland." *Yearbook for Traditional Music* 27 (1995): 90–103.

Vamvarakis, Markos. *Autobiographia*. Ed. Ageliki-Bellou-Keil. Athens: Ekdoseis Papazisi, 1978.

Velkova, Sanya. "Dancing and the Modern Greek Self-Consciousness: Path, Measure, Truth and Harmony." *Etudes balkaniques* 42, Part 3/4 (2006): 338–343.

DVD

Ferris, Costas. *I istoria tou rebetikou tragoudiou* (The History of *Rebetiko* Song). Athens: Victory Media, 2006.

WEB SITES

Note: Many contemporary Greek musicians and performers have excellent Web sites with musical samples. These can be found on the Internet by searching under the artist's name.

All About Greek and Turkish Clarinet, www.gtc-music1.com/.

Cretan Music, www.cretan-music.gr/.

Dora Stratou, http://www.grdance.org/.

Folk with Dunav, The Sharing Place for Balkan Music and Dance, www.dunav. org.il/balkan_music_greek.html.

Greek Dances, http://www.btinternet.com/~argyros.argyrou/dances/Dances.htm.

Greek Music Information Center, http://www.musicportal.gr.

Kithara.vu Greek Lyrics, www.kithara.vu.

"Portrait of Greek Dance," Nostos, Hellenic Information Society UK, www.enostos. net/dance/.

"Rebetika and Greek Popular Music," Matt Barett's Greek Travel Guides, www. greecetravel.com/music/rembetika/.

Rebetiko.gr, database for *rebetika*, www.rebetiko.gr.

Stixoi.info Greek lyrics, http://www.stixoi.info.

CHAPTER 7: MEDIA, THEATER, AND CINEMA

Bacopoulou-Halls, Aliki. "Greece." In *The World Encyclopedia of Contemporary Theatre*, ed. Don Rubin, Peter Nagy, and Philippe Rouyer, 402–426. London: Routledge, 1994.

Bacopoulou-Halls, Aliki. "The Theatre System in Greece." In *Theatre Worlds in Motion*, ed. H. Van Maanen and S. E. Wilmer, 259–308. Amsterdam: Rodopi, 1998.

Constantinidis, Stratos E. "Greek Film and the National Interest." *Journal of Modern Greek Studies* 18, no. 1 (May 2000): 1–12.

Constantinides, Stratos E. "The Greek Studio System (1950–1970)." *Film Criticism* 27, no. 2 (2002): 9–30.

Constantinidis, Stratos E. *Modern Greek Theatre: A Quest for Hellenism.* Jefferson, NC: McFarland, 2001.

Georgakas, Dan. "Greek Cinema For Beginners: A Thumbnail History." *Film Criticism* 27, no. 2 (2002): 2–8.

"Greek Film." Special Issue of *Journal of Modern Greek Studies* 18, no. 1 (May 2000).

"Modern Greek Drama." Special issue of *Journal of Modern Greek Studies* 14, no. 1 (May 1996).

"Modern Greek Theater." Special issue of *Journal of Modern Greek Studies* 25, no. 2 (October 2007), ed. Stratos E. Constantinidis and Walter Puchner.

Myrsiades, Kostas. *Cultural Representation in Historical Resistance.* Lewisburg, PA: Bucknell University Press, 1999.

Papadimitriou, Lydia. "More Than a Pale Imitation: Narrative, Music and Dance in Two Greek Film Musicals of the 1960s." In *Musicals: Hollywood and Beyond*, ed. Bill Marshall and Robynn Jeananne Stilwell, 117–124. Bristol, UK: Intellect, 1999.

Papathanassopoulos, Stylianos. "The Decline of Newspapers: The Case of the Greek Press." *Journalism Studies* 2, no. 1 (February 2001): 109–123.

Papathanassopoulos, Stylianos. "Greece." In *The Media in Europe: The Euromedia Handbook*, ed. Mary Kelly et al, 91–102 London: Sage Publications, 2004.

Papathanassopoulos, Stylianos. "The Politics and the Effects of the Deregulation of Greek Television." *European Journal of Communication* 12, no. 3 (August 1997): 351–368.

Van Steen, Gonda. "Forgotten Theater, Theater of the Forgotten: Classical Tragedy on Modern Greek Prison Islands." *Journal of Modern Greek Studies* 23, no. 2 (October 2005): 335–395.

Van Steen, Gonda. *Venom in Verse: Aristophanes in Modern Greece*. Princeton, NJ: Princeton University Press, 2000.

Yoder, Andrew. *Pirate Radio Stations: Tuning In to Underground Broadcasts in the Air and Online*. New York: McGraw-Hill, 2002.

Zaharopoulos, Thimios, and Manny Paraschos. *Mass Media in Greece: Power, Politics, and Privatization*. New York: Praeger, 1993

WEB SITES

Arkas the Official Website, http://www.arkas.gr/.

The Art Theatre Karolos Koun, http://www.theatro-technis.gr.

CorfuFestival, http://www.corfufestival.gr/.

Greece 2001 Frankfurt Book Fair, http://www.greece2001.gr.

Dimitris Papaioannou, http://www.dimitrispapaioannou.com/.

ELIA (Hellenic Literary and Historical Archive), http://www.elia.org.gr.

ERT Online, http://www.ert.gr/.

ERT Audio-Visual Archive, http://www.ert-archives.gr/wpasV2/public/index.aspx.

Greek Cartoonists Association, http://www.cartoonists.gr/.

Greek Movies, http://www.greek-movies.com/movies.php.

Hellenic Festival, http://www.greekfestival.gr.

Hellenic Radio Portal, http://www.e-radio.gr/.

International Thessaloniki Film Festival, http://www.filmfestival.gr/.

Kalamata International Dance Festival, http://www.kalamatadancefestival.gr.

Lakis Lazopoulos, www.lakislazopoulos.gr/.

Lucia Rikaki, http://www.luciarikaki.gr.

National Theatre of Greece, http://www.n-t.gr/.

Renaissance Festival Rethymnon http://www.rfr.gr.

River Party, http://www.riverparty.org/.

Theo Angelopoulos, http://www.theoangelopoulos.com.

CHAPTER 8: ARCHITECTURE AND ART

Aesopos, Yannis, and Yorgos Simeoforidis, eds. *The Contemporary (Greek) City*. Athens: Metapolis Press, 2001.

Bastéa, Eleni. *The Creation of Modern Athens: Planning the Myth*. New York: Cambridge University Press, 2000.

Beard, Mary. *The Parthenon*. London: Profile Books, 2002.

Bires, Manos, and Maro Kardamitse-Adame. *Neoclassical Architecture in Greece.* Los Angeles: J. Paul Getty Museum, 2004.

Brown, K. S., and Yannis Hamilakis, eds. *The Usable Past: Greek Metahistories.* Lanham, MD: Lexington Books, 2002.

Condaratos, Savas, and Manos Bires. *Twentieth Century Architecture: Greece* [on the occasion of the exhibition "20th Century Architecture, Greece," Deutsches Architektur-Museum, Frankfurt am Main, July 9–September 19, 1999]. Munich: Prestel, 1999.

Dictionary of Greek Artists—Painters, Sculptors, Engravers, 16th-20th Century, 4 vols. Athens: 1997–2000.

Doxiades, Konstantinos Apostolou. *Destruction of Towns and Villages in Greece.* Athens: Ypourgeion Anoikodomiseo, 1947.

Doxiadis, Konstantinos Apostolou. *Thysies tes Hellados: aitemata kai epanorthoseis ston defteron Pankosmio Polemo* [The sacrifices of Greece in the Second World War]. Athens: Ypourgeion Aoikodomiseos, 1947.

Ebony, David. "Chryssa at Castelli." *Art in America* 84 (October 1996): 117–118.

Ferlenga, Alberto. *Dimitris Pikionis, 1887–1968.* Milan: Electa, 1999.

Fessas-Emmanouil, Helen. *Essays on Neohellenic Architecture.* Athens: A. P. Christakis, 2001.

Hamalidi, Elena, ed. *Contemporary Greek Artists.* Athens: Melissa, 2004.

Hitchens, Christopher, Robert Browning, and Graham Binns. *The Elgin Marbles.* London: Verso, 1997.

Ioannou, Andreas. *Greek Painting: The 19th Century.* Athens: Melissa, 1999.

Korres, M., and Charalampos Bouras. *Athens: From the Classical Period to the Present Day (5th Century B.C.– A.D. 2000).* New Castle, DE: Oak Knoll Press, 2003.

Loukaki, Argyro. *Living Ruins, Value Conflicts. Heritage, Culture and Identity.* Aldershot, UK: Ashgate, 2008.

St. Clair, William. *Lord Elgin and the Marbles.* Oxford: Oxford University Press, 1998.

Skousbøll, Karin. *Greek Architecture Now.* Athens: Studio Art Bookshop, 2006.

Tournikiotis, Panayotis. *The Historiography of Modern Architecture.* Cambridge, MA: MIT Press, 1999.

Tournikiotis, Panayotis. *The Parthenon and Its Impact in Modern Times.* Athens: Melissa, 1996.

Vakalo, Eleni. *I fysiognomia tis metapolemikis technis stin Ellada* (The physiognomy of postwar art in Greece). Vols. 1–4, *Abstraction; Expressionism, Surrealism; The Myth of Hellenicity; After Abstraction.* Athens: Kedros, 1981–1985.

Vatopoulos, Nikos. *Facing Athens: The Façades of a Classical City.* Athens: Potamos, 2003.

Yalouri, Eleana. *The Acropolis: Global Fame, Local Claim, Materializing Culture.* Oxford, UK: Berg, 2001.

WEB SITES

Archaeology of the City of Athens, http://www.eie.gr/archaeologia/En/Index.aspx.
Artforum Culture Foundation, http://artforum-culture-foundation.com/.

Artopos Online Cultural Center, www.eikastikon.gr.

"Arts Program," Metro and Culture, Attiko Metro, www.ametro.gr/page.

Atalier Spirou Vassiliou, http://www.spyrosvassiliou.org/.

Benaki Museum, http://www.benaki.gr.

Ilias Lalaounis Jewelry Museum, http://www.lalaounis-jewelrymuseum.gr/eng.

Kathimerini (archive of the newspaper *Kathimerini*), http://www.kathimerini.com
(Nikos Vatopoulos's regular columns in the newspaper offer a wealth of information and reflection on Greece's architecture).

Municipal Art Gallery of Rhodes, http://www.helios.gr/dis/rhodes/artgallery/.

National Gallery of Greece, http://www.nationalgallery.gr.

New Acropolis Museum, http://www.newacropolismuseum.gr/eng/.

Yiannis Tsarouchis Foundation, http://www.tsarouchis.gr/.

Index

Acropolis of Athens, 2, 19, 197; buildings on, 197; built into foundations of modern city, 202; Dionysiou Areopagitou street, 198–200, 222, 209, 222; excavation of, 202–203; landscaping by Dimitris Pikionis, 211; Nelly's photographs on, 216; New Acropolis Museum, 198–201, 214, 221–22; Parthenon, 178, 181, 197, 198, 210, 214, 216, 217, 221; Parthenon Marbles, 198–99; poem by Nicolas Calas, 116; view of, 197–200

Aegean, 2–6, 117; architecture inspired by, 210; artisans from, 209; cooking of, 93; islands of, 7–8, 16, 29, 35, 88; music and dance of, 139; theater of, 179, 181, 185

Aegina, 5, 159–61, 200

Aeschylus, 102, 108, 174, 175, 181; *Oresteia* in film, 185–86; riots over modern Greek translation of, 102, 179

Africa, 8; immigrants from, 10, 35, 70; African, 181, African American, 145, 174

Agriculture and livestock breeding, 4–8; changing conditions of working the land, 97 n.21; European Union subsidies, 11–12, 25; grape vines, 4, 5, 77, 87, 92; *tsiflikia*, 15

Akrotiri, 1

Albania, 3

Albanian, 9, 55, 139; in cinema, 189–90; immigrants from, 10, 70; immigrant music, 144; immigrant writing, 129–30

Alexakis, Vassilis, 128

Alexandrakis, Alekos, 178, 186, 188

Alexandria, Egypt, 114, 176, 178

Alexandrou, Aris, 125

Alexandroupolis, 5, 156

Alexiadou, Vefa, 93

Alexiou, Haris, 137, 152, 156

Ali Pasha, 13

Altamura, Eleni, 127, 216

About the Author

ARTEMIS LEONTIS is an Associate Professor of Modern Greek at the University of Michigan.